World Water and Food to 2025

World Water and Food to 2025: Dealing with Scarcity

Mark W. Rosegrant
Ximing Cai
and Sarah A. Cline

International Food Policy Research Institute
Washington, D.C.

Library of Congress Cataloging-in-Publication Data

Rosegrant, Mark W.
    World water and food to 2025 : Dealing with Scarcity / Mark W. Rosegrant,
Ximing Cai, Sarah A. Cline.
    p. cm.
Includes bibliographical references.
ISBN 0-89629-646-6 (alk. paper)
    1. Water-supply—Forecasting—Econometric models. 2. Food supply—Forecasting—
Econometric models. 3. Twenty-first century—Forecasts. I. Cai, Ximing, 1966- II. Cline,
Sarah A., 1974-. III. Title.

HD1691 .R66 2002
333.91'001'12—dc21   2002015170

International Food Policy Research Institute
2033 K Street, NW, Washington, DC 20006-1002, USA
Telephone: +1-202-862-5600; Fax: +1-202-467-4439
www.ifpri.org

Contents

Tables

Figures

Boxes

Foreword

The story of food security in the 21st century is likely to be closely linked to the story of water security. In the coming decades the world's farmers will need to produce enough food to feed many millions more people, yet there are virtually no untapped, cost-effective sources of water for them to draw on as they face this challenge. Moreover, farmers will face heavy competition for this water from households, industries, and environmentalists.

By analyzing various policy and investment scenarios, the authors of this book show that how policymakers and water users manage this scarce resource can help make the difference between a food-secure world and one in which water shortages could lead to hunger, poverty, and conflict. With better water management, sound policies, and increased investment in water, farmers and other water users can get more use out of each unit of water and the amount of water reserved for the environment can increase substantially. Continued complacency over the water situation, on the other hand, is likely to lead to a water crisis that will have the direst consequences for the world's poor.

This book is an outgrowth of the shared interest of the International Food Policy Research Institute (IFPRI) and the International Water Management Institute (IWMI) in how water- and food-related policies will affect global, regional, and local water scarcity, food production, food security, the environment, and livelihoods in the long term. In the past four years, IFPRI has developed the IMPACT-WATER model, which is presented and applied in this book to examine water and food policy and investment issues. At the same time IWMI has developed PODIUM, the Policy Dialogue model that can help explore critical planning questions in water and food.

Future collaboration between IFPRI and IWMI will build on the work presented here to further enhance policymakers' understanding of critical water and food issues for the future. In January 2002 the two institutes joined forces on a program to model and analyze water resources and food policy at the river basin, country, regional, and global levels. Ultimately this program will also analyze the effects of climate change on water and agriculture over longer time periods; develop investment and cost functions for water storage, new irrigation infrastructure, and efficiency improvements in existing water and irrigation systems; and offer more detailed assessments of the effects of water quality and pollution.

This work should further clarify the policy choices laid out in this book. Although there is still much to learn about the future water situation, we already know for certain that if we are to avoid a devastating water crisis, policy and management reforms are needed now.

To share the key findings from this important research with a wider audience, we are publishing a more popular version of this book as a food policy report titled *Global Water Outlook to 2025: Averting an Impending Crisis.*

Joachim von Braun
Director General
International Food Policy Research Institute

Frank Rijsberman
Director General
International Water Management Institute

Acknowledgments

The authors benefited from the contributions of many colleagues. Andrew Keller of Keller-Bliesner Engineering provided important methodological insights early in the modeling development, and helpful comments on the first draft of this book. Joseph Alcamo and Thomas Henrichs of the Center for Environmental Systems Research (CESR), University of Kassel, provided the authors with outputs from the WaterGAP model, including global runoff and reference evapotranspiration. Frank Rijsberman, director general of the International Water Management Institute (IWMI); Sandra Postel, director of the Global Water Policy Project; Ariel Dinar of the World Bank; and Kenneth Strzepek of Colorado University also provided valuable comments. As in previous global analyses, Per Pinstrup-Andersen, then director general of IFPRI, and Rajul Pandya-Lorch, head of its 2020 Vision Initiative, provided institutional support, encouragement, and detailed and insightful comments. Financial support for this work was received from the Secretariat of the Consultative Group on International Agricultural Research, the Ford Foundation, IFPRI and its 2020 Vision Initiative, and IWMI and its Comprehensive Assessment of Water Management in Agriculture.

Siet Meijer provided essential research and editorial assistance. Claudia Ringler assisted with data collection in the early stages of the work and provided excellent editorial assistance. Uday Mohan and Evelyn Banda efficiently managed the editorial and production processes, respectively. Maria Esteban provided excellent administrative support and processed several drafts of the manuscript. Mary Jane Banks did a superb job of editing the manuscript. Remaining deficiencies are the responsibility of the authors.

Acronyms

BE	Basin (water use) efficiency (the ratio of beneficial consumption over total consumption)
CRWR	Center for Research in Water Resources
CRU	Climate Research Unit of the University of East Anglia, England
DC	Consumption coefficient (the ratio of water consumption over water withdrawal)
FAO	Food and Agriculture Organization of the United Nations
EWIR	Effective water supply for irrigation
ECOSOC	Economic and Social Council of the United Nations
GCM	Global climate models
GIS	Geographic Information Systems
GDP	Gross domestic product
GMAWW	Groundwater maximum allowable water withdrawal
GNP	Gross national product
GPS	Global positioning systems
IWMI	International Water Management Institute
IWSR	Irrigation water supply reliability index
LA	Latin America
M&I	Municipal and industrial
MCM	Million cubic meters
NGO(s)	Nongovernmental organization(s)
NIWSR	Non-irrigation water supply reliability
OECD	Organisation for Economic Co-Operation and Development
O&M	Operations and maintenance
RBOs	River basin organizations
SMAWW	Surface maximum allowable water withdrawal
SPAR	Soil-plant-atmosphere-research
SSA	Sub-Saharan Africa
UFW	Unaccounted-for water
UN	United Nations

UNCED   United Nations Conference on Environment and Development
UNESCO   United Nations Educational Scientific and Cultural Organization
WANA   West Asia and North Africa
WRI   World Resources Institute
WUA(s)   Water user associations
WWV   World Water Vision

Note: See Table 1.1 for scenario abbreviations and descriptions and Boxes 2.1 and 2.2 for water demand and water supply definitions, respectively.

Water Resources and Food Production

INTRODUCTION

Water is essential for growing food; for household water uses, including drinking, cooking, and sanitation; as a critical input into industry; for tourism and cultural purposes; and for its role in sustaining the earth's ecosystems. But this essential resource is under threat. Growing national, regional, and seasonal water scarcities in much of the world pose severe challenges for national governments and international development and environmental communities. The challenges of growing water scarcity are heightened by the increasing costs of developing new water, degradation of soil in irrigated areas, depletion of groundwater, water pollution and degradation of water-related ecosystems, and wasteful use of already developed water supplies, often encouraged by the subsidies and distorted incentives that influence water use.

Water development is critical for food security in many regions of the world. Today's 250 million hectares of irrigated area, worldwide, is nearly five times the amount that existed at the beginning of the twentieth century. Without irrigation, increases in agricultural yields and outputs that have fed the world's growing population would not have been possible. Further, irrigation has stabilized food production and prices by enabling greater production control and scope for crop diversification. Thus, irrigation has been vital to food security and sustainable livelihoods, especially in developing countries during the Green Revolution, through increased income and improved health and nutrition, locally, and by bridging the gap between production and demand, nationally.

Irrigated agriculture is the dominant user of water, accounting, for example, for about 80 percent of global and 86 percent of developing country water consumption in 1995. Population and income growth will boost demand for irrigation water to meet food production requirements and household and industrial water demand. By 2025, global population will likely increase to 7.9 billion, more than

80 percent of whom will live in developing countries and 58 percent in rapidly growing urban areas. In response to population growth and rising incomes, worldwide cereal demand will grow by a projected 46 percent between 1995 and 2025, and in developing countries by 65 percent; meat demand is projected to grow by 56 percent worldwide and more than double in the developing world; and calorie requirements and dietary trends will translate to even greater water demand if the food produced is to supply adequate nutrition.

The success of irrigation in ensuring food security and improving rural welfare has been impressive, but past experiences also indicate that inappropriate management of irrigation has contributed to environmental problems including excessive water depletion, water quality reduction, waterlogging, and salinization. Long-term hydrological records have shown a marked reduction in the annual discharge on some of the world's major rivers. In some basins, excessive diversion of river water has led to environmental and ecological disasters for downstream areas, and pumping groundwater at unsustainable rates has contributed to the lowering of groundwater tables and to saltwater intrusion in some coastal areas. Many water quality problems have also been created or aggravated by changes in stream flows associated with water withdrawals for agriculture. Moreover, poor irrigation practices accompanied by inadequate drainage have often damaged soils through oversaturation and salt build-up. It is estimated that on a global scale there are about 20–30 million hectares of irrigated lands severely affected by salinity. An additional 60–80 million hectares are affected to some extent by waterlogging and salinity (FAO 1996).

In addition to irrigation, water is essential for drinking and household uses, as an input into industrial production, and for environmental and ecosystem services. Although the domestic and industrial sectors use far less water than agriculture, growth in water consumption in these sectors has been rapid. Globally, withdrawals for domestic and industrial uses grew four-fold between 1950 and 1995, compared with just over a doubling for agricultural uses (Cosgrove and Rijsberman 2000; Shiklomanov 1999). Domestic water is used for drinking, cooking, bathing, and cleaning. Access to safe drinking water and sanitation is critical in terms of health—particularly for children. Unsafe drinking water contributes to numerous health problems in developing countries, such as the one billion or more incidents of diarrhea that occur annually. For more than one billion people across the globe, safe water is available in insufficient quantities to meet minimum levels of health and income. Contaminated water supplies also impact health through food consumption because untreated wastewater or contaminated surface water is often used for irrigation in poor communities.

Water is also valued for environmental and ecosystem uses, and ecosystems are valued for regulating water quality and quantity. Recognition of the importance of reserving water for environmental purposes has come late in much of the world, and only in recent years have environmental uses of water received policy recognition in much of the developing world. It has been estimated that, during the twentieth century, more than half the world's wetlands were lost, (Bos and Bergkamp 2001).

Continued rapid growth of domestic and industrial water uses, growing recognition of environmental demands for water, and the high cost of developing new water resources threaten the availability of irrigation water to meet growing food demands. A crucial and urgent question for the world, therefore, is whether water availability for irrigation—together with feasible production growth in rainfed areas—will provide food to meet growing demand and ultimately improve national and global food security. This book attempts to answer this question by addressing the relationship between water availability and food production including the following key issues.

• How will water availability and demand evolve over the next three decades, accounting for availability and variability in water resources, water supply infrastructure, and irrigation and nonagricultural water demands?

• How will water scarcity affect food production and the availability of water for environmental purposes?

• How much of future food production will come from rainfed and irrigated areas?

• What are the impacts of alternative water policies and investments on water supply and demand, food production and demand, and food security?

ISSUES AND CHALLENGES

Increasing Costs of Water Development

New sources of water are increasingly expensive to exploit, limiting the potential for expansion in new water supplies. Real costs of Indian and Indonesian new irrigation more than doubled from 1970 to 1990 (Rosegrant and Svendsen 1993); and in Pakistan they more than doubled between 1980 and 1990 (Dinar and Subramanian 1997). In the Philippines costs have increased by more than 50 percent, in Thailand they have increased by 40 percent, and in Sri Lanka they have tripled. These increases in costs, together with declining cereal prices, result in low rates of economic return for new irrigation construction.

In Africa, irrigation construction costs are even higher than in Asia because of numerous physical and technical constraints. The average investment cost for medium- and large-scale irrigation with full water control was estimated to be $8,300 per hectare in 1992 dollars (FAO 1992). However, the average cost of irrigation systems in Sub-Saharan Africa increases to $18,300 per hectare if the typically high indirect costs of social infrastructure, including roads, houses, electric grids, and public service facilities, are included. Latin America has had lower irrigation costs than Africa, but much higher costs than Asia and other regions, with average expenses for constructing new irrigation infrastructure estimated to be $10,000 per hectare (Jones 1995).

In addition to the ever-increasing financial costs of building new irrigation and dams, the development of new dams often imposes high environmental and human resettlement costs. Dam building can have extensive negative impacts on ecosystems including loss of habitat, species, and aquatic diversity. It is estimated that 40–80 million people have been displaced by dam projects (Bird and Wallace 2001). The controversy over the Narmada Valley Development Program in western India starkly illustrates the issues to be resolved if large-scale irrigation projects are to play a role in future water development. The projects are designed to bring irrigation to almost two million hectares of arid land. They promise drinking water for 30 million people in drought-prone areas, and 1,200 million watts of electricity for agriculture, cities, and industry. But they require resettlement of more than 140,000 people, mostly poor tribal villagers, in the areas to be flooded by the Sardar Sarovar dam and displaced by the building of canals. The projects also may have negative environmental consequences. Upstream effects may include siltation, salination, and deforestation; downstream effects are more difficult to assess because they are generally less immediate and visible, but could involve water quality and temperature changes, depleted fish stocks, effects on wetlands, and reduction in silt carried out to the estuary and the sea (Curtin 2000; World Bank 1995; Berger 1994; Seckler 1992).

The cost of supplying water for household and industrial uses is also increasing rapidly, as each successive investment to supply more water to expanding cities must typically tap water at a greater distance from the city, and often with increasing hydrologic and engineering difficulty. Rogers, de Silva and Bhatia (2002) cite an Asian Development Bank study that estimated the average tariff charged by water utilities in 38 large Asian cities rose 88 percent between 1993 and 1997. In Hyderabad, India, the average financial supply cost of water more than tripled between 1989 and 1995, from $0.05 to $0.17 per cubic meter (Saleth and Dinar 1997). In Amman, Jordan, the average incremental cost of water from groundwater sources was $0.41 per cubic meter during the 1980s, but with shortages of groundwater in the 1990s the city began to rely on surface water pumped from a site 40 kilometers away at an average incremental cost of $1.33 per cubic meter. In Yingkou, China, pollution of the water supply source has forced a shift to a new source that increased the average incremental cost from about $0.16–0.30 per cubic meter. In Mexico City, water is being pumped over an elevation of 1,000 meters into the Mexico Valley from the Cutzamala River through a pipeline about 180 kilometers long at an average incremental cost of $0.82 per cubic meter of water. This is almost 55 percent more than the cost of the previous source, the Mexico Valley aquifer (World Bank 1993).

The increasing costs of water from traditional sources could open a greater opportunity for improved nontraditional technologies such as desalination. While desalination through evaporative techniques has proven too expensive for all but the richest, water-scarce countries, the emerging technique of membrane desalination through reverse osmosis offers significant cost advantages. Despite these promising prospects, however, desalination today contributes only about 0.2 percent of global water withdrawals, and perhaps one percent of drinking water (Martindale and Gleick 2001). It is likely that this technology will remain concentrated in the coastal regions of developed countries, the water-scarce Persian Gulf, and island nations given the substantial transportation costs involved in pumping desalinated water inland, the high capital and energy costs, and the potential environmental damages from generated wastes.

Wasteful Use of Existing Water Supplies

One of the most important challenges is to generate water savings from existing agricultural, household, and industrial uses. Although individual irrigation system performance varies considerably, average irrigation efficiency (the product of irrigation system efficiency and field application efficiency) is low in developing countries ranging from 25–40 percent for the Philippines, Thailand, India, Pakistan, and Mexico, to 40–45 percent in Malaysia and Morocco. These efficiencies are well below what is achievable, as seen by the average irrigation efficiencies of 50–60 percent in Taiwan, Israel, and Japan (Rosegrant and Shetty 1994).

Water is also wasted in domestic and industrial uses. "Unaccounted-for water" (UFW) typically constitutes a high proportion of urban water supply. UFW is usually defined as the difference between water supplied to a system and water sold, as a proportion of water supplied (Gleick et al. 2002). Although some UFW is unmeasured beneficial use, much of it constitutes real water losses to non-beneficial uses and salt sinks. UFW rates should be 10–15 percent in well-managed systems. But the average UFW for large cities in Africa was 39 percent in the 1990s, for large cities in Asia, 35 to 42 percent, and for large cities in Latin America, 40 percent (WHO 2000, cited by Gleick et al. 2002). Even in the water-scarce Middle East, UFW is high—51 percent in Algiers and 52 percent in Amman in the 1990s (Saghir, Schiffler, and Woldu 1999). The average level of UFW in World Bank-assisted urban water projects was about 36 percent in the early 1990s. In Jakarta, where water loss through leakage was estimated at 41 percent of total supply, it was estimated that nearly half of these losses could be eliminated cost-effectively (Bhatia and Falkenmark 1993). Some municipalities have been able to decrease the level of UFW by changes in management. In Murcia, Spain, the UFW level dropped from 44 percent in 1989 to 23 percent in 1994 with the institution of management changes to reduce commercial losses, improve metering, and reduce leaks (Yepes 1995).

These inefficiencies in irrigation and urban systems seem to imply potential huge savings from existing water uses; however, the potential savings are not as dramatic in all regions or delivery systems because much of the water "lost" is reused elsewhere within the river basin. Unmeasured downstream recovery of "waste" drainage water and recharge and extractions of groundwater can result in actual basinwide efficiencies substantially greater than the nominal values for particular systems. For example, estimates of overall water use efficiencies for individual systems in the Nile Basin in Egypt are as low as 30 percent, but the overall efficiency for the entire Nile system in that country is estimated at 80 percent (Keller 1992). At the river basin level, the actual physical water losses comprise the water that flows to water sinks including water vapor lost to the atmosphere through surface and plant evaporation; flows of water to oceans or inland seas; and pollution of surface and groundwater by salts or toxic elements (Seckler 1996). Water can also become economically unrecoverable. If the cost of reusing drainage water is high enough a threshold is passed whereby water becomes uneconomical to use and is effectively sequestered (Rosegrant 1997). The main sources of water savings from existing uses through improved river basin efficiency therefore include boosting output per unit of evaporative loss, increasing water utilization before it reaches salt sinks, reducing water pollution, and increasing the proportion of economically recoverable drainage water. Important research remains to be done on these issues because it is unclear how large each of these potential savings are; nevertheless, considerable scope for water savings and economic benefits from improvements in water use efficiency appears to exist in many river basins.

Groundwater Overdrafting and Degradation of Irrigated Cropland

Groundwater is depleted when pumping rates exceed the rate of natural recharge. While mining of both renewable and nonrenewable water resources can be an optimal economic strategy, it is clear that groundwater overdrafting is excessive in many instances. Overdraft or mining of groundwater at a higher rate than recharge increases pumping lifts and costs from the lowered water table, causes land to subside (sometimes irreversibly damaging the aquifer), and induces saline intrusion and other degradation of water quality in the aquifer.

In parts of the North China Plain, groundwater levels are falling by as much as one meter per year. In the west Indian state of Gujarat, overpumping from coastal aquifers drove a rapid expansion of agricultural production in the 1960s and 1970s. But the overpumping caused saltwater to invade the aquifers, leading to a similarly rapid collapse of production (Molden, Amarasinghe, and Hussain 2001). At the same time, in a number of regions in India water tables have been falling at average rates of two to three meters per year as the number of irrigation wells grows. The resultant depletion of groundwater aquifers has some analysts predicting that 25 percent of India's harvest may be at risk in the coming years (Brown 2000; Gleick 2000).

According to the World Resources Institute (WRI 2000), around 66 percent of agricultural land has been degraded to varying degrees by erosion, salinization, nutrient depletion, compaction, biological degradation, or pollution over the past 50 years. Poor policies and inappropriate incentives for intensification of agriculture have been major contributors to land degradation. Salinization, as a result of poor irrigation management, is a particular culprit in the degradation of irrigated croplands. Salinization is caused by intensive use of irrigation water in areas with poor drainage, which leads to a rise in the water table from the continual recharge of groundwater. In the semi-arid and arid zones this results in salinity buildup, while in the humid zone it results in waterlogging. Soil salinity is induced by an excess of evapotranspiration over rainfall causing a net upward movement of water through capillary action and the concentration of salts on the soil surface. The groundwater itself need not be saline for salinity to build up; it can occur from the long-term evaporation of continuously recharged water of low salt content (Moorman and van Breemen 1978 cited in Pingali and Rosegrant 2000). High water tables prevent salts from being flushed from surface soil. In fact, about one tenth of global irrigated lands are affected by soil salinity and could be threatening ten percent of the global grain harvest (FAO 2002).

Threats to Ecosystems, Increasing Pollution, and Declining Water Quality

In addition to its value for direct human consumption, water is integrally linked to the provision and quality of ecosystem services. On the one hand, water is vital to the survival of ecosystems and the plants and animals that live in them; on the other, ecosystems regulate the quantity and quality of water. Wetlands retain water during high rainfall and release it during dry periods, purifying it of many contaminants. Forests reduce erosion and sedimentation of rivers and recharge groundwater (Bos and Bergkamp 2001). Ecosystem services can be defined as the conditions and processes through which ecosystems sustain and fulfill human life, including the provision of food and other goods (Carpenter et al. 2002). Ecosystem services are not generally traded in markets, have no price, and therefore are not properly valued in economic decisionmaking, but they are essential for human life and welfare. Important interlinked categories of ecosystem services include:

- provisioning of food, freshwater, and other biological products (including fiber, biochemicals/medicine, fuels and energy, and nonliving materials);

- supporting regulation functions (including soil formation, nutrient cycling, waste treatment, climate regulation, atmospheric composition, flood and erosion control, and pollination) and organization and structure (including biodiversity, landscape interconnections and structure, and space); and

- enriching cultural life, recreation, and tourism (Carpenter et al. 2002).

But water and the ecosystems it supports are under increasing threat, leading to deterioration in the quality and quantity of ecosystem services. The Organisation of Economic Co-Operation and Development (OECD 1996) cited in Wetlands International (1996) mentions that no direct measures of worldwide wetland losses are available. However, as the principal cause of wetland losses, drainage for agricultural production can give a rough estimation. By 1985 it was estimated that 56–65 percent of the available wetlands were lost to agriculture in Europe and North America. In Asia, South America, and Africa, wetland losses from agricultural drainage were estimated to be 27, 6, and 2 percent, respectively, bringing global wetland loss to a total of 26 percent. The pressure to drain land for agriculture is still intensifying in these regions (Wetlands International 1996).

In addition to wetland loss, deforestation—which can lead to excess erosion and sedimentation of rivers and storage reservoirs—is occurring at an accelerated rate. Forests provide a wide range of invaluable environmental, social, and economic benefits of which timber production is only a minor element. Natural forests are essential to maintaining ecosystems at the local, regional, and global levels. They provide habitat to half of the world's species, regulate climate, and protect soils and water systems. Although increasing slightly in developed countries since the 1980s, forested area declined by an estimated 10 percent in developing countries. The majority of the forest depletion is caused by agricultural expansion, logging, and road construction. Mining is a significant catalyzing factor because not only does it open up forests through logging and road construction but also by increasing pioneering settlement, hunting activities, fires, and new diseases in flora and fauna (WRI 2000).

Moreover, a growing number of the world's rivers, lakes, and groundwater aquifers are being severely contaminated by human, industrial, and agricultural wastes. High withdrawals of water and heavy pollution loads have already caused widespread harm to a number of ecosystems. This has resulted in a wide range of health effects in which humans have been harmed by waterborne illness and contaminated food. Rising human demands only increase pressure on ecosystems and intensify the need to maintain an adequate water supply to wetlands, lakes, rivers, and coastal areas to ensure the healthy functioning of ecosystems (UN 1997).

Water-related diseases place an excessive burden on the population and health services of many countries worldwide, and in particular on those in developing countries (WHO 2000). Some significant improvements have been achieved in water quality, however, particularly resulting from government and industry responses to citizen-applied pressure for cleanups. Most developed countries have begun treating an increasing part of their municipal sewage, and a number of their industries are reducing discharges of many toxic substances. Hence risks to human health have been reduced and the health of some wildlife species has improved (UN 1997).

Nevertheless, unsafe drinking water combined with poor household and community sanitary conditions remains a major contributor to disease and malnutrition, particularly among children. These poor water quality and sanitation conditions contribute to the approximately 4 billion cases of diarrhea each year, which lead to 2 million deaths, mostly among children under the age of five (WHO and UNICEF 2000). In the year 2000, 1.1 billion people were without access to an improved water supply and 2.4 billion had inadequate sanitation facilities (WHO and UNICEF 2000). The majority of these under-served people are in developing regions, particularly in Asia and Africa, with two-thirds of those without access to clean water and three-fourths of those without access to adequate sanitation residing in Asia (WHO and UNICEF 2000).

Contaminated wastewater is often used to irrigate food crops, creating significant risks for human health and well being. Scott, Zarazúa and Levine (2000, citing Moscosco 1996) note that at least 500,000 hectares of cropland are irrigated with untreated wastewater in Latin America alone. Natural contamination of water supplies combined with new technology for extracting water can also have devastating effects. Arsenic contamination has affected many people in Bangladesh and the state of West Bengal in India. It has been estimated that 1.1 million people in West Bengal obtain their drinking water from an arsenic-contaminated well (Revenga et al. 2000) and between 35 and 77 million people in Bangladesh are at risk of drinking from an arsenic-contaminated well (Smith, Lingas, and Rahman 2000). In Bangladesh, this problem has occurred mainly within the last 30 years as tube-wells were installed intending to provide clean drinking water for residents since the surface water was contaminated with microorganisms (Smith, Lingas, and Rahman 2000). The excessive groundwater withdrawal and drilling of boreholes enable oxygen to react with the naturally existing arsenopyrites, however, thus releasing arsenic into the water. This arsenic-contaminated water then infiltrates into the shallow tube-wells, leading to adverse health effects. Exposure to arsenic can result in many health effects including skin lesions, skin and internal cancers, as well as neurological and other effects.

Subsidies, Distorted Incentives, and Poor Cost Recovery

Despite increasing water scarcity and the wasteful use of existing water supplies, water is not generally treated as a scarce commodity. In most developing (and many developed) countries, both domestic and irrigation water users are provided with large subsidies on water use. Higher water prices could raise incentives for efficient water use, increase cost recovery in the water sector, and enhance the financial sustainability of urban water supply systems and irrigation, including the ability to raise capital for expansion of services to meet future demand.

Many factors contribute to the persistent use of subsidies and the lack of aggressive use of water pricing to encourage water conservation. Water pricing possibly conflicts with the idea of water services as a basic right of all individuals. The high costs of measuring and monitoring water use where infrastructure and institutions are weak can also be a major constraint in implementing water pricing. Adding to the difficulty of pricing reform, both long-standing practice and cultural and religious beliefs have treated water as a free good and entrenched interests benefit from the existing system of subsidies and administered allocations of water.

But low water charges and poor cost recovery risk the efficient maintenance of existing water infrastructure, as well as the additional investments in future water development projects, and encourage wasteful use of irrigation water (Saleth 2001). Moreover—contrary to stated equity goals— subsidies tend to worsen rather than improve equity. In most countries, water subsidies go disproportionately to the better off: urban water users connected to the public system and irrigated farmers. The urban poor who rely on water vendors, therefore, often pay far more for water than the generally better-off residents who receive subsidized water from the public piped water systems. At the national level, for example, the richest 20 percent get about twice the amount of subsidized water services as the poorest 20 percent in Ghana, Guatemala, Mexico, and Peru. In the Côte d'Ivoire more than 60 percent of the rich receive subsidies for their water services compared with a negligible amount of the poor. In the urban areas this difference is less striking but access to water service subsidies is still much lower for the poorest quintile compared with the richest. This results in poor people spending proportionally up to three times as much on water bills as the rich spend (de Moor and Calamai 1997). The equity impacts of subsidies are worsened even further when the subsidies are financed from regressive general taxes, as is often the case in developing countries. To improve both efficiency and equity in such situations urban water prices could be increased to cover the costs of delivery and to generate adequate revenues to finance growth in supplies. General subsidies could be replaced with subsidies targeted to the urban poor.

Subsidies for drinking water and irrigation have been estimated at $45 billion per year in developing countries alone (de Moor and Calamai 1997). New water supply connections for residential consumers in Sri Lanka cost the National Water Supply and Drainage Board US$714.28 on average, while consumers usually pay less than US$285 for the connections (Gunatilake, Gopalakrishnan, and Chandrasena 2001). In Mexico during the mid-1990s the annual subsidy for operations and maintenance (O&M) of water systems (not including capital costs) was one-half of one percent of gross domestic product (GDP)—far more than was spent on the agricultural research system (Rosegrant, Schleyer, and Yadav 1995). Annual irrigation subsidies have been estimated at US$0.6 billion in Pakistan, US$1.2 billion in India, and US$5.0 billion in Egypt (Bhatia and Falkenmark 1993). In the mid-1980s, average irrigation subsidies in six Asian countries covered an average of 90 percent or more of total O&M costs (Repetto 1986). During the 1990s, subsidies have declined somewhat because most countries worldwide have officially adopted the stated goal of full recovery of O&M costs. O&M cost recovery remains dismal, however, in most developing countries. In Pakistan, for example, the cost recovery for O&M expenditures in the Punjab region was 26 percent in 1995–96, while the Sindh region's performance over the same period was even worse, with a cost recovery of 12 percent (Dinar, Balakrishnan, and Wambia 1998). At the national level in developing countries, the recovery of irrigation O&M ranges from 20 to 30 percent in India and Pakistan to 75 percent in Madagascar, and depreciation is virtually uncovered (Dinar and Subramanian 1997).

Pricing irrigation water to recover full capital costs appears unlikely in existing systems in most of the developing world (even developed countries have rarely attempted full capital cost recovery for irrigation), but pricing to cover O&M costs and capital asset replacement or depreciation costs may be feasible. Even the recovery of O&M costs would require a major reform in pricing policy, monitoring, and enforcement (Rosegrant and Cline 2002).

Low Rainfed Crop Yields

Rainfed areas accounted for 58 percent of world cereal production in 1995, and thus are essential to meeting future food production needs. But in developing countries rainfed crop yields remain far below irrigated crop yields. Rainfed cereal yields averaged 1.5 metric tons per hectare in the developing world in 1995, less than half the developing country irrigated cereal yield of 3.3 metric tons per hectare (and also less than half the 3.2 metric tons per hectare of rainfed yields achieved on average in the developed world). To increase production, rainfed farmers have two options: extensive systems, which expand the area planted, or intensive systems, which increase inputs on a planted area in order to increase yields. To meet immediate food demands, farmers in many rainfed areas have expanded production into marginal lands. These fragile areas are susceptible to environmental degradation—

particularly erosion—from intensified farming, grazing, and gathering. This problem may be especially severe in areas of Africa where the transfer from extensive to intensive systems was slower than in other regions (de Haen 1997).

The environmental consequences of area expansion make crop yield growth a better solution to increasing production. Sustainable intensification of rainfed agriculture development can increase production while limiting environmental impacts. The three primary ways to enhance rainfed agricultural production through higher crop yields are to increase effective rainfall use through improved water management, to increase crop yields through agricultural research, and to reform policies and increase investment in rainfed areas (Rosegrant et al. 2002).

OVERVIEW OF THE BOOK

The challenges addressed in this introduction provide the focus for the modeling results presented in the remainder of the book. Prior to presenting the scenario results, however, we describe the methodology for the integrated water and food supply and demand model (the IMPACT-WATER model) in Chapter 2. The model is the primary tool used to explore a variety of possible futures for water and food to 2025. Then in Chapter 3, we describe—both qualitatively and quantitatively—the three primary scenarios for water and food futures—business-as-usual, water crisis, and sustainable water use.

Presentation of scenario results begins in Chapter 4 with outcomes under the business-as-usual scenario (BAU), representing our best estimate of future water and food supply and demand outcomes if present trends and policies continue. BAU is also used as a benchmark against which all other scenarios are analyzed and assessed. Chapter 5 examines the impacts of pessimistic and optimistic alternatives to BAU on water demand and supply and food production, prices, and trade (water crisis, or CRI, and sustainable water use, or SUS, respectively).

Chapters 6–8 use additional scenarios to focus on specific policy, investment, and management interventions to explore their individual influence on future developments. Chapter 6 explores the impacts of increasing water prices on water demand, environmental water use, and agricultural production for both agricultural and nonagricultural sectors. Chapter 7 explores the impact of reducing groundwater overdrafting on agriculture and on water demand from other sources. Chapter 8 explores the potential for rainfed agriculture to play an enhanced role in meeting future food production needs and conserving water. Finally, Chapter 9 synthesizes the results to discuss the likely implications for policy options toward ensuring a water and food secure future. Table 1.1 provides a summary of all the scenarios underpinning the projection results in each of these chapters.

Table 1.1—Scenario groupings, names, abbreviations, and descriptions

Group/Name	Abbreviation	Description
Benchmark (Chapter 4)		
Business as usual	BAU	Projects the likely water and food outcomes for a future trajectory based on the recent past, whereby current policy trends for water investments, water prices, and management are broadly maintained. BAU is used as the benchmark against which all other scenarios are compared so as to quantify the likely effects of the specific policy changes being models.
Pessimistic/optimistic (Chapter 5)		
Water crisis	CRI	Projects overall deterioration of current trends and policies in the water sector.
Sustainable water use	SUS	Projects overall improvements in a wide range of water sector policies and trends.
Higher water pricing (Chapter 6)		
Higher water prices	HP	Implements higher water prices with water use efficiency stable at BAU levels, and allocates a large portion of the conserved water to environmental uses.
Higher water price, lower environmental water share	HP-LENV	Implements higher water prices with water use efficiency stable at BAU levels, but allocates none of the conserved water to the environment.
Higher water price, higher basin efficiency	HP-HE	Implements higher water prices with higher water use efficiency than under BAU and allocates a large portion of the conserved water to environmental uses.
Higher water price, higher basin efficiency, lower environmental water share	HP-HE-LENV	Implements higher water prices with higher water use efficiency than under BAU, but allocates none of the conserved water to the environment.
Environmental flow reservation (Chapter 7)		
Low groundwater pumping	LGW	Projects the effects of the global elimination of groundwater overdraft.
Higher environmental flow	HENV	Projects a global increase in water reserved as committed flows for the environment without improved river basin efficiency.
Higher environmental flow and higher irrigation efficiency	HENV-HE	Projects a global increase in water reserved as committed flows for the environment with improved river basin efficiency.
Investment and effective rainfall use (Chapter 8)		
Low investment in irrigation development and water supply	LINV	Projects the impact of low irrigation and water supply investments on food production.
No improvement in effective rainfall use	NIER	Projects the effects of no improvement in effective rainfall use.
Low investment in irrigation development and water supply but high increases in rainfed area and yield	LINV-HRF	Projects the effects of high increases in rainfed area and yield to counteract reduced irrigated production from low irrigation and water supply investments.
Low investment in irrigation development and water supply but high increase of effective rainfall use	LINV-HIER	Projects the effects of increasing effective rainfall use to counteract reduced irrigated production from low irrigation and water supply investments.

Chapter 2

The Water and Food Model

This chapter presents a detailed description of the global water and food model, IMPACT-WATER, along with a brief review of relevant global modeling work focusing on state-of-the-art developments in global water modeling, particularly as they relate to agriculture. Appendix A provides more detailed technical documentation of the model for those interested, including the equations for the relationships incorporated in the model.

LITERATURE REVIEW

Global water models have taken advantage of recent developments in hydrological science, and system modeling technology, as well as numerous international and national efforts in global and regional water resources and food production assessments. Over the past ten years, hydrological and meteorological sciences have made great advances in land surface hydrology, and in providing knowledge, techniques, and prediction capabilities that are particularly useful in water resource applications. New technologies in remote sensing, radar, and geophysical exploration at multiple scales have been applied in data collection and modeling. The development of datasets and routing methods for the characterization of water movement over the land surface at the global scale has been particularly important to global freshwater assessment (Maidment 1999).

One comprehensive global hydrologic database is the climate data series provided by Climate Research Unit (CRU) of the University of East Anglia in England, which includes a 0.5-degree 1901–95 monthly climate time-series with precipitation, temperature, wind speed, net radiation, vapor pressure, and other data. The *Digital Atlas of the World Water Balance* developed at the Center for Research in Water Resources (CRWR) of the University of Texas at Austin features a compilation of global climate data in Geographic Information Systems (GIS) format, for use in characterizing the water balance of the earth, including both the description of vertical and horizontal processes affecting the movement of water over the land surface. The *World Water & Climate Atlas* developed at the International Water Management Institute (IWMI) is another data source, presenting rapid access of key climate variables for agriculture and water resources management including 30-year data from 30,000 meteorology stations around the world. Ongoing research has focused on improving databases, taking into account the impact of land uses and climate change.

Global climate models (GCM), or continental hydrologic models, have been created based on global climate datasets such as those described above (Asante 2000). Models such as those by Vorosmarty, Fekete, and Tucker (1996); Miller, Russell, and Caliri (1994); Lohmann et al. (1998); Alcamo et al. (1998); and Asante (2000) have been applied to calculate runoff and water storage at the global or continental scale. These models provide runoff generation and water balance at a scale around 10,000 square kilometers, and runoff at the river basin scale can also be extracted (Alcamo et al. 1998).

Several global water resources overviews have been published based on these global datasets and models and observed records. Margat (1995) studied the global water situation in 1990 and 2025, developing a set of global maps indicating regional variability of various water-related characteristics. Raskin, Hansen, and Margolis (1995) examined the future of water assuming a business-as-usual scenario based on anticipated economic development measured in terms of gross national product (GNP) growth and its past correlation with water demands. Gleick et al. (2002) summarize a wide range of global water resources data including both water supply from various sources and water demand in various sectors. Seckler et al. (1998) developed some scenarios of water demand and supply to 2025, identified countries and regions that will face serious water shortages in the next 25 years, and discussed some potential solutions to eliminate water scarcity including improving irrigation water use effectiveness and water supply expansion. WRI (1998) publishes water supply and demand data by country, which is updated annually. The Economic and Social Council of the United Nations (ECOSOC) presented the Comprehensive Assessment of the Freshwater Resources of the World to the UN (ECOSOC 1997). Goals of ongoing research in global freshwater assessment include improving long-term prediction with consideration of the change in global climate and the growing human impacts, improving the prediction of seasonal and interannual climate variability, and developing the relationship between hydrological and biochemical processes and food production (SCOWR 1997).

The United Nations Conference on Environment and Development (UNCED) held in Rio de Janeiro in 1992 concluded that water should be considered an integral part of the ecosystem and sustainable water resources development and management should be achieved at regional, national, and global scales. Since then, numerous international and national efforts have been undertaken to evaluate current water demand and supply situations and search for future solutions. Since agriculture has been, and will continue to be, the largest water consumer in most countries, global and regional water development and management for agriculture has been given high priority. Recently, the United Nations Educational Scientific and Cultural Organization (UNESCO) launched an investigation project, World Water Vision (WWV), which involved many national and international research and consulting agencies. Several documents based on this project were published in 2000, including an overall project report (Cosgrove and Rijsberman 2000), a specific report describing a vision of water for food and rural development (van Hofwegen and Svendsen 2000), and additional country reports (see Cosgrove and Rijsberman 2000 for details). See also Chapter 3 for more discussion of the WWV work as it relates to scenario development.

Besides global water modeling and assessments, other studies that contribute to water development and management include integrated basin management, field water management, crop water modeling, and system analysis techniques. Integrated basin/catchment management has been recognized as an important strategy for managing water uses and dealing with water scarcity at the river basin scale (Batchelor 1999). IWMI has completed substantial work on identifying ways to improve the productivity of water within basins (Molden, Sakthivadivel, and Habib 2001) and in modeling natural and artificial processes in river basins (Kite and Droogers 2001). The International Food Policy Research Institute (IFPRI) has developed integrated basinwide hydrologic-agronomic-economic models for efficient water allocation and economic water use efficiency analysis (Rosegrant et al. 2000). To deal with multiple objectives at the basin level, new problem-solving technologies in the areas of systems analysis, operations research, and decision support systems have emerged and been applied to deal with the growing complexities in water resources systems (McKinney et al. 1999). These types of basin studies will provide more detailed support for global water resources assessment.

Water resources research has also given priority to agricultural water management issues. Soil-plant-atmosphere-research (SPAR) provides an excellent opportunity to develop databases and modeling tools for field water management and crop water modeling. For practical purposes, the set of Irrigation and Drainage Papers published by FAO has guided crop field water management widely. Doorenbos and Pruitt (1977) and Allen et al. (1998) offer guidelines for computing crop water requirements. Doorenbos and Kassam (1979) established an empirical relationship between crop yield response and water stress that has been widely used because it is very simple and uses the most complete summary of available data for implementation of crop-water relationships (from FAO). Further, the data have been widely used for planning, designing, and operating irrigation supply systems and take account of the effect of the different water regimes on crop production (Perry and Narayanamurthy 1998).

Obviously, plentiful information exists for both global and regional water development and management analysis; however, the increased complexity of the physical aspects of water resources development introduces other economic, legal, social, and political intricacies. In recent decades, environmental concern, protection, and enhancement issues created additional complications. Furthermore, multiple objectives involved in water development are often disparate or incompatible, and water allocation conflicts between upstream and downstream users and between different sectors have materialized. New problem-solving technologies such as systems analysis, operations research, and decision support systems have emerged and have been applied to deal with these growing complexities in water resources systems (Yevjevich 1991; and McKinney et al. 1999). However, additional research is still necessary to conceptualize and quantify humanity's dependence on water today and in the future (SCOWR 1997); and policy analysis must integrate pieces of information into a consistent analytical framework and combine international and national efforts for policy-relevant regional and global water resources research.

The modeling exercise presented in this book attempts to draw upon these modeling efforts and integrate available information in water resources, agronomy, and economics in a comprehensive framework to analyze 30-year projections of domestic, industrial, livestock, and irrigation water demand and supply for 69 individual or aggregated river basins at a global scale, incorporating seasonal and interannual climate variability. Concepts related to water demand and supply in different sectors are presented and a systematic approach is developed to analyze the interrelationships among water availability, water infrastructure development, water management polices, and water demand, regionally and globally, in terms of sector, water scarcity, food production, demand, and trade.

The global modeling framework—IMPACT-WATER—combines an extension of the International Model for Policy Analysis of Agricultural Commodities and Trade (IMPACT) with a newly developed Water Simulation Model (WSM), based on state-of-the-art global water databases and models, integrated basin management, field water management and crop water modeling.

IMPACT-WATER MODEL

The IMPACT model provides a consistent framework for examining the effects of various food policies, the impact of different rates of agricultural research investment on crop productivity growth, and income and population growth on long-term food demand and supply balances and food security. The model comprises a set of 36 country or regional submodels, each determining supply, demand, and prices for

16 agricultural commodities, including eight crops. The country and regional agricultural submodels are linked through trade—a specification that highlights the interdependence of countries and commodities in global agricultural markets. The model uses a system of supply and demand elasticities incorporated into a series of linear and nonlinear equations to approximate the underlying production and demand functions. Details of the IMPACT methodology can be found in Rosegrant, Agcaoili-Sombilla, and Perez (1995) and Rosegrant, Meijer, and Cline (2002).

The primary IMPACT model simulates annual food production, demand, and trade over a 30-year period based on a calibrated base year. In calculating crop production, however, IMPACT assumes a "normal" climate condition for the base year as well as for all subsequent years. Impacts of annual climate variability on food production, demand, and trade are therefore not captured in the primary IMPACT model.

In reality, however, climate is a key variable affecting food production, demand, and trade. Consecutive droughts are a significant example, especially in areas where food production is important to local demand and interregional or international trade. More importantly, water demand is potentially increasing but supply may decline or may not fully satisfy demand because of water quality degradation, source limits (deep groundwater), global climate change, and financial and physical limits to infrastructure development. Therefore future water availability—particularly for irrigation—may differ from water availability today. Both the long-term change in water demand and availability and the year-to-year variability in rainfall and runoff will affect food production, demand, and trade in the future. To explore the impacts of water availability on food production, water demand and availability must first be projected over the period before being incorporated into food production simulation. This motivates an extension of IMPACT using WSM at the global scale.

WSM simulates water availability for crops accounting for total renewable water, nonagricultural water demand, water supply infrastructure, and economic and environmental policies related to water development and management at the river basin, country, and regional levels. Crop-specific water demand and supply are calculated for the eight crops modeled in IMPACT—rice, wheat, maize, other coarse grains, soybeans, potatoes, sweet potatoes and yams, and cassava and other roots and tubers—as well as for crops not considered (which are aggregated into a single crop for water demand assessment). Water supply in irrigated agriculture is linked with irrigation infrastructure, permitting estimation of the impact of investment on expansion of potential crop area and improvement of irrigation systems.

IMPACT-WATER—the integration of IMPACT and WSM—incorporates water availability as a stochastic variable with observable probability distributions to examine the impact of water availability on food supply, demand, and prices. This framework allows exploration of water availability's relationship to food production, demand, and trade at various spatial scales—from river basins, countries, or regions, to the global level—over a 30-year time horizon.

Although IMPACT divides the world into 36 spatial units, significant climate and hydrologic variations within large countries or regions make large spatial units inappropriate for water resources assessment and modeling. IMPACT-WATER, therefore, conducts analyses using 69 basins, with many regions of more intensive water use broken down into several basins. China, India, and the United States (which together produce about 60 percent of the world's cereal) are disaggregated into 9, 13, and 14 major river basins, respectively. Water supply and demand and crop production are first assessed at the river-basin scale, and crop production is then summed to the national level, where food demand and trade are modeled. Other countries or regions considered in IMPACT are combined into 33 aggregated "basins."

WATER DEMAND

The term water demand is often used inconsistently in the literature, sometimes referring to water withdrawal and other times to water consumption or depletion. The specific definitions of water demand terms used in our model are listed in Box 2.1. The concepts of water demand included in this discussion are all defined at the basin scale, unless otherwise stated. Water demand is classified as irrigation demand and non-irrigation demand, the latter further disaggregated into domestic, industrial, and livestock water demand. More detailed descriptions of the different types of water demand and their inclusion in the model are discussed in the following sections. (See Appendix A for detailed technical documentation with equations of the relationships incorporated in the model.)

Irrigation Water Demand

Irrigation water demand is projected based on irrigated area, crop evapotranspiration requirements, effective rainfall, soil and water quality (salinity), and basin-level irrigation-water-use efficiency. Basin efficiency in future years is assumed to increase at a prescribed rate in a basin, depending on water infrastructure investment and water management improvement in the basin.

Estimation of irrigation water demand requires extensive hydrologic and agronomic data support. Irrigated harvested crop area was assessed by Cai and Rosegrant (1999), crop growth periods in different countries or basins are collected from USDA–WAOB (1998), and the value of crop evapotranspiration coefficients by crop growth stages are estimated based on Doorenbos and Kassam (1979) and FAO

Box 2.1—Water demand definitions

Water Withdrawal. Water removed from a source and used for human needs, some of which may be returned to the original source and reused downstream with changes in water quantity and quality (Gleick 1998).

Water Consumption. Water withdrawn from a source and made unusable for reuse in the same basin through irrecoverable losses including evapotranspiration, seepage to a saline sink, or contamination (Gleick 1998).

Beneficial Water Consumption. Water consumption that contributes to various benefits of water use; crop evapotranspiration in agriculture, for example, is considered to be beneficial water consumption.

Nonbeneficial Water Consumption. Water depleted from the source but not used for productive purposes, such as "salt sinks" (drainage with high salt concentration), evaporation loss of field drainage, and seepage in distribution systems that cannot be returned to a source for potential reuse.

Basin Efficiency (BE). Water use efficiency assessed at the river basin scale, taking account of return flow reuse. For irrigation, BE measures the ratio of beneficial water consumption to total irrigation water consumption at the river-basin scale.

Consumption Coefficient (DC). The ratio of water consumption over water withdrawal. The value of (1-DC) indicates the fraction of water returned to the water supply system.

(1998a). Reference evapotranspiration is taken from a half-degree grid of monthly average reference evapotranspiration on agricultural land for 1961–90 calculated by Alcamo et al. (1998) using a Taylor method based on global climate datasets (CRU and GIS coverage of croplands).

The projection of irrigation water demand thus depends on changes in irrigated area and cropping patterns, water use efficiency, and rainfall harvest technology. Global climate change can also affect future irrigation water demand through changes in temperature and precipitation but is not considered in the current modeling framework.

Livestock Water Demand

Livestock water demand in the base year is assessed based on livestock production, water price, and water consumptive use per unit of livestock production including beef, milk, pork, poultry, eggs, sheep and goats, and aquaculture fish production.

Consumptive use coefficients for water for livestock are estimated for the United States from Solley, Pierce, and Perlman (1998), Mancl (1994), and Beckett and Oltjen (1993) and are adapted to other countries based on FAO (1986). For all livestock products except fish it is assumed that the projections of livestock water demand in each basin, country, or region follow the same growth rate as livestock production. Livestock production is endogenously determined in the IMPACT-WATER model as a function of livestock prices, feed prices, and technological change in the livestock sector. Water demand for fish production is assumed to grow at the weighted average rate of livestock water demand growth.

Municipal and Industrial Water Demand

Industrial water demand depends on income (GDP per capita), water use technology improvements, and water prices. A linear relationship is assumed between industrial water demand intensity (cubic meters of water per $1,000 GDP), GDP per capita, and a technology variable that varies with time. The impact of water prices is captured through a specified elasticity of industrial demand with respect to water price. Domestic water demand includes municipal water demand and rural domestic water demand. Domestic water demand is estimated based on projections of population, income growth, and water prices. In each country or basin, income and price elasticities of demand for domestic use are synthesized based on available estimates from the literature. These elasticities of demand measure the propensity to consume water with respect to increases in per capita income and prices. Projections of consumptive use of water by municipal and industrial sectors are adjusted for the fraction of population living in coastal areas (that is, within 50 kilometers of the coast). For these areas, we assume that discharge from municipal and industrial water use systems goes to the ocean and will not be reused.

Committed Flow for Environmental, Ecological, and Navigational Uses

Rising public awareness of the fragility of environmental and ecological systems over the last two decades has generated demand for committed water flow for environmental and ecological purposes, political purposes, and instream uses such as recreation, hydropower generation, and navigation. Committed flow is defined here as the quantity of water set aside or otherwise managed for environmental purposes and instream use that cannot be used for other purposes in the locations where the water has been reserved. Much of the committed flow is brought about by legislative or regulatory processes. In this modeling framework, committed flow is estimated as a portion of average annual runoff.

WATER SUPPLY

Water supply refers to water available for use from many sources. Water supply concepts are also simulated at the basin scale in the model and are described in the following sections. Box 2.2 provides a list of definitions of the water supply terms used in the model.

Effective Rainfall and Rainfall Harvest

Effective rainfall is rainfall that can be effectively used for crop growth and is generally the only water source for rainfed crops. Effective rainfall can be increased through rainfall harvesting—the capture, diversion, and storage of rainwater for plant growth and other uses. Rainfall harvesting can increase water availability, soil

---

Box 2.2—Water supply definitions

Renewable Water. Water that can be renewed by natural cycling through the atmosphere and the earth. For each region, total renewable water includes internal renewable water (the flow of rivers and recharges of groundwater generated from endogenous precipitation) and the inflow of surface and groundwater from other regions.

Total Water Availability. For each region, total water availability is the sum of renewable water, artificial basin/regional water transfer, desalinated water, nonrenewable groundwater (available only for a limited period), and salt water (available only for limited uses).

Maximum Allowable Water Withdrawal (MAWW). Water withdrawal capacity available for agricultural and municipal and industrial water uses, based on physical capacity (surface water diversion capacity and groundwater pumping capacity) and environmental constraints.

Effective Rainfall. Rainfall that can be effectively used for crop growth, including rainfall intercepted by plant foliage, rainfall that can enter and be stored in the root zone, and artificial rainfall harvested.

Effective Water Supply for Irrigation (EWIR). Field water supply that can be fully used for crop evapotranspiration. For each region and time period, *EWIR* is subject to water availability, maximum allowed water withdrawal, water allocation between sectors, water quality (such as salt concentration), and water use efficiency. For crops, *EWIR* is further subject to crop acreage and crop patterns.

Irrigation Water Supply Reliability (IWSR). Ratio of actual irrigation water consumption over the gross irrigation requirement, which depends on net irrigation requirement and irrigation efficiency.

fertility, and crop production and can also provide broader environmental benefits through reduced soil erosion especially in arid and semi-arid regions. Although improved rainfall harvesting is often considered in connection with traditional agriculture, it also has potential in highly developed agriculture. Advanced tillage practices, contour plowing (typically a soil-preserving technique), and precision leveling are all examples of practices that can improve infiltration and evapotranspiration, thus increasing the share of rainfall that can be used effectively for crop growth.

Effective Water Supply for Irrigation

Effective water supply for irrigation (EWIR) is calculated at the basin level and depends on hydrologic processes such as precipitation, evapotranspiration, and runoff, as well as anthropogenic impacts. Anthropogenic impacts include water demand in agricultural, domestic, and industrial sectors; flow regulation through storage and flow diversion and groundwater pumping, water pollution, and other water sinks; and water allocation policies such as committed flows for environmental purposes or water transfers from agricultural to municipal and industrial uses.

WATER SIMULATION MODEL

River Basin Aggregation

The WSM uses river basins as the spatial element of modeling. For each basin, all surface reservoirs, along both the main river and its tributaries, are aggregated into an "equivalent basin reservoir," and all groundwater sources are aggregated into a single groundwater source. Water demands in each basin are estimated separately for agricultural and nonagricultural uses (the latter including industrial and municipal uses) as well as committed flow for the environment. This aggregation assumes full water transfer capacity within each basin; water in one subbasin may be used for other subbasins where needed. Although defined in the model at the basin scale, water demands in the real world are generally located in proximity to the water source, and full water transfer between subbasins and different water supply systems is often constrained by engineering and economic feasibility. To avoid the potential "aggregation fallacy" created by this degree of basin aggregation, we introduce the concept of maximum allowable water withdrawal (MAWW), as defined in Box 2.2. The MAWW for a basin depends on source availability (including surface and groundwater), the physical capacity of water withdrawal for agricultural, domestic and industrial uses, instream flow requirements for navigation, hydropower generation, recreation, environmental purposes, and water demand. Total water withdrawal in each basin is constrained by its MAWW, which prevents water withdrawal beyond the basin's engineering capacity. With this constraint, the river basin aggregation method should be valid for modeling water supply and demand at the basin scale but this method is mainly used for global modeling. For detailed single-basin scale studies, spatial distribution of water supply and demand should be explicitly implemented with any analytical framework.

Model Formulation and Implementation

Based on the concepts discussed above, the WSM generates projections of water demand and water supply based on changes in water supply infrastructure and water allocation and management policy. The model is designed to simulate water demand and supply year by year (up to 30 years) for each basin or aggregated basin used in IMPACT-WATER. The model assumes that nonagricultural water demand, including municipal and industrial water demand and committed flow for instream uses, is satisfied as the first priority, followed by livestock water demand. The effective water supply for irrigation is the residual claimant, simulated by allowing a deficit between water supply and demand.

A traditional reservoir operation model is used (see Loucks, Stedinger, and Douglas 1981), incorporating all the previously discussed components of natural water availability, storage regulation, withdrawal capacity, and committed flow requirement. The objective of this optimization model is to maximize the reliability of water supply (that is, the ratio of water supply to demand). The model is applied for a monthly water balance within one year, and is run through a series of years by solving individual years in sequence and connecting the outputs from year to year. The ending storage of one year is taken as the initial storage of the next, with assumed initial water storage for the base year. For those basins with large storage capacity, interyear flow regulation will be active.

The time series of climate parameters is derived from 30-year historic records for the period 1961–90. In addition to a basic scenario that overlays the single historic time series over the 1995–2025 projection period, a number of alternative scenarios of hydrologic time series are generated by changing the sequence of the yearly historic records. These scenarios are used in WSM to generate alternative scenarios of water availability for irrigation. The model is run for individual basins but with interbasin and international flows simulated. The outflow from one basin becomes a source to downstream basins, which is important in many international river basins (such as the Nile, Mekong, Amazon, Indus, and Ganges-Brahmaputra).

Because of its global scope, the WSM relies more heavily on simplifying assumptions than do single-basin models. These assumptions include the aggregation of water storage at the river basin scale, the absence of irrigation effects on hydrologic processes, the priority of municipal and industrial water demands, and other assumptions noted above. The main advantage of the WSM is its integration of essential hydrologic and agronomic relationships with policy options for water resources development and management, mainly for irrigation. As such, the WSM is an effective tool for estimating irrigation water availability in the context of river basins for analysis at the global scale.

EXTENSION OF THE IMPACT MODEL

The original IMPACT model is updated to assess the effect of water availability on food production, demand, and prices by revising and adding several functional relationships. IMPACT examines supply and demand relationships for cereals, soybeans, roots and tubers, meats, milk, oils, and oilcakes and meals. Of these commodities, the treatment of cereals, soybeans, and roots and tubers is extended to include detailed analysis of the effects of water availability on commodity supply and demand and incorporates the following features.

1) Separate area and yield functions for rainfed and irrigated crops.

    • Water availability for irrigated area includes irrigation water and effective rainfall and groundwater extraction from the root zone.

    • Crop yields and yield growth rates are estimated separately for irrigated and rainfed areas based on differing inputs, investment, and agricultural research.

    • Farmers' responses to drought differ for irrigated and rainfed areas. In the case of drought, for example, farmers in rainfed areas generally maintain cultivated area while sacrificing yields, while farmers in irrigated areas tend to reduce cultivated area to maintain high yields.

2) Updated crop area and yield functions including water availability as a variable.

    • Potential irrigated crop area in the absence of water stress is a function of crop prices and potential irrigated area; actual crop area is a function of potential area and water-limited actual evapotranspiration relative to potential evapotranspiration.

    • Potential rainfed area in the absence of water stress is a function of crop prices; actual rainfed area is a function of potential rainfed area and water-limited actual evapotranspiration relative to potential evapotranspiration.

    • Potential irrigated and rainfed crop yields in the absence of water stress are a function of crop price, labor price, capital price, and technological change; actual irrigated and rainfed crop yields are a function of the potential yields and their respective water-limited evapotranspiration relative to potential evapotranspiration.

To determine the reduction of crop area harvested when water is limiting, a threshold level of relative evapotranspiration, E^*, is defined, below which farmers reduce crop area rather than impose additional moisture stress on existing crop area. The parameter E^* is an important policy and behavioral parameter that varies across countries and possibly across basins within countries. In developed countries characterized by large farms, E^* is assumed to be relatively higher, especially for irrigated crops. Water shortages are generally handled in these countries by fallowing a portion of the land while maintaining yields on remaining area, either by small reductions in area by most farmers or by some farmers fallowing all of their land with compensation from short-term sale of water rights, government drought insurance, or other mechanisms.

In developing countries characterized by many small farmers, on the other hand, E^* will likely be much lower, approaching the 0.60 considered the reference threshold level. In these countries, reduction in area caused by water shortages would imply complete fallowing of many small farms, eliminating the entire means of livelihood for these farmers. Under such circumstances, government irrigation management and local customs often favor spreading the water over as broad an area as possible to maintain some level of yield and income for the largest possible number of farms. For example, the *warabandi* system that governs many irrigation systems in India formally specifies that shortages be widely shared across farms.

LINKING IMPACT AND WSM

Figure 2.1 shows the integration of the water and food components in a consistent framework. IMPACT includes food production, demand, and trade components. Initial inputs into IMPACT, including growth in urban areas, income, and population, are used to project food and calorie demands, which in turn affect crop and livestock supply, demand, and prices. Elasticities for crop area, livestock number, and crop and livestock yield, as well as area and yield growth rates, are used in area and yield projections, which are in turn used in the calculations of crop and livestock supply. These projections of area, yield, and supply and demand are used in the WSM. The WSM includes functions of precipitation, runoff, evapotranspiration, water supply infrastructure, and socioeconomic and environmental policies. Water supply for irrigation is simulated accounting for year-by-year hydrologic fluctuations, irrigation development, growth of industry and domestic water uses, livestock water demand, environmental and other flow requirements (committed flow), and water supply and use infrastructure. This effective water supply for irrigation is then used as a variable in the irrigated and rainfed area and crop yield projections in IMPACT, and in the water supply and demand balance equations.

Figure 2.1—IMPACT-WATER: The structure and integration of the IMPACT and water simulation models

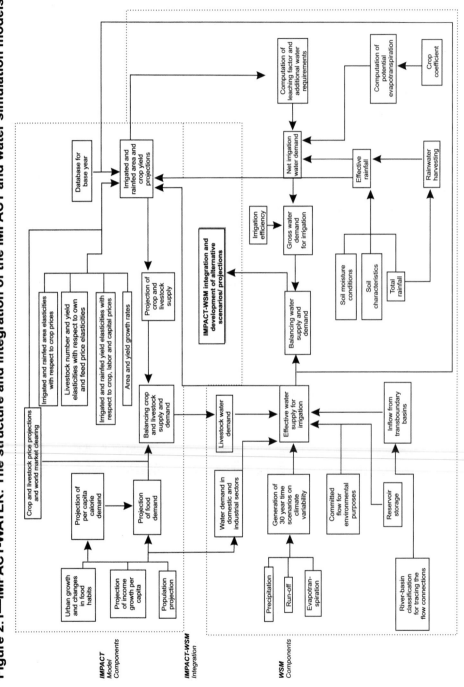

WSM first computes total EWIR in each time period, and then allocates the total EWIR to specific crops based on crop profitability, sensitivity to water stress, and irrigation water demand. Higher priority is given to crops that are more profitable, more drought sensitive, or require more irrigation water. WSM thus generates monthly effective irrigation water supply by crop and by basin over a 30-year time horizon and provides these variables as inputs into IMPACT. Other water parameters input into IMPACT include effective rainfall and maximum crop evapotranspiration by month, year, and basin.

The effective water supply for irrigation and rainfed agriculture is then entered into the crop model. For each year it is initially assumed that there is no water shortage so that crop area and yield are at their potential levels fully determined by prices, irrigation investment, and technological change. Water availability for crops is then computed, and crop area and yield are adjusted based on relative evapotranspiration. Next, crop production and stocks are updated, food demand is computed, and net food trade and global trade balances are calculated. Global net trade should equal zero; if the trade balance condition is violated crop prices are adjusted and the model undertakes a new iteration. The loop stops when net trade for all commodities equals zero. Crop area, yield, production, and prices are thus determined endogenously.

Data requirements for the modeling are extensive and relate to agronomy, economics, engineering, and public policy. Appendix A provides a description of the data requirements for this study.

The integrated model provides a wide range of opportunities to analyze water availability and food security at the basin, country, and global levels. Many policy-related water variables are involved in this modeling framework including potential irrigated area and cropping patterns, water withdrawal capacity for both surface and groundwater, water use efficiency, water storage and interbasin transfer capacity, rainfall harvest technology, allocation of agricultural and nonagricultural uses, and allocation of instream and offstream uses. Investment and management reform can influence the future paths of these variables, which in turn influence food security at both national and global levels.

Figure 2.2 shows a framework for the scenario analysis based on the primary driving forces in IMPACT-WATER. Four classes of driving factors influence the amount of water available for irrigation including agroclimatic variables, water management and investment in infrastructure, water allocation and incentives, and economic and demographic factors. Some of these drivers—such as increases in infrastructure investment, water management improvement, and development of new water sources—may increase water availability for irrigation, while others—such as faster urbanization and increased committed flows for environmental purposes—may decrease water availability for irrigation. These driving forces can be varied in WSM, the output of which—reflecting the effects of these driving forces

Figure 2.2—IMPACT-WATER: Driving forces for scenario analysis

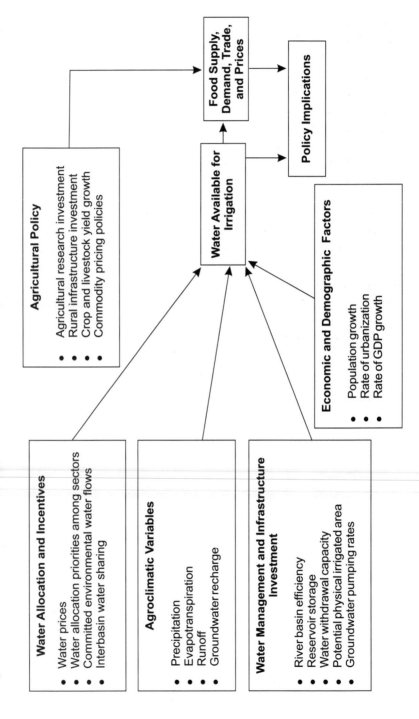

on effective water supply for irrigation and rainfed agriculture—can then be incorporated into IMPACT-WATER to compute food supply, demand, trade, and food prices. Additional agricultural policy drivers, such as investments in agricultural research and rural infrastructure, commodity pricing policies, and crop and livestock yield growth also directly affect food supply, demand, trade and prices. Policy implications related to these scenarios can then be explored based on outputs from both WSM and IMPACT-WATER. Further discussion of the use of critical drivers to develop alternative scenarios is provided in Chapter 3.

The purpose of this modeling exercise is to develop a tool for policy analysis in regional and global water resources development and management. As stated, many policy-related water variables are involved in this modeling framework including potential irrigated area and cropping patterns, MAWW for both surface and groundwater, water use efficiency, water storage and interbasin transfer facility, rainfall harvest technology (that is, to increase effective rainfall for crops), allocation of water to agricultural and nonagricultural uses, and committed instream flow requirements. In particular, water supply in irrigated agriculture is integrated with irrigation infrastructure, which permits the estimation of the impact of investment on expansion of potential crop area and improvement of irrigation systems. The remainder of this book consists of a series of different scenarios—including holistic alternative futures as well as assessments of the impacts of changes in policy and investment—and conclusions based on the scenario results.

Chapter 3

Potential Water Worlds:
Future Scenarios

he future of water and food is highly uncertain. Relatively uncontrollable factors like weather are partially the cause but the fundamental policy choices
that drive water and food supply and demand long-term are key to determining actual outcomes. Such policies address income and population growth,
investment in water supply, urban water systems, dams, irrigation, and other water
infrastructure; relative allocations of water to irrigation, domestic, industrial, and
environmental uses; reform of river basin, irrigation, and municipal and industrial
water management; water prices; and technological change in agriculture. Three possible futures for global water and food markets are presented in this and the next
two chapters.

1) The business-as-usual scenario (BAU) projects the likely water and food outcomes for a future trajectory based on the recent past, whereby current trends
   for water investments, water prices, and management are broadly maintained.

2) The water crisis scenario (CRI) projects deterioration of current trends and
   policies in the water sector.

3) The sustainable water use scenario (SUS) projects improvements in a wide
   range of water sector policies and trends.

SCENARIO ANALYSIS

A scenario is a coherent, internally consistent, and plausible description of a possible future state of the world (Carter et al. 1994). A scenario is not a forecast but
rather a snapshot of how the future could unfold. Scenario analysis of future outcomes encompasses a wide range of methodological approaches from sensitivity
analysis—based on changes in one underlying variable within a single formal

model—to holistic qualitative scenarios that create a narrative from a logical plot that governs the way events will unfold and then employ other models and quantitative tools, such as accounting frameworks and mathematical simulation models, to assess the quantitative aspects of the scenarios (Gallopin and Rijsberman 2001).

The strength of sequential sensitivity analysis of specific underlying variables within a single modeling framework is that it employs an internally consistent framework allowing assessment of the individual contributions of important underlying variables on future outcomes. The strength of the broad-based holistic scenario approach is that it incorporates quantitative insights from available data, numerical calculations, and mathematical models but also gives weight to the comprehensive underlying narrative and to key elements that are not quantifiable either in principle—such as cultural influences, behavior, and institutional responses to change—or in practice—as a result of inadequacies in data or scientific theory (Gallopin and Rijsberman 2001).

The analysis in our three primary scenarios represents a middle ground between these two approaches. A broad-based narrative describes the projected policy, management, and investment environment underlying the changing drivers (variables) explicitly represented in the model to provide a plausible backdrop of food and water policy for each scenario. The projected changes in the explicit model drivers are then quantified for each scenario.

The narratives developed in this book owe an intellectual debt to the water scenarios developed under the World Water Vision (Cosgrove and Rijsberman 2000); they also differ in important respects. The WWV process used mostly qualitative scenarios to help people think about future water worlds with selective quantitative assessments playing a supporting role (Gallopin and Rijsberman 2001). The Water Vision scenario narratives extend far beyond issues specific to water, including lifestyle choices, technology, demographics, and economics (Raskin 2002). Certain water and food related issues were then quantified using a variety of models—but no single integrated modeling framework was used to generate full quantitative scenarios.

Like the WWV scenarios, those here start with holistic narratives but we limit the variables across scenarios (both in the narrative and in the model parameters) to the underlying drivers that directly influence the water and food sectors.[1] We further limit the food sector variables to those directly related to water.[2] This method focuses the analysis on how policies, investments, and management reform—specific to water—influence future outcomes for water and food.

SCENARIO NARRATIVES

The primary drivers in the model are used as the building blocks for the scenarios. The drivers were identified in the discussion of the model in Chapter 2 but are worth summarizing here.

- *Economic and demographic drivers* include population growth, rate of urbanization, and rate of growth in GDP, and GDP per capita. The projected outcomes on the economic and demographic drivers are held constant across scenarios.

- *Climate and hydrological parameters* include precipitation, evapotranspiration, runoff, and groundwater recharge. These are likewise held constant across the three scenarios.

- *Technological, management, and infrastructural drivers* include river basin efficiency, reservoir storage, water withdrawal capacity, potential physical irrigated area, and crop and animal yield growth.[3]

- *Policy drivers* include water prices, water allocation priorities among sectors, committed water flows for environmental purposes, interbasin water shares, commodity price policy as defined by taxes and subsidies on commodities.

A wide range of actions can induce changes in the value of these drivers across the business-as-usual, water crisis, and sustainable water use scenarios. The narratives, next described, provide storylines of how these actions unfold and their qualitative impact on the model drivers.

THE BUSINESS-AS-USUAL SCENARIO

The business-as-usual scenario (BAU) assumes a continuation of current trends and existing plans in water and food policy, management, and investment. Continued complacency by international donors and national governments about agriculture and irrigation results in continued declining investment in these sectors. Limited and piecemeal implementation of institutional and management reform continues, with only mixed success in both urban water supply and drainage systems and in the irrigation sector. The combination of slowing investment and sporadic policy reform results in only slow progress in meeting major challenges in the water and food sectors.

In the food crop sector under BAU, both irrigated and rainfed harvested area grow at a slow rate in most of the world over the coming decades. Given a high proportion of land suitable for agricultural use is already being harvested and other factors such as urbanization, slow growth in irrigation investment, and soil degradation hinder additional growth of harvested area, yield improvements are a larger source of the additional agricultural production. Cereal prices further affect crop area expansion because steady or declining real cereal prices make it unprofitable to expand harvested area.

This slow rate of area expansion causes production growth to be based primarily on yield increases but crop yield growth also continues to slow. Slowing growth in public investment in agricultural research and rural infrastructure over recent decades continues into the future contributing to accompanying slowing yield growth in many regions and for many commodities. The very success of the Green Revolution in rice and wheat makes future crop yield gains for these crops more difficult because many sources of yield gains in recent decades are not readily repeatable—such as increasing crop-planting density through changes to plant architecture, raising the weight of usable food product as a fraction of total plant weight, introducing strains with greater fertilizer responsiveness, and improving management practices. Moreover, in the most productive regions, high existing levels of fertilizer use make it difficult to further boost yields through additional fertilizer use.

In the water sector under BAU, river basin and irrigation water management efficiency increase—but relatively slowly. At the mainstream level in most countries, public agencies continue to manage bulk water distribution between sectors, as well as primary irrigation canals. Technological innovations are introduced in some major systems, particularly those facing growing water shortages. Such innovations as real-time management of water releases from dams, keyed to telemetric monitoring of weather and streamflow conditions improve water use efficiency in some water-scarce basins.

Some river basins make progress toward more integrated river basin management through establishment of river basin organizations (RBOs) that promote greater stakeholder involvement, serve as a problem solving mechanism and provide a forum for dispute resolution. RBOs also facilitate information gathering and exchange through standardization of data collection, initiation of water quality and quantity monitoring, and the exchange of hydrologic and other information among various stakeholder groups. But in many cases, the functions of organizations constituting the RBO overlap and conflicts over coordination, disputes over budgetary authority, and loopholes in the laws and regulations cause serious problems. Furthermore, decentralization of government functions in some countries causes a breakdown in management at the river basin scale that transcends local and regional governments. These problems, combined with continued declines in operational budgets for RBOs, result in relatively slow overall progress in integration of river basin management.

Spurred by the often disappointing results achieved in publicly managed irrigation systems, by the expectation of benefits from decentralized management, and by the desire to transfer operations and maintenance cost to farmers to reduce budget transfers, governments under BAU continue recent trends in turnover of irrigation to farmer organizations and water user associations. But the benefits of system turnover continue to be mixed. System turnover is relatively successful and contributes to water efficiency gains in those instances where it is built on existing patterns of cooperation, backed by a supportive policy and legal environment that includes establishing secure water rights and providing technical and organizational training and support. But just as often, these policy and legal supports are lacking, and turnover has mixed success in improving management.

Increasing water scarcity and gradual introduction of small water price increases in some agricultural areas induce farmers in these regions to use water more efficiently by adopting improved technology (such as furrow, sprinkler, and drip irrigation) and improving onfarm water management. But continued political opposition prevents vigorous implementation of economic incentives that could better induce gains in water management and technology adoption. Opposition to pricing arises both from concerns over the impact of higher prices on farm income and from entrenched interests that benefit from existing systems of allocating water by bureaucratic decisions.

Water management also improves slowly in rainfed agriculture under BAU, with effective water use for rainfed crops improving gradually. Advancements in water harvesting and better onfarm management techniques— as well as some success in the development of shorter duration crop varieties that allow crop growth periods to shift to better utilize rainfall—lead to marginal enhancements in rainfall use efficiency. But with little progress in effective water harvesting systems, the high costs and labor constraints of implementing water harvesting prevents widespread use.

Public investment in irrigation expansion and reservoir storage continues to decline as the capital costs of building new irrigation systems escalate and the prices of cereals and other crop outputs of irrigation continue to decline. In addition to the direct cost of new systems, concerns over high environmental and social costs, including dislocation of persons displaced from dam and reservoir sites, results in a slowdown in investment. Nevertheless, many governments proceed with construction of dams where they judge benefit-cost ratios to be adequate. As a result, reservoir storage and water withdrawal capacity for irrigation water increase at a slow-to-moderate level in the coming decades.

However, with relatively slow growth in investment in expansion of potential irrigated area from surface water and a failure to establish higher prices for pumping of groundwater or to effectively regulate groundwater, farmers continue to expand pumping from groundwater. As a result, regions that are currently pumping groundwater at rates higher than recharge continue to do so. Unsustainable groundwater pumping therefore continues in a number of basins in the western United States, northern China, northern and western India, Egypt and other areas in the West Asia and North Africa (WANA) region under BAU. Groundwater extraction continues to grow significantly in other basins as well.

Environmental and other interest groups continue to press for increased allocation of water for environmental and instream uses including supplying water to wetlands, diluting pollutants, maintaining riparian flora and other aquatic species, and for tourism and recreation. With the relatively slow progress in policy reform and in improving basin water use efficiency, however, the need for water for domestic, industrial, and agricultural uses remains high, and no increases are given in committed environmental water allocations relative to total renewable water.

As in the irrigation sector, the cost of supplying water to domestic and industrial users also increases dramatically under BAU, with new supplies coming on stream at two to three times the cost per liter of existing water supplies. Improvement in the delivery and efficiency of use in the domestic sector is relatively slow but does lead to some increase in the proportion of households connected to piped water. However, the number of unconnected households remains large. With industrial water use intensity in developing countries three times as high as in developed countries in 1995, substantial room exists for conserving water supplies as industrialization proceeds. After a first use, freshwater can be recycled in the same home or factory, or wastewater can be collected, treated, and redistributed for use in another location. Industrial water use intensity drops in response to small price increases, improved pollution-control regulation and enforcement, and improved technology transferred through new industrial plants and retrofitted into many older plants. Significant additional potential gains are, however, foregone because industrial water prices remain relatively low and pollution regulations are often not enforced.

THE WATER CRISIS SCENARIO

BAU shows a mixed picture combining some successes with worrying trends. The water crisis scenario (CRI) examines the impact of a deterioration of current trends in water and food policy and investment. Moderate deterioration of many of these trends builds sufficiently to tip the scale to genuine water crisis.

Under CRI, government budget problems worsen and competing claims on slowly growing revenues draw funds away from the water sector, resulting in dramatic government cuts on irrigation systems expenditures and accelerated turnover of irrigation systems to farmers and farmer groups, devolving O&M to water users. But this rapid turnover is not accompanied by the necessary reform of water rights and often fails to gain support. At the same time prices for water delivery to secondary canals increase in an attempt to fund administrative and O&M delivery costs in the main system. Water users fight price increases, and a high degree of conflict translates to lack of local water-user cooperation about cost-sharing arrangements. With public investments declining, devoid of compensating increases in farmer and community funding, expenditures on O&M for secondary and tertiary systems similarly decline dramatically. Rapidly deteriorating infrastructure and poor management reduce system-level and basin-level water use efficiency.

Concomitant with the failure of decentralized management, central management also loses capability. Attempts to develop integrated river basin management by establishing RBOs fail from lack of funding from both general revenues and fee collections from water delivery, and because of high levels of conflict among water stakeholders within the basin as water scarcity grows.

National budget constraints and declining international interest in agriculture result in further declines in public investment in crop breeding for rainfed agriculture in developing countries, especially for staple crops such as rice, wheat, maize, other coarse grains, potatoes, cassava, yams, and sweet potatoes. Contrary to some expectations, the investment gap for these commodities is not filled by private agricultural research, which focuses mainly on developed country commodities and commercial crops in developing countries. The fall in research funding causes further declines in productivity growth in rainfed crop areas, particularly in more marginal areas. Despite rapid migration to cities, the absolute population of marginal rainfed areas increases, and the slow growth in rainfed productivity is inadequate to support these populations. In search of improved incomes, people turn to slash and burn agriculture, resulting in deforestation in the upper watersheds of many basins. Deforestation causes rapid increases in erosion and sediment loads in rivers, in turn causing faster sedimentation of reservoir storage. With a growing crisis in food and water, encroachment into wetlands for both land and water increases drastically. Encroaching settlements and pollution accelerate degradation of the integrity and health of aquatic ecosystems. The amount of water reserved for environmental purposes—such as minimum instream flows and wetlands maintenance—declines dramatically as unregulated and illegal withdrawals increase.

The cost of building new dams continues to increase rapidly, discouraging new investment in many proposed dam sites. Governments push forward with plans to build at other sites but are met with mounting—often violent—opposition from indigenous groups and nongovernmental organizations (NGOs) calling for a moratorium on all dam building given concerns over environmental impacts and the cost and impact of human resettlement. In the face of these protests and high costs, new investment in medium and large dams and storage reservoirs is virtually halted; combined with increased sedimentation of existing storage, net water storage declines in developed countries and in developing countries remains static.

With surface water supply declining and basin water use efficiency dropping, farmers turn to faster exploitation of groundwater. Overdrafting of groundwater is intensified in river basins in northern India, northern China, some countries in WANA, and in several basins in the western United States compared with BAU. For several years, rates of groundwater extraction increase, driving down water tables. But after about 2010, key aquifers in northern China, northern India, and WANA begin to fail; declining water tables make extraction costs too high for continued pumping, causing a big drop in groundwater extraction from these regions, further reducing water availability for all uses.

As under BAU, the rapid increase in urban populations—particularly in the burgeoning mega-cities of Asia, Africa, and Latin America—results in rapidly growing demand for domestic water use. But with tightening budget constraints, governments lack public funds to make the investments to extend piped water and sewage disposal to meet the population influx, and turn instead to a massive but rushed and inadequately planned privatization of urban water and sanitation services. The newly privatized urban water and sanitation firms are unable to hit their revenue targets because of underestimation of the backlog of investments needed just to bring the existing system up to grade. Seeking to raise more money, major price increases for connected households are implemented, but users respond by increasing unauthorized use of water, leaving revenues inadequate. Firms remain undercapitalized and do little to connect additional populations to piped water. A rapidly increasing number and percentage of the urban population must rely on high-priced water from vendors, or spend many hours fetching often-dirty water from standpipes and wells—time that is taken from child care and income-earning opportunities. Both water quantity and quality are inadequate to support healthy living standards for the growing urban masses that do not have access to piped water and sewer services, so disease and malnutrition increase dramatically.

THE SUSTAINABLE WATER USE SCENARIO

The sustainable water use scenario (SUS) explores the potential for dramatically increasing environmental water allocations and achieving full connection of all urban households to piped water and higher per capita domestic water consumption, while maintaining food production at BAU levels. It postulates the achievement of greater social equity and environmental protection through both careful market-oriented reform in the water sector and more comprehensive and coordinated government action. This includes greater investment in infrastructure and water management reform to improve water management efficiency, and investment in efficiency-and productivity-enhancing water and agricultural technology, particularly in rainfed areas.

In the food sector, increased crop research investments, technological change, and policy and water management reform boost water productivity and crop yield growth in rainfed agriculture. The high heterogeneity and erratic rainfall of rainfed environments make plant breeding a difficult task, and until recently, potential cereal yield increases appeared limited in the less favorable rainfed areas with poor soils and harsh environmental conditions. However, accumulating evidence shows dramatic increases in yield potential—even in drought-prone and high temperature rainfed environments—inducing a change in breeding strategy to directly target rainfed areas rather than relying on "spill-ins" from breeding for irrigated areas as a key to this faster growth. Increased agricultural research investments in both conventional breeding and in the tools of biotechnology—such as marker-assisted selection and cell and tissue culture techniques—ultimately lead to improved cereal yield growth in rainfed environments. Such growth comes both from incremental increases in the yield potential and from improved stress resistance including improved drought tolerance. Yields are further enhanced through participatory plant breeding that helps tailor new crop varieties to the multitude of rainfed microenvironments. Improved policies and increased investment in rural infrastructure helps to exploit remaining yield gaps by linking remote farmers to markets and reducing the risks of rainfed farming.

In the water sector under SUS, the effective price of water to the agricultural sector is gradually increased to induce water conservation and free up agricultural water for environmental, domestic, and industrial uses. By 2025 agricultural water prices are twice as high in developed countries, and three times as high as the very low levels in developing countries under BAU. These agricultural water price increases are implemented through incentive programs that provide farmers with income for the water they save, such as negative pricing or charge subsidy schemes that pay farmers for reducing water use, and through the establishment, purchase, and trading of water use rights. In cases where direct establishment of water rights to farmers is not feasible (for example, in large rice-based irrigation systems that serve many small farmers), water rights are established for communities and water user associations, which, with better knowledge of local farming conditions, pass on the change in price incentives to their members. The devolution of water rights to communities and water user associations (WUAs) is accompanied in many regions with turnover of O&M to these groups. The integrated devolution of water rights and systems results in more effective management of secondary and tertiary irrigation systems. This combination of water rights-based price increases with system turnover leads farmers to increase their onfarm investment in irrigation and water management technology significantly. With the public sector increasing direct investments and farmers and community boosting their private investments, irrigation system efficiency and basin water use efficiency increases significantly.

The successful decentralization of a number of significant water management functions through community and incentive-based management is supported at the river basin level with the establishment of effective RBOs for the management of mainstream water allocation for coordination of stakeholder interests. Higher funding and reduced water conflicts—a result of the overall improvement in water management—facilitate effective stakeholder participation in RBOs.

Breakthroughs in water harvesting systems including low-cost, labor-saving techniques and construction materials for building water catchment bunds and distributing water induce a more rapid adoption of water harvesting technologies in developing countries, improving the effective use of rainfall in crop production and increasing crop evapotranspiration per unit of rainfall. In addition to water harvesting, the more rapid adopting of advanced farming techniques helps to conserve soil and make more effective use of rainfall. While traditional agricultural techniques have tended to apply the same management to an entire field, precision agriculture methods focus on information technology using site-specific soil, crop, and other environmental data to determine specific inputs required for certain sections of fields. Many of these methods involve the use of technologies like global positioning systems (GPS), satellites, and remote sensing. Precision agriculture directly increases crop yields and also improves water availability through greater relative infiltration of rainfall. Initially adopted in the United States, it spreads more rapidly there and in developed countries given cost-reducing advances in information and communications technology and begins to penetrate commercial farming in developing countries including Argentina, Brazil, China, and India. Adoption rates of other improved techniques also accelerate, including contour plowing and precision land leveling that act to detain and infiltrate a higher share of the precipitation. Conservation tillage technologies, such as minimum till and no till, that began to spread in South Asian rice-wheat farming systems in the late twentieth century continue to expand their coverage. Adoption of conservation tillage practices increases the share of rainfall that goes to infiltration and evapotranspiration. The combination of water harvesting, precision agriculture, and conservation tillage increases the effective rainfall used for crop production.

Spurred by the rapidly escalating costs of building new dams and the increasingly apparent environmental and human resettlement costs, developing (and developed) countries undertake a comprehensive reassessment of reservoir construction plans involving both new analysis of the costs and benefits of proposed projects—including environmental externalities—and consultation with multiple stakeholders—including potential beneficiaries such as farmers who would receive new irrigation water, potential flood control beneficiaries, and those who could be adversely affected by new dams such as persons who would have to be relocated and environmental advocacy groups. As a result of this process, a large number of planned storage projects are taken off the drawing boards. The cutback is partly compensated by reduced rates of sedimentation of reservoirs given more rapid growth in rainfed crop yields (see above), which slows the movement of farmers to clear forests for cultivation in fragile upper watersheds.

The rapidly increasing cost of groundwater pumping, together with the decline in water tables, and increasing degradation of overdrafted aquifers induces a significant change in policy toward groundwater extraction. A combination of market-based approaches that assign water rights to groundwater based on annual withdrawals and the renewable stock of groundwater—together with the passage of stricter regulations and better enforcement of these regulations—results in a phasing-out of all groundwater overdrafting in excess of natural recharge.

Similar to the case for agricultural water management, dramatic reform is undertaken in the domestic and industrial water demand sectors. A doubling of water prices for connected households is phased-in gradually, with targeted subsidies retained for low-income households. The increase in revenue from higher water prices is invested to reduce water losses in existing water supply systems and to expand water supply to households that were previously not connected to piped water systems. In many major cities, water systems are privatized, and additional investment funds are obtained through private capital markets. In many other cities, the water supply stays under public management but the regulatory system is separated from service delivery and is greatly improved. With improved performance, public systems are able to raise the needed new capital through issuance of municipal bonds or, in the case of smaller cities, bonds backed by regional water-development boards supported by national general revenues and international development assistance. The strong evidence that access to clean water dramatically reduces child malnutrition and mortality motivates this increase in national and international public funding.   The same findings spur dramatic increases in public provision of standpipes in areas that are not yet serviced by piped water, thus improving access and reducing the price of unconnected water, ultimately boosting water consumption for unconnected households. As water supply expansion continues, the number of unconnected households declines over time until all households are connected by 2020. Industries respond to higher prices, particularly in developing countries, by dramatically increasing in-plant recycling of water, reducing consumptive use of water. The technological backlog on water recycling in developing countries means that considerable potential for improvement exists, and industrial demand in response to prices is relatively high.

With strong societal pressure for improved environmental quality, allocations for environmental uses of water are increased. Moreover, pressure on wetlands and on other environmental purposes for water are reduced by many of the reforms undertaken in the agricultural and nonagricultural water sectors. All water savings from both domestic and urban water conservation resulting from higher water prices are fully allocated to instream environmental uses. Improvement in water use efficiency resulting from higher investment and better water management means that more water is left instream for environmental purposes.

SCENARIO SPECIFICATION

The scenarios are implemented in the model through changes in the assumptions regarding underlying drivers. This section summarizes the projected values of the drivers for the various scenarios.

Population and Income Growth

Population and income growth are crucial determinants of water and food supply and demand. A world population of 3 billion people in 1960 doubled to 6 billion by 1999, with population growth rates peaking at 2.1 percent annually between 1965 and 1970, and declining progressively since then to 1.4 percent annually between 1997 and 1998. The population projections in the scenarios are based on the medium variant UN projections (UN 1998), and are disaggregated over separate five-year periods. As noted above, population (and income) projections are the same across scenarios to focus the analysis on the impact of changes in direct water-related factors. Projected population for all countries and regions covered in the model are shown in Table 3.1. Further declines in global population growth rates are projected, with growth rates declining in later periods as birth rates fall in virtually all regions and declining mortality rates level off. The developing countries are projected to account for 98 percent of world population growth through 2025. Despite the impact of HIV/AIDS, the population of Sub-Saharan Africa (SSA), estimated at 532 million in 1995, is projected to grow at 2.5 percent per year, more than doubling to 1.1 billion people in 2025. Among other regions, Pakistan, South Asia, and WANA have relatively high population growth rates. The two most populous countries—India and China—will average only 1.3 and 0.6 percent per year, respectively. Nevertheless, because the population bases of these countries are so large, they will still account for about 30 percent of the total world population increase during 1995–2025.

Closely related to population and income changes is the transformation of demographic patterns. The most vital of these demographic characteristics, particularly in terms of projecting future water and food needs in fast-growing economies, is the rate of urbanization. Urbanization accelerates changes in diet away from basic staples like sorghum, millet, maize, and root crops, to cereals requiring less preparation (such as wheat), fruits, livestock products, and processed foods (Rosegrant et al. 2001). Moreover, urbanization influences the rate of growth in

Table 3.1—Rural, urban, and total population, 1995 and 2025

Country/Region	1995 baseline estimates (millions)			2025 projections (millions)		
	Rural	Urban	Total	Rural	Urban	Total
United States	64	205	269	58	289	347
European Union 15	80	293	373	56	316	372
Japan	28	98	125	20	104	124
Australia	3	15	18	3	21	24
Other developed countries	32	59	90	27	79	106
Eastern Europe	54	83	137	33	81	114
Central Asia	31	23	54	37	35	72
Rest of former Soviet Union	67	172	239	40	162	202
Mexico	24	67	91	25	105	130
Brazil	34	125	159	26	193	219
Argentina	4	31	35	3	44	47
Colombia	11	28	39	11	48	59
Other Latin America	53	99	152	57	177	234
Nigeria	60	39	99	79	124	203
Northern Sub-Saharan Africa	104	29	133	174	114	288
Central and western Sub-Saharan Africa	84	47	131	132	150	282
Southern Sub-Saharan Africa	55	24	80	75	80	154
Eastern Sub-Saharan Africa	70	19	89	112	73	184
Egypt	34	27	62	41	54	95
Turkey	19	43	61	12	75	87
Other West Asia/North Africa (WANA)	84	127	212	107	275	382
India	679	248	927	777	575	1,352
Pakistan	81	42	124	118	133	251
Bangladesh	97	27	124	125	85	211
Other South Asia	48	10	58	72	35	107
Indonesia	127	70	198	107	166	273
Thailand	47	12	59	50	28	77
Malaysia	9	11	20	9	22	31
Philippines	31	37	68	30	77	107
Viet Nam	59	14	73	73	32	105
Myanmar	33	11	44	34	26	60
Other Southeast Asia	14	3	16	21	10	32
China	857	369	1,226	778	702	1,480
Korea, Republic of	10	35	45	5	47	52
Other East Asia	10	14	24	9	21	29
Rest of the World	5	2	6	7	4	11
Developing countries	2,774	1,634	4,408	3,106	3,510	6,616
Developed countries	327	925	1,251	237	1,051	1,288
World	**3,101**	**2,559**	**5,659**	**3,343**	**4,561**	**7,903**

Sources: 1995 data are from FAO (2000); 2025 data are authors' projections based on UN (1998) medium scenario.

Table 3.2—Gross domestic product per capita in 1995 and 2025

Country/Region	Gross domestic product (GDP) per capita (U.S. dollars)		Projected annual growth rate 1995–2025 (percent per year)
	1995 baseline estimates	2025 projections	
United States	27,700	50,410	2.0
European Union 15	21,820	42,430	2.2
Japan	38,430	76,460	2.3
Australia	19,880	32,400	1.6
Other developed countries	13,830	21,360	1.5
Eastern Europe	2,510	8,430	4.1
Central Asia	950	1,700	2.0
Rest of former Soviet Union	1,970	3,830	2.2
Mexico	3,810	7,710	2.4
Brazil	4,180	8,830	2.5
Argentina	8,210	22,660	3.4
Colombia	2,200	4,330	2.3
Other Latin America	2,090	3,910	2.1
Nigeria	270	450	1.7
Northern Sub-Saharan Africa	110	140	0.8
Central and western Sub-Saharan Africa	390	570	1.3
Southern Sub-Saharan Africa	450	610	1.0
Eastern Sub-Saharan Africa	240	350	1.3
Egypt	960	2,030	2.5
Turkey	2,640	6,890	3.2
Other West Asia/North Africa (WANA)	1,630	2,590	1.6
India	360	1,470	4.8
Pakistan	430	840	2.3
Bangladesh	240	660	3.4
Other South Asia	300	610	2.4
Indonesia	1,020	2,760	3.4
Thailand	2,840	10,490	4.5
Malaysia	4,230	12,580	3.7
Philippines	1,090	2,980	3.4
Viet Nam	270	990	4.4
Myanmar	170	390	2.8
Other Southeast Asia	610	1,190	2.3
China	670	3,060	5.2
Korea, Republic of	9,820	36,270	4.5
Other East Asia	610	1,140	2.1
Rest of the World	2,910	5,500	2.1

Sources: 1995 data are from World Bank (2000); 2025 data are authors' projections.

domestic and industrial water demand, as well as agriculural water demand through changes in the food demand. Rural-to-urban migration—and its attendant significant effect on demand structures—increased quite rapidly over the past few decades throughout the developing world and will continue to grow over the projection period. About 37 percent of the population of developing countries resided in urban areas in 1995, up from 22 percent in 1960 and 30 percent in 1980 (Table 3.1 and World Bank 2000). Urbanization is projected to accelerate in the future, with the urban population of developing countries more than doubling between 1995 and 2025, while the rural population increases by 12 percent. By 2025, 53 percent of the population in developing countries will reside in urban areas (Table 3.1).

GDP per capita in 1995 and 2025 and the annual rate of growth between 1997 and 2025 are shown in Table 3.2. GDP per capita growth rate disparities among countries in the developing world are projected to remain high. Growth rates will be highest in Asia, ranging from 2.1 to 5.2 percent per year; with growth rates in Latin America (LA) of 2.1 to 3.4 percent per year. GDP growth for SSA is projected to be between 0.8 and 1.7 percent per year between 1995 and 2025, with lower aggregate growth further suppressed by rapid population growth.

Water Infrastructure, Policy, and Management

The key drivers influenced by water policy, management, and infrastructure investment include river basin efficiency, reservoir storage capacity, physical potential irrigated area, and allowable water withdrawal.

Basin Efficiency. Depending on the local conditions in the irrigation system, agronomic, technical, managerial, and institutional improvements can have large positive impacts on irrigation system water use efficiencies (Batchelor 1999). However, improvement in river basin efficiency is more difficult because much of water "lost" from individual irrigation systems is in the form of return flows that are reused downstream. Rapid improvement in basin efficiency would require a significant commitment to water policy reform and investment—a commitment not apparent in current trends in the water sector. Under BAU, it is projected that basin efficiency (*BE*) will improve relatively slowly. The estimated and projected values of *BE* for selected countries and regions in 1995 and 2025 are shown in Table 3.3. In 1995, the average *BE* was assessed at 0.56 globally, 0.53 in developing countries, and 0.64 in developed countries. By 2025, the average *BE* is projected to reach 0.61 worldwide, 0.59 in developing countries and 0.69 in developed countries, representing relatively small—but important—improvements over efficiency levels in 1995 (Table 3.3). Relatively high increases in *BE* are projected for developed and developing countries in which renewable water supply infrastructure is highly developed, including India, China, and WANA, while smaller increases are projected for areas where water supply facilities are relatively underdeveloped, including SSA and Southeast Asia. Excluding China and India, the developing countries are projected to display slow improvements in *BE*, from 0.53 in 1995 to 0.56 in 2025.

Table 3.3—Basin efficiency and reservoir storage for irrigation and water supply under business-as-usual, water crisis, and sustainable water use scenarios,1995 and 2025

| Country/Basin(s) | Basin efficiency | | | | Reservoir storage (km³) | | | |
| | 1995 baseline estimates | 2025 projections | | | 1995 baseline estimates | 2025 projections | | |
		BAU	CRI	SUS		BAU	CRI	SUS
Basins in the United States								
Ohio and Tennessee	0.61	0.62	0.58	0.65	2	2	2	2
Rio Grande River	0.74	0.78	0.66	0.85	4	4	4	4
Columbia	0.69	0.75	0.64	0.83	18	18	16	18
Colorado	0.82	0.90	0.71	0.90	55	55	48	55
Great Basin	0.71	0.76	0.65	0.86	3	3	3	3
California	0.76	0.84	0.68	0.90	31	31	28	31
Arkansas-White-Red	0.70	0.74	0.65	0.79	20	20	18	20
Mid Atlantic	0.61	0.62	0.58	0.69	8	8	7	8
Mississippi								
Downstream	0.67	0.71	0.62	0.77	1	1	1	1
Upstream	0.61	0.64	0.58	0.71	2	2	2	2
Great Lakes	0.61	0.64	0.58	0.73	2	2	2	2
South Atlantic-Gulf	0.61	0.64	0.58	0.68	15	15	13	15
Texas-Gulf	0.73	0.76	0.66	0.83	40	40	35	40
Missouri	0.71	0.76	0.65	0.81	60	60	53	60
United States					**263**	**263**	**230**	**263**
Basins in China								
HuaiHe	0.60	0.67	0.45	0.82	137	156	136	143
HaiHe	0.70	0.78	0.48	0.86	110	117	106	114
HuangHe	0.58	0.64	0.44	0.79	80	98	78	88
ChangJiang	0.52	0.58	0.41	0.79	325	363	327	336
SongLiao	0.54	0.61	0.42	0.81	153	185	153	162
Inland	0.47	0.52	0.38	0.81	38	51	39	45
Southwest	0.47	0.53	0.38	0.78	6	7	6	6
ZhuJiang	0.47	0.53	0.38	0.75	152	173	155	159
Southeast	0.47	0.53	0.39	0.75	63	72	63	68
China					**1,064**	**1,221**	**1,063**	**1,122**
Basins in India								
Sahyadri Ghats Mountains	0.57	0.63	0.43	0.71	16	23	16	19
Eastern Ghats Mountains	0.52	0.56	0.41	0.64	9	14	9	11
Cauvery River Basin	0.52	0.57	0.41	0.69	7	11	7	9
Godavari River Basin	0.53	0.58	0.42	0.65	24	35	24	29
Krishna River Basin	0.53	0.58	0.41	0.67	23	34	23	28
Coastal drainage (Indian)	0.60	0.66	0.45	0.76	19	33	19	25
Chotanagpur Plateau coastal	0.55	0.61	0.43	0.69	4	5	4	4
Brahmari River Basin	0.60	0.66	0.45	0.77	21	36	21	27
Luni River Basin	0.61	0.67	0.45	0.80	21	38	21	28
Mahi Tapti Narmada, and Purna	0.55	0.61	0.42	0.69	17	30	17	22
Brahmaputra River Basin	0.55	0.60	0.42	0.66	2	3	2	3
Indus River Basin	0.55	0.61	0.43	0.75	21	31	21	25
Ganges River Basin	0.59	0.65	0.44	0.75	50	74	50	59
India					**232**	**367**	**233**	**287**

(continued)

Table 3.3—Continued

Country/Basin(s)	Basin efficiency				Reservoir storage (km³)			
	1995 baseline estimates	2025 projections			1995 baseline estimates	2025 projections		
		BAU	CRI	SUS		BAU	CRI	SUS
Other countries/regions								
European Union 15	0.55	0.58	0.53	0.59	56	61	54	58
Japan	0.56	0.59	0.53	0.61	4	4	4	4
Australia	0.73	0.79	0.65	0.86	65	75	63	70
Other developed countries	0.55	0.60	0.53	0.64	257	274	254	266
Eastern Europe	0.60	0.64	0.56	0.68	28	32	28	32
Central Asia	0.55	0.61	0.42	0.70	93	98	89	98
Rest of former Soviet Union	0.60	0.63	0.44	0.68	122	131	118	131
Mexico	0.51	0.56	0.40	0.64	104	122	101	113
Brazil	0.41	0.42	0.34	0.51	96	108	93	103
Argentina	0.42	0.44	0.35	0.50	60	71	58	67
Colombia	0.41	0.43	0.35	0.50	5	7	5	7
Other Latin America	0.41	0.42	0.35	0.49	99	118	96	107
Nigeria	0.45	0.48	0.37	0.57	37	51	40	51
Northern Sub-Saharan Africa	0.42	0.43	0.35	0.51	16	21	17	21
Central and western Sub-Saharan Africa	0.45	0.46	0.37	0.65	145	174	153	164
Southern Sub-Saharan Africa	0.49	0.51	0.39	0.60	153	178	160	166
Eastern Sub-Saharan Africa	0.40	0.42	0.34	0.50	3	4	3	4
Egypt	0.70	0.75	0.57	0.88	146	155	140	151
Turkey	0.60	0.64	0.45	0.74	139	197	144	157
Other West Asia/North Africa (WANA)	0.69	0.75	0.57	0.89	32	47	32	37
Pakistan	0.50	0.52	0.40	0.61	21	26	21	24
Bangladesh	0.46	0.47	0.37	0.53	12	17	12	15
Other South Asia	0.43	0.44	0.35	0.50	5	8	5	7
Indonesia	0.46	0.47	0.37	0.55	55	72	55	64
Thailand	0.50	0.53	0.40	0.60	31	38	30	36
Malaysia	0.52	0.55	0.41	0.66	15	19	15	18
Philippines	0.47	0.49	0.38	0.56	2	3	2	2
Viet Nam	0.45	0.48	0.37	0.55	1	2	1	2
Myanmar	0.45	0.47	0.37	0.55	3	5	3	4
Other Southeast Asia	0.50	0.53	0.40	0.64	10	15	10	13
South Korea	0.62	0.65	0.45	0.75	15	20	15	19
Other East Asia	0.42	0.44	0.35	0.50	28	34	28	32
Rest of the World	0.43	0.45	0.36	0.50	8	11	8	10
Developing countries	0.53	0.59	0.57	0.72	2,632	3,209	2,634	2,903
Developed countries	0.64	0.69	0.42	0.69	796	840	751	823
World	**0.56**	**0.61**	**0.44**	**0.70**	**3,428**	**4,049**	**3,385**	**3,727**

Source: IMPACT-WATER projections, 2002.
Notes: BAU indicates business-as-usual scenario; CRI, water crisis scenario; SUS, sustainable water use scenario; and km³, cubic kilometers.

Reservoir Storage. For most basins and countries, surface reservoir storage in the base year is estimated on values from the International Committee of Large Dams (ICOLD 1998), while ESCAP (1995) provides estimates for non-ICOLD member countries. Changes in reservoir storage to 2025 are based on assessments by Wallingford (2000), and on our estimates of future investments in storage. Reservoir storage for selected countries and regions in 1995 and for alternative scenarios in 2025 are shown in Table 3.3. The total global reservoir storage for irrigation and water supply is estimated at 3,428 cubic kilometers in 1995 (47 percent of total reservoir storage for all purposes), and under BAU, is projected to reach 4,049 cubic kilometers by 2025, representing a net increase of 621 cubic kilometers over the next 25 years. Only 44 cubic kilometers of the net storage increase will be in developed countries, with the major increases occurring in China, with a storage increase of 15 percent to 1,221 cubic kilometers; India, with an increase of 58 percent to 367 cubic kilometers; SSA, with an increase of 21 percent to 425 cubic kilometers; Asian countries excluding China and India, with an increase of 36 percent to 132 cubic kilometers; and LA, with an increase of 17 percent to 62 cubic kilometers.

Under CRI, net reservoir storage for irrigation and water supply will stay at 1995 levels for developing countries as a whole, and it will slightly decline (by 2 percent or 40 cubic kilometers) for developed countries from 1995 levels. In 2025, world reservoir storage for irrigation water supply will be only 3,385 cubic kilometers, 16 percent less than under BAU. Under SUS, the net increase of global reservoir storage for irrigation and water supply will be about 300 cubic kilometers, less than half the increase under BAU. Of this increase, about 19 percent is in China, 18 percent in India, 18 percent in Sub-Saharan Africa, and 45 percent in other countries and regions.

Maximum Allowable Water Withdrawals. As described in Chapter 2, actual water withdrawals are constrained by allowable water withdrawal for surface water and groundwater. Total allowable water withdrawal in the base year is estimated based on Gleick (1999), Shiklomanov (1999), and WRI (2000). In the model, projected allowable water withdrawal is governed by a combination of "hard" infrastructure constraints such as physical diversion structures and pumping capacities, and "soft" policy constraints such as the amount of water that must be left instream for environmental purposes and regulations on groundwater extraction. Maximum allowable water withdrawals for surface water (SMAWW) and groundwater (GMAWW) under BAU are projected to 2025, respectively, according to the current water withdrawal capacity, the growth of water demand, physical constraints on pumping, and projected investments in infrastructure in future years. Table 3.4 shows the SMAWW and GMAWW for the 1995 baseline year and projected to 2025 for selected countries and regions under our three primary scenarios.

Table 3.4—Annual maximum allowable water withdrawal for surface and groundwater under business-as-usual, water crisis, and sustainable water use scenarios,1995 and 2025

Country/Region	SMAWW (km³) 1995 baseline estimates	2025 projections BAU	CRI	SUS	GMAWW (km³) 1995 baseline estimates	2025 projections BAU	CRI	SUS
Asia	1,919	2,464	2,926	2,464	478	542	519	389
China	584	764	916	764	138	171	176	137
India	573	735	872	735	237	255	235	163
Southeast Asia	194	286	375	286	22	32	41	32
South Asia excluding India	318	390	444	390	57	58	41	32
Latin America (LA)	251	358	452	358	65	79	90	79
Sub-Saharan Africa (SSA)	73	141	222	141	63	87	109	90
West Asia/North Africa (WANA)	246	302	348	302	72	74	60	45
Developed countries	976	1,131	1,247	1,131	255	278	293	267
Developing countries	2,425	3,197	3,875	3,197	670	773	769	594
World	3,401	4,327	5,122	4,327	925	1,051	1,062	861

Source: Authors' estimates and IMPACT-WATER projections, 2002.
Notes: SMAWW indicates surface maximum allowable water withdrawal; GMAWW groundwater maximum allowable water withdrawal; and km³ indicates cubic kilometers. BAU indicates business-as-usual scenario; CRI, water crisis scenario; and SUS, sustainable water use scenario.

The utilization of groundwater is determined by the change in GMAWW and groundwater extraction rates relative to GMAWW. Many countries and basins currently exploit their groundwater reserves at a rate substantially exceeding recharge. For these "overdrafting" basins, particularly the overexploited aquifers in northern India, northern China, WANA, and the western United States, a slight decline in GMAWW is assumed for the baseline. Conversely, for aquifers worldwide that are currently underutilized relative to GMAWW, a gradual increase in extraction is projected under the baseline.

Under CRI, for countries and river basins currently pumping in excess of recharge, the growth in extraction continues at BAU rates until 2010. Then, beginning in 2010, a rapid decline in GMAWW begins, until, in 2025, GMAWW declines to below physical recharge rates, as saltwater intrusion, subsidence of aquifers, and depth to the declining water table makes it uneconomic to pump groundwater. For other countries and river basins, where overdrafting is not occurring, the growth in GMAWW and extraction rates under CRI is more rapid than the same under BAU, as farmers seek to access more water to make up for declining water use efficiency and declining availability of water from reservoir storage. The balance of these effects leaves total GMAWW for the developing countries in 2025 virtually the same as under BAU.

In the SUS scenario, groundwater overdrafting is phased out over the next 25 years through a reduction in the ratio of annual groundwater pumping to recharge at the basin or country level to 0.55. Compared with 1995 levels, under SUS, groundwater pumping in these countries/regions declines by 163 cubic kilometers including a reduction of 30 cubic kilometers in China, 69 in India, 29 in WANA, 11 in the United States, and 24 cubic kilometers in other countries. The projected increase in pumping for areas with more plentiful groundwater resources remains virtually the same as under BAU. For developing countries as a whole under SUS, allowable groundwater pumping in 2025 falls to 594 cubic kilometers representing a decline of 11 percent from the value in 1995 and a drop from the 2025 BAU value of 23 percent (Table 3.4).

Potential Irrigated Area. Two concepts need to be distinguished with respect to irrigated area: potential irrigated area and actual or realized irrigated area. Potential irrigated area is the area that can be irrigated in the absence of any water supply constraints at the prevailing level of irrigation infrastructure and commodity prices. Actual irrigated area is the irrigated area harvested under the prevailing hydrological conditions in any given year, and is therefore a function of both potential and available water. Potential and actual irrigated area by crop in 1995 is modeled based on data from FAO (1999) and Cai and Rosegrant (1999). Projected actual irrigated area for the three scenarios is reported in the model outcomes in Chapters 4 and 5. Growth rates for potential irrigated area between 1995 and 2025 are estimated based on FAO (1999) and on our estimation of the impact of investment on expansion in irrigation infrastructure (Rosegrant et al. 2001). For the scenario analysis, we want to isolate the direct impact of changes in water scarcity on the growth in actual irrigated area, rather than driving the results by changing the potential area irrigated. We therefore assume the same potential irrigation water demand by projecting the same potential irrigated area under each scenario, and allow the endogenous outcomes on irrigation water availability to drive the irrigated area outcome. Results for actual irrigated area under the three scenarios are provided in Chapters 4 and 5. Table 3.5 shows the 1995 estimated and 2025 projected potential irrigated area. Potential irrigated area growth is projected to be relatively slow, with a total increase of 28 million hectares for irrigated cereals by 2025, and an increase in potential irrigated area for all crops from 375 million hectares in 1995 to 441 million hectares in 2025.

Environmental, Ecological, and Navigational Flow Commitments. Committed flow is estimated as a portion of total renewable water, depending on availability of runoff and relative demands of these instream uses in different basins. Some basins already have legislative requirements for environmental and instream flows. In the California water basin in the model, for example, legal committed flows represent

Table 3.5—Potential irrigated area under the business-as-usual scenario, 1995 and 2025

Country/Region	Cereals (million ha)		Other crops (million ha)		Total (million ha)	
	1995 baseline estimates	2025 BAU projections	1995 baseline estimates	2025 BAU projections	1995 baseline estimates	2025 BAU projections
Asia	157.0	175.3	74.5	99.6	231.5	274.9
China	64.1	69.3	27.4	38.4	91.5	107.7
India	38.3	48.0	20.7	28.3	59.0	76.3
Southeast Asia	19.2	20.8	5.6	7.3	24.8	28.1
South Asia excluding India	20.0	21.4	9.3	13.5	29.3	34.9
Latin America (LA)	7.8	10.2	9.0	11.8	16.8	22.0
Sub-Saharan Africa (SSA)	3.3	5.0	21.7	26.5	25.0	31.6
West Asia/North Africa (WANA)	12.6	14.7	13.1	16.6	25.6	31.3
Developed countries	46.2	48.2	36.2	38.5	82.4	86.7
Developing countries	176.7	201.6	116.3	152.6	293.0	354.1
World	222.9	249.8	152.5	191.1	375.4	440.8

Source: Authors' estimates and IMPACT-WATER projections, 2002.
Notes: BAU indicates business-as-usual scenario; million ha, million hectares.

46 percent of renewable water. In river basins that have high hydropower generation and navigation requirements, the fraction of committed flow is relatively high. For example, in 1995, the estimate is 48 percent for Yangtze River Basin in China and 45 percent for Brazil. In the dry areas in developing countries, the committed flow is as low as 6 percent, and generally varies from 15 to 30 percent (Table 3.6).

For the BAU scenario, the fraction of renewable water committed to environmental, ecological, and navigational flow is assumed to remain constant through 2025. Under the other two scenarios, committed flows remain at BAU levels through 2000, then decrease or increase. Under CRI, the minimum flow committed to environmental use in developing countries declines significantly as farmers and urban water supply systems seek to exploit additional water from rivers and wetlands to counteract declining basin efficiency and water storage. In most developing countries, committed flows fall to half to one-third of BAU levels. For example, in dry areas in China, the minimum flow committed to environmental use is only about 5–7 percent of the total renewable water, and in dry areas in India, the committed flow is below 5 percent (Table 3.6). Under SUS, the committed flows increase by five to ten percentage points compared with BAU, and are three to four times higher than under CRI.

Table 3.6—Minimum committed flow for environment as percent of annual total renewable water under business-as-usual, water crisis, and sustainable water use scenarios,1995 and 2025

Region/Country/Basins	1995 baseline estimates	2025 projections		
		BAU	CRI	SUS
Basins in the United States				
Ohio and Tennessee	35	35	35	40
Rio Grande River	20	20	20	23
Columbia	35	35	35	40
Colorado	16	16	16	18
Great Basin	30	30	30	35
California	25	25	25	29
Arkansas-White-Red	30	30	30	35
Mid Atlantic	30	30	30	35
Mississippi				
Downstream	30	30	30	35
Upstream	35	35	35	40
Great Lakes	30	30	30	35
South Atlantic-Gulf	30	30	30	35
Texas-Gulf	25	25	25	29
Missouri	30	30	30	35
Basins in China				
HuaiHe	25	25	7	30
HaiHe	25	25	7	30
HuangHe	27	27	19	32
ChangJiang	45	45	24	50
SongLiao	30	30	11	36
Inland	15	15	5	18
Southwest	35	35	16	42
ZhuJiang	35	35	15	42
Southeast	30	30	15	36
Basins in India				
Sahyadri Ghats Mountains	10	10	4	13
Eastern Ghats Mountains	10	10	4	13
Cauvery River Basin	10	10	4	13
Godavari River Basin	10	10	4	13
Krishna River Basin	10	10	4	13
Coastal drainage (Indian)	6	6	2	8
Chotanagpur Plateau coastal	6	6	2	8
Brahmari River Basin	6	6	2	8
Luni River Basin	6	6	2	8
Mahi Tapti Narmada, and Purna	15	15	5	19
Brahmaputra River Basin	15	15	5	19
Indus River Basin	10	10	4	13
Ganges River Basin	15	15	5	19

(continued)

Table 3.6—Continued

Region/Country/Basins	1995 baseline estimates	2025 projections		
		BAU	CRI	SUS
Other countries and regions				
European Union 15	45	45	45	54
Japan	30	30	11	38
Australia	23	23	23	28
Other developed countries	35	35	35	44
Eastern Europe	25	25	9	31
Central Asia	28	28	9	34
Rest of former Soviet Union	28	28	10	35
Mexico	25	25	7	31
Brazil	45	45	14	54
Argentina	30	30	11	38
Colombia	35	35	12	44
Other Latin America	35	35	11	44
Nigeria	10	10	4	13
Northern Sub-Saharan Africa	10	10	4	13
Central and western Sub-Saharan Africa	25	25	9	31
Southern Sub-Saharan Africa	35	35	11	44
Eastern Sub-Saharan Africa	30	30	11	38
Egypt	16	16	6	18
Turkey	20	20	7	25
Other West Asia/North Africa (WANA)	15	15	5	19
Pakistan	20	20	7	25
Bangladesh	30	30	11	35
Other South Asia	25	25	9	31
Indonesia	35	35	11	40
Thailand	25	25	9	31
Malaysia	30	30	11	38
Philippines	20	20	7	25
Viet Nam	25	25	9	31
Myanmar	30	30	11	35
Other Southeast Asia	30	30	11	35
South Korea	25	25	7	31
Other East Asia	25	25	9	31
Rest of the World	25	25	9	31

Source: Authors' estimates and IMPACT-WATER projections, 2002.
Notes: BAU indicates business-as-usual scenario; CRI, water crisis scenario; and SUS, sustainable water use scenario.

Table 3.7—Percentage of households with access to piped water under business-as-usual, water crisis, and sustainable water use scenarios,1995 and 2025

	Rural households				Urban households			
	1995 baseline estimates	2025 projections			1995 baseline estimates	2025 projections		
Country/Region		BAU	CRI	SUS		BAU	CRI	SUS
United States	100	100	100	100	100	100	100	100
European Union 15	100	100	100	100	100	100	100	100
Japan	100	100	100	100	100	100	100	100
Australia	100	100	100	100	100	100	100	100
Other developed countries	81	90	100	100	97	98	78	100
Eastern Europe	51	89	71	100	94	97	86	100
Central Asia	78	86	70	100	97	100	66	100
Rest of former Soviet Union	97	97	92	100	98	98	100	100
Mexico	30	69	32	100	86	92	61	100
Brazil	39	70	49	100	85	88	61	100
Argentina	30	61	36	100	85	97	64	100
Colombia	52	62	52	100	96	99	62	100
Other Latin America	56	75	57	100	84	91	53	100
Nigeria	36	69	31	100	80	88	33	100
Northern Sub-Saharan Africa	17	51	12	100	74	90	24	100
Central and western Sub-Saharan Africa	30	51	21	100	66	77	24	100
Southern Sub-Saharan Africa	43	68	35	100	81	88	32	100
Eastern Sub-Saharan Africa	40	74	28	100	83	88	29	100
Egypt	86	97	83	100	97	95	54	100
Turkey	70	88	90	100	82	92	55	100
Other West Asia/North Africa (WANA)	57	85	47	100	92	94	50	100
India	11	47	13	100	66	90	36	100
Pakistan	28	56	32	100	86	97	37	100
Bangladesh	36	69	36	100	80	87	32	100
Other South Asia	33	63	24	100	62	77	21	100
Indonesia	48	75	61	100	82	92	45	100
Thailand	73	93	76	100	86	97	43	100
Malaysia	94	97	97	100	100	98	55	100
Philippines	68	91	74	100	89	95	53	100
Viet Nam	45	84	43	100	81	88	39	100
Myanmar	39	68	39	100	65	79	33	100
Other Southeast Asia	17	47	12	100	55	74	19	100
China	21	70	27	100	63	85	40	100
Korea, Republic of	70	88	86	100	76	92	62	100
Other East Asia	90	92	90	100	93	94	68	100
Rest of the World	39	66	29	100	74	83	33	100
Developing countries	29	64	30	100	76	89	43	100
Developed countries	89	97	95	100	99	99	97	100
World	**35**	**66**	**34**	**100**	**85**	**92**	**55**	**100**

Source: Authors' estimates based on WHO and UNICEF (2000) and IMPACT-WATER projections, 2002.
Notes: BAU indicates business-as-usual scenario; CRI, water crisis scenario; and SUS, sustainable water use scenario.

Domestic Water Access

Household access to piped water in 1995 is estimated at 29 percent in rural areas and 76 percent for urban areas in developing countries.[4] The detailed breakdown of household access by country is shown in Table 3.7. Under BAU, access to piped water is projected to increase to 64 percent in rural areas and 89 percent in urban areas in developing countries. Under CRI, it is assumed that there will be no increase in the number of households with access to piped water after 2000, so there will be a significant decline in the percentage of households connected compared with BAU. The rural access to piped water will therefore be only 30 percent in 2025 and the urban access 43 percent in developing countries, less than half the 2025 levels under BAU. In sharp contrast, under SUS it is assumed that all domestic households attain full access to piped water beginning in 2020 (Table 3.7).

Water Prices

Under BAU, real water prices are projected to change little, increasing by ten percent between 1995 and 2025. Under CRI, the real effective water price for industrial and connected domestic households increases gradually to 2020, reaching 50 percent and 25 percent higher than BAU prices in the developing and the developed world, respectively. No change is projected for agricultural water prices and unconnected household water prices compared with BAU.

Under SUS, water prices are increased more dramatically. In the industrial sector, water prices increase gradually from 2000 to 2025; in developed countries they are 75 percent higher than BAU prices by 2025; and in developing countries they are 125 percent higher. In the agriculture sector, where 1995 water prices are very low particularly in the developing countries, price increases are also phased in, and by 2025 are double the BAU prices in developed countries and three times the BAU prices in developing countries. In the domestic sector, for connected households, water price increases gradually increase from 2000 to 2020, reaching a level 40 percent higher than BAU prices in developed countries, and 80 percent higher in developing countries. For unconnected households, water prices are far higher in 1995 than for connected households. Under SUS, these unconnected water prices gradually decline, converging toward the connected price as higher prices for connected households and industry free up water that is accessed by unconnected households. After 2020, the prevailing water prices are 50 percent higher than the BAU connected water price in developed countries, and twice the BAU connected water price in developing countries for all households in the domestic sector, which by that time are 100 percent connected (see above).

Rainfed Crop Yield

Crop yields in the model are determined by the rates of technological change resulting from investment in crop research and crop management, by the prevailing crop prices, and by the availability of water. The crop price and water availability effects on crop yields are determined endogenously in the model simulations, while the effect of technological change is projected exogenously as a key driver. The rate of technological change in crop yield growth in irrigated areas is assumed to be the same across the scenarios. This assumption is made so that, in irrigated crop production, the changes in crop yield are determined only by the direct impacts of changes in water availability and the feedback effects of crop price changes.

However, the rates of technological change in rainfed crop yields are assumed to vary across the three scenarios, following their three different narratives. Under CRI, it is assumed that rainfed crop yields grow at a rate that is 25 percent less than yield growth under BAU (that is, if the BAU growth rate in crop yield is 1.00 percent per annum, the growth rate under CRI is set at 0.75 percent per annum). Under SUS, rainfed crop yield growth is assumed to be 25 to 50 percent higher than under BAU, with the bigger increases in growth rates occurring in the more water scarce areas.

Water Harvesting and Effective Rainfall

Under BAU, it is projected that effective rainfall use for rainfed crops will increase 3–5 percent by 2025 because of improved water harvesting and onfarm water management, as well as varietal improvements that shift crop growth periods to better utilize rainfall. Under CRI, it is assumed that there is no improvement in effective rainfall use, with levels remaining the same as in 1995.

Under SUS, a more rapid phased improvement in effective rainfall use occurs compared with BAU. In those basins/countries with severe rainwater shortages for crop production, including river basins in the western United States, northern and western China, northern and western India, and countries in northern SSA and WANA, effective rainfall use increases by 10–15 percent between 1995 and 2025. For other regions that face less severe water shortages, the increase in effective rainfall use ranges from 5–10 percent.

This chapter has sketched the backdrop, in narrative and quantitative terms, for three very different—but highly plausible—scenarios for the future water and food situation. Chapters 4 and 5 provide a detailed assessment of the impact of these different policies, investments, and management choices on water supply and demand, food production and demand, prices, and trade. Chapter 4 analyzes outcomes under the business-as-usual scenario, then Chapter 5 presents results under the water crisis and sustainable water use scenarios, comparing them with BAU levels to quantify the differences.

NOTES

1. Gallopin and Rijsberman (2001) make the important point that the con-
    struction and interpretation of a scenario are influenced by the beliefs and the-
    oretical assumptions of the analyst. The account of the mechanisms leading to
    alternative scenarios and judgment of the efficacy of alternative actions are guid-
    ed by one's analytical understanding. The narrative storyline is inherently sub-
    jective; therefore, we believe that the ultimate plausibility of the scenarios rests
    fundamentally on the plausibility of their quantification within the model so
    as to capture the range of outcomes.

2. For a detailed analysis of more comprehensive alternative scenarios for the
    food sector, see Rosegrant et al. 2001.

3. Drivers are not further subdivided among technology, management, and infra-
    structure because the outcomes on the drivers are a function of all three of these
    factors.

4. Estimates for access to piped water in 1995 include access to in-house piped
    water and standpipes because comprehensive data was unavailable for house-
    holds with in-house piped connections. Thus the percentage of households with
    access to piped water (connected households) is higher than typically cited for
    household connections. 1995 estimates of per capita water consumption for
    each group (see Chapter 4) have been adjusted accordingly.

Maintaining the Status Quo:
The Business-as-Usual Scenario

The business-as-usual scenario (BAU), as described in Chapter 3, projects the future of the food and water sectors if current planning and trends in policies, management, and investments were to continue to 2025. BAU is used throughout the book as a benchmark against which the results of other scenarios are compared.[1]

THE WATER STORY

"Water demand," as discussed in Chapter 2, can be defined and measured in terms of withdrawals and actual consumptive uses (See Box 2.1). While water withdrawal is the most commonly estimated figure, consumptive use best captures actual water use, and most of our analysis utilizes this concept. Total global water withdrawal in 2025 is projected to increase 22 percent above 1995 levels under BAU to 4,772 cubic kilometers—consistent with other recent projections to 2025 including the Alcamo et al. (1998) medium scenario of 4,580 cubic kilometers, the Seckler et al. (1998) business-as-usual scenario of 4,569 cubic kilometers, and the Shiklomanov (1999) forecast of 4,966 cubic kilometers (excluding reservoir evaporation) (Table 4.1). The increase is much higher in developing countries, at 27 percent over the 30-year projection period.

The "criticality ratio," or the ratio of water withdrawal to total renewable water, is an indicator of water scarcity stress at the basin level (Alcamo, Henrichs, and Rösch 2000; Raskin 1997). The higher the criticality ratio, the more intensive the use of river basin water, and the lower the water quality for downstream users. Hence at high criticality ratios, water usage by downstream users can be impaired, and during low flow periods, the chance of absolute water shortages increases. There is no objective basis for selecting a threshold between low and high water stress, but the literature indicates that criticality ratios equal to or greater than 0.4

are considered "high water stress," and 0.8 "very high water stress" (Alcamo, Henrichs, and Rösch 2000).

Under BAU, the criticality ratio increases globally from 0.08 in 1995 to 0.10 in 2025 (Table 4.1) Although the criticality ratio is relatively low globally and for large aggregated regions because of the abundance of water in some of the component countries and basins that make up these aggregates, it is far higher for dry regions. In China, the criticality ratio increases from 0.26 in 1995 to 0.33 in 2025 (a 27 percent increase), and in India, the criticality ratio increases from 0.30 to 0.36 (a 20 percent increase). Water-scarce basins in northern China and northern and northwestern India have criticality ratios several times higher than these values (see also Boxes 4.1 and 4.2). In West Asia and North Africa (WANA), the ratio increases by 32 percent, from 0.69 to 0.90. While water stress is not particularly excessive at the global level under BAU, many regions and people face high and significantly worsening water stress over the projection period.

Table 4.1—Total water withdrawal by volume and as a percentage of renewable water

Region/Country	Total water withdrawal (km³)			Total withdrawal as a percentage of renewable water (%)		
	1995 baseline	BAU projections 2010	2025	1995 baseline	BAU projections 2010	2025
Asia	2,165	2,414	2,649	17	19	20
China	679	759	846	26	29	33
India	674	750	815	30	33	36
Southeast Asia	203	240	287	4	4	5
South Asia excluding India	353	391	421	18	20	22
Latin America (LA)	298	354	410	2	2	3
Sub-Saharan Africa (SSA)	128	166	214	2	3	4
West Asia/North Africa (WANA)	236	266	297	69	81	90
Developed countries	1,144	1,223	1,265	9	9	10
Developing countries	2,762	3,134	3,507	8	9	10
World	3,906	4,356	4,772	8	9	10

Sources: 1995 baseline data for total withdrawals are author estimates based on Shiklomanov (1999) and Gleick (1993) for individual countries and regions; HPDGJ (1989), Qian (1991), NIHWR (1998), and CMWR (1990–98) for river basins in China; USGS (1998) for river basins in the United States; ESCAP (1995) and IMWR (1998–2000) for river basins in India. 1995 baseline data for renewable water are from Alcamo et al. (1998). 2025 data are IMPACT-WATER projections, 2002.
Notes: BAU indicates business-as-usual scenario; km³, cubic kilometers.

Box 4.1—Water scarce basins

The analysis in this book primarily focuses on water and food futures at the global scale and for major countries and regions, but it is also essential to assess how changes in trends, policies, and investments will affect important water scarce river basins, where the impacts of changes may be particularly high. Therefore, selected results for individual river basins will be highlighted throughout the analysis, including the Yellow (Huanghe) and Haihe River basins in northern China, the parts of the Ganges and Indus River basins that lie within India. In addition, we highlight alternative futures for Egypt, which is virtually coterminous with the Nile River basin.

The Yellow River is the second largest river in China, traversing nine provinces on its 5,464 kilometer course through the northern heartland of China. The Yellow River basin is of utmost importance for China in terms of food production, natural resources, and socioeconomic development: it covers 7 percent of China's land area and supports 136 million people, or 11 percent of China's population. The total physical crop area in the basin is 12.9 million hectares, of which 31 percent is irrigated, but while it contains 13 percent of the total cultivated area in China, it holds only 3 percent of the country's water resources (CMWR 2002). Increased water scarcity in this basin is shown by interruption of flow in the lower Yellow River, declining groundwater levels, disappearing lakes, and silting up of river beds (Dialogue on Water and Climate 2002).

The Haihe River basin covers eight provinces and cities, including China's capital city of Beijing and China's fourth largest city, Tianjin, and has a population of 90 million. The basin extends over 3.3 percent of China's total area, supports about 10 percent of China's population, and holds 15 percent of China's industrial production and 10 percent of the country's total agricultural output. Total physical crop area amounts to 10.8 million hectares, 7.1 million hectares of which are irrigated (CMWR 2002). However, the Haihe basin has had a water deficit for over 25 years, potentially leading to significant water quality and quantity problems in this basin (Working Group on Environment in U.S.-China Relations 1998).

The Indus basin begins in Tibet and flows through India and Pakistan. In India, about 60 million people reside in the basin area, which covers the northern and northwestern states. The drainage area of 321,289 square kilometers of the Indus River basin encompasses nearly 10 per-

(continued)

Box 4.1—Continued

cent of the total geographical area of India. Cropland in the basin is
about 9.6 million hectares, 5 percent of the total cropland of the country, of which about 30 percent is irrigated (IMWR 2002). The fight for
water has been ongoing in the Indus, with water tables dropping
because of groundwater overpumping and basins running dry the for
portions of the year (Postel 2002). Water scarcity is an international
issue in the Indus; after the Independence of India and Pakistan, they
nearly went to war over this basin, a water treaty was established in
1960 that has proven resilient (Postel and Wolf 2001).

The Ganges, the subcontinent's largest and most important river, rises
in Nepal and flows 1,400 miles through three densely populated Indian
states—Uttar Pradesh, Bihar, and West Bengal—before entering
Bangladesh and flowing into the Bay of Bengal (Hinrichsen, Robey,
and Upadhyay 1998). The Ganges River basin within India encompasses nearly 26 percent of the total geographical area of the country, and is
inhabited by 323 million people. Physical cropland in the Indian part
of the basin is estimated to be 58 million hectares or 30 percent of the
total cropland of the country of which 20 percent is irrigated (IMWR
2002). Even though the Ganges does not seem water-scarce based on
total annual flows, it often experiences severe water stress from January
to April, and floods during other months (Biswas, Uitto, and
Nakayama 1998).

The Nile River, the longest river in the world, flows from its major
source Lake Victoria in east central Africa, north through Uganda and
into Sudan where it meets the Blue Nile at Khartoum, which rises in
the Ethiopian highlands. From the confluence of the White and Blue
Nile, the river continues to flow northwards into Egypt and on to the
Mediterranean Sea (Nile Basin Initiative 2002). Egypt gets 97 percent
of its water from this river. However, as the countries in the upper Nile
basin continue to use more water given rising population and increasing
economic growth, Egypt's water share could decline (McNeeley 1999).
In 1995, the cultivated area in Egypt was 3.3 million hectares, or 3.2
percent of the total area and almost all cropland is irrigated. As mentioned above, the Nile River is by far the dominant water source of
water for Egypt and 90 percent of the cropland is in the Nile Valley and
delta area (FAO 1995). Thus the results presented for Egypt are closely
indicative of change in the Nile River basin within Egypt.

Non-Irrigation Water Demand-Consumptive Use

Non-irrigation consumptive use varies by sector and at the basin, country, and regional levels (Table 4.2). At a global level, all non-irrigation uses increase 225 cubic kilometers over the period, an increase of 62 percent by 2025. All non-irrigation uses are projected to increase significantly, with a large share of the increase occurring in developing countries.

Box 4.2—Water scarce basins under the business-as-usual scenario: Growing scarcity

Income and population growth drive rapid increases in water consumption in the domestic, industrial, and livestock sectors. Total non-irrigation water consumption increases by 75 percent in the Yellow River basin, 83 percent in the Haihe River basin, 88 percent in Egypt, and by over 100 percent in the Indus and the Ganges compared with 1995 levels. With limited water supply growth, this increase in non-irrigation demand is in large part at the expense of water supply for irrigation.

Water stress at the basin level, measured by the criticality ratio (ratio of withdrawals to total renewable water), also increases significantly from the already high levels in these basins under BAU. Even in 1995, the criticality ratios for these basin are high a) based on world and developing country averages, b) relative to the thresholds for all the selected basins compared with global and developing country averages, and c) relative to the indicative threshold levels of 0.40 for high water stress and 0.80 for very high water stress. And under BAU, these high stress levels intensify, with Egypt increasing from 0.99 to 1.08, the Yellow River basin from 0.89 to 1.11, the Haihe from 1.40 to 1.49, the Indus from 0.72 to 0.90, and the Ganges from 0.50 to 0.57. The level of water stress increases greatly across all basins in 2025, however. This critical level of water stress signals increasingly serious water scarcity problems in the future with probable poor water quality from high water reuse rates.

Although irrigated area increases by 23 percent in the Yellow River basin, 15 percent in the Haihe, 15 percent in Egypt, 28 percent in the Indus, and 29 percent in the Ganges, irrigation water consumption declines or barely increases. Compared with 1995, irrigation water consumption in 2025 declines by 19 percent in the Haihe and 6 percent in the Ganges; and increases by 7 percent in Egypt, 5 percent in the Yellow, and 12 percent in the Indus. Irrigation water supply reliability (IWSR) declines between 1995 and 2025 in each of the basins and

(continued)

Box 4.2—Continued

Egypt, with particularly large drops in the Haihe (22 percent) and the Ganges (19 percent).

Under BAU, crop yields increase through agricultural research and growth of fertilizer use and other inputs, raising total cereal production in each of the water scarce basins between 1995 and 2025. Cereal production is projected to increase by 48 percent in the Haihe, 45 percent in the Yellow, 54 percent in the Indus, and 50 percent in the Ganges River basins. But increasing water scarcity slows cereal production growth significantly. With the decline in IWSR, relative irrigated yields (compared to full water adequacy) decline dramatically. The relative irrigated cereal yield declines between 1995 and 2025 from 0.91 to 0.71 in the Yellow River basin, from 0.80 to 0.70 in the Haihe, from 0.88 to 0.71 in the Indus, from 0.83 to 0.67 in the Ganges, and from 0.66 to 0.59 in Egypt. Irrigated cereal yields in these basins thus range from 11 percent lower (Egypt) to 22 percent lower (Yellow) in 2025 than they would have been if irrigation water scarcity had been maintained at 1995 levels.

Domestic water demand makes up 8 percent of total potential demand in 1995, and is projected to increase to 11.5 percent by 2025 under BAU. Domestic demand rises rapidly with a projected global increase of 71 percent, and a doubling of demand in developing countries. Faster growth in developing countries results from their higher population growth and a relatively rapid increase of per capita water use from the existing low levels caused by income growth (Table 4.3). About 97 percent of population growth occurs in developing countries, and per capita domestic water use in developing countries is projected to increase by 8.3 cubic meters per year. In contrast, population in developed countries increases only 4.6 percent between 1995 and 2025, and per capita domestic water use increases by 6.4 cubic meters per year over the initial 48 cubic meter level. Per capita domestic water use declines under BAU in developed countries with the highest per capita water demand—a result of conservation and technological improvements. Hence, total domestic water demand in developed countries grows much more slowly than in developing countries at just 10 cubic kilometers by 2025.

Domestic water demand is differentiated as connected and unconnected households in both rural and urban areas.[2] We assessed the percentage of population connected and unconnected in rural and urban areas for various countries from 1995

Table 4.2—Non-irrigation consumptive water use, 1995, 2010, and 2025

Region/Country	Domestic (km³)			Industrial (km³)			Livestock (km³)			Total Non-Irrigation (km³)		
	1995 baseline estimates	BAU projections 2010	2025	1995 baseline estimates	BAU projections 2010	2025	1995 baseline estimates	BAU projections 2010	2025	1995 baseline estimates	BAU projections 2010	2025
Asia	79.1	121.8	156.7	48.3	75.3	90.7	11.7	17.9	25.6	139.1	215.0	273
China	30.0	48.0	59.4	13.1	24.5	31.1	3.4	5.3	7.4	46.5	77.8	97.9
India	21.0	32.1	40.9	7.2	13.8	15.7	3.3	5.3	8.1	31.5	51.2	64.6
Southeast Asia	13.9	21.4	30.4	11.2	15.3	20.9	1.7	2.8	4.1	26.8	39.5	55.4
South Asia excluding India	7.0	11.5	16.2	1.9	3.2	4.7	1.7	2.7	3.9	10.6	17.4	24.7
Latin America (LA)	18.2	25.0	30.7	17.9	25.3	29.9	6.9	9.5	12.5	43.1	59.8	73
Sub-Saharan Africa (SSA)	9.5	16.0	23.9	0.9	1.6	2.4	1.6	2.6	4.1	12	20.2	30.4
West Asia/North Africa (WANA)	7.1	10.2	13.1	4.6	6.9	8.7	1.8	2.5	3.3	13.4	19.6	25.1
Developed countries	58.7	64.5	68.6	94.7	112.8	113.8	15.3	16.9	18.2	168.6	194.2	200.6
Developing countries	110.6	169.5	221.0	62.2	98.3	121.4	21.8	32.1	45.2	194.5	299.9	387.5
World	169.2	234.0	289.6	156.9	211.0	235.2	37.0	49.0	63.4	363.1	494.0	588.2

Sources: 1995 baseline data for water consumption by sector are author estimates based on Shiklomanov (1999) and Gleick (1993) for individual countries and regions; HPDGJ (1989), Qian (1991), NIHWR (1998), and CMWR (1990-98) for river basins in China; USGS (1998) for river basins in the United States; ESCAP (1995) and IMWR (1998-2000) for river basins in India. Livestock data are from FAO (1986), Mancl (1994), and Beckett and Oltjen (1993). 2010 and 2025 data are IMPACT-WATER projections, 2002.
Notes: BAU indicates busines-as-usual scenario; km³, cubic kilometers.

Table 4.3—Per capita domestic water demand

	Per capita consumption (m³/person/year)		
	Baseline estimates	BAU projection	
Region/Country	1995	2010	2025
Asia	24.8	32.9	36.9
China	24.5	35.8	41.2
India	22.6	28.1	30.7
Southeast Asia	29.9	37.2	45.6
South Asia excluding India	23.7	27.4	29.6
Latin America (LA)	24.8	32.5	36.9
Sub-Saharan Africa (SSA)	18.3	21.2	21.9
West Asia/North Africa (WANA)	21.2	23.0	23.4
Developed countries	47.8	51.8	54.4
Developing countries	25.6	31.4	33.9
World	**30.3**	**35.0**	**37.2**

Sources: 1995 baseline data for total domestic water consumption are author estimates based on Shiklomanov (1999) and Gleick (1993) for individual countries and regions; HPDGJ (1989), Qian (1991), NIHWR (1998), and CMWR (1990–98) for river basins in China; USGS (1998) for river basins in the United States; ESCAP (1995) and IMWR (1998–2000) for river basins in India. Connected population are estimates based on WHO and UNICEF (2000) and FAO (2000). 2010 and 2025 data are IMPACT-WATER projections, 2002.
Notes: BAU indicates business-as-usual scenario; m³/person/year, cubic meters per person per year.

to 2025 using data on the percentage of population connected (WHO and UNICEF 2000) the projected total urban and rural population in each country (FAO 2000), and on our assessment of recent trends in development of urban water systems.

Table 4.4 shows the per capita water demand for connected and unconnected rural and urban areas in selected countries and regions. Per capita demand is higher in urban than in rural areas, and connected demand is higher than unconnected demand.[2] Worldwide, the 1995 per capita demand in unconnected rural households is 55 percent of the connected demand, increasing to 60 percent by 2025; the per capita demand in unconnected urban households is 57 percent of the connected demand and decreases to 52 percent by 2025 as a result of large increases in urban population—especially in developing countries.

The growth in global industrial water demand is also rapid, with demand increasing by 50 percent for the world as a whole. (Table 4.2). The majority of this increase also occurs in developing countries, where demand almost doubles. The 1995 estimate for industrial water consumption in the developed world is much greater than that of the developing world; however, by 2025 developing world industrial water demand is projected to increase to 121 cubic kilometers, 7 cubic kilometers greater than the level in the developed world. The intensity of industrial water use (water demand per $1,000 of GDP) decreases significantly worldwide, especially

Table 4.4—Per capita domestic water demand for connected/unconnected households in rural and urban areas under the business-as-usual scenario, 1995 and 2025

	Annual consumption (m³/person/year)							
	1995 baseline estimates				2025 BAU projections			
	Rural		Urban		Rural		Urban	
Region/Country	Connected	Unconnected	Connected	Unconnected	Connected	Unconnected	Connected	Unconnected
Asia	27.1	17.6	41.8	25.5	29.7	18.9	52.4	27.8
China	25.7	17.1	44.3	26.9	27.6	18.4	64.4	28.7
India	26.8	17.9	38.7	23.4	27.8	18.4	43.0	24.1
Southeast Asia	29.6	19.2	43.3	26.1	38.2	23.6	56.8	32.0
South Asia excluding India	25.7	17.3	36.4	23.2	28.2	18.9	36.0	27.5
Latin America	27.2	17.6	41.7	25.5	29.7	18.9	52.4	27.8
Sub-Saharan Africa	18.8	12.8	29.2	17.8	19.5	13.1	29.1	18.0
West Asia/North Africa (WANA)	18.3	10.6	25.7	17.8	17.0	10.0	27.0	15.8
Developed countries	47.0	22.3	49.3	28.6	48.8	33.9	55.7	34.8
Developing countries	25.2	16.9	39.1	24.7	27.0	17.6	45.5	24.9
World	31.0	17.0	43.4	24.8	29.3	17.7	48.1	25.1

Sources: 1995 baseline data for total domestic water consumption are author estimates based on Shiklomanov (1999) and Gleick (1993) for individual countries and regions; HPDGJ (1989), Qian (1991), NIHWR (1998), and CMWR (1990–98) for river basins in China; USGS (1998) for river basins in the United States; ESCAP (1995) and IMWR (1998-2000) for river basins in India; and WHO and UNICEF(2000) for connected and unconnected households. 2025 data are IMPACT-WATER projections, 2002.

Notes: BAU indicates business-as-usual scenario; m³/person/year, cubic meters per person per year.

in developing countries (where initial intensity levels are very high) because of improved water-saving technology and demand policy in this sector (Table 4.5). The increase of total industrial production, however, still leads to an increase in total industrial water demand. Globally, industrial water demand is 7.4 percent of total potential demand in 1995, and is projected to increase to 9.4 percent of the total in 2025.

Direct water consumption by livestock is very small, but given the rapid increase of livestock production, particularly in developing countries, livestock water demand is projected to increase 71 percent from 1995 to 2025 (Table 4.2). Livestock water demand is a very small fraction of total consumptive water use in 1995 at only 2 percent, and increases only slightly to 3 percent by 2025 under BAU. Regionally, however, livestock can have much larger impacts on water use, and is becoming an even greater consumer of water, particularly in the developing world. While livestock water demand increases only 19 percent in the developed world, it is projected to more than double in the developing world, from 22 cubic kilometers in 1995 to 45 cubic kilometers in 2025.

Irrigation Water Demand: Consumptive Use

The potential demand or consumptive use for irrigation water is defined as the irrigation water requirement to meet full evapotranspirative demand of all crops included in the model, over the full potential irrigated area. Potential demand is thus the

Table 4.5—Industrial water use intensity

	Industrial water use intensity (m³/$1,000 of GDP)		
	1995	BAU projection	
Region/Country	baseline estimates	2010	2025
Asia	16.2	13.9	6.7
China	16.0	12.1	6.2
India	19.6	16.3	7.9
Southeast Asia	20.4	13.4	8.9
South Asia excluding India	18.3	15.6	11.7
Latin America (LA)	10.6	8.7	5.9
Sub-Saharan Africa (SSA)	6.3	6.3	5.8
West Asia/North Africa (WANA)	8.4	7.2	5.1
Developed countries	4.3	3.5	2.5
Developing countries	13.2	10.5	6.4
World	5.9	5.1	3.6

Sources: 1995 baseline data for total industrial water consumption are author estimates based on Shiklomanov (1999) and Gleick (1993) for individual countries and regions; HPDGJ (1989), Qian (1991), NIHWR (1998), and CMWR (1990–98) for river basins in China; USGS (1998) for river basins in the United States; ESCAP (1995) and IMWR (1998–2000) for river basins in India. 2025 data are IMPACT-WATER projections, 2002. GDP for all years is from World Bank (1998).

Notes: BAU indicates business-as-usual scenario; m³, cubic meters; GDP, gross domestic product.

Table 4.6—Potential and actual consumptive use of water for irrigation and irrigation water supply reliability, 1995, 2010, and 2025

Region/Country	Potential irrigation consumption (km³)			Actual irrigation consumption (km³)			Irrigation water supply reliability index (IWSR)		
	1995 baseline estimates	BAU projections 2010	2025	1995 baseline estimates	BAU projections 2010	2025	1995 baseline estimates	BAU projections 2010	2025
Asia	1,130.1	1,197.9	1,230.2	920.2	910.4	933.3	0.81	0.76	0.76
China	279.4	285.4	291.2	244.2	225.5	230.9	0.87	0.79	0.79
India	399.6	440.5	465.9	321.3	321.6	331.7	0.80	0.73	0.71
Southeast Asia	98.2	102.1	106.3	85.5	87.8	91.9	0.87	0.86	0.86
South Asia excluding India	205.3	215.5	225.0	163.2	168.1	169.4	0.79	0.78	0.75
Latin America (LA)	106.8	121.1	128.8	88.3	89.6	96.9	0.83	0.74	0.75
Sub-Saharan Africa (SSA)	68.5	78.0	87.3	50.3	55.4	62.9	0.73	0.71	0.72
West Asia/North Africa (WANA)	156.1	170.7	184.2	121.6	128.0	137.1	0.78	0.75	0.74
Developed countries	312.8	314.2	308.2	271.7	267.1	276.9	0.87	0.85	0.90
Developing countries	1,444.8	1,557.7	1,615.6	1,163.8	1,168.3	1,215.5	0.81	0.75	0.75
World	1,757.6	1,864.3	1,923.8	1,435.5	1,435.5	1,492.3	0.82	0.77	0.78

Sources: 1995 baseline data for irrigation water consumption are author estimates based on Shiklomanov (1999) and Gleick (1993) for individual countries and regions; HPDGJ (1989), Qian (1991), NIHWR (1998), and CMWR (1990–98) for river basins in China; USGS (1998) for river basins in the United States; ESCAP (1995) and IMWR (1998-2000) for river basins in India. 2025 data are IMPACT-WATER projections, 2002.
Notes: BAU indicates business-as-usual scenario; km³, cubic kilometers.

demand for irrigation water in the absence of any water supply constraints. Actual irrigation consumptive use is the realized water demand, given the limitations of water supply for irrigation. The proportion of potential demand realized in actual consumptive use is the irrigation water supply reliability index (IWSR), which is defined as the ratio of water supply available for irrigation over potential demand for irrigation water. The average potential and actual irrigation water demands and the IWSR resulting from the 30 climate scenarios are shown in Table 4.6. Compared with other sectors, the growth of irrigation water potential demand is much lower, with 12 percent growth in potential demand during 1995–2025 in developing countries, and a slight decline in potential demand in developed countries.

Under BAU, Sub-Saharan Africa (SSA) is projected to have the highest percentage increase in potential irrigation water demand, at 27 percent, while Latin America (LA) experiences the second highest growth, at 21 percent. Each of these regions has a high percentage increase in irrigated area from a relatively small 1995 level. India is projected to have by far the highest absolute growth in potential irrigation water demand—66 cubic kilometers (17 percent)—given relatively rapid growth in irrigated area from an already high 1995 level. WANA increases by 18 percent (28 cubic kilometers, mainly in Turkey), and China experiences a much smaller increase of 4 percent (12 cubic kilometers).

Water for Irrigation: Increasing Scarcity

Actual consumptive use of irrigation water worldwide is projected to grow more slowly than potential consumptive use, with an increase of only 4 percent (Table 4.6). In developing countries, consumptive use for irrigation increases from 1,164 cubic kilometers in 1995 to 1,216 cubic kilometers in 2025, an increase of 4 percent. This is of critical importance because irrigation water demand in developing countries is projected to be increasingly supply-constrained, with a declining fraction of potential demand being met over time.

For developing countries, the IWSR declines from 0.81 in 1995 to 0.75 in 2025 (Table 4.6). Relatively dry basins that face rapid growth in domestic and industrial demand, or experience slow improvement in river basin efficiency, or have rapid expansion in potential irrigated area without adequate increase in storage or withdrawal capacity, show even greater declines in water supply reliability. For example, in China's Yellow River basin, which mainly grows wheat and maize, the IWSR is projected to decline from 0.80 to 0.75, and in the Ganges of India the IWSR declines from 0.83 to 0.67. More severe increases in water scarcity occur in both China and India than in the developing countries as a whole.

In the developed world, water-scarce basins such as the Colorado and White-Red basins in the United States also face increasing water scarcity in the future. Developed countries as a whole, however, show a sharp contrast to the developing world in that their irrigation water supply is projected to grow faster than potential demand, partially compensating at the global level for shortfalls in the developing world. Over the full projection period, irrigation water supply in the developed world increases by 5.2 cubic kilometers, while the corresponding demand decreases by 4.6 cubic kilometers. Irrigation demand in the developed world as a whole declines because basin efficiency increases sufficiently to more than offset the very small increase in irrigated area. As a result, after initially declining from 0.87 to 0.85 in 2010, the IWSR improves to 0.90 in 2025 as a result of slowing domestic and industrial demand growth in later years (and actual declines in total domestic and industrial water use in the United States and Europe) and improved efficiency in irrigation water use. The divergence between trends in developing and developed countries indicates that agricultural water shortages become worse in the former even as they improve in the latter, providing a major impetus for the expansion in virtual water transfers through agricultural trade.

By 2025 under BAU, basins and countries with IWSR values less than 0.75 (a 25 percent water shortage relative to potential irrigation demand) include the Huaihe River basin, Haihe River basin, the Yellow River basin, most basins in India (including the Ganges River basin), as well as basins in central Asia, and most countries in LA, SSA, and WANA. IWSR remains above 85 percent in most developed countries and basins because of slow growth or declining water demand for domestic and industrial uses; however, even when the IWSR remains relatively high over time, irrigation is susceptible to considerable downside risk. Some basins in the United States, including the Colorado, Rio Grande, downstream Mississippi, Missouri, Texas Gulf, and White-Red-Arkansas River basins have an IWSR as low as 0.60 in some dry years in the latter stages of the projection period, which means as much as 40 percent of irrigation water demand cannot be satisfied in those years.

River basins in northern China display different water supply trends than those in the south. The ratio of irrigation water supply to demand in northern China is projected to remain below 0.8 in most years, and falls as low as 0.50 in some dry years. Southern China has IWSR values above 0.85 in most years, although this ratio falls as low as 0.50 in some particularly dry years.

The IWSR falls as low as 0.30 to 0.40 in some basins in western and northwestern India, particularly after 2015. Dramatic drops to approximately 30 percent may occur in some dry years or years with uneven intrayear rainfall distribution in other Indian basins. For the major cereal production basin, the Ganges, the IWSR is projected to decline from 0.83 in 1995 to below 0.67 percent by 2025.

LA countries maintain their base year water supply reliability under BAU, which measures below 0.75 in Mexico, Brazil, Argentina, and Colombia, and 0.79 percent in other LA countries—with Mexico undergoing slight declines. SSA countries, however, are projected to have widely varying agricultural water supply conditions. Nigeria has a low reliability of 0.57 along with considerable downside variance, and northern SSA undergoes a slight decline from 0.74 in 1995 to 0.69 in 2025. Central and western SSA undergo a larger decline from 0.90 to 0.80, while southern and eastern SSA maintain an average annual reliability of 0.77 with a relatively high variance. In WANA, the year-to-year variability is relatively small, but all countries experience declining reliability over the projection period with a decrease of 3 percent in Egypt, 4 percent in Turkey, and 5 percent in other countries in WANA.

Among South Asian countries, Bangladesh experiences the highest variance in water supply reliability with an average of around 75 percent between 1995 and 2010, declining to 70 percent between 2010 and 2025. Pakistan and other South Asian countries (excluding India) have relatively low variances, but average reliability is projected to decline from 80 to 70 percent in Pakistan and from 88 to 83 percent in other countries.

All Southeast Asian countries have high water supply reliability with averages between 0.67 and 0.88, depending on the country and time period. Water supply variances are also high and widen in the latter years of the projection period. In east Asia, excluding China, South Korea is projected to have a high variance in annual water supply reliability and a high average of 0.78 to 0.96.

Causes of Water Supply Constraints

Water shortages are caused by different factors in different countries. In the modeling framework, the causes of water shortages can be classified as source limits and infrastructure constraints. Source limits for irrigation water supply may come from fluctuation of natural sources (precipitation and runoff), and from increased non-irrigation water demands including domestic, industrial, and environmental water demand. Infrastructure constraints can be caused by insufficient reservoir storage or withdrawal facilities. The relative importance of these factors in a specific basin can help prioritize the need for different water development policies including infrastructure investment and policy reform that enhance basin efficiency. In the model, the relative importance of these factors can be identified through the constraint equations related to each of the factors such as infrastructure capacity, environmental requirements, and source balance. After the model is solved, the status of all the constraints and the IWSR can be examined. If the IWSR is below 0.95 and one of the corresponding constraints is contingent (reaching the lower or upper bound), then we conclude that the water shortage is caused by the factor(s) with the contingent constraint(s). For example, if the IWSR is 0.85, and the water supply reaches the source limit, then the water shortage is caused by the source limit.

In the United States, source limits occur in the Rio Grande and Colorado River basins in some dry years. Late in the projection period, the Missouri, Texas Gulf, and White-Red-Arkansas River basins may suffer water shortages of up to 40 percent in some dry years to maintain non-irrigation demands and environmental water requirements. Australia also has source shortages in some dry years. In China, serious source shortages are possible in the Haihe River basin, inland basins of northwest China, the Yellow River basin, and the Huaihe River basin. The Huaihe River basin and the Yellow River basin also have infrastructure constraints in some dry years (when water requirement from irrigation is large to make up for lack of rainfall) because the limits of withdrawal capacity are reached. Although it is seemingly paradoxical that withdrawal capacity could be a constraint when water supply is low, low rainfall also increases the proportion of crop water demand that must be met from irrigation. Basins in south and southeast China experience a dramatic drop (as much as 50 percent) in water supply in some years because of lack of storage capacity to deliver water during the dry season.

Infrastructure constraints cause water shortages of as much as 60–70 percent in some basins in western and northwestern India after 2015, especially because of insufficient reservoir storage. The same problem could occur in some basins in southern and eastern India where internal rainfall distribution is uneven. The Ganges River basin is also constrained by storage and water withdrawal capacity in later years, particularly after 2015.

Many LA countries face water withdrawal capacity constraints, with Mexico and Argentina requiring more storage for intra and interyear regulation in later years. The countries in WANA require more storage (with the exception of Egypt), and Turkey is also constrained by the water withdrawal capacity limit. Egypt has substantial source problems under BAU, particularly after 2010. All regions of SSA and most Asian countries need more storage or larger withdrawal capacity to meet growing demands for water. For other developed countries and regions (including western and eastern Europe, Russia, Australia, Oceania, and Japan) agricultural water shortages occur in some dry years, mainly as a result of the need to meet environmental and other non-irrigation demands and water withdrawal capacity limitations.

Variability in Irrigation Water Demand and Supply

Climate variability leads to variability and risk to irrigation water supply availability under existing and projected water supply infrastructure. Low rainfall years can lead to severe water shortages even in regions in which water is relatively plentiful in most years. Water supply variability in a specific year can be assessed based on the multiple climate simulations or through changes in year-to-year variation in supply for a single climate run. Variability in irrigation water supply tends to be higher at smaller spatial scales because as the size of the spatial unit increases, local variability within the component units of the larger spatial unit is often counterbalanced by negative covariation between the component spatial units. This tendency is shown in Figure 4.1, which shows the standard deviation in irrigation water supplies from the 30 different climate scenarios at three spatial scales, the Luni River basin in India, India, and the world. The variability, as shown by the standard deviation in irrigation water supply, decreases as spatial scale increases. However, it is important to note that variability in irrigation water supply increases over time at all spatial scales. From 1995 to 2025, the standard deviation (variance divided by mean) of irrigation water supply increases from 4.1 percent to 5.0 percent in the world, 7.2 percent to 9.4 percent in India, and 34.2 percent to 37.2 percent in the Indian Luni River basin. Figure 4.2 shows the increase in variability even more dramatically for the year-to-year irrigation water supply in the Indian Ganges River basin under the climate regime of 1961–90. Irrigation water supply variability in the Ganges—and more generally in many relatively dry basins—becomes larger in later years because of the increase in non–irrigation water demand combined with water supply constraints—further illustrated below.

Figure 4.1—Coefficient of variation of irrigation water supply for the world, India, and the Indian Luni River Basin

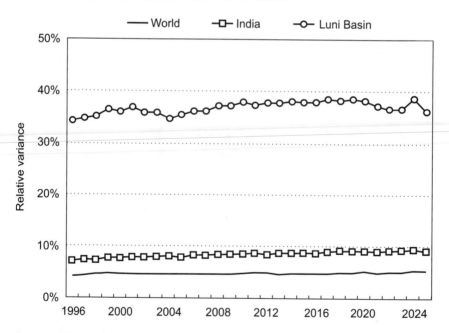

Source: IMPACT-WATER assessments and projections, 2002.
Note: Coefficient of variation is the ratio of standard deviation over the average irrigation water supply.

Figure 4.2—Irrigation water depletion in the Indian Ganges River Basin under the climate regime of 1961–90

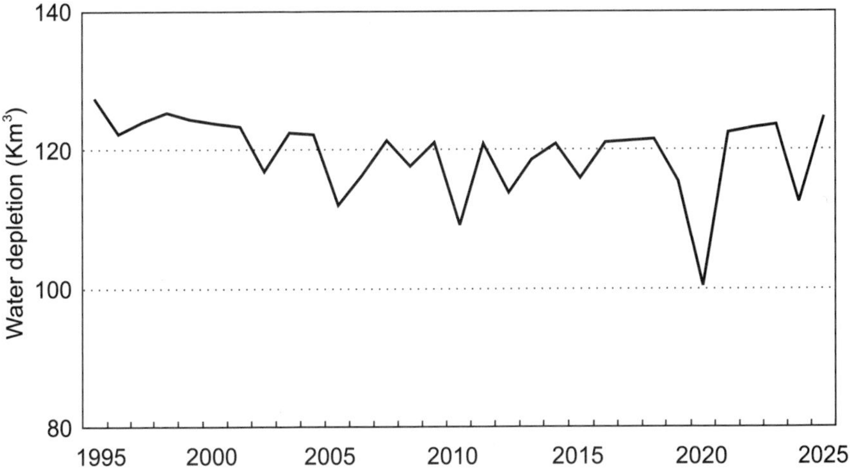

Source: IMPACT-WATER assessments and projections, 2002.

The degree and impact of irrigation water supply variability depends on climate variability, the degree of water scarcity, and the adequacy of water supply infrastructure. It is a fundamental problem that, in general, irrigation water supply variability increases precisely in those basins in which water scarcity is severe and increasing, such as river basins in the western United States, WANA, and northern China and India. Under these conditions, natural climate variability can cause severe shortages in irrigation water supply. On the other hand, in basins where water supply is relatively plentiful, the impact of climate variability may be low because inadequate water storage and withdrawal facilities are the dominant constraint on water supply even in dry years. In such basins or countries, annual climate variability barely affects agricultural water supply, although further development of water supply infrastructure raises water supply variability along with the average supply level from the climatic variability at higher levels of water supply. Nigeria typifies this situation, where the variability in irrigation water supply is very small until late in the projection period, when growth in both demand and supply bring source limitations into play. Figure 4.3 shows the average irrigation water consumption and the coefficient of variation in Nigeria. As can be seen, the variability increases with years. This can be explained by Figure 4.4, which presents water withdrawal capacity, computed average water withdrawal, and withdrawal under a single one climate scenario. In earlier years, actual water withdrawal reaches the capacity, and with little or no variability in water withdrawal. With the increase of water withdrawal capacity, variability with the actual water withdrawal increases, which leads to some significant variability in later years.

Figure 4.3—Coefficient of variation of irrigation water supply and the average supply in Nigeria during 1995–2025

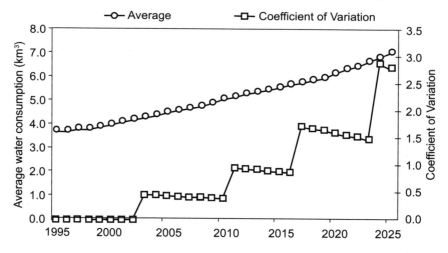

Source: IMPACT-WATER assessments and projections, 2002.

Figure 4.4—Comparison of withdrawal capacity, average computed withdrawal, and withdrawal under one hydrologic scenario under the climate regime of 1961–90

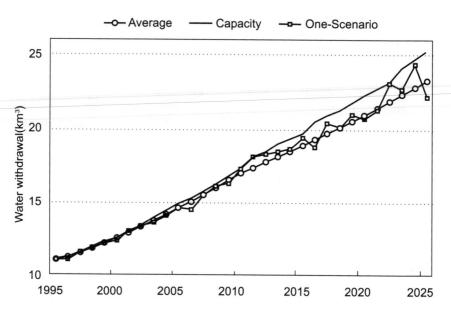

Source: IMPACT-WATER assessments and projections, 2002.

WATER PRODUCTIVITY

One important strategy to increase food production in the face of increasing water scarcity is to increase the water productivity[3] (Molden 1997; Molden, Sakthivadivel, and Habib 2001; Barker and Kijne 2001). Water productivity (WP) is defined more specifically as crop yield (*P*) per cubic meter of water consumption including "green" water (effective rainfall) for rainfed areas and both green and "blue" water (diverted water from water systems) for irrigated areas (Equation 4.1). Water consumption (*WC*) includes beneficial (*BWC*) and nonbeneficial (*NBWC*) consumption (Equation 4.2). BWC directly contributes to crop growth at a river basin scale, and NBWC includes distribution and conveyance losses to evaporation and sinks, which are not economically reusable. BWC is characterized by water use efficiency in agriculture.

We use effective efficiency at the river basin scale, or basin efficiency (*BE*), (Keller, Keller, and Seckler 1996) to represent water use efficiency, which is a ratio of BWC to WC.

$$WP_{(kg/m^3)} = \frac{P_{(kg)}}{WC_{(m^3)}} \tag{4.1}$$

$$WC = BWC + NBWC = \frac{BWC}{BE} \tag{4.2}$$

Water productivity, defined above, varies from region to region and field to field, depending on many factors such as crop and climate patterns (if rainfall fits crop growth), irrigation technology and field water management, land and infrastructure, and input including labor, fertilizer, and machinery. Water productivity can be increased by either increasing crop yield (that is, increasing the numerator in Equation 4.1 through other inputs while maintaining constant water use level, or reducing water consumption and maintaining the yield level (that is, decreasing denominator), or both.

Water Productivity in 1995

Figure 4.5 shows a global map of water productivity of irrigated rice, and Figure 4.6 shows a similar map of water productivity for irrigated cereals excluding rice. The basic elements of these maps are 36 countries and aggregated regions used in IMPACT (Rosegrant et al. 2001). Because rice usually consumes more water than other crops, the water productivity of rice is significantly lower than that of other cereals. The water productivity of rice ranges from 0.15 to 0.60 kilograms per cubic meter, while that of other cereals ranges from 0.20 to 2.40 kilograms per cubic meter. For both rice and other cereals, water productivity in SSA is the lowest in the world. The water productivity of rice is 0.10–0.25 kilograms per cubic meter in this region, with average yield of 1.4 metric tons per hectare and water consumption per hectare close to 9,500 cubic meters. For other cereals in SSA, the average yield is 2.40 metric tons per hectare, the water consumption per hectare is 7,700 cubic meters, and the average water productivity is 0.30 kilograms per cubic meter (ranging from 0.10 to 0.60 kilograms per cubic meter). Among developing countries, China and some Southeast Asian countries have higher water productivity for rice, ranging from 0.4 to 0.6 kilograms per cubic meter; however, the average for the developed world, 0.47 kilograms per cubic meter, is higher than the 0.39 kilograms per cubic meter for the developing world. For other cereals, water productivity is lower than 0.4 kilograms per cubic meter in South Asia, central Asia, northern and central SSA; ranges from 1.0–1.7 kilograms per cubic meter in China, the United States, and Brazil; and ranges from 1.7–2.4 kilograms per cubic meter in western European countries. The average water productivity of other cereals in the developed world is 1.0 kilograms per cubic meter, while in the developing world it is 0.56 kilograms per cubic meter.

Figure 4.5—Water productivity of rice, 1995

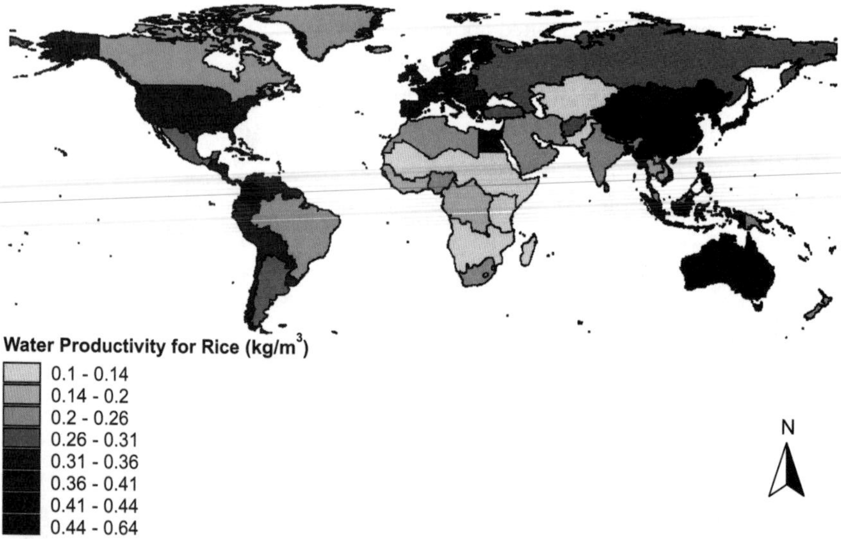

Water Productivity for Rice (kg/m^3)

- 0.1 - 0.14
- 0.14 - 0.2
- 0.2 - 0.26
- 0.26 - 0.31
- 0.31 - 0.36
- 0.36 - 0.41
- 0.41 - 0.44
- 0.44 - 0.64

N

Source: IMPACT-WATER assessments, 2002.

Figure 4.6—Water productivity of total cereals excluding rice, 1995

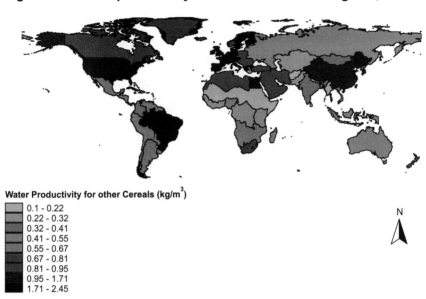

Water Productivity for other Cereals (kg/m³)

0.1 - 0.22
0.22 - 0.32
0.32 - 0.41
0.41 - 0.55
0.55 - 0.67
0.67 - 0.81
0.81 - 0.95
0.95 - 1.71
1.71 - 2.45

N

Source: IMPACT-WATER assessments, 2002.

It should be noted that because of the level of aggregation, the numbers shown on these maps do not show the variation of water productivity within individual countries. Within some large countries, water productivity varies significantly. Figure 4.7 shows the water productivity of all cereals excluding rice in major river basins in China, India, and the United States. In China, water productivity for non-rice cereals ranges from 0.4 to 1.4 kilograms per cubic meter, with higher water productivity in the Yangtze River basin and northeast China (the Song-Liao River basin). Crop yields in these areas are relatively higher and water availability is relatively less restricted. However, in India, where nonrice cereal productivity ranges from 0.2 to 0.7 kilograms per cubic meter, higher water productivity occurs in the north (0.4–0.7 kilograms per cubic meter), where crop yield is higher but water availability is more restricted than in other areas. In the United States, water productivity ranges from 0.9–1.9 kilograms per cubic meter, with higher values in the north than in the south, and the highest in the northwestern regions.

Figure 4.7—Water productivity of total cereals in river basins in China, India, and the United States excluding rice, 1995

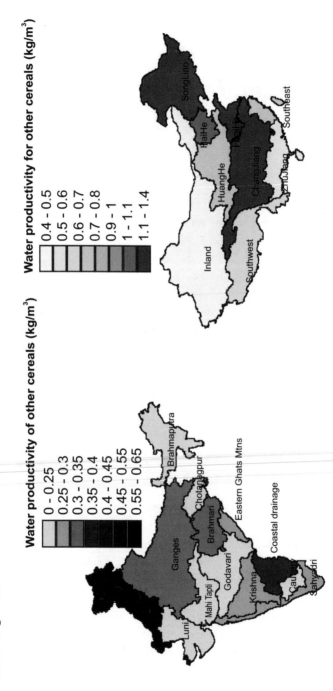

Source: IMPACT-WATER assessments, 2002.

Figure 4.7—Continued

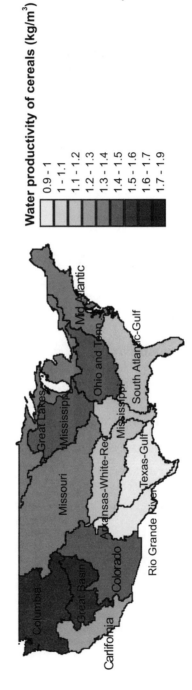

Source: IMPACT-WATER assessments, 2002.

Changes In Water Productivity between 1995 and 2025

To show the year-to-year variability of water productivity between 1995 and 2025, we report BAU results with one hydrologic regime, which regenerates the monthly hydrologic records for 1961–90. Our projections of water productivity show variation from 1995 to 2025 for both irrigated rice and other cereals, both in developed and developing countries and worldwide (Figures 4.8 and 4.9). This year-to-year variation is caused by climate variability, which affects water availability, and thus water productivity. Based on assumptions of area and yield growth and water supply enhancement, water productivities are projected to increase significantly between 1995 and 2025. For example, water productivity of other cereals will increase from 1.0 to 1.4 kilograms per cubic meter in developed countries, 0.6 to 1.0 kilograms per cubic meter in developing countries, 0.7 to 1.1 kilograms per cubic meter globally.

Figures 4.10 and 4.11 compare crop yield and water consumption between 1995 and 2025 for rice and other cereals, respectively, to give insight into the major cause of water productivity increases over the period. As can be seen, crop yield increases and water consumption per hectare decreases. Water consumption per hectare depends on the change in total consumption and the change in crop area.

Figure 4.8—Water productivity of irrigated rice, 1995–2025

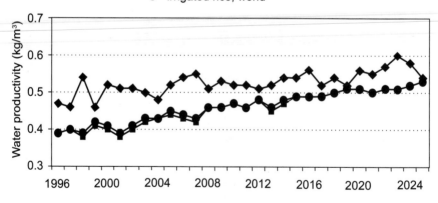

Source: IMPACT-WATER assessments and projections, 2002.

Figure 4.9—Water productivity of irrigated cereals excluding rice, 1995–2025

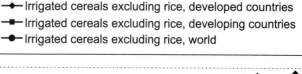

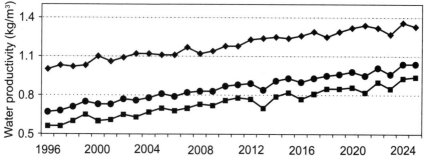

Source: IMPACT-WATER assessments and projections, 2002.

The model projects a relatively small increase in irrigated cereal crop area at 24 million hectares (10 percent) worldwide from 1995 to 2025. Total realized crop water consumption is further determined by the change in water withdrawal capacity, basin efficiency, rainfall harvest, crop consumption requirements, and the amount of water taken by non-irrigation sectors. Under BAU, total global water withdrawals are projected to increase by 23 percent from 1995 to 2025, with the increase mainly used for non-irrigation sectors (increasing by 62 percent worldwide from 1995 to 2025), leading to an increase in total consumption. Water consumption can be reduced, however, because the projected increase of effective river basin water use efficiency will decrease crop demand. All of these factors result in a 3.9 percent increase in consumptive water use for irrigation worldwide. Overall, as can be seen in Figures 4.10 and 4.11, the change of water consumption per hectare is small compared with the change of crop yield. The increase of water productivity results mainly from increases in crop yield.

Water productivity for irrigated crops is higher than that of rainfed crops in developing countries (Figures 4.12 and 4.13). The difference becomes larger over time because of the higher increase in irrigated yield and the increase in water use efficiency over time. However, the water productivity of irrigated crops is not higher than that of rainfed crops everywhere in the world. As observed in Figures 4.14

Figure 4.10—Crop yield and water consumption of rice per hectare, 1995 and 2025

(a) Crop yield

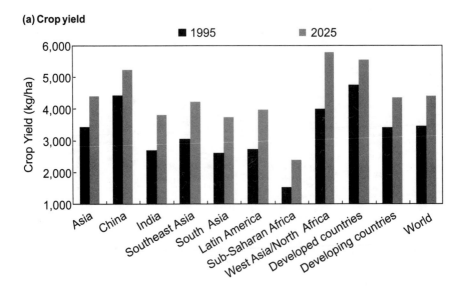

(b) Water consumption per hectare

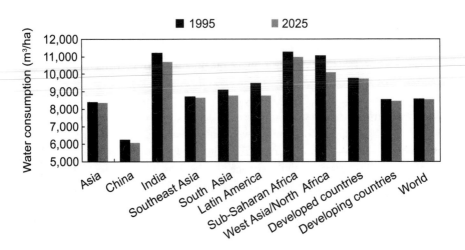

Source: IMPACT-WATER assessments and projections, 2002.

Figure 4.11—Crop yield and water consumption of cereals excluding rice per hectare, 1995 and 2025

(a) Crop yield

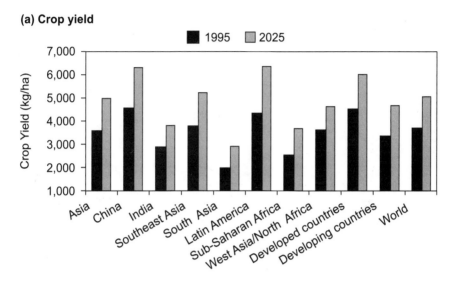

(b) Water consumption

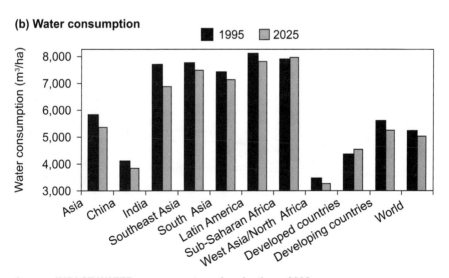

Source: IMPACT-WATER assessments and projections, 2002.

Figure 4.12—Water productivity for irrigated and rainfed rice in developing countries, 1995–2025

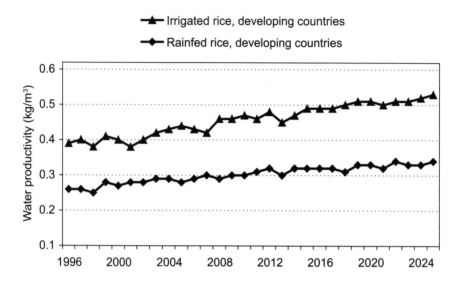

Source: IMPACT-WATER assessments and projections, 2002.

Figure 4.13—Water productivity for irrigated and rainfed cereals excluding rice in developing countries, 1995–2025

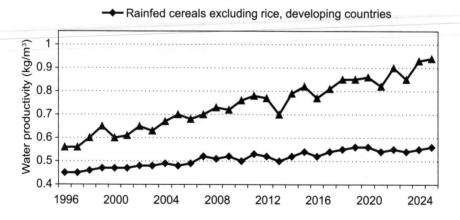

Source: IMPACT-WATER assessments and projections, 2002.

Figure 4.14—Water productivity for irrigated and rainfed rice in developed countries, 1995–2025

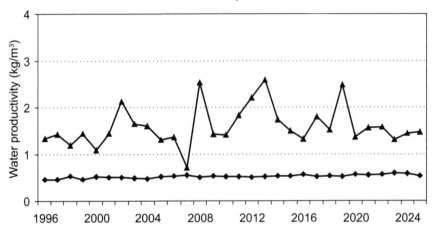

Source: IMPACT-WATER assessments and projections, 2002.

and 4.15, the curve of irrigated crops is below the curve of rainfed crops in developed countries for both rice and other cereals over the same period. This indicates the existence of relatively favorable rainfall conditions for crop growth and high rainfed crop yields associated with infrastructure and other inputs to rainfed crops in developed countries, compared with those in developing countries.

THE FUTURE FOR FOOD

Food Demand

With slowing population growth rates and increasing diversification of diets away from cereals given rising prosperity and changing dietary preferences, annual growth in cereal demand is projected to decline worldwide to 1.3 percent between 1995 and 2025 from 2.2 percent in 1965–95 (and 1.7 percent, 1970–2000). Nevertheless, the projected absolute increase in cereal demand of 828 million metric tons (Table 4.7) is nearly as large as the 846 million metric ton increase of the

Figure 4.15—Water productivity for irrigated and rainfed cereals excluding rice in developed countries, 1995–2025

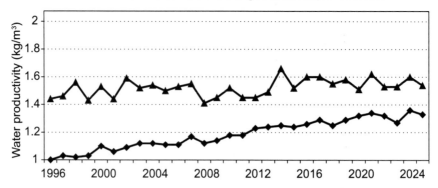

Source: IMPACT-WATER assessments and projections, 2002.

preceding 30 years. Growth in food demand is concentrated in developing countries, which also undergo a change in the composition of cereal demand from rising incomes and rapid urbanization. Per capita food consumption of maize and coarse grains declines as consumers shift to wheat and rice, livestock products, and fruits and vegetables. In much of Asia, an additional shift occurs from rice to wheat. The projected strong growth in meat consumption, in turn, substantially increases cereal consumption for animal feed, particularly maize. The developing country presence in global food markets increases substantially. Under BAU, 86 percent of the projected increase in global cereal consumption between 1995 and 2025 comes from developing countries. Because of their larger, more urbanized populations and rapid economic growth, developing countries in Asia account for just over half the increase in global demand for cereals, with China alone accounting for one-quarter (Table 4.7).

Global demand for meat will grow much faster than that for cereals. Worldwide, demand for meat is forecast to increase by 70 percent between 1995 and 2025, with 86 percent of the increase occurring in developing countries, where meat demand more than doubles over 30 years (Table 4.8). China alone accounts for 39 percent of this increase, compared with India's 4 percent.

Poultry accounts for 41 percent of the global increase in demand for meat under BAU, reaching 33 percent of total meat demand in 2025, significantly higher than the 28 percent of total meat it accounted for in 1995, reflecting a dramatic shift in

Table 4.7—Cereal demand and total cereal production under the business-as-usual scenario, 1995 and 2025

| | Cereal demand (million mt) | | | | | | Cereal production (million mt) | |
| | 1995 baseline estimates | | | 2025 BAU projections | | | 1995 baseline estimates | 2025 BAU projections |
Region/Country	Food	Feed	Total	Food	Feed	Total		
Asia	554.7	157.7	794.3	751.1	348.5	1,228.2	726.5	1,092.8
China	230.9	105.8	375.0	264.6	253.8	581.4	357.6	541.6
India	152.0	6.7	171.3	231.4	22.7	274.7	174.8	256.8
Southeast Asia	84.3	15.0	113.5	123.7	31.1	176.0	106.4	170.2
South Asia excluding India	49.2	1.7	54.9	89.4	4.1	101.6	51.1	80.9
Latin America (LA)	58.4	58.2	137.4	86.5	116.7	238.7	117.0	222.4
Sub-Saharan Africa (SSA)	61.5	3.8	78.4	134.6	9.2	172.4	67.8	137.7
West Asia/North Africa (WANA)	72.9	30.9	120.2	117.5	58.0	202.0	82.4	119.5
Developed countries	154.0	412.2	686.4	164.4	497.1	802.5	794.0	1,050.0
Developing countries	731.7	233.4	1,092.2	1,074.7	514.9	1,803.9	983.8	1,564.2
World	885.7	645.7	1,778.6	1,239.0	1,011.9	2,606.4	1,777.7	2,614.2

Sources: 1995 baseline data are author estimates based on FAO (1998b), 2025 data are IMPACT-WATER projections, 2002.

Notes: BAU indicates business-as-usual scenario; million mt, million metric tons.

taste from red meat to chicken. Increasingly, cereal crops are grown for animal feed to fuel the explosive rise in demand for meat rather than for direct human consumption. As a result, maize rises in importance relative to wheat and rice, accounting for 45 percent of the incremental cereal demand during 1995–2025 and reaching 35 percent of total cereal demand in 2025 compared with 31 percent in 1995. Soybeans and meals also show fast demand growth, increasing by 77 percent and 70 percent, respectively, between 1995 and 2025 (Table 4.8).

Demand growth for noncereal staple food commodities is also strong in developing countries under BAU. In many parts of SSA, roots and tubers—especially cassava, sweet potatoes, and yams—are a major source of sustenance. In the late 1990s, they accounted for 20 percent of calorie consumption in the region, with an even higher concentration in the diets of the poor. In much of Asia and LA, roots and tubers provide an important, supplemental source of carbohydrates, vitamins, and amino acids in food systems that are dominated by other commodities. These patterns are projected to continue, with total root and tuber demand in the developing world increasing by 65 percent (282 million tons) between 1995 and 2025. SSA is projected to account for 47 percent of this increase, indicating that roots and tubers will continue to be of crucial importance to the diet in that region (Table 4.8). Asia also accounts for a significant amount of the total increase, with east Asia accounting for 21 percent, and South Asia 14 percent.

Production, Area, and Yield

Production growth in meat, soybeans, meals, and roots and tubers generally follows the trends in demand growth (Table 4.9). However, for meats, meals, and roots and tubers, production growth in developing countries as a group is somewhat slower than demand growth, which leads to increasing imports as shown below. Soybean production growth lags demand in Asia, but outpaces demand growth in LA.

Cereal production in developing countries as a group will not keep pace with increases in demand. Cereal harvested area is expected to grow only slowly in the coming decades, by 0.40 percent per year in developing countries and 0.29 percent per year in the world as a whole (Table 4.10). Both irrigated and rainfed cereal areas harvested grow slowly, as will be discussed in more detail below. A large share of the most suitable land is already under cultivation, and factors limiting further land expansion include the slow projected growth of irrigation investment (see below), soil degradation, and rapid urbanization leading to conversion of cropland for other uses. The primary constraint to further crop area expansion is not purely a physical limit, however, but rather the projected flat or slowly declining real cereal prices that render expansion of cropland unprofitable in many cases (see discussion of cereal prices below). In Asia, cereal area is projected to increase by only 8 million

Table 4.8—Demand for meat, soybeans, meals, and roots and tubers under the business-as-usual scenario, 1995 and 2025

Region/Country	1995 baseline estimates (million mt)				2025 BAU projections (million mt)			
	Meat	Soybeans	Meals	Roots and tubers	Meat	Soybeans	Meals	Roots and tubers
Asia	72.1	32.4	45.2	245.1	153.8	68.6	101.4	354.9
China	47.4	16.9	16.2	170.8	101.9	38.8	38.7	218.9
India	4.1	4.7	10.3	25.0	10.1	11.5	27.6	60.0
Southeast Asia	8.0	3.7	6.2	31.0	19.4	7.5	15.5	48.0
South Asia excluding India	2.7	0.0	1.8	5.1	6.9	0.1	4.6	12.0
Latin America (LA)	23.0	36.4	13.1	49.6	46.4	69.7	27.1	76.3
Sub-Saharan Africa (SSA)	5.1	0.5	2.2	130.9	12.2	1.1	5.7	262.4
West Asia/North Africa (WANA)	6.9	0.6	5.0	14.3	14.6	1.4	10.0	27.3
Developed countries	96.4	66.4	83.2	198.0	115.5	97.9	104.9	203.8
Developing countries	101.6	64.9	59.5	435.2	220.5	133.9	138.1	717.1
World	198.0	131.3	142.7	633.3	336.0	231.8	243.0	920.9

Sources: 1995 baseline data are author estimates based on FAO (1998b); 2025 data are IMPACT-WATER projections, 2002.
Notes: BAU indicates busines-as-usual scenario; million mt, million metric tons.

Table 4.9—Production of meat, soybeans, meals, and roots and tubers under the business-as-usual scenario, 1995 and 2025

Region/Country	1995 baseline estimates (million mt)				2025 BAU projections (million mt)			
	Meat	Soybeans	Meals	Roots and tubers	Meat	Soybeans	Meals	Roots and tubers
Asia	69.3	21.9	45.5	255.7	147.9	44.6	80.0	340.9
China	47.5	14.3	16.7	168.9	101.9	27.1	30.3	211.4
India	4.3	4.7	14.4	25.2	10.6	11.6	26.8	48.3
Southeast Asia	8.0	2.2	5.2	45.8	19.2	4.6	8.6	54.6
South Asia excluding India	2.7	0.0	1.8	5.0	6.6	0.0	3.4	11.5
Latin America (LA)	23.6	40.3	31.1	49.5	48.0	95.6	53.6	82.3
Sub-Saharan Africa (SSA)	4.9	0.5	2.6	130.9	12.0	1.0	4.4	248.0
West Asia/North Africa (WANA)	5.9	0.3	2.3	14.7	11.9	0.5	4.0	29.6
Developed countries	97.4	68.4	65.9	186.1	119.4	90.3	107.9	223.6
Developing countries	100.6	62.9	76.8	447.2	216.5	141.5	135.1	697.2
World	198.0	131.3	142.7	633.3	336.0	231.8	243.0	920.9

Source: 1995 baseline data are author estimates based on FAO (1998b). 2025 data are IMPACT-WATER projections, 2002.
Notes: BAU indicates busines-as-usual scenario; million mt, million metric tons.

hectares, with an actual decline in rainfed cereal area (Table 4.10). SSA and LA have more potential for area expansion, with area under cereal production projected to expand by 30 million hectares in SSA (of which 28 million is rainfed area) and by 16 million hectares in LA during 1995–2025 (Table 4.10).

With slow growth in area, increases in cereal production are thus highly dependent on increases in productivity. But increases in crop yields are slowing across all cereals and all regions, with the notable exception of SSA, where yields are projected to recover from past stagnation. Yield growth rates in most of the world have been slowing since the early 1980s. In the developed world, the slowdown was primarily policy-induced, as North American and European governments reduced cereal stocks and scaled back farm-price support programs in favor of direct payments to farmers, while in Eastern Europe and the former Soviet Union economic collapse and subsequent economic reforms further depressed productivity. Factors contributing to the slowdown in cereal productivity growth in developing countries, particularly in Asia, include high levels of input use (meaning that it takes increasing input requirements to sustain yield gains), slowing public investment in crop research and irrigation infrastructure, and growing water shortages as irrigation development slows and nonagricultural water demand diverts water from agriculture. This slowdown is projected to continue, with the global yield growth rate for

Table 4.10—Irrigated and rainfed cereal area under the business-as-usual scenario, 1995 and 2025

Region/Country	Irrigated area (million ha)		Rainfed area (million ha)		Total cereal area (million ha)	
	1995 baseline estimates	2025 BAU projections	1995 baseline estimates	2025 BAU projections	1995 baseline estimates	2025 BAU projections
Asia	152.9	168.5	136.9	129.4	289.7	297.9
China	62.4	67.1	26.2	29.0	88.6	96.1
India	37.8	47.1	62.3	48.9	100.1	96.0
Southeast Asia	19.2	20.3	29.8	32.2	48.9	52.5
South Asia excluding India	19.9	21.0	5.6	5.5	25.5	26.5
Latin America (LA)	7.5	9.8	41.8	55.6	49.3	65.4
Sub-Saharan Africa (SSA)	3.3	4.9	69.8	97.7	73.0	102.6
West Asia/North Africa (WANA)	9.8	10.8	34.0	36.0	43.7	46.8
Developed countries	41.8	44.9	192.1	195.7	233.9	240.6
Developing countries	171.3	192.6	282.2	318.5	453.5	511.1
World	213.1	237.5	474.3	514.12	687.4	751.7

Sources: 1995 baseline data are based on FAO (1999) for cereals in developing countries and Cai and Rosegrant (1999) for crops in basins in the United States, China, and India, and noncereal crops in all countries and regions. 2025 data are IMPACT-WATER projections, 2002.
Notes: BAU indicates busines-as-usual scenario; million ha, million hectares.

Table 4.11—Irrigated and rainfed cereal yield under the business-as-usual scenario, 1995 and 2025

Region/Country	Irrigated yield (mt/ha)		Rainfed yield (mt/ha)		Total cereal yield (mt/ha)	
	1995 baseline estimates	2025 BAU projections	1995 baseline estimates	2025 BAU projections	1995 baseline estimates	2025 BAU projections
Asia	3.23	4.57	1.70	2.50	2.51	3.67
China	4.23	6.02	3.59	4.74	4.04	5.64
India	2.65	3.74	1.20	1.65	1.75	2.67
Southeast Asia	3.05	4.39	1.61	2.53	2.17	3.25
South Asia excluding India	2.19	3.34	1.24	1.94	1.98	3.05
Latin America (LA)	4.07	5.66	2.07	3.00	2.37	3.40
Sub-Saharan Africa (SSA)	2.16	3.23	0.85	1.25	0.91	1.34
West Asia/North Africa (WANA)	3.58	4.91	1.40	1.85	1.88	2.56
Developed countries	4.44	6.13	3.17	3.96	3.39	4.36
Developing countries	3.25	4.60	1.51	2.13	2.17	3.06
World	**3.48**	**4.89**	**2.18**	**2.83**	**2.58**	**3.48**

Sources: 1995 baseline data are based on FAO (1999) for cereals in developing countries and Cai and Rosegrant (1999) for crops in basins in the United States, China, and India, and noncereal crops in all countries and regions. 2025 data are IMPACT-WATER projections, 2002.
Notes: BAU indicates busines-as-usual scenario; mt/ha, metric tons per hectare.

all cereals declining from 1.5 percent per year during 1982–95 to 1.0 percent per year during 1995–2025; and average crop yield growth in developing countries, declining from 1.9 percent per year to 1.2 percent.

Growing water shortages are a particularly important source of yield growth decline, and a declining fraction of this irrigation water demand is met over time because irrigation water supply is increasingly being constrained, as indicated in the IWSR discussion above. Increasing water scarcity for irrigation directly contributes to slowing cereal yield growth in developing countries, as can be seen in the projected relative crop yields for irrigated cereal. Relative crop yield is the ratio of projected crop yield to the maximum economically attainable yield at given crop and input prices under zero water stress conditions. The fall in the relative crop yield index significantly hinders future yield growth. For developing countries as a group in 2025, the drop from 0.86 to 0.75 represents an annual 0.68 million tons per hectare in crop yield foregone through increased water stress or an annual loss of cereal production of 130 million metric tons—equivalent to China's annual rice crop and double the U.S. wheat crop in the late 1990s (Table 4.12).

Table 4.12—Relative irrigated cereal crop yields under the business-as-usual scenario, 1995 and 2025

	Relative irrigated cereal crop yields	
Region/Country	1995 baseline estimates	2025 BAU projections
Asia	0.87	0.76
China	0.89	0.78
India	0.84	0.72
Southeast Asia	0.97	0.87
South Asia excluding India	0.87	0.73
Latin America (LA)	0.94	0.76
Sub-Saharan Africa (SSA)	0.96	0.77
West Asia/North Africa (WANA)	0.68	0.57
Developed countries	0.89	0.87
Developing countries	0.86	0.75
World	**0.87**	**0.77**

Sources: Authors' estimates and IMPACT-WATER projections, 2002.
Note: BAU indicates busines-as-usual scenario.

International Trade and Prices

By 2020 under BAU, with developing countries unable to meet cereal demand from their own production, international trade becomes even more vital in providing food to many regions of the globe. Net cereal import demand from the developing world is projected to increase from 107 million metric tons in 1995 to 245 million metric tons in 2025, with Asian nations—particularly China—boosting their imports enormously. Developing countries as a group also increase their imports of meat and roots and tubers, and shift from net exporters of meals to net importers. Asia significantly increases the import of soybeans, while LA dramatically increases soybean exports (Table 4.13).

The substitution of cereal and other food imports for irrigated agricultural production (so-called imports of "virtual water") can be an effective means for reducing agricultural water use (Allan 1996). The virtual water concept is based on the principle of comparative advantage in international trade. Maize is exported from the United States in significant part because it can be grown without irrigation given the exceptionally favorable agroclimatic conditions of the "corn belt." Water-scarce countries, such as much of WANA, have a disadvantage in growing water-intensive crops such as cereals, and could improve water availability for other crops and other sectors by increasing their reliance on cereal imports. Countries with relatively plentiful water, such as Viet Nam, Thailand, and Myanmar, in turn have a comparative advantage in exporting water-intensive crops, like rice, to water-scarce countries (IWMI 2000).

Table 4.13—Net food trade under the business-as-usual scenario, 1995 and 2025

Region/Country	1995 baseline estimates (million mt)					2025 BAU projections (million mt)				
	Cereals	Meat	Soybeans	Meals	Roots and tubers	Cereals	Meat	Soybeans	Meals	Roots and tubers
Asia	-67.7	-2.8	-10.5	0.3	10.6	-139.7	-5.9	-24.0	-21.4	-14.0
China	-17.4	0.1	-2.6	0.5	-1.9	-42.0	0.0	-11.7	-8.4	-7.5
India	3.6	0.2	0.0	4.1	0.2	-19.1	0.5	0.1	-0.8	-11.7
Southeast Asia	-7.0	0.0	-1.5	-1.0	14.8	-6.2	-0.2	-2.9	-6.9	6.6
South Asia excluding India	-3.8	0.0	0.0	0.0	-0.1	-21.0	-0.3	-0.1	-1.2	-0.5
Latin America (LA)	-20.4	0.6	3.9	18.0	-0.1	-16.8	1.6	25.9	26.5	6.0
Sub-Saharan Africa (SSA)	-9.8	-0.2	0.0	0.4	0.0	-34.9	-0.2	-0.1	-1.3	-14.4
West Asia/North Africa (WANA)	-37.8	-1.0	-0.3	-2.7	0.4	-83.0	-2.7	-0.9	-6.0	2.3
Developed countries	107.5	1.0	2.0	-17.3	-11.9	245.2	4.0	-7.6	3.0	20.6
Developing countries	-107.5	-1.0	-2.0	17.3	11.9	-245.2	-4.0	7.6	-3.0	-20.6
World	0.0	0.0	0.0	0.0	0.0	0.0	0.0	0.0	0.0	0.0

Sources: 1995 baseline data are author estimates based on FAO (1998b). 2025 data are IMPACT-WATER projections, 2002.

Note: Negative values indicate net imports; positive values, net exports. BAU indicates business-as-usual scenario; million mt, million metric tons.

BAU shows the vital importance of trade in relation to virtual water. The increase in developing country cereal imports by 138 million metric tons between 1995 and 2025 is equivalent to saving 147 cubic kilometers of water at 2025 water productivity levels, or 8 percent of total water consumption and 12 percent of irrigation water consumption in developing countries in 2025. The water (and land) savings from projected large increases in food imports by developing countries are particularly beneficial if they are the result of strong economic growth that generates the necessary foreign exchange to pay for the food imports. However, even when rapidly growing food imports are primarily a result of rapid income growth, they often act as a warning signal to national policymakers concerned with heavy reliance on world markets, and can induce pressure for trade restrictions that can threaten growth and food security in the longer term. More serious food security problems arise when high food imports are the result of slow agricultural and economic development that fails to keep pace with basic food demand growth driven by population growth. Under these conditions, it may be impossible to finance the required imports on a continuing basis, further deteriorating the ability to bridge the gap between food consumption and food required for basic livelihood. As such, "hot spots" for food trade gaps occur in SSA, where cereal imports are projected to more than triple by 2025 to 35 million metric tons, and in WANA, where cereal imports are projected to increase from 38 million metric tons in 1995 to 83 million metric tons in 2025. The reliance on water-saving cereal imports in WANA makes economic and environmental sense, but must be supported by enhanced nonagricultural growth. It is highly unlikely that SSA could finance the projected level of imports internally; instead international financial or food aid would be required. Failure to finance these imports would further increase food insecurity and pressure on water resources in this region.

Sharp decreases in food prices over the last three decades were a great benefit to the poor, who spend a large share of income on food. Real world prices of wheat, rice, and maize fell by 47, 59, and 61 percent, respectively, between 1970 and 2000. But international cereal prices are projected to decline much more slowly during the next two decades, a significant break from past trends, with a projected increase in the price of maize (Table 4.14). Prices of meat and other commodities also decline far less than in previous decades. This tighter predicted future price scenario indicates additional shocks to the agricultural sector—particularly shortfalls in meeting agricultural water and other input demands—that could seriously pressure food prices upward.

Irrigated and Rainfed Production, 1995

Rainfed and irrigated cereal area and yield for the 1995 baseline were estimated based on data from FAO (1999) and Cai and Rosegrant (1999).[4] Figures 4.16 to 4.18

Table 4.14—World food prices under the business-as-usual scenario, 1995 and 2025

	World food prices (US$/mt)	
Commodity	1995 baseline estimates	2025 BAU projections
Rice	285	221
Wheat	133	119
Maize	103	104
Other coarse grains	97	82
Beef	1,808	1,660
Pork	2,304	2,070
Sheep	2,918	2,621
Poultry	735	700
Potatoes	209	180
Sweet potatoes	134	90
Other roots and tubers	106	81
Soybeans	247	257
Meals	199	262

Sources: 1995 baseline data are based on FAO (1998c), IMF (1997), USDA-NASS (1998), and World Bank (1997). 2025 data are IMPACT-WATER projections, 2002.
Note: BAU indicates business-as-usual scenario; US$/mt, U.S. dollars per metric ton.

Figure 4.16—Cereal area, 1995

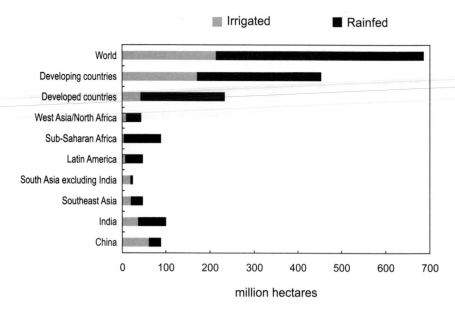

Source: Author estimates based on FAO (1999) and Cai and Rosegrant (1999).

Figure 4.17—Cereal yield, 1995

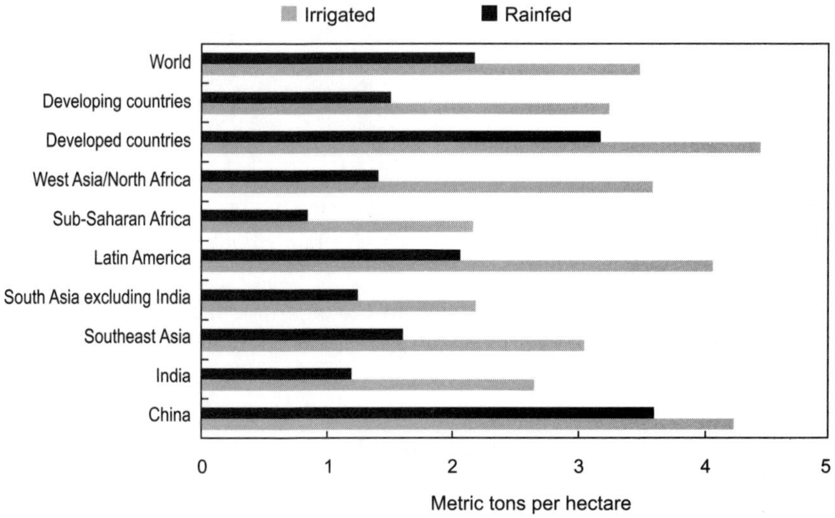

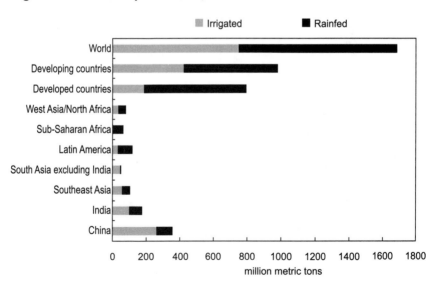

Source: Author estimates based on FAO (1999) and Cai and Rosegrant (1999).

Figure 4.18—Cereal production, 1995

Source: Author estimates based on FAO (1999) and Cai and Rosegrant (1999).

show rainfed and irrigated cereal area, yield, and production in selected countries and aggregated regions in 1995. Developing countries rely substantially more on irrigated agriculture than developed countries, with 38 percent of all cereal area irrigated, accounting for 59 percent of total cereal production. Conversely, only 18 percent of all cereal area is irrigated in the developed world, accounting for 23 percent of total cereal production. Rainfed cereal yield in the developed world is almost double the rainfed yield in the developing world, and is only slightly lower than the irrigated yield in the developing world. As a result, rainfed cereal production in the developed world contributes 59 percent of global rainfed production, and 34 percent of total cereal production.

For some countries and regions with an arid or semi-arid climate, the fraction of rainfed crops is very low, for example, zero percent of the cereal area harvested in Egypt and 7.4 percent in Pakistan is rainfed.[5] Because rice is the dominant crop in Japan and South Korea, rainfed cereal harvested area occupies only 10 and 16 percent, respectively, of the total area harvested. Other countries in which the fraction of rainfed harvested cereal area is below 50 percent include Bangladesh, China, Malaysia, Indonesia, and Viet Nam. The fraction of rainfed cereal harvested area in Nigeria, all SSA countries, and some South American countries such as Argentina and Brazil is over 90 percent, while in LA as a whole the percentage is a slightly lower 85 percent.

Globally, 69 percent of cereal area planted is rainfed including 40 percent of rice, 66 percent of wheat, 82 percent of maize, 86 percent of other grains, and 85 percent of soybeans. The global rainfed harvested area of rice, wheat, maize, other cereals, soybeans, potatoes, sweet potatoes, and cassava and other roots is 560 million hectares in 1995, with cereals representing 85 percent of this total. Worldwide rainfed cereal yield is about 2.2 metric tons per hectare, which is about 65 percent of the irrigated yield. Rainfed cereal production accounts for 58 percent of worldwide cereal production.

Globally, the harvested area of rice is 146 million hectares, of which approximately 87 million hectares are irrigated, and 59 million hectares are rainfed. Developed countries plant very little rainfed rice, while it occupies approximately 42 percent, or 59 million hectares of the total rice area, in developing countries. Developing countries are also responsible for almost all production worldwide, with 97 percent of the total world rice yield coming from those countries. Rainfed rice yield in developing countries is 1.4 tons per hectare or about 44 percent of the total irrigated rice yield in developing countries; this amounts to 24 percent of the developing country total, and 23 percent of world production.

In 1995, 222 million hectares of wheat was harvested globally, 66 percent of which was rainfed, the remaining 34 percent irrigated. About 83 percent of the area planted to wheat in developed countries was rainfed, while in developing countries slightly less than half the total wheat area planted was rainfed. Rainfed wheat yields in developed and developing countries are approximately 2.5 and 1.2 tons per hectare, respectively, while the irrigated yields are slightly higher at 2.9 and 1.7 tons per hectare, respectively. Rainfed wheat production contributes 33 percent of the total yield in developing countries, 81 percent in developed countries, and 52 percent worldwide.

Maize is grown under rainfed conditions more often than rice and wheat. Of the roughly 138 million hectares sown to maize in the world, 82 percent is rainfed, while 18 percent is irrigated. Over 60 percent of the total maize area worldwide is in developing countries, where the average rainfed maize yield is 3.4 tons per hectare; developing countries lag behind at 1.8 tons per hectare. Irrigated yields are higher at 4.2 tons per hectare in developed countries and 2.9 tons per hectare in developing countries. Rainfed maize production contributes 66 percent of the total yield in developing countries, 81 percent in developed countries, and 74 percent globally.

Global production of other coarse grains including barley, millet, oats, rye, and sorghum is predominantly rainfed, with 156 million rainfed hectares, accounting for 86 percent of the total world harvested area. In contrast to wheat and maize, other grains have a lower fraction of rainfed area in developed countries (80 percent) compared with developing countries (91 percent). The average rainfed yield of other grains in developed countries is 2.1 tons per hectare, while that of developing countries is much lower at 0.9 tons per hectare. Irrigated areas yield 3.5 tons of other grains per hectare in developed countries and 2.2 tons per hectare in developing countries. Rainfed production of other coarse grains contributes 80 percent of total yield in developing countries, 71 percent in developed countries, and 74 percent globally.

Approximately 62 million hectares of soybeans are harvested worldwide of which 53 million hectares are rainfed. Developed countries cultivate 91 percent of the total soybean area using rainfed agriculture, while 80 percent of the area in developing countries is rainfed. Unlike cereal crops, rainfed and irrigated soybean yields are similar. In developed countries, the irrigated soybean yield is 2.7 tons per hectare, slightly higher than the rainfed yield of 2.2 tons per hectare; in developing countries the irrigated yield is only slightly higher than the rainfed yield with both at approximately 1.8 tons per hectare.

Rainfed Agriculture versus Irrigated Agriculture—Changes to 2025

Total world irrigated area is projected to increase by 59 million hectares to 420 million hectares—just 16 percent—between 1995 and 2025. Cereals accounted for an

Table 4.15—Irrigated and rainfed cereal production under the business-as-usual scenario, 1995 and 2025

Region/Country	Irrigated production (million mt)		Rainted production (million mt)		Share of rainfed production (%)	
	1995 baseline estimates	2025 BAU projections	1995 baseline estimates	2025 BAU projections	1995 baseline estimates	2025 BAU projections
Asia	493	769	233	323	32	30
China	264	404	94	138	26	25
India	100	176	75	81	43	31
Southeast Asia	59	89	48	81	45	48
South Asia excluding India	44	70	7	11	14	13
Latin America (LA)	31	55	86	167	74	75
Sub-Saharan Africa (SSA)	7	16	59	122	89	89
West Asia/North Africa (WANA)	35	53	48	67	58	56
Developed countries	186	275	608	775	77	74
Developing countries	557	886	425	678	43	43
World	**742**	**1,161**	**1,033**	**1,453**	**58**	**56**

Sources: 1995 baseline data are based on FAO (1999) for cereals in developing countries and Cai and Rosegrant (1999) for crops in basins in the United States, China, and India. 2025 data are IMPACT-WATER projections, 2002.
Notes: BAU indicates business-as-usual scenario; million mt, million metric tons.

estimated 59 percent of world irrigated area in 1995; under BAU, in 2025 they account for 57 percent. Irrigated cereal area increases by 24.4 million hectares, an 11 percent increase over 1995 levels. Nearly all of this increase occurs in developing countries, with the largest increases in India and China. Developed country irrigation increases by only 5.4 million hectares, with a 3.1 million hectare increase in cereal irrigated area.

A more detailed breakdown of irrigated and rainfed cereal area, yield, and production is provided in Tables 4.10, 4.11, and 4.15. Worldwide, rainfed cereal area in 2025 is projected to be 514 million hectares, an 8 percent increase over 1995 levels (Table 4.10). Rainfed cereal area accounts for 68 percent of the total harvested area in 2025, down only slightly from 69 percent in 1995. In developing countries, the rainfed fraction of total area remains the same as 1995 levels at 62 percent. Developed countries, on the other hand, show a slight decrease from 82 percent of the total area planted using rainfed methods in 1995 to 81 percent in 2025.

The global average rainfed cereal yield under BAU is 2.8 metric tons per hectare in 2025, 30 percent higher than in 1995 (Table 4.11). Globally, irrigated cereal yield increases even more, with an overall increase of 40 percent (from 3.5 tons per hectare in 1995 to 4.9 tons per hectare in 2025). The developing world shows a rainfed yield increase of 0.6 metric tons per hectare (a 41 percent increase over 1995 levels), while irrigated yields increase 39 percent (from 3.3 to 4.6 metric tons per hectare). Rainfed yield in the developed world increases 0.8 metric tons per hectare over the period (an increase of 25 percent), while irrigated yields increase 1.7 metric tons or 38 percent.

Global rainfed production increases 41 percent over 1995 values, while irrigated production increases 56 percent (Table 4.10). Relative production increases are more pronounced in developing countries (particularly for rainfed production) at 60 and 59 percent for rainfed and irrigated production, respectively. Developed countries increase rainfed production by 27 percent, while irrigated production increases by 48 percent. Rainfed production accounts for 56 percent of total cereal production worldwide, down slightly from 58 percent in 1995. The developing world maintains its share of rainfed production (43 percent), and rainfed production in the developed world slightly decreases its share, from 77 percent in 1995 to 74 percent in 2025.

Figure 4.19 shows the sources of increased global cereal production during 1995–2025. Under BAU, irrigated and rainfed production each account for about half the total increase in cereal production between 1995 and 2025.

Figure 4.19—Share of irrigated and rainfed production in cereal production increase under the business-as-usual scenario, 1995–2025

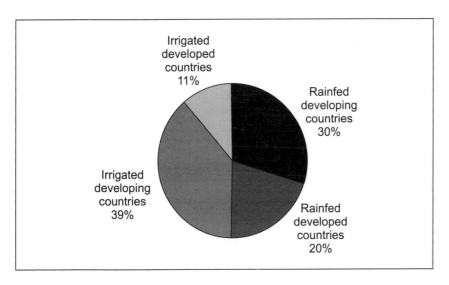

Source: IMPACT-WATER assessments and projections, 2002.

Irrigation plays a dominant role in cereal production in developing countries, accounting for 57 percent of future cereal production growth in developing countries and four-fifths of the growth in global irrigated cereal production. The importance of rainfed cereal production at the global scale is in part a result of the dominance of rainfed agriculture in developed countries. More than 80 percent of cereal area in developed countries is rainfed, much of which is highly productive maize and wheat land such as that in the midwestern United States and parts of Europe. Rainfed cereal yields in developed countries averaged 3.2 metric tons per hectare in 1995, nearly as high as irrigated cereal yields in developing countries, and grow to 4 metric tons per hectare by 2025 under BAU. Rainfed agriculture remains important in developing countries as well. While rainfed yields in developing countries only increase from 1.5 metric tons per hectare to 2.1 metric tons per hectare by 2025, rainfed cereal production still accounts for 43 percent of the developing country total, the same percentage as in 1995.

SUMMARY

Water demand is projected to grow rapidly, particularly in developing countries. Irrigation remains the single largest water user over the 30-year projection period, but the increase in demand is much faster for domestic and industrial uses than for agriculture. Modeling results under BAU also show declining water supply reliability and relative crop yields, as well as worsening agricultural production vulnerability from water scarcity. Food production, demand, and trade and food prices are increasingly affected by declining water availability for irrigation. Given significantly faster growth in water demand in all sectors, developing countries are substantially more negatively affected by declining water availability for irrigation and other uses than developed countries. This is especially so for developing countries with arid climates, poor infrastructure development, and rapidly increasing populations. The increase in imports of "virtual water" through the import of water-intensive cereals is an important safety valve for many developing countries but does not fully compensate declining relative water supply for irrigation.

Rainfed agriculture contributes half the additional cereal production during 1995–2025, showing significant potential for maintaining food security and, importantly, implying the need to improve rainfed agriculture through rainfall harvesting and other means. Our projections indicate that water productivity of irrigated crops is also higher than that of rainfed crops in developing countries, but lower in developed countries. This shows that in developing countries irrigated agriculture is more efficient than rainfed agriculture in resource utilization and food production but also points to the untapped potential to increase the water productivity of rainfed crops through research and infrastructure investment. (The potential for increasing food production from rainfed agriculture is discussed further in Chapters 5 and 8).

Both the increase of crop yield and the reduction of water consumption through basin efficiency improvements contribute to increased water productivity, but the major contribution comes from increased crop yields. Therefore, investments in agricultural infrastructure and research are an essential complement to efforts to improve water use efficiency through investments in water management and infrastructure.

Worldwide and in large aggregated regions, water withdrawal is a small fraction of total renewable water, but for some countries and river basins (especially those arid and semi-arid regions) water withdrawal increasingly seems to threaten the minimum required environmental flow during 1995–2025. The conflict between irrigation and environmental uses and possible solutions for the resolution of this conflict is further addressed in Chapters 5 and 7.

Overall, to meet food demand and sustain minimum required environmental flow to 2025, investments, technology adoption, and policy reform in water and irrigation management are all necessary to maintain water supply reliability and to reduce water supply vulnerability for irrigation, especially in developing countries. More comprehensive analysis through alternative scenarios in terms of investment, technology, and policy variables follows in subsequent chapters.

NOTES

1. All results except when noted are based on the mean of 30 hydrologic samples specified based on the hydrologic regime between 1961 and 1990. The thirty hydrologic scenarios operate under the same assumptions but with various year sequences as given below:

Scenario 1:	1961,	1962...	1990,		
Scenario 2:	1962,	1963...	1990,	1961,	
Scenario 3:	1963,	1964...	1990,	1961,	1962

    ...

    | Scenario 30: | 1961, | 1962... | 1988, | 1989, | 1990 |

    The projected results are reported as the mean across the 30 scenarios for each year during 1996–2025.

2. As noted in Chapter 3, estimates for connected households include households with access to both in-house piped water and to standpipes because comprehensive data was unavailable for households with in-house piped connections.

Thus the per capita water consumption differential between connected and unconnected households, while substantial, is lower than some estimates based on only in-house piped water connections.

3.   Water productivity is generally defined as physical or economic output per unit of water application.

4.   1995 is the most recent year for which it was possible to assemble adequate data.

5.   WANA as a whole is much more reliant on rainfed cereals, which account for 78 percent of harvested area.

Chapter 5

Sustainable Water
World or Water Crisis?

Two alternatives to the business-as-usual scenario were described in Chapter 3—the water crisis scenario (CRI), projecting a worsening of the current situation for water and food policy, and the sustainable water use scenario (SUS), projecting a more positive future with greater environmental water reservation, greater domestic consumption from full water connection of urban and rural households, and maintenance of BAU levels of food production. This chapter presents results for these scenarios and compares them with BAU.[1]

THE WATER STORY

The CRI and SUS scenarios influence the use of water dramatically—but obviously very differently. Under CRI, consumptive water use increases significantly, and under SUS substantial water savings occur. By 2025, total worldwide water consumption under CRI is 13 percent (or 261 cubic kilometers) higher than that under BAU, while under SUS it is 20 percent (or 408 cubic kilometers) lower (Table 5.1). This reduction in consumption frees water for environmental uses. Virtually all the difference in water consumption between the CRI and BAU scenarios is in the irrigation sector—253 cubic kilometers worldwide—mainly a result of declining water use efficiency, in turn causing higher losses through nonbeneficial water consumption and greater water withdrawals to compensate for these losses. Under SUS, however, irrigation water consumption declines by 296 cubic kilometers compared with BAU levels (mainly through reduction in nonbeneficial consumption) because of higher water prices and higher water use efficiency. In each scenario, greater changes occur in the developing as opposed to the developed world, so the former is inversely affected—that is, the developing world is more negatively affected under CRI and more positively affected under SUS. Total water consumption in the developing world increases under CRI by 14 percent (or 225 cubic kilometers) over BAU levels and by 8 percent (or 36 cubic kilometers) in the developed world. Conversely, total water consumption in the developing world decreases

Table 5.1—Total and irrigation water consumption under business-as-usual, water crisis, and sustainable water use scenarios, 1995 and 2025

Region/Country	Total water consumption (km³)				Total irrigation water consumption (km³)			
	1995 baseline estimates	2025 projections			1995 baseline estimates	2025 projections		
		BAU	CRI	SUS		BAU	CRI	SUS
Asia	1,059	1,206	1,371	949	920	933	1,087	727
China	291	329	385	258	244	231	264	179
India	353	396	446	293	321	332	387	234
Southeast Asia	112	147	175	120	86	92	124	81
South Asia excluding India	174	194	214	157	163	169	193	136
Latin America (LA)	131	170	205	136	88	97	132	86
Sub-Saharan Africa (SSA)	62	93	123	76	50	63	102	47
West Asia/North Africa (WANA)	135	162	160	111	122	137	137	92
Developed countries	440	478	514	426	272	277	304	258
Developing countries	1,358	1,603	1,828	1,246	1,164	1,216	1,440	939
World	**1,799**	**2,081**	**2,342**	**1,673**	**1,436**	**1,492**	**1,745**	**1,196**

Source: IMPACT-WATER assessments and projections, 2002.
Notes: BAU indicates business-as-usual scenario; CRI, water crisis scenario; SUS, sustainable water use scenario; and km³, cubic kilometers.

under SUS by 22 percent (or 357 cubic kilometers) and by 11 percent (or 52 cubic kilometers) in the developed world.

West Asia and North Africa (WANA) is the only region in Table 5.1 that does not increase water consumption under CRI because of source limits on water supply. Sub-Saharan Africa (SSA) has the largest water consumption increase at 32 percent, while Latin America (LA) has an increase of 21 percent. Under SUS, all regions show lower water consumption than under BAU, with the largest decline occurring in WANA at 33 percent. The decline in the irrigation water supply reliability index (IWSR) is largest in WANA because, even under SUS, basin water use efficiency (*BE*) improves less than in other regions given already high initial levels, and because tight water supply constraints mean that water diverted for environmental use directly reduces water availability for irrigation.

Water withdrawal patterns directly follow water consumption patterns. Compared with BAU, water withdrawal patterns are also significantly higher under CRI and significantly lower under SUS. Under CRI, 2025 global water withdrawal is 10 percent (or 459 cubic kilometers) higher than BAU, while under SUS, it is 22 percent (1,029 cubic meters) lower (Table 5.2).

Irrigation

Table 5.3 indicates that, under CRI, beneficial irrigation water consumption is lower than BAU levels for all regions except Southeast Asia, LA, and SSA. The beneficial

Table 5.2—Total mean water withdrawal under business-as-usual, water crisis, and sustainable water use scenarios, 1995 and 2025

| Region/Country | Total mean water withdrawal (km³) | | | |
| | 1995 baseline estimates | 2025 projections | | |
		BAU	CRI	SUS
Asia	2,165	2,649	2,943	2,039
China	679	846	978	644
India	674	815	889	602
Southeast Asia	203	287	323	222
South Asia excluding India	353	421	449	335
Latin America (LA)	298	410	477	302
Sub-Saharan Africa (SSA)	128	214	247	173
West Asia/North Africa (WANA)	236	297	289	199
Developed countries	1,144	1,265	1,342	1,085
Developing countries	2,762	3,507	3,889	2,659
World	**3,906**	**4,772**	**5,231**	**3,743**

Source: IMPACT-WATER assessments and projections, 2002.
Notes: BAU indicates business-as-usual scenario; CRI, water crisis scenario; SUS, sustainable water use scenario; and km³, cubic kilometers.

Table 5.3—Beneficial irrigation water consumption under business-as-usual, water crisis, and sustainable water use scenarios, 1995 and 2025

| Region/Country | Beneficial irrigation water consumption (km³) | | | |
| | 1995 baseline estimates | 2025 projections | | |
		BAU	CRI	SUS
Asia	492	541	450	504
China	132	138	109	143
India	184	208	167	172
Southeast Asia	40	45	47	46
South Asia excluding India	79	85	74	78
Latin America (LA)	39	45	47	46
Sub-Saharan Africa (SSA)	22	29	37	26
West Asia/North Africa (WANA)	83	100	73	79
Developed countries	175	190	174	187
Developing countries	627	707	599	646
World	**802**	**897**	**773**	**833**

Source: IMPACT-WATER assessments and projections, 2002.
Notes: BAU indicates business-as-usual scenario; CRI, water crisis scenario; SUS, sustainable water use scenario; and km³, cubic kilometers.

irrigation water consumption value is determined using total irrigation consumption and *BE*. CRI has lower *BE* values than BAU, as specified in Chapter 3. Hence beneficial irrigation water consumption is 8 percent (16 cubic kilometers) lower than BAU in the developed world and 16 percent (108 cubic kilometers) lower in the developing world.

Under SUS, despite a large decline in total irrigation water consumption, the beneficial irrigation consumption is much closer to BAU levels because SUS has a higher *BE*. Beneficial irrigation water consumption under SUS is 2 percent (3 cubic kilometers) lower than BAU in the developed world and 9 percent (61 cubic kilometers) lower in developing countries. For some countries and regions, including China, Southeast Asia, and LA, the beneficial irrigation water consumption is slightly higher under SUS than CRI, a result of more rapid improvement in basin irrigation efficiency over initial levels.

Under CRI, IWSR reduces significantly for all countries and regions except in Southeast Asia, LA, and SSA (Table 5.4), indicating more severe water scarcity for irrigation in most of the world. In these regions however, IWSR values are higher under CRI because increased diversion of water from environmental uses more than compensate for the reduced water use efficiency. In the developing countries as a whole, however, IWSR is significantly lower under CRI than BAU, at 0.65 under CRI compared with 0.75 under BAU. Developed countries and the world as a whole also show lower IWSR values under CRI than BAU, at 0.82 compared with 0.90 for developed countries and 0.67 compared with 0.78 worldwide.

IWSR values under SUS are also lower than under BAU except in Southeast Asia and LA where water resources are relatively plentiful. The average developing country IWSR under SUS is 0.69, compared with 0.75 under BAU; in the developed world, the IWSR is only slightly lower than BAU; and globally, it is 0.73 compared with 0.78 under BAU. Although the decline in IWSR relative to BAU may

Table 5.4—Irrigation water supply reliability under business-as-usual, water crisis, and sustainable water use scenarios, 1995 and 2025

	1995 baseline estimates	2025 projections					
		Mean IWSR			Minimum IWSR		
Region/Country		BAU	CRI	SUS	BAU	CRI	SUS
Asia	0.81	0.76	0.63	0.71	0.71	0.58	0.66
China	0.87	0.80	0.64	0.82	0.67	0.52	0.68
India	0.80	0.71	0.58	0.59	0.65	0.50	0.51
Southeast Asia	0.87	0.87	0.90	0.89	0.75	0.79	0.76
South Asia excluding India	0.79	0.76	0.66	0.69	0.67	0.59	0.61
Latin America (LA)	0.83	0.76	0.80	0.78	0.65	0.70	0.66
Sub-Saharan Africa (SSA)	0.73	0.72	0.92	0.65	0.63	0.88	0.57
West Asia/North Africa (WANA)	0.78	0.75	0.55	0.59	0.64	0.51	0.53
Developed countries	0.87	0.90	0.82	0.89	0.85	0.78	0.83
Developing countries	0.81	0.75	0.65	0.69	0.71	0.61	0.65
World	**0.82**	**0.78**	**0.67**	**0.73**	**0.74**	**0.63**	**0.70**

Source: IMPACT-WATER assessments and projections, 2002.
Notes: BAU indicates business-as-usual scenario; CRI, water crisis scenario; SUS, sustainable water use scenario; and IWSR, irrigation water supply reliability index.

seem surprising, it directly follows the high priority given environmental flows under SUS. As discussed below, SUS reduces irrigation water use so as to increase committed flows for the environment, and improved rainfed agriculture compensates for the deficit in irrigated crop production. Nevertheless, despite the large diversion of water to environmental uses under SUS, the relative water supply reliability for irrigation in developing countries stabilizes in 2016 and actually begins to increase in 2021, as shown in Figure 5.1. Over time, the continued increase in *BE* under SUS counterbalances the transfer of water to the environment and provides IWSR increases.

The minimum IWSR value for a given basin (the basic spatial unit in the model) results from the most unfavorable hydrologic scenario applied to the basin. For each of the 30 hydrologic scenarios, water supply and demand are scaled up to country and regional levels through data aggregation, and minimum IWSRs are

Figure 5.1—Mean irrigation water supply reliability in developing countries under business-as-usual, water crisis, and sustainable water use scenarios, 1995–2025

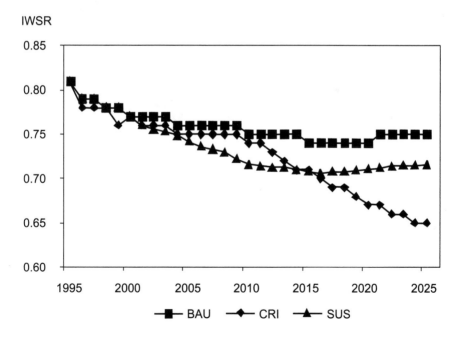

Source: IMPACT-WATER assessments and projections, 2002.
Notes: BAU indicates business-as-usual scenario; CRI, water crisis scenario; SUS, sustainable water scenario; and IWSR, irrigation water supply reliability index.

chosen from the 30 samples. Hence the minimum IWSR for an aggregated spatial unit reflects the most unfavorable condition for the unit as a whole but should not be taken to mean that all the component spatial units simultaneously experience the worst condition. The minimum IWSR values in Table 5.4 indicate the vulnerability of irrigation water supply under each scenario. CRI represents the "worst" hydrologic condition with actual water supply reaching only 60 percent of demand for the developing world as a whole, and only 50 percent for China, India, and WANA.

Domestic Sector

Table 5.5 compares the total domestic water demand in 1995 and 2025 under the three scenarios. Total domestic demand under CRI is 160 cubic kilometers in developing countries (28 percent less than under BAU); 63 cubic kilometers in developed countries (8.5 percent less than under BAU); and 223 cubic kilometers globally (28 percent less than under BAU). Under SUS in 2025, total domestic water demand is 10 percent less than under BAU for developing countries, 4 percent less for developed countries, and 9 percent less globally.

The reasons for these shortfalls in domestic consumption, however, are very different for SUS than for CRI, as seen in Table 5.6, which compares the per capita domestic water demand for connected and unconnected households in rural and urban areas in 1995 and 2025 under each of the three scenarios. Domestic water supply for disadvantaged households improves under SUS through the universal extension of household water connections, while the initially connected households

Table 5.5—Domestic water consumption under business-as-usual, water crisis, and sustainable water use scenarios, 1995 and 2025

	Domestic water demand (km³)			
	1995 baseline	2025 projections		
Region/Country	estimates	BAU	CRI	SUS
Asia	79.1	156.7	113.0	143.9
China	30.0	59.4	42.3	54.3
India	21.0	40.9	27.7	42.0
Southeast Asia	13.9	30.4	23.6	23.8
South Asia excluding India	7.0	16.2	11.1	15.3
Latin America (LA)	18.2	30.7	24.7	22.8
Sub-Saharan Africa (SSA)	9.5	23.9	15.2	23.8
West Asia/North Africa (WANA)	7.1	13.1	9.9	11.2
Developed countries	58.7	68.6	62.8	65.8
Developing countries	110.6	221.0	159.7	198.7
World	**169.3**	**289.6**	**222.5**	**264.5**

Source: IMPACT-WATER assessments and projections, 2002.
Notes: BAU indicates business-as-usual scenario; CRI, water crisis scenario; and SUS, sustainable water use scenario.

reduce consumption in response to higher prices and improved water savings technology. In the rural areas, this leads to an actual increase in the overall per capita domestic consumption compared with BAU. In urban areas overall per capita consumption declines because of the greater weight of initially connected households in urban areas (Table 5.6).

Under CRI, however, domestic water supply conditions continually worsen because the proportion of population in households connected to the water supply declines sharply compared with BAU. Per capita demand under CRI for both

Table 5.6—Per capita potential domestic water demand for connected/unconnected households in rural and urban areas under business-as-usual, water crisis, and sustainable water use scenarios, 1995 and 2025

Region/Country	Connected (m³/yr/person)				Unconnected (m³/yr/person)			
	1995 baseline estimates	2025 projections			1995 baseline estimates	2025 projections		
		BAU	CRI	SUS		BAU	CRI	SUS
Rural areas								
Asia	27.1	29.7	27.5	33.5	17.6	18.9	17.1	n.a.
China	25.7	27.6	26.7	36.9	17.1	18.4	17.8	n.a.
India	26.8	27.8	24.2	31.4	17.9	18.4	16.4	n.a.
Southeast Asia	29.6	38.2	33.1	34.7	19.2	23.6	20.0	n.a.
South Asia excluding India	25.7	28.2	22.1	27.1	17.3	18.9	15.3	n.a.
Latin America (LA)	27.2	29.7	27.5	33.4	17.6	18.9	17.1	n.a.
Sub-Saharan Africa (SSA)	18.8	19.5	16.5	21.5	12.8	13.1	12.0	n.a.
West Asia/North Africa (WANA)	18.3	17.0	16.2	19.9	10.6	10.0	8.0	n.a.
Developed countries	47.0	48.8	47.2	51.2	22.3	33.9	24.1	n.a.
Developing countries	25.2	27.0	24.7	30.2	16.9	17.6	15.8	n.a.
World	**31.0**	**29.3**	**29.2**	**33.7**	**17.0**	**17.7**	**15.8**	**n.a.**
Urban areas								
Asia	41.8	52.4	47.0	33.5	25.5	27.8	24.4	n.a.
China	44.3	64.4	57.6	36.9	26.9	28.7	28.0	n.a.
India	38.7	43.0	31.0	31.4	23.4	24.1	21.1	n.a.
Southeast Asia	43.3	56.8	55.3	34.7	26.1	32.0	28.8	n.a.
South Asia excluding India	36.4	36.0	34.0	27.1	23.2	27.5	17.0	n.a.
Latin America (LA)	41.7	52.4	46.9	33.4	25.5	27.8	24.3	n.a.
Sub-Saharan Africa (SSA)	29.2	29.1	19.8	21.5	17.8	18.0	12.5	n.a.
West Asia/North Africa (WANA)	25.7	27.0	26.2	19.9	17.8	15.8	12.3	n.a.
Developed countries	49.3	55.7	51.2	51.2	28.6	34.8	23.0	n.a.
Developing countries	39.1	45.5	41.3	30.2	24.7	24.9	21.1	n.a.
World	**43.4**	**48.1**	**45.3**	**33.7**	**24.8**	**25.1**	**21.4**	**n.a.**

Source: IMPACT-WATER assessments and projections, 2002.
Notes: BAU indicates business-as-usual scenario; CRI, water crisis scenario; SUS, sustainable water use scenario; n.a., not applicable; and m³/yr/person, cubic meters per year per person.

connected and unconnected households is significantly lower than under BAU in both rural and urban areas of most regions including the developed and developing worlds as a whole (Table 5.6). In the developing world, per capita demand declines by 9 percent for connected rural households, by 9 percent for connected urban households, by 10 percent for unconnected rural households, and by 15 percent for unconnected urban households.

Industrial Sector
Under SUS, industrial water demand declines compared with BAU, through technological improvements in water use and recycling and increased water prices that induce reductions in demand (as discussed in Chapter 3). Under CRI, with weakened incentives and regulations and lower investment in technology, industrial water demand increases compared with BAU, as more water is needed to produce a unit of output. In 2025, total worldwide industrial water demand under CRI is 80 cubic kilometers (or 33 percent) higher than under BAU, while it is 85 cubic kilometers (or 35 percent) lower under SUS (Table 5.7). Compared with BAU global industrial water use intensity is 1.2 cubic meters per thousand U.S. dollars higher under CRI, and 1.3 cubic meters per thousand U.S. dollars lower under SUS.

Non-Irrigation Water Supply Reliability
Non-irrigation water supply reliability (NIWSR) is expressed as the ratio of actual water consumption over potential demand for the industrial, domestic, and

Table 5.7—Total industrial water demand and industrial water use intensity under business-as-usual, water crisis, and sustainable water use scenarios, 1995 and 2025

	Industrial water demand (km³)				Industrial water use intensity (m³/1,000 US$)			
	1995 baseline estimates	2025 projections			1995 baseline estimates	2025 projections		
Region/Country		BAU	CRI	SUS		BAU	CRI	SUS
Asia	48.9	92.6	148.5	55.1	16.2	6.7	11.3	3.8
China	13.2	32.1	74.8	18.5	16.0	6.2	14.5	3.6
India	7.3	16	23.1	9.8	19.6	7.9	11.5	4.9
Southeast Asia	11.5	21.3	23.2	11.6	20.4	8.9	9.7	4.9
South Asia excluding India	1.9	4.7	5.7	2.6	18.3	11.7	14.0	6.5
Latin America (LA)	18	30.2	36.7	16.1	10.6	5.9	7.1	3.1
Sub-Saharan Africa (SSA)	0.9	2.5	2.3	1.3	6.3	5.8	6.2	3.0
West Asia/North Africa (WANA)	4.6	8.8	9.7	4.5	8.4	5.1	5.7	2.6
Developed countries	96.6	115.7	133.2	85.6	4.3	2.5	2.8	1.8
Developing countries	62.9	123.8	186.4	69.1	13.2	6.4	9.6	3.6
World	**159.5**	**239.5**	**319.6**	**154.6**	**5.9**	**3.6**	**4.8**	**2.3**

Source: IMPACT-WATER assessments and projections, 2002.
Notes: BAU indicates business-as-usual scenario; CRI, water crisis scenario; SUS, sustainable water use scenario; km³, cubic kilometers; and m³/1,000 US$, cubic meters per thousand U.S. dollars.

Table 5.8—Non-irrigation water supply reliability under business-as-usual, water crisis, and sustainable water use scenarios, 1995 and 2025

Region/Country	1995 baseline estimates	2025 projections Mean NIWSR BAU	CRI	SUS	Minimum NIWSR BAU	CRI	SUS
Asia	0.99	0.98	0.95	0.99	0.97	0.92	0.99
China	0.98	0.97	0.93	0.99	0.95	0.90	0.99
India	0.99	0.98	0.96	0.99	0.97	0.91	0.98
Southeast Asia	0.97	0.98	0.97	1.00	0.95	0.93	1.00
South Asia excluding India	0.98	0.97	0.96	0.99	0.95	0.92	0.99
Latin America (LA)	0.99	0.99	0.97	1.00	0.98	0.94	1.00
Sub-Saharan Africa (SSA)	0.98	0.97	0.97	0.99	0.96	0.89	0.98
West Asia/North Africa (WANA)	0.99	0.99	0.97	1.00	0.98	0.89	1.00
Developed countries	0.98	0.98	0.98	1.00	0.98	0.95	0.99
Developing countries	0.99	0.98	0.95	0.99	0.97	0.90	0.99
World	**0.98**	**0.98**	**0.95**	**1.00**	**0.98**	**0.91**	**0.99**

Source: IMPACT-WATER assessments and projections, 2002.
Notes: BAU indicates business-as-usual scenario; CRI, water crisis scenario; SUS, sustainable water use scenario; and NIWSR, non-irrigation water supply reliability index.

livestock sectors. Table 5.8 shows NIWSR values for 1995 and 2025 for each scenario, including the mean and minimum values of the 30 sample hydrologic scenarios. CRI has the lowest reliability and SUS the highest. The worst case among the 30 samples under CRI indicates a 9 percent worldwide water supply deficit for the non-irrigation sectors; by contrast, SUS virtually eliminates non-irrigation water supply shortage even in years of severe water scarcity.

Environmental Committed Flow
As discussed above, total water withdrawals are largest under CRI and smallest under SUS (See Table 5.2). This results in sharply reduced environmental committed flow in 2025 under CRI, with 380 cubic kilometers less in the developing world, 80 cubic kilometers less in the developed world, and 460 cubic kilometers less in the world. SUS, on the other hand, results in higher environmental committed flows, with an 850 cubic kilometer increase in the developing world, a 180 cubic kilometer increase in the developed world, and a 1,030 cubic kilometers increase globally. SUS has a much greater level of committed environmental flow than CRI, at 1,490 cubic kilometers, equivalent to 31 percent of the total water withdrawals under BAU.

Table 5.9 shows the criticality ratio—the ratio of water withdrawal over total renewable water—in 1995 and 2025 under the three scenarios. As noted in Chapter 4, the criticality ratio is indicative of the intensity of human water use. As expected, the ratios for the world under CRI are the highest and those under SUS are the lowest. Globally, CRI results in a ratio that is 3-percentage points (but 34 percent) higher than under SUS, CRI results in significantly higher ratios in 2025 than 1995, while SUS maintains 1995 levels. For very high water stress areas, such as WANA, CRI results in a slightly lower ratio in 2025 than under BAU, because lower *BE* under CRI causes a greater amount of water is be lost to nonbeneficial consumption, reducing return flows and withdrawals downstream. The ratio is relatively low globally and for large aggregated regions because abundant water in some countries masks scarcity in others, but the ratio is far higher for individual dry regions. It is in these dry regions that the impact of SUS is most beneficial. For example, in 2025, in WANA the ratio is 0.90 under BAU compared with 0.61 under SUS, and in China and India the ratios decline from 0.33 to 0.25 and from 0.36 to 0.26, respectively; in the Yellow River and Haihe River basins in northern China, the ratios drop from 1.11 to 0.71 and from 1.49 to 0.93, respectively; and in the Indus and Ganges in India the ratios fall from 0.90 to 0.62, and 0.57 to 0.41, respectively (see also Box 5.1).

THE FUTURE FOR FOOD

In 2025, CRI results in lower harvested cereal area for both irrigated and rainfed areas in both the developing and the developed world. Compared with BAU, total harvested cereal area in the developing world under CRI is 17.7 million hectares (or 3 percent) lower than BAU, 8.9 million hectares (or 4 percent) lower in the developed world, and 26.6 million hectares (or 4 percent) lower globally (Table 5.10). The total harvested area under SUS is only slightly lower than under BAU.

Table 5.9—Ratio of water withdrawal to total renewable water under business-as-usual, water crisis, and sustainable water use scenarios, 1995 and 2025

	1995 baseline estimates	2025 projections		
Region/Country		BAU	CRI	SUS
Asia	0.17	0.20	0.23	0.16
China	0.26	0.33	0.38	0.25
India	0.30	0.36	0.39	0.26
Southeast Asia	0.04	0.05	0.06	0.04
South Asia excluding India	0.18	0.22	0.23	0.17
Latin America (LA)	0.02	0.03	0.03	0.02
Sub-Saharan Africa (SSA)	0.02	0.04	0.05	0.03
West Asia/North Africa (WANA)	0.69	0.90	0.88	0.61
Developed countries	0.09	0.10	0.10	0.08
Developing countries	0.08	0.10	0.11	0.08
World	**0.08**	**0.10**	**0.11**	**0.08**

Source: IMPACT-WATER assessments and projections, 2002.
Notes: BAU indicates business-as-usual scenario; CRI, water crisis scenario; and SUS, sustainable water use scenario.

Table 5.10—Irrigated and rainfed cereal area under business-as-usual, water crisis, and sustainable water use scenarios, 1995 and 2025

Region/Country	Irrigated cereal area (million ha)				Rainfed cereal area (million ha)				Total cereal area (million ha)			
	1995 baseline estimates	2025 projections			1995 baseline estimates	2025 projections			1995 baseline estimates	2025 projections		
		BAU	CRI	SUS		BAU	CRI	SUS		BAU	CRI	SUS
Asia	152.9	168.5	154.4	163.7	136.9	129.4	125.6	127.9	289.7	297.9	280.0	291.6
China	62.4	67.1	60.4	64.1	26.2	29.0	28.0	28.6	88.6	96.1	88.4	92.6
India	37.8	47.1	44.9	46.3	62.3	48.9	48.3	48.7	100.1	96.0	93.1	95.0
Southeast Asia	19.2	20.3	19.5	20.3	29.8	32.2	30.7	31.5	48.9	52.5	50.2	51.8
South Asia excluding India	19.9	21.0	18.8	20.0	5.6	5.5	5.6	5.5	25.5	26.5	24.4	25.5
Latin America (LA)	7.5	9.8	9.4	9.7	41.8	55.6	54.8	54.3	49.3	65.4	64.2	64.1
Sub-Saharan Africa (SSA)	3.3	4.9	4.8	4.6	69.8	97.7	99.9	96.7	73.0	102.6	104.7	101.3
West Asia/North Africa (WANA)	9.8	10.8	10.1	10.3	34.0	36.0	35.9	35.9	43.7	46.8	46.0	46.1
Developed countries	41.8	44.9	43.8	44.5	192.1	195.7	187.9	190.8	233.9	240.6	231.7	235.3
Developing countries	171.3	192.6	177.4	186.9	282.2	318.5	316.0	314.7	453.5	511.1	493.4	501.6
World	213.1	237.5	221.3	231.4	474.3	514.2	503.8	505.5	687.4	751.7	725.1	736.9

Source: IMPACT-WATER assessments and projections, 2002.

Notes: BAU indicates business-as-usual scenario; CRI, water crisis scenario; SUS, sustainable water use scenario; and million ha, million hectares.

Table 5.11—Irrigated and rainfed cereal yield under business-as-usual, water crisis, and sustainable water use scenarios, 1995 and 2025

Region/Country	Irrigated cereal yield (kg/ha)				Rainfed cereal yield (kg/ha)				Total cereal yield (kg/ha)			
	1995 baseline estimates	2025 projections			1995 baseline estimates	2025 projections			1995 baseline estimates	2025 projections		
		BAU	CRI	SUS		BAU	CRI	SUS		BAU	CRI	SUS
Asia	3,227	4,565	4,357	4,434	1,699	2,500	2,416	2,787	2,505	3,668	3,486	3,712
China	4,225	6,023	5,762	5,973	3,585	4,739	4,614	5,203	4,036	5,638	5,400	5,739
India	2,653	3,739	3,379	3,449	1,197	1,652	1,597	2,018	1,747	2,674	2,456	2,715
Southeast Asia	3,054	4,386	4,444	4,394	1,609	2,529	2,439	2,662	2,174	3,245	3,216	3,339
South Asia excluding India	2,187	3,343	3,234	3,213	1,239	1,938	1,779	2,232	1,979	3,051	2,902	3,002
Latin America (LA)	4,066	5,660	5,646	5,696	2,067	3,004	2,913	3,137	2,373	3,401	3,314	3,528
Sub-Saharan Africa (SSA)	2,157	3,232	3,597	3,118	848	1,249	1,194	1,311	907	1,343	1,306	1,393
West Asia/North Africa (WANA)	3,578	4,910	4,826	4,824	1,397	1,845	1,757	2,849	1,884	2,557	2,431	3,294
Developed countries	4,439	6,129	5,764	6,089	3,167	3,960	3,635	4,029	3,394	4,364	4,038	4,417
Developing countries	3,249	4,599	4,423	4,481	1,506	2,130	2,041	2,401	2,165	3,061	2,897	3,177
World	3,483	4,888	4,689	4,790	2,179	2,826	2,635	3,015	2,583	3,478	3,262	3,573

Source: IMPACT-WATER assessments and projections, 2002.

Notes: BAU indicates business-as-usual scenario; CRI, water crisis scenario; SUS, sustainable water use scenario; and kg/ha, kilograms per hectare.

Average irrigated cereal yield is lower for developing and developed countries and the world as a whole in 2025 because of the lower IWSR under the CRI and SUS compared with BAU. Globally, irrigated cereal yields are 4 percent lower under CRI, and 2 percent lower under SUS (Table 5.11). However (as previously discussed) IWSR values under CRI or SUS are even higher than under BAU for some specific regions, hence irrigated yields in these regions are even higher than under BAU (Southeast Asia and SSA are examples).

Global rainfed yields under SUS are 189 kilograms per hectare or 7 percent higher than BAU because of higher yields from improved rainfall harvesting and greater investment in crop research. The rainfed yield under CRI, however, results in a decrease of 191 kilograms per hectare (7 percent) compared with BAU given no improvement in rainfall harvesting and lower rainfed crop yield growth from 1995 to 2025. As a result, with faster rainfed yield growth compensating for slower irrigated yield growth under SUS, the average total cereal yield in 2025 is slightly higher under SUS than under BAU but is 216 kilograms per hectare (6 percent) lower under CRI than under BAU.

The impact of irrigation and rainfall use on crop yield is further explored in Table 5.12, which compares relative irrigated and rainfed yields to their potential yields under each scenario. Aggregated results for developed and developing countries show BAU to have the highest relative irrigated yield, while SUS has the highest relative rainfed yield. CRI results in the lowest relative yield for both irrigated and rainfed cereals; however, the relative irrigated yield varies over the regions shown in the table depending on IWSR (Table 5.4).

In 2025, irrigated production is 123 million metric tons (11 percent) lower under CRI than under BAU, and 53 million metric tons (5 percent) lower under SUS than under BAU (Table 5.13). Compared with BAU, rainfed production in 2025 declines by 126 million metric tons (9 percent) under CRI, and increases by 71 million metric tons (5 percent) under SUS. As a result, total cereal production under CRI is 249 million metric tons (10 percent) less than under BAU and, under SUS, 19 million metric tons (1 percent) more than under BAU.

Rainfed agriculture's contribution to total additional cereal production varies significantly across regions and scenarios during 1995–2025 (Figure 5.2). In the developed world, rainfed agriculture contributes 50 percent of the total under BAU and CRI, and 57 percent under SUS. In the developing world, rainfed agriculture's contribution to additional cereal production is 43 percent under BAU, 50 percent under CRI, and 54 percent under SUS. However, the increase of rainfed contribution under CRI is mainly the result of declines in irrigated production compared with BAU; while the increase of rainfed contribution under SUS is a result of improved rainfall harvesting and larger increases in rainfed yields.

Table 5.12—Ratio of irrigated and rainfed yield to potential yield under business-as-usual, water crisis, and sustainable water use scenarios, 1995 and 2025

	Relative irrigated yield				Relative rainfed yield			
	1995 baseline estimates	2025 projections			1995 baseline estimates	2025 projections		
Region/Country		BAU	CRI	SUS		BAU	CRI	SUS
Asia	0.87	0.76	0.72	0.73	0.83	0.64	0.62	0.71
China	0.89	0.78	0.74	0.77	0.86	0.61	0.60	0.67
India	0.84	0.72	0.65	0.67	0.78	0.68	0.66	0.84
Southeast Asia	0.97	0.87	0.89	0.87	0.98	0.85	0.82	0.89
South Asia excluding India	0.87	0.73	0.70	0.70	0.86	0.76	0.69	0.87
Latin America (LA)	0.94	0.76	0.76	0.77	0.94	0.75	0.72	0.78
Sub-Saharan Africa (SSA)	0.96	0.77	0.80	0.74	0.89	0.65	0.62	0.68
West Asia/North Africa (WANA)	0.68	0.57	0.56	0.56	0.78	0.60	0.57	0.81
Developed countries	0.89	0.87	0.82	0.87	0.90	0.84	0.77	0.85
Developing countries	0.86	0.75	0.72	0.73	0.86	0.67	0.64	0.75
World	**0.87**	**0.77**	**0.74**	**0.75**	**0.88**	**0.74**	**0.69**	**0.79**

Source: IMPACT-WATER assessments and projections, 2002.

Notes: BAU indicates business-as-usual scenario; CRI, water crisis scenario; and SUS, sustainable water use scenario.

Hydrologic and water supply variability can significantly affect food production in both irrigated and rainfed areas, as shown in Figures 5.3 and 5.4. Under all three scenarios, potential irrigated production in developing countries tends to decline from increasing water stress (Figure 5.3). CRI shows the fastest drop in relative irrigated production, while under BAU and SUS, declines occur at a slightly less drastic rate. Corresponding to the increase of the irrigation water supply reliability after 2016 under SUS (Figure 5.1), relative irrigated production under SUS shifts from decreases to increases around the same year. Relative rainfed production in developing countries tends to decline under CRI, while the BAU and SUS show some increase in later years from improved rainfall harvest (Figure 5.4).

Food Prices

As with food production, crop prices under BAU and SUS are similar, declining slowly under both scenarios from 1995 to 2025, except for small price increases for maize and soybeans under BAU (Table 5.14). Under CRI, however, 2025 prices show dramatic increases over those of 1995—40 percent for rice; 80 percent for wheat; 120 percent for maize; 85 percent for other coarse grains; 70 percent for soybeans; and 50–70 percent for potatoes, sweet potatoes, and other roots and tubers. Compared with BAU, 2025 crop prices under CRI show tremendous increases—1.8 times higher for rice, 1.7 times higher for potatoes, 1.6 times higher for soybeans, and more than double for all other crops.

Table 5.13—Irrigated, rainfed, and total cereal production under business-as-usual, water crisis, and sustainable water scenarios, 1995 and 2025

	Irrigated cereal production (million mt)				Rainfed cereal production (million mt)				Total cereal production (million mt)			
	1995 baseline estimates	2025 BAU	CRI	SUS	1995 baseline estimates	2025 BAU	CRI	SUS	1995 baseline estimates	2025 BAU	CRI	SUS
Region/Country												
Asia	493.3	769.4	672.6	726.0	232.6	323.4	303.5	356.5	725.9	1,092.8	976.1	1,082.5
China	263.6	404.2	348.1	383.1	94.0	137.5	129.0	148.6	357.6	541.7	477.1	531.7
India	100.3	175.9	151.6	159.6	74.6	80.8	77.1	98.3	174.9	256.7	228.7	257.9
Southeast Asia	58.5	88.9	86.7	89.0	47.9	81.3	74.7	83.8	106.4	170.2	161.4	172.8
South Asia excluding India	43.6	70.2	60.7	64.2	6.9	10.7	10.0	12.3	50.5	80.9	70.7	76.5
Latin America (LA)	30.6	55.2	53.3	55.4	86.4	167.1	159.4	170.6	117.0	222.3	212.7	226.0
Sub-Saharan Africa (SSA)	7.0	15.7	17.4	14.2	59.2	122.0	119.3	126.8	66.2	137.7	136.7	141.0
West Asia/North Africa (WANA)	34.9	53.0	48.5	49.6	47.5	66.6	63.3	102.4	82.4	119.6	111.8	152.0
Developed countries	185.6	275.1	252.6	270.7	608.3	774.9	682.9	768.7	793.9	1,050.0	935.5	1,039.4
Developing countries	556.7	885.9	784.7	837.8	425.0	678.4	644.8	755.6	981.7	1,564.3	1,429.5	1,593.4
World	742.3	1,161.0	1,037.3	1,108.5	1,033.3	1,453.3	1,327.7	1,524.3	1,775.6	2,614.3	2,365.0	2,632.8

Source: IMPACT-WATER assessments and projections, 2002.

Notes: BAU indicates business-as-usual scenario; CRI, water crisis scenario; SUS, sustainable water use scenario; and million mt, million metric tons.

Figure 5.2—Contribution of rainfed cereals to additional cereal production globally and in developed and developing countries under business-as-usual, water crisis, and sustainable water use scenarios, 1995–2025

(a) Global

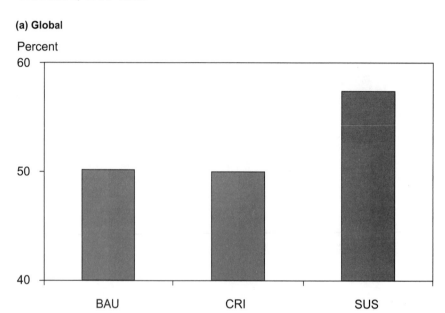

(b) Developed countries

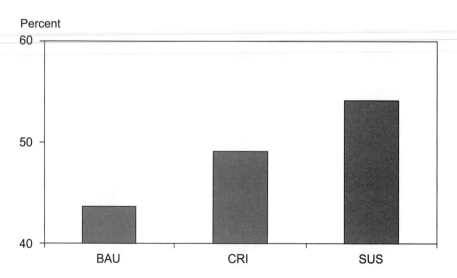

Figure 5.2—Continued

(c) Developing countries

Percent

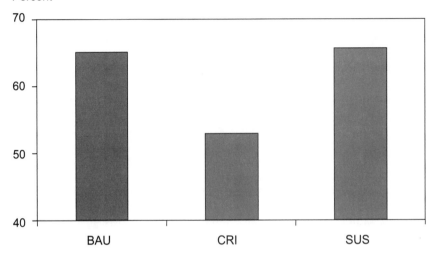

Source: IMPACT-WATER assessments and projections, 2002.
Notes: BAU indicates business-as-usual scenario; CRI, water crisis scenario; and SUS, sustainable water scenario.

Hydrologic and water supply variability can also have a significant impact on food prices—particularly under CRI. CRI's "worst" climate condition of the 30 samples results in 2025 rice prices as high as US$446 per metric ton for rice (1.6 times the 1995 price), US$282 per metric ton for wheat (2.1 times the 1995 price), US$246 per metric ton for maize (2.4 times the 1995 price), and US$472 per metric ton for soybeans (2.1 times the 1995 price).

Figure 5.5(a–d) compares mean global prices under CRI, SUS, and BAU for rice, wheat, maize, and soybeans from 1995 to 2025. For all these crops, CRI prices go up over time while SUS prices go down. Further illustrating this variation under BAU and CRI, Figures 5.6, 5.7, and 5.8(a–b) present the minimum, mean, and maximum global prices for rice, wheat, and soybeans, respectively. Not only do mean prices go down under BAU but the spread between the mean and maximum prices stays constant or declines slightly over time. In contrast, under CRI, both the mean price and the spread between the mean and maximum prices increase significantly, indicating

BOX 5.1—Irrigation, environment and food production in water scarce basins

In the focal water-scarce basins under CRI—although water withdrawal is even higher than under BAU, as irrigators tap environmental flows to try to compensate for lower basin efficiency—irrigation supply reliability drops sharply in 2025. Compared with BAU, IWSR in 2025 falls by 39 percent in the Haihe, 40 percent in the Yellow, 22 percent in the Ganges, and 20 percent in the Indus river basins, and 13 percent in Egypt. With increasing water scarcity, irrigated cereal areas and yields drop significantly compared with BAU. Rainfed yields also fall relative to BAU because of failure to improve rainfall harvesting and declining research investment. Cereal production thus drops sharply in 2025 compared with BAU—by 32 percent in the Haihe, 31 percent in the Yellow, 23 percent in the Indus, and 12 percent in the Ganges river basins, and 9 percent in Egypt. Water shortages occur even in non-irrigation uses in the basins in northern China, with the median non-irrigation water supply deficit increasing to 12 percent in Haihe and 11 percent in Huanghe river basins. And in poor rainfall years, all four basins have shortages in domestic and urban water use, 15 percent in the Haihe, 14 percent in the Yellow, 11 percent in the Indus, and 8 percent in the Ganges river basins, and 2 percent in Egypt. Large amounts of water are depleted from what were previously environmental uses. Compared with total withdrawal under BAU, environmental water flows decline by the equivalent of 12 percent of total BAU water withdrawal in the Yellow River basin, 18 percent in the Indus, 13 percent in the Ganges, and 8 percent in Egypt, with the Haihe losing a relatively small 1 percent.

Under SUS, in stark contrast, there are large improvements in environmental flows and reductions in water stress at the basin level. Domestic and industrial water demands are fully met. The ratio of water withdrawal to total renewable water in 2025 drops 28-36 percent compared with BAU in the four basins and by 28 percent in Egypt. The drop in withdrawals saves a large amount of water for environmental uses, equivalent to 38 percent of BAU withdrawals in the Haihe, 36 percent in the Yellow, 31 percent in the Indus, 28 percent in Egypt, and 27 percent in the Ganges. Compared with the BAU, irrigated crop yields decline only slightly because higher basin efficiency largely compensates for the reduced withdrawals for irrigation. Rainfed yields increase because of the improvement in rainfall harvesting and higher rainfed yield and area growth rate. Therefore, the total cereal production under SUS is 1-4 percent less than under BAU in 2025 for the four basins and Egypt.

Table 5.14—World food prices under business-as-usual, water crisis, and sustainable water use scenarios, 1995 and 2025

Commodity	1995 baseline estimates	World food prices (US$/mt)					
		2025 projections					
		Mean			Maximum		
		BAU	CRI	SUS	BAU	CRI	SUS
Rice	285	221	397	215	240	446	235
Wheat	133	119	241	111	140	282	124
Maize	103	104	224	98	114	246	106
Other coarse grains	97	82	180	74	92	204	80
Soybeans	247	257	422	253	282	472	283
Potatoes	209	180	317	166	202	355	178
Sweet potatoes	134	90	233	77	168	332	100
Other roots and tubers	106	81	167	69	95	208	83

Source: IMPACT-WATER assessments and projections, 2002.
Notes: BAU indicates business-as-usual scenario; CRI, water crisis scenario; SUS, sustainable water use water scenario; and US$/mt, U.S. dollars per metric ton.

Figure 5.3—Relative irrigated cereal production in developing countries under business-as-usual, water crisis, and sustainable water use scenarios, 1995–2025

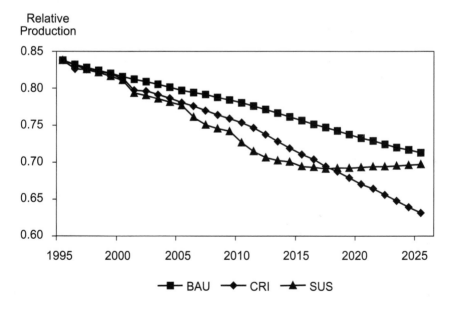

Source: IMPACT-WATER assessments and projections, 2002.
Notes: BAU indicates business-as-usual scenario; CRI, water crisis scenario; and SUS, sustainable water scenario.

Figure 5.4—Relative rainfed cereal production in developing countries under business-as-usual, water crisis, and sustainable water use scenarios, 1995–2025

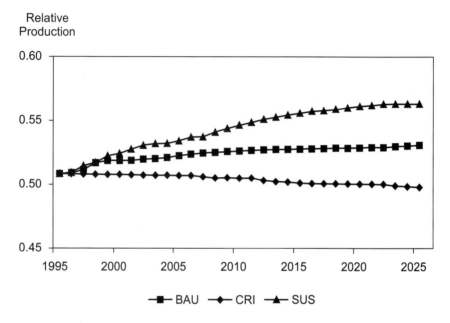

Source: IMPACT-WATER assessments and projections, 2002.
Notes: BAU indicates business-as-usual scenario; CRI, water crisis scenario; and SUS, sustainable water scenario.

a significant increase in price variation from 1995 to 2025 and an even more negative impact on consumers during unfavorable weather years than under BAU.[3]

Food Demand

High prices unsurprisingly dampen food demand. Under CRI—with prices much higher than under BAU—cereal demand declines by 55 million metric tons (7 percent) in the developed world, 192 million metric tons (11 percent) in the developing world, and 246 million metric tons (9 percent) globally (Table 5.15). For the worst case in the 30 hydrologic samples (the minimum in Table 5.15), cereal demand declines by 54 million metric tons (7 percent) in developed countries, 184 million metric tons (10 percent) in developing countries, and 237 million metric tons (9 percent) worldwide compared with the mean under BAU.

Table 5.16 shows per capita cereal consumption under the three scenarios. CRI's 2025 per capita cereal consumption is 7 percent lower than under BAU in the developed world, 11 percent lower in the developing world, and 9 percent lower globally. The reduction in consumption under CRI is so severe that 2025 per

Table 5.15—Cereal demand under business-as-usual, water crisis, and sustainable water use scenarios, 1995 and 2025

Region/Country	1995 baseline estimates	2025 projections					
		Mean (million mt)			Minimum (million mt)		
		BAU	CRI	SUS	BAU	CRI	SUS
Asia	794	1,228	1,116	1,236	1,209	1,101	1,219
China	375	581	535	584	576	529	577
India	171	275	243	278	268	238	273
Southeast Asia	113	176	162	177	174	160	175
South Asia excluding India	55	102	86	103	98	84	101
Latin America (LA)	137	239	207	241	234	203	237
Sub-Saharan Africa (SSA)	78	172	138	176	164	131	171
West Asia/North Africa (WANA)	120	202	184	204	198	180	201
Developed countries	686	803	748	806	790	736	796
Developing countries	1,092	1,804	1,612	1,819	1,768	1,584	1,791
World	**1,779**	**2,606**	**2,360**	**2,625**	**2,557**	**2,320**	**2,587**

Source: IMPACT-WATER assessments and projections, 2002.
Notes: BAU indicates business-as-usual scenario; CRI, water crisis scenario; SUS, sustainable water use scenario; and million mt, million metric tons.

capita cereal consumption in the developing world is actually 2 percent lower than 1995 levels; hence, under CRI, poor water policies cause serious food security problems, especially in developing countries.

Compared with BAU, under CRI, soybean demand decreases by 26 million metric tons (25 percent) in developed countries, by 34 million metric tons (27 percent) in developing countries, and by 60 million metric tons (26 percent) globally; potato demand reduces by 13 million metric tons (7 percent) in the developing world, by 8 million metric tons (4 percent) in the developed world, and by 21 million metric tons (5 percent) worldwide; root and tuber demand reduces by 18 million metric tons (2 percent) in developing countries, 13 million metric tons (4 percent) in developed countries, and 31 million metric tons (4 percent) globally.

Food Trade
Compared with BAU, net trade declines under both CRI and SUS scenarios (Table 5.17). Exports from the developed world, or imports to the developing world, decline under CRI by 58 million metric tons (23 percent), and under SUS by 14 million metric tons (6 percent); however, these declines have different implications. Declines under CRI imply that high prices dampen crop demand leading to trade reductions, while declines under SUS reflect different rates of food production adjustment between the food importing and exporting countries. As shown in Table 5.13, cereal production under the SUS is 11 million metric tons less in developed countries, and 29 million metric tons more in developing countries than under the BAU scenario.

Table 5.16—Per capita cereal consumption under business-as-usual, water crisis, and sustainable water use scenarios, 1995 and 2025

Region/Country	1995 baseline estimates	Per capita cereal consumptions (kg/year) 2025 projections BAU	CRI	SUS
Asia	264.3	294.7	267.7	296.5
China	305.9	392.8	361.7	394.3
India	184.7	203.2	179.9	205.3
Southeast Asia	237.2	256.6	236.7	257.9
South Asia excluding India	180.0	178.6	151.4	181.1
Latin America (LA)	46.8	58.4	50.8	59.0
Sub-Saharan Africa (SSA)	147.4	155.0	124.1	158.5
West Asia/North Africa (WANA)	358.7	358.8	326.6	362.2
Developed countries	548.5	623.2	580.5	625.5
Developing countries	247.8	272.7	243.7	275.0
World	**314.3**	**329.8**	**298.6**	**332.1**

Source: IMPACT-WATER assessments and projections, 2002.
Notes: BAU indicates business-as-usual scenario; CRI, water crisis scenario; SUS, sustainable water use scenario; and kg/year, kilograms per year.

Table 5.17—Net trade under business-as-usual, water crisis, and sustainable water use scenarios, 1995 and 2025

Region/Country	1995 baseline estimates	Net trade (million mt) 2025 projections BAU	CRI	SUS
Asia	-67.7	-139.7	-141.8	-156.9
China	-17.4	-42.0	-58.5	-53.2
India	3.6	-19.1	-15.7	-20.4
Southeast Asia	-7.0	-6.2	-1.1	-4.7
South Asia excluding India	-3.8	-21.0	-15.7	-27.1
Latin America (LA)	-20.4	-16.8	4.7	-16.1
Sub-Saharan Africa (SSA)	-9.8	-34.9	-3.3	-35.7
West Asia/North Africa (WANA)	-37.8	-83.0	-72.3	-52.6
Developed countries	107.5	245.2	187.7	231.6
Developing countries	-107.5	-245.2	-187.7	-231.6
World	**0.0**	**0.0**	**0.0**	**0.0**

Source: IMPACT-WATER assessments and projections, 2002.
Notes: Negative values indicate net imports; positive values, net exports. BAU indicates business-as-usual scenario; CRI, water crisis scenario; SUS, sustainable water use scenario; and million mt, million metric tons.

Figure 5.5—World prices for rice, wheat, maize, and soybeans under business-as-usual, water crisis, and sustainable water scenarios, 1995–2025

(a) Rice

Price US$/mt

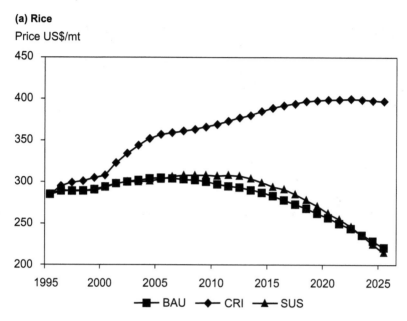

(b) Wheat

Price US$/mt

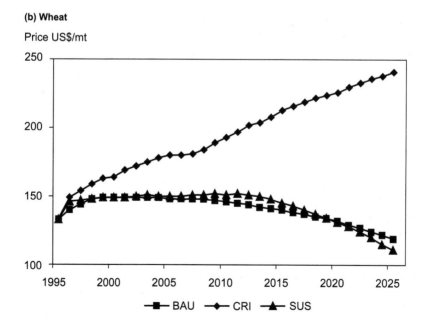

Figure 5.5—Continued

(c) Maize

Price US$/mt

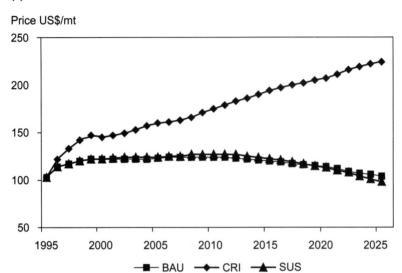

(d) Soybeans

Price US$/mt

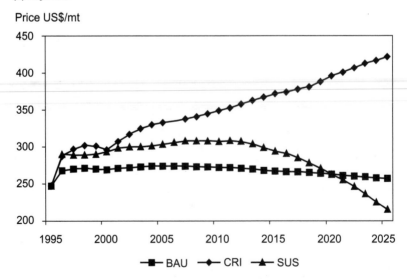

Source: IMPACT-WATER assessments and projections, 2002.
Note: BAU indicates business-as-usual scenario; CRI, water crisis scenario;
SUS, sustainable water scenario; and US$/mt, U.S. dollars per metric ton.

Figure 5.6—Average, maximum, and minimum world rice prices for 30 hydrologic scenarios under business-as-usual and water crisis scenarios, 1995–2025

(a) Business-as-usual

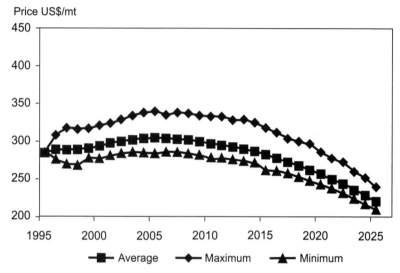

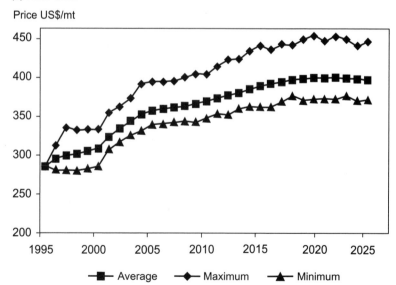

Source: IMPACT-WATER assessments and projections, 2002.
Notes: US$/mt indicates U.S. dollars per metric ton.

Figure 5.7—Average, maximum, and minimum world wheat prices for 30 hydrologic scenarios under business-as-usual and water crisis scenarios, 1995–2025

(a) Business-as-usual

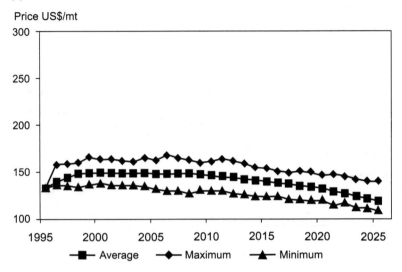

(b) Water crisis

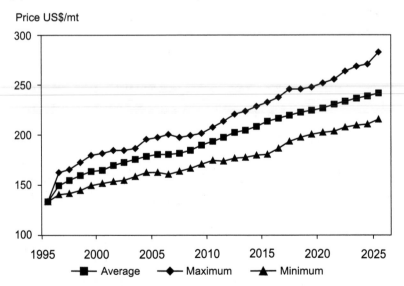

Source: IMPACT-WATER assessments and projections, 2002.
Notes: US$/mt indicates U.S. dollars per metric ton.

Figure 5.8—Average, maximum, and minimum world soybean prices for 30 hydrologic scenarios under business-as-usual and water crisis scenarios, 1995–2025

(a) Business-as-usual

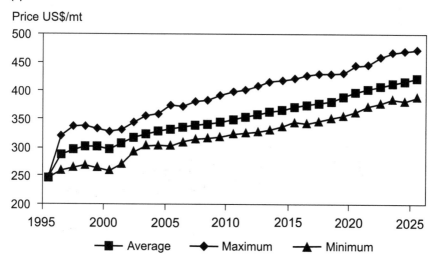

(b) Water crisis

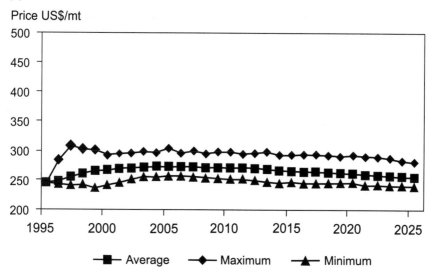

Source: IMPACT-WATER assessments and projections, 2002.
Notes: US$/mt indicates U.S. dollars per metric ton.

SUMMARY

The alternative scenarios show that plausible changes in water policies and invest-ments would make dramatic differences in outcomes on water and food supply and demand to 2025. Growing water resource scarcity combined with continuing dete-rioration in water policies and investments under CRI would significantly reduce environmental water flows, endangering wetlands and the minimum stream flows required to maintain biodiversity. Food prices for major crops under CRI are more than double those under SUS and BAU, yet 2025 world cereal production under CRI is 270 million metric tons less than under SUS—equivalent to an annual loss of production close to India's total 2025 cereal crop or the combined total of WANA and Sub-Saharan Africa. These enormous increases in cereal and other food prices would significantly constrain the real incomes of poor consumers leading to substantial increases in malnutrition considering the poorest people in low-income developing countries spend more than half their income on food. Sharp price increases can also fuel inflation, severely pressure foreign exchange reserves, and have adverse effects on macroeconomic stability and investment in developing countries. Such worsening food security would be accompanied by a dramatic declines in access to water for drinking and other household uses, escalating malnutrition and disease.

Conversely, with improved water policies and investments, and improved rain-fed cereal crop management and technology, food production growth could be maintained concurrently with universal access to piped water and dramatic increas-es in environmental water flows. The large reduction in water withdrawals for human uses reduces water stress at the river basin scale, cutting the reuse of water and improving water quality. Compared with CRI, the increase in environmental flows under SUS is about 1,490 cubic kilometers—equivalent to five times the annual flow of the Mississippi River or four times that of the Ganges River.

NOTES

1. As described in the beginning of Chapter 4, each of these scenarios is run through the 30 hydrologic conditions, from which the mean and variation of water and food items are derived for the following discussion.

2. See Table 3.7 for a percentage comparison of households with access to piped water under BAU, CRI, and SUS.

3. Graphs of mean, maximum, minimum prices are not shown for SUS because they are virtually identical to the BAU.

Chapter 6

Water Prices, Water Demand, Food Production, and Environmental Flows

The introductory chapter to this book described the major problems in water pricing policy in much of the world: prevailing low water prices and high subsidies for capital investment and O&M costs threaten the financial viability of irrigation and urban water supplies, creating a particularly serious problem given the huge financial resources that these sectors will require in the future. Low water prices and poor cost recovery compromise the efficient maintenance of existing water infrastructure as well as the additional investments necessary to develop future water projects. Perhaps even more fundamentally, low water prices encourage misallocation and wasteful water use in all sectors. A key motive for reforming water pricing policies is the growing competition between domestic, industrial, irrigation and environmental uses, especially in arid or semi-arid regions. If higher water prices could substantially reduce the withdrawal of water in other sectors, the savings would be available for environmental uses.

Despite the potential benefits of higher water prices, policymakers have found it difficult to raise them, especially in the agricultural sector, because of concerns over impacts on food production and farmer and poor household incomes, and about the associated political risk of increasing water charges (Molle 2001 and 2002; de Fraiture and Perry 2002). Adding to the difficulty of pricing reform, both long-standing practice and cultural and religious beliefs have treated water as a free resource, and entrenched interests benefit from the existing system of subsidies and administered allocations of water. Equity concerns are intensified by evidence that the responsiveness of agricultural water demand to changes in water prices is generally very low, and that price increases sufficient to reduce demand significantly could greatly depress farm incomes (Berbel and Gomez-Limon 2000; Rosegrant et al. 2000; Perry 1996).

The purpose of this chapter is to explore the potential of higher water prices in achieving water conservation and balancing direct human consumptive water uses with environmental water uses globally. Detailed discussion of the pros and cons, feasibility, and appropriate institutional design of water pricing, water markets, and water trading is beyond the scope of this book; these issues have been treated extensively in the literature (Molle 2002; Perry 2001; Johansson 2000; Dinar and Subramanian 1997; Easter, Rosegrant, and Dinar 1998; Rosegrant and Binswanger 1994). It is important, however, to briefly discuss policy options in response to the problems of implementing water pricing policy reform.

Most obviously, equity issues must be addressed to ensure water provision to low-income households harmed by high water prices; but current pricing systems are themselves highly inequitable with the bulk of subsidies going to the relatively well-off (as summarized in Chapter 1). Water pricing systems could be designed and implemented to provide increased incentives for water conservation without reducing incomes, and possibly even enhancing the incomes of the poor. In the domestic and industrial water sectors, water price increases could be made directly, replacing existing generalized subsidies with subsidies targeted to the poor.

Designing a water pricing system for agriculture to protect farm incomes is more challenging. Direct water price increases are likely to be punitive to farmers because water is such a significant input to production. Nevertheless, pricing schemes could be designed that, rather than charging farmers for using water, pay them for reducing water use (Pezzey 1992; Rosegrant and Cline 2002). Higher water prices establishing incentives for more efficient use could also be achieved through the development of water markets and water trading (Easter, Rosegrant, and Dinar 1998). See Chapter 9 for a discussion of water pricing and incentive mechanisms that we consider both feasible and able to protect or enhance the incomes of the poor.

INCREASED WATER PRICING SCENARIOS

A key motive for reforming water pricing policies is the growing competition between irrigation and environmental uses, especially in arid or semi-arid regions. We examine several scenarios where water prices are higher than those under BAU. Using available data and various policy assumptions, our analysis focuses on the impacts on food security and environmental water reservation given the irrigation sector will continue to be the major water user and the conflict between irrigation demand and environmental requirements is growing. The scenarios are analyzed based on varying levels of water use efficiency, measured as basin efficiency (*BE*), and the proportion of conserved water allocated to the environment. The four scenarios presented here use the climate regime of 1961–90 as compared with the 30 climate scenario simulations used in the BAU, CRI, and SUS scenarios of the previous chapters. This format simulates a normal weather pattern over the projection period. Specific projection results are annual average values for the period 2021–25.[1]

Higher Water Pricing Scenario Specification

The four higher price scenarios are defined based on the extent to which water use efficiency improvements are induced by higher prices and the redistribution of conserved water from the non-irrigation sectors to irrigation and environmental uses. Depending on policy assumptions, water savings from domestic and industrial sectors resulting from the higher water prices can be reserved for environmental uses or be fully used for irrigation. If some fraction of the amount released from non-irrigation sectors is allocated to irrigation, actual water consumption for irrigation can increase in water-scarce basins constrained by water availability rather than price, despite the higher irrigation water prices.

The four higher water price scenarios are:

1) The higher price scenario (HP) under which higher water prices are implemented, water use efficiency remains the same as under the BAU scenario, and a large portion of the conserved water is allocated to environmental uses;

2) The higher price, lower environmental water share scenario (HP-LENV), under which higher water prices are implemented, water use efficiency remains the same as under the BAU scenario, but irrigation has first priority on conserved water from domestic and industrial sectors.

3) The higher price, higher basin efficiency scenario (HP-HE) under which higher water prices are implemented, water use efficiency is higher than under the BAU scenario, and a large portion of the conserved water is allocated to environmental uses; and

4) The higher price, higher basin efficiency, lower environmental water share scenario (HP-HE-LENV) under which higher water prices are implemented, water use efficiency is higher than under the BAU scenario, but irrigation has first priority on conserved water from domestic and industrial sectors.

Note that given the large share of water allocated to the environment under the HP and HP-HE scenarios, we don't present scenarios with 100 percent of conserved water allocated to the environment. The specific values for *BE* and the share of water reserved for environmental uses for each scenario for various regions are shown in Table 6.1.

Table 6.1—Selected assumptions for the four higher water price scenarios

Region/Country	HP BE (ratio)	HP Priority environ-mental share (%)	HP-LENV BE (ratio)	HP-LENV Priority environ-mental share (%)	HP-HE BE (ratio)	HP-HE Priority environ-mental share (%)	HP-HE-LENV BE (ratio)	HP-HE-LENV Priority environ-mental share (%)
United States	0.77	89	0.77	0	0.82	89	0.82	0
Central Asia	0.61	87	0.61	0	0.70	87	0.70	0
India	0.63	62	0.63	0	0.73	62	0.73	0
China	0.60	79	0.60	0	0.68	79	0.68	0
South Asia excluding India	0.49	50	0.49	0	0.55	51	0.55	0
Southeast Asia	0.50	60	0.50	0	0.56	60	0.56	0
Asia	0.58	70	0.58	0	0.66	70	0.66	0
Sub-Saharan Africa (SSA)	0.46	55	0.46	0	0.52	55	0.52	0
Latin America (LA)	0.47	90	0.47	0	0.53	90	0.53	0
West Asia/North Africa (WANA)	0.73	53	0.73	0	0.86	53	0.86	0
Developed countries	0.69	88	0.69	0	0.72	88	0.72	0
Developing countries	0.58	72	0.58	0	0.67	72	0.67	0
World	**0.61**	**77**	**0.61**	**0**	**0.68**	**77**	**0.68**	**0**

Source: Authors' estimates.
Notes: HP indicates the higher price scenario; HP-LENV, the higher price, lower environmental water share scenario; HP-HE, the higher price, higher basin efficiency scenario; and HP-HE-LENV, the higher price, higher basin efficiency, lower environmental water share scenario. BE is basin efficiency and environmental share, the share of total water savings from the non-irrigation sector that goes to the environment as a result of higher water prices.

Water Prices

Compared with BAU, under all four higher water price scenarios, water prices for agriculture, industry, and connected households are assumed to increase gradually during 2000–25. By 2025, water prices are 1.75–2.25 times higher for industrial water use, 1.5–2.0 times higher for domestic water use, and 2–3 times higher for agricultural water use than under BAU.

Price Elasticity of Water Demand

The price elasticity of water demand is very important to water demand management and public policies related to water use.[2] These values allow policymakers to determine the level at which consumers will respond to changes in water price and hence to adopt the most effective policies. We assessed water price elasticities and compiled results from estimates in relevant empirical studies for domestic, industrial, and agricultural water demand. Many studies have been conducted, but the majority of estimates are for the domestic sector in developed countries, particularly the United States.

Many factors influence values for water price elasticity including sector, season, region (developed versus developing, rural versus urban, and so on), and, for domestic demand, indoor versus outdoor use. The available evidence shows that the elasticity of water demand in terms of water prices is relatively low, particularly in the agricultural sector. Gracia, Garcia Valinas, and Martinez-Espineira (2001) present a survey of the main issues involved in the estimation of residential water demand, and Dalhuisen et al. (2002) and Espey, Espey, and Shaw (1997) provide meta-analyses of price elasticities of residential water demand. The elasticities used in our model are summarized in Table 6.2. Agricultural elasticities include both irrigated crop agriculture and livestock. Where a range of values is shown for a country or region, the different values refer to different river basins or subregions.

Figures 6.1 and 6.2 illustrate the aggregate impact of water prices on industrial and domestic water demand respectively, under the specified water demand elasticities, for both the developing and developed world in 2025.

The industrial, household, and livestock water demand elasticities in terms of water prices shown here are long-term elasticities reflecting full adjustment in water demand to changes in water prices. The irrigation water demand elasticities are short-term elasticities that reflect the change in water withdrawal and total water consumption in response to changes in water prices, including substitution of variable inputs such as labor and fertilizer for water. The longer term response of

Table 6.2—Water price elasticities

Region/Country	Domestic	Industrial	Agriculture
United States	-0.30 to -0.50	-0.45 to -0.72	-0.08 to -0.14
China	-0.35 to -0.55	-0.55 to -0.80	-0.09 to -0.16
India	-0.30 to -0.55	-0.50 to -0.80	-0.08 to -0.16
European Union 15	-0.16	-0.45	-0.04
Japan	-0.22	-0.45	-0.06
Australia	-0.45	-0.67	-0.11
Other developed countries	-0.31	-0.53	-0.08
Eastern Europe	-0.24	-0.44	-0.06
Central Asia	-0.45	-0.77	-0.11
Rest of former Soviet Union	-0.35	-0.67	-0.09
Latin America (LA)	-0.40 to -0.50	-0.70 to -0.80	-0.07 to -0.12
Sub-Saharan Africa (SSA)	-0.45 to -0.55	-0.60 to -0.8	-0.10 to -0.15
West Asia/North Africa (WANA)	-0.44 to -0.57	-0.75 to -0.85	-0.10 to -0.20
South Asia	-0.35 to -0.40	-0.65 to -0.75	-0.08 to -0.11
Southeast Asia	-0.35 to -0.45	-0.65 to -0.80	-0.09 to -0.12

Source: Author estimates based on Dalhuisen et al. (2002); Espey, Espey, and Shaw (1997); Gracia, Garcia Valinas, and Martinez-Espineira (2001).
Notes: Ranges indicate different river basins or subregions.

Figure 6.1—Industrial water demand as a function of water prices, 2025

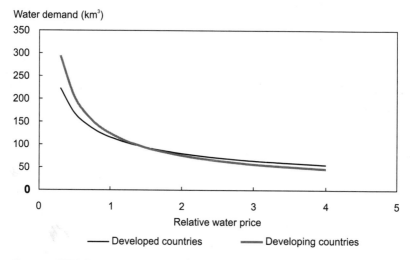

Water demand (km³)

Source: IMPACT-WATER projections, 2002.
Notes: A relative water price of 1.0 corresponds to the business-as-usual
scenario level. Km³ indicates cubic kilometers.

Figure 6.2—Domestic water demand as a function of water prices, 2025

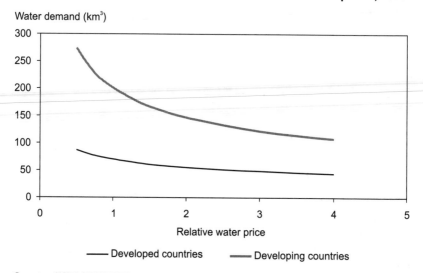

Water demand (km³)

Source: IMPACT-WATER projections, 2002.
Notes: Domestic water represents connected households only; a relative water
price of 1.0 corresponds to the business-as-usual scenario level. Km³ indicates
cubic kilometers.

beneficial irrigation water demand to water prices is determined also by the response of water use efficiency to water prices.

Farmers respond to higher water prices not only by a direct reduction in water withdrawals and consumption but also by improving water use efficiency so that a greater portion of water is used beneficially for crop production (Varela-Ortega et al. 1998; Zilberman, Chakravorty, and Shah 1997; Shah, Zilberman, and Chakravorty 1995; Caswell and Zilberman 1985, 1986). Water use efficiency can be increased by investment in water-conserving irrigation technology, such as drip and sprinkler irrigation, or by improving the on-farm management of the water to reduce losses to nonbeneficial consumption. In the context of the IMPACT-WATER model, the longer term efficiency response to water prices is represented by the elasticity of basin efficiency in terms of water prices. The literature cited immediately above shows that higher water prices induce improvements in irrigation technology and reductions in water use. Direct estimates of basin efficiency elasticities are not, however, available from the literature, so we examine two efficiency responses through the scenario variants HP and HP-HE. HP is a "worst-case" scenario, with an assumed basin efficiency response to water prices of 0.0. For the HP-HE scenario, the basin efficiency elasticities are set at what we regard as medium values. Under HP-HE the values of the elasticity of basin efficiency with respect to water prices average 0.04 for developed countries and 0.08 for developing countries, with the regional values ranging from 0.06 in Southeast Asia to 0.09 in West Asia and North Africa (WANA) (Table 6.3).

Table 6.3—Elasticity of basin efficiency in terms of irrigation water pricing, various scenarios

Region/Country	HP, HP-LENV, and BAU	HP-HE and HP-HE-LENV
Asia	0.0	0.069
China	0.0	0.067
India	0.0	0.079
Southeast Asia	0.0	0.060
South Asia excluding India	0.0	0.061
Latin America (LA)	0.0	0.064
Sub-Saharan Africa (SSA)	0.0	0.065
West Asia/North Africa (WANA)	0.0	0.089
Developed countries	0.0	0.043
Developing countries	0.0	0.078
World	**0.0**	**0.065**

Source: Authors' estimates.
Notes: BAU indicates the business-as-usual scenario; HP, the higher price scenario; HP-LENV, the higher price, lower environmental water share scenario; HP-HE, the higher price, higher basin efficiency scenario; and HP-HE-LENV, the higher price, higher basin efficiency, lower environmental water share scenario.

Non-Irrigation Water Demand

Non-irrigation consumptive water uses include industrial, domestic, and livestock water demand. Under the higher price scenario, water demand in 2021–25 decreases by large amounts compared with BAU levels for all regions (Table 6.4). Total non-irrigation consumptive water use declines from 599 to 449 cubic kilometers worldwide, from 395 to 285 cubic kilometers in developing countries, and from 204 to 164 cubic kilometers in developed countries. These numbers correspond, approximately, to water withdrawal decreases for non-irrigation sectors of 345 cubic kilometers globally, 110 cubic kilometers in developed countries, and 235 cubic kilometers in developing countries compared with BAU.

The changes in total domestic water consumption result from the changes in per capita water demand for connected and unconnected households. More detailed data on per capita domestic demand for connected and unconnected households are presented in Table 6.5.

In 1995, per capita water demand in urban and rural areas is 1.5 to 2.0 times higher for connected than for unconnected households in developing countries; in developed countries, it is estimated at 1.7 times higher for connected households in urban areas and 2.1 times higher for connected households in rural areas (see also

Table 6.4—Consumptive water use for non-irrigation sectors under business-as-usual and higher price scenarios, 2021–25

Region/Country	Consumptive water use (km³)							
	Domestic		Industrial		Livestock		Total Non-Irrigation	
	BAU	HP	BAU	HP	BAU	HP	BAU	HP
Asia	160.2	126.2	92.6	55.1	26.2	23.2	279.0	204.5
China	60.9	46.2	32.1	18.5	7.6	6.7	100.6	71.3
India	41.4	34.0	16.0	9.8	8.3	7.4	65.7	51.2
Southeast Asia	31.2	24.0	21.3	11.6	4.2	3.7	56.7	39.3
South Asia excluding India	16.7	13.8	4.7	2.6	3.9	3.5	25.4	20.0
Latin America (LA)	31.0	23.4	30.2	16.1	12.7	11.2	73.8	50.6
Sub-Saharan Africa (SSA)	24.5	19.5	2.5	1.3	4.3	3.7	31.3	24.5
West Asia/North Africa (WANA)	13.2	9.3	8.8	4.5	3.3	2.8	25.3	16.6
Developed countries	69.9	61.3	115.7	85.6	18.5	17.5	204.0	164.4
Developing countries	225.5	175.2	123.8	69.1	46.2	40.6	395.4	284.9
World	**295.3**	**236.5**	**239.5**	**154.6**	**64.6**	**58.1**	**599.4**	**449.2**

Source: IMPACT-WATER projections, 2002.
Notes: Data are annual averages. BAU indicates business-as-usual scenario; HP, higher price scenario; and km³, cubic kilometers.

Table 6.5—Per capita domestic water demand under business-as-usual and higher price scenario, 1995 and 2021–25

Region/Country	Per capita domestic water demand (m³/capita/year)					
	1995 baseline estimates		2021–25 projections			
			BAU		HP	
	Connected	Unconnected	Connected	Unconnected	Connected	Unconnected
Asia	35.1	18.7	42.2	20.7	31.1	22.7
China	36.1	18.8	46.9	21.6	32.7	25.8
India	35.0	18.6	36.7	19.1	27.5	20.7
Southeast Asia	35.6	20.2	48.7	26.2	35.9	26.7
South Asia excluding India	30.7	17.8	32.4	20.3	26.4	20.6
Latin America (LA)	39.4	20.9	49.1	24.1	32.7	26.3
Sub-Saharan Africa (SSA)	24.1	13.5	25.0	14.4	18.6	14.7
West Asia/North Africa (WANA)	23.2	12.6	24.3	13.4	16.5	14.7
Developed countries	48.7	23.8	54.5	34.3	47.7	34.4
Developing countries	33.7	18.2	38.3	19.4	28.1	21.1
World	**39.3**	**18.3**	**41.6**	**19.6**	**32.0**	**21.2**

Source: IMPACT-WATER assessments and projections, 2002.
Notes: Data are annual averages. BAU indicates business-as-usual scenario; HP, higher price scenario; and m³/capita/year, cubic meters per capita per year.

Table 5.6). Given a relative reduction in water demand in the connected sectors from higher water prices, making more water available for the unconnected sector, we assume that per capita water demand for unconnected households is at least 60 percent of the connected household demand by 2010 and is a minimum of 75 percent of the connected household demand by 2021–25.

Under the higher price scenarios, domestic demand for connected households decreases sharply causing water savings, which in turn cause unconnected demand to increase slightly. For example in 2021–25 in Latin America (LA), per capita water demand for connected households is one-third less, and for Sub-Saharan Africa (SSA), it is one-quarter less. In developing countries, per capita water demand in connected households declines from 38.3 cubic meters under BAU to 28.1 cubic meters, but unconnected households increase per capita consumption from 19.4 to 21.1 cubic meters (Table 6.5).

Higher Water Pricing Scenarios: Environmental Flows and Food Production

All the higher water price scenarios show lower levels of water withdrawal and water consumption in 2021–25 than under BAU (Tables 6.6 and 6.7). Among the higher water pricing scenarios, HP and HP-HE have the lowest global water withdrawal and consumption levels with reductions of 839 cubic kilometers in water withdrawal and 287 cubic kilometers in water consumption compared with BAU. These water savings from water price increases—18 percent of BAU withdrawals in 2021–25 and 14 percent reduction in consumptive use—represent a major increase in water allocated to environmental flows.

Even for the scenarios where non-irrigation water conservation is not committed on a priority basis to environmental uses—HP-LENV and HP-HE-LENV—water withdrawal is 730 cubic kilometers less and water consumption 238 cubic kilometers less than under BAU. The reduction in water withdrawals remains high under these scenarios because only basins with severe, absolute annual or seasonal water shortages tap water saved from non-irrigation sources because water demand for irrigation is also reduced by higher water prices. The reductions in water withdrawal (and resultant increases in environmental flows) are even greater in some regions, with reductions in withdrawals of more than 20 percent in China, Southeast Asia, LA, and WANA.

Although the total water consumption in 2021–25 under HP-HE is the same as under HP (Table 6.7), the beneficial water consumption for irrigation is substantially higher, generating significant crop production gains. Total irrigation consumption is 1,393 cubic kilometers under both HP and HP-HE, which is lower than the 1,493 cubic kilometers under BAU. Within the IMPACT-WATER model,

Table 6.6—Water withdrawal under business-as-usual and four higher price scenarios, 2021–25

Region/Country	Water withdrawal (km³)				
	BAU	HP	HP-LENV	HP-HE	HP-HE-LENV
Asia	2,420	1,995	2,041	1,994	2,040
China	844	676	703	676	703
India	822	692	700	692	699
Southeast Asia	278	222	228	222	228
South Asia excluding India	416	360	364	360	365
Latin America (LA)	402	302	332	302	332
Sub-Saharan Africa (SSA)	207	172	176	172	176
West Asia/North Africa (WANA)	294	230	234	230	234
Developed countries	1,272	1,080	1,103	1,080	1,103
Developing countries	3,481	2,834	2,920	2,833	2,920
World	**4,752**	**3,913**	**4,023**	**3,913**	**4,022**

Source: IMPACT-WATER projections, 2002.
Notes: Data are annual averages. BAU indicates the business-as-usual scenario; HP, the higher price scenario; HP-LENV, the higher price, lower environmental water share scenario; HP-HE, the higher price, higher basin efficiency scenario; HP-HE-LENV, the higher price, higher basin efficiency, lower environmental water share scenario; and km³, cubic kilometers.

Table 6.7—Water consumption under business-as-usual and four higher price scenarios, 2021–25

Region/Country	Water consumption (km³)				
	BAU	HP	HP-LENV	HP-HE	HP-HE-LENV
Asia	1,090	937	958	936	958
China	329	277	289	277	289
India	402	349	353	349	353
Southeast Asia	144	121	125	120	124
South Asia excluding India	192	171	172	170	172
Latin America (LA)	167	135	149	135	149
Sub-Saharan Africa (SSA)	91	79	81	79	81
West Asia/North Africa (WANA)	161	132	134	132	134
Developed countries	479	429	438	429	438
Developing countries	1,595	1,359	1,399	1,359	1,399
World	**2,075**	**1,788**	**1,837**	**1,788**	**1,837**

Source: IMPACT-WATER projections, 2002.
Notes: Data are annual averages. BAU indicates the business-as-usual scenario; HP, the higher price scenario; HP-LENV, the higher price, lower environmental water share scenario; HP-HE, the higher price, higher basin efficiency scenario; HP-HE-LENV, the higher price, higher basin efficiency, lower environmental water share scenario; and km³, cubic kilometers.

the share of total irrigation water consumption that is beneficial to crop growth equals the total irrigation water consumption multiplied by the *BE*. Because global basin efficiency under HP-HE is higher than that under HP (0.68 versus 0.61, see Table 6.1), beneficial irrigation water consumption under HP-HE is substantially higher—947 compared with 850 cubic kilometers under HP, and higher even than the 912 cubic kilometers under BAU.

At a global level, the criticality ratio of water withdrawal to total renewable water under HP is 8 percent compared with 10 percent under BAU (Table 6.8). The most significant changes in the ratios of water withdrawal to total renewable water occur under HP and HP-HE compared with BAU. In China and India, for example, the ratio is 0.06 lower under HP and HP-HE than under BAU, and in WANA 0.19 and 0.17 lower under HP and HP-HE, respectively, than under BAU. As shown in Box 6.1, the criticality ratio drops dramatically in the severely water-scarce basins, indicative of the drop in water withdrawals for human uses, causing increased environmental flows and reduced reuse of water, ultimately improving the quality of water in the river basin.

The irrigation water supply reliability index (IWSR) varies across scenarios depending on *BE* improvement and the share of water conservation from non-irrigation sectors. IWSR values under HP-HE and HP-HE-LENV are close to those under BAU. Under these two scenarios, we assume agricultural *BE* increases in response to the increase in water prices, with the relative magnitude of the response given by the *BE* elasticities in Table 6.3. Under HP-HE-LENV, under which no

Table 6.8—Ratio of water withdrawal to total renewable water under business-as-usual and four higher price scenarios, 2021–25

Region/Country	Ratio of water withdrawal to total renewable water				
	BAU	HP	HP-LENV	HP-HE	HP-HE-LENV
Asia	0.20	0.16	0.17	0.16	0.17
China	0.33	0.27	0.28	0.27	0.28
India	0.36	0.30	0.31	0.30	0.31
Southeast Asia	0.05	0.04	0.04	0.04	0.04
South Asia excluding India	0.21	0.18	0.17	0.18	0.17
Latin America (LA)	0.03	0.02	0.02	0.02	0.02
Sub-Saharan Africa (SSA)	0.04	0.03	0.03	0.03	0.03
West Asia/North Africa (WANA)	0.86	0.67	0.69	0.67	0.69
Developed countries	0.10	0.09	0.09	0.09	0.09
Developing countries	0.10	0.08	0.09	0.08	0.09
World	**0.10**	**0.08**	**0.09**	**0.08**	**0.09**

Source: IMPACT-WATER projections, 2002.
Notes: Data are annual averages. BAU indicates the business-as-usual scenario; HP, the higher price scenario; HP-LENV, the higher price, lower environmental water share scenario; HP-HE, the higher price, higher basin efficiency scenario; and HP-HE-LENV, the higher price, higher basin efficiency, lower environmental water share scenario.

water is committed to the environment from non-irrigation water conservation, *BE* values are the same as those under HP-HE, but IWSR values are higher than under BAU and HP-HE in most regions (Table 6.9).

Under HP and HP-LENV, where *BE* levels are the same as under BAU, IWSR values are lower than BAU levels. When irrigation has first priority over the water conserved from the non-irrigation sector—as under HP-LENV—IWSR values improve but are still lower than those under BAU (0.69 compared with 0.75 in the developing world). Hence on an aggregate basis for developing countries, water savings from the non-irrigation sectors used for irrigation in supply-constrained river basins only partly compensate reduced irrigation water demand resulting from higher agricultural water prices.

Under HP-HE, the change in irrigated and total cereal production is slight because the increase in *BE* almost fully compensates the reduction in total water consumption, maintaining beneficial water consumption close to BAU levels (Table 6.10). Some regions have slight improvements in production, such as LA and Southeast Asia. Other regions still show small declines in cereal production, including WANA, China, and India. But even in very water-scarce basins such as the Yellow and the Indus, cereal production is restored to nearly BAU production levels under HP-HE (see Box 6.1). HP-HE-LENV shows an increase in irrigated cereal production of about 2 percent compared with BAU because of the efficiency improvements and the access of supply-constrained basins to water conserved from non-irrigation sectors. Under HP and HP-LENV, where *BE* is the same as under

Table 6.9—Irrigation water supply reliability under business-as-usual and four higher price scenarios, 2021–25

Region/Country	Irrigation water supply reliability				
	BAU	HP	HP-LENV	HP-HE	HP-HE-LENV
Asia	0.76	0.68	0.70	0.76	0.78
China	0.77	0.69	0.72	0.77	0.81
India	0.73	0.64	0.65	0.73	0.74
Southeast Asia	0.84	0.77	0.81	0.85	0.89
South Asia excluding India	0.75	0.68	0.68	0.75	0.76
Latin America (LA)	0.74	0.67	0.77	0.75	0.86
Sub-Saharan Africa (SSA)	0.71	0.64	0.66	0.71	0.73
West Asia/North Africa (WANA)	0.73	0.62	0.63	0.72	0.73
Developed countries	0.90	0.85	0.88	0.89	0.92
Developing countries	0.75	0.67	0.69	0.75	0.78
World	**0.77**	**0.70**	**0.72**	**0.77**	**0.80**

Source: IMPACT-WATER projections, 2002.
Notes: Data are annual averages. BAU indicates the business-as-usual scenario; HP, the higher price scenario; HP-LENV, the higher price, lower environmental water share scenario; HP-HE, the higher price, higher basin efficiency scenario; and HP-HE-LENV, the higher price, higher basin efficiency, lower environmental water share scenario.

BAU, irrigated cereal production declines. HP has the largest negative impact on irrigated production of these scenarios. Compared with BAU, the irrigated cereal production in developing countries under HP declines by nearly 5 percent. The biggest percentage reduction in irrigated production is in WANA (9 percent), where a large proportion of the decline in consumption is beneficial because *BE* is high (Table 6.10).

Under HP-LENV, where irrigation has first access to water saved from non-irrigation sectors, irrigated production in developing countries declines by only 2.4 percent. It appears surprising that LA, which is not generally water-scarce, increases production significantly under HP-LENV compared with HP, while India gains little. But non-irrigation water consumption in LA is much higher relative to India (43 percent of total water consumption compared with 19 percent), so that greater water savings are available for irrigation through water price increases. And although water is not generally scarce in LA, seasonal water shortages are met with water from non-irrigation savings.

Net cereal trade in 2021–25 is affected under all scenarios compared with BAU, but the changes are not large (Table 6.11). HP-HE-LENV shows net cereal imports declining by 4.2 million metric tons in the developing world compared with BAU. The scenarios with *BE* values the same as BAU (HP and HP-LENV) show increased net cereal imports in developing countries. HP-LENV projects an increase in net cereal imports in the developing world of 5 million metric tons over BAU levels by 2021–25, and HP shows a 10 million metric ton increase.

Box 6.1—The role of water pricing in water scarce basins

Increased water prices have a strong impact on water withdrawals in water scarce basins and countries. As evidenced by the ratio of water withdrawal to renewable water, withdrawals drop significantly under HP and HP-HE compared with BAU, including declines of 23 percent in the Haihe, 19 percent in the Yellow, 20 percent in the Indus, and 15 percent in the Ganges river basins, and 23 percent in Egypt.

Although the irrigation water supply reliability index (IWSR) is reduced significantly under HP compared with BAU, the increasing basin efficiency implemtented under HP-HE replenishes IWSR in these basins and countries. IWSR values decline for all the focal water scarce basins under HP, with reductions of 0.08 to 0.12. Under HP-HE, however, with increases in basin efficiency in response to higher water prices, IWSR only declines by 0.02 compared with BAU in the Haihe river basin and in Egypt, and remains the same or slightly increases in the remaining basins. Correspondingly, irrigated cereal yields relative to potential yields decline under HP but generally increase under HP-HE. The relative irrigated cereal yields decline 5-13 percent under HP compared with BAU, while they remain the same as BAU under HP-HE for the Haihe and Egypt, and increase slightly for the Yellow, Indus, and Ganges river basins. These impacts on irrigated yields in the water scarce basins lead to decreased total cereal production under HP-HE. Impacts on cereal production under HP are higher in water scarce basins because a high proportion of consumption is used beneficially. Shortfalls in total cereal production compared with BAU range from 4 to 9 percent for the Haihe, Yellow, Indus. and Ganges river basins, and are 9 percent for Egypt. But under HP-HE, these basins are able to use increased efficiency to reduce or eliminate production shortfalls. The Yellow and Indus river basins have slightly higher cereal production under HP-HE than under BAU. Cereal production in Egypt recovers significantly from HP levels but remains 3 percent below BAU levels, while it is less under HP-HE in the Haihe and Ganges river basins than under BAU (1.5 and 0.5 percent, respectively).

Table 6.10—Change in irrigated cereal production relative to the business-as-usual level for four higher price scenarios, 2021–25

| | Change in Irrigated cereal production relative to BAU levels | | | | | | | |
| | HP | | HP-LENV | | HP-HE | | HP-HE-LENV | |
Region/Country	(million mt)	(%)	(million mt)	(%)	(million mt)	(%)	(million mt)	(%)
Asia	-32.5	-4.3	-17.1	-2.3	0.1	0.0	14.5	1.9
China	-16.7	-4.3	-2.6	-0.7	-0.3	-0.1	13.5	3.4
India	-10.1	-5.7	-10.0	-5.6	-0.2	-0.1	-0.2	-0.1
Southeast Asia	-1.6	-1.8	-0.6	-0.7	0.2	0.2	1.1	1.3
South Asia excluding India	-3.7	-5.4	-3.6	-5.2	0.3	0.4	0.1	0.1
Latin America (LA)	-2.2	-4.1	1.0	1.9	0.2	0.4	3.9	7.3
Sub-Saharan Africa (SSA)	-0.2	-1.4	0.0	0.0	0.1	0.7	0.4	2.7
West Asia/North Africa (WANA)	-4.7	-8.9	-4.6	-8.7	-1.2	-2.3	-0.9	-1.7
Developed countries	-2.8	-1.0	1.2	0.4	0.3	0.1	4.2	1.6
Developing countries	-40.1	-4.6	-21.1	-2.4	-0.9	-0.1	18.1	2.1
World	**-42.9**	**-3.8**	**-19.9**	**-1.7**	**-0.6**	**-0.1**	**22.2**	**2.0**

Source: IMPACT-WATER projections, 2002.
Notes: Data are annual averages. BAU indicates the business-as-usual scenario; HP, the higher price scenario; HP-LENV, the higher price, lower environmental water share scenario; HP-HE, the higher price, higher basin efficiency scenario; HP-HE-LENV, the higher price, higher basin efficiency, lower environmental water share scenario; and million mt, million metric tons.

Table 6.11—Net cereal trade under business-as-usual and four higher price scenarios, 2021–25

| | Net cereal trade (million mt) | | | | |
Region/Country	BAU	HP	HP-LENV	HP-HE	HP-HE-LENV
Asia	-136.8	-150.5	-143.5	-135.6	-128.6
China	-47.3	-56.5	-45.3	-46.6	-34.2
India	-10.5	-15.3	-17.6	-10.7	-13.5
Southeast Asia	-8.9	-7.5	-8.0	-8.8	-9.2
South Asia excluding India	-19.5	-21.3	-22.1	-19.2	-20.8
Latin America (LA)	-17.9	-14.0	-13.4	-17.6	-16.5
Sub-Saharan Africa (SSA)	-26.9	-22.5	-24.4	-26.5	-28.5
West Asia/North Africa (WANA)	-81.5	-84.5	-86.2	-84.1	-85.6
Developed countries	233.9	243.4	239.1	234.7	229.7
Developing countries	-233.9	-243.4	-239.1	-234.7	-229.7
World	**0.0**	**0.0**	**0.0**	**0.0**	**0.0**

Source: IMPACT-WATER projections, 2002.
Notes: Data are annual averages. BAU indicates the business-as-usual scenario; HP, the higher price scenario; HP-LENV, the higher price, lower environmental water share scenario; HP-HE, the higher price, higher basin efficiency scenario; HP-HE-LENV, the higher price, higher basin efficiency, lower environmental water share scenario; and million mt, million metric tons.

Figure 6.3—World food prices under business-as-usual and four higher water price scenarios, 2021–25

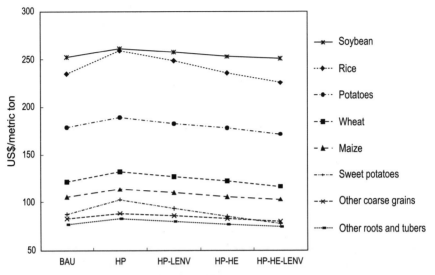

Source: IMPACT-WATER projections, 2002.
Notes: Data are annual averages. BAU indicates the business-as-usual scenario; HP, the higher price scenario; HP-LENV, the higher price, lower environmental water share scenario; HP-HE, the higher price, higher basin efficiency scenario; and HP-HE-LENV, the higher price, higher basin efficiency, lower environmental water share scenario.

World food prices are affected in all higher price scenarios compared with BAU; (Figure 6.3). HP and HP-LENV, with *BE* values the same as BAU, generally show the most significant increases for most crops. HP projects an increase in world food prices of 9–13 percent for cereals and 4 percent for soybeans. HP-HE and HP-HE-LENV, having higher *BE* values than BAU, tend to have similar prices to BAU (or lower for certain crops). HP-HE-LENV results in decreases in world prices, with declines of 3–5 percent for all major cereal crops.

SUMMARY

The results presented in this chapter show that water prices are a powerful tool for influencing water demand in domestic, industrial, and agricultural sectors—and therefore in determining the availability of water for the environment. Even though the water demand response to water prices is relatively small in agriculture, the total amount of water saved through water price increases is large because irrigation accounts for such a large share of water use. Conversely, although water consumption in domestic and industrial sectors is relatively small, the price response is high, so these sectors also contribute substantially to water savings.

Even under the worst-case where water prices have no impact on basin efficiency, the large percentage changes in water prices have relatively modest impacts on food production. These modest impacts occur because the water price response is low in agriculture and the declines in irrigated production cause increases in food prices that induce more rainfed production (and partially mitigate the fall in irrigated production). Also, in a few water-scarce regions where water use is constrained by water availability rather than water prices, a portion of the water released from nonagricultural uses provides additional water for irrigation.

In the more likely case that there are at least moderate increases in *BE* in response to increases in agricultural water prices, beneficial water consumption for irrigation is maintained at nearly the BAU levels, even though total consumption declines when water prices increase. Even severely water-scarce river basins such as the Yellow and the Indus basins are able to compensate for water price increases and achieve water use efficiencies, irrigation reliability, and cereal production nearly equal to—and in some cases slightly higher than—BAU levels. The major beneficiary in the higher price scenarios is the environment. The dramatic reduction in the ratio of withdrawals to total water availability in response to price increases means a significant improvement in water quality as the reuse of water declines, and the reduction in water withdrawals provides a major increase in environmental flows.

NOTES

1. The single-climate scenarios conserve simulation time and resources. Comparative analysis of BAU, SUS, and CRI single-climate runs versus 30-climate runs indicated that the relative impacts of alternative scenarios on the outcomes were virtually identical. Hence, single-climate runs were used for the remaining scenarios.

2. The elasticity of water demand in terms of water price represents the responsiveness of water demand to a change in the price of water. It is expressed as percentage change in water demand in response to a percentage change in water price. Thus an elasticity of 0.50 means that a 10 percent increase in water price would result in a 5 percent decrease in water demand.

Chapter 7

Balancing Water for Food and the Environment

Water, the environment, and food production are closely interrelated at the local, regional, and global levels—as discussed extensively in previous chapters. Rapidly increasing water demands and competition among household, industrial, environmental, and agricultural uses have escalated in many regions. Long-term hydrological records show a marked reduction in the annual discharge on some of the world's major rivers (OECD 1998) resulting largely from the growth of agricultural water consumption.

Balancing water uses between agriculture, the environment, and other sectors can be tricky to say the least. Growing irrigation water use and prescribed water reservation for environmental uses could jeopardize the long-term availability of water for food production, raising the question of whether water scarcity will constrain food production growth, particularly in the developing world. In this chapter we assess the impact of water supply on future food production growth and examine the trade-offs among increasing water allocation for the environment, eliminating groundwater overdraft, and producing food.

UNSUSTAINABLE GROUNDWATER USE

Unsustainable groundwater use is often associated with irrigation. It is a concern in numerous areas around the globe because it can lead to both water scarcity and water quality problems. Groundwater overdraft occurs when groundwater pumping exceeds the rate of natural recharge. Overdrafting leads to a lowered water table, which in turn increases the depth of pumping, boosting pumping costs. Additional environmental problems may also occur from groundwater overdrafting including decreased water quality, subsiding land, and saline intrusion into aquifers. Salt intrusion into aquifers as a result of groundwater overdraft is of particular concern in coastal regions.

Estimates indicate that irrigated cropland has degraded significantly over the past decade through waterlogging and salinization. Waterlogging develops when the soil becomes saturated because of a high or perched water table. It often occurs in more humid regions and is generally caused by over-irrigation or inadequate drainage. It leads to poor plant growing conditions. Salinization—or the accumulation of salts in the soil through water evaporation from the upper soil layers—can occur naturally but is generally a problem under irrigated conditions. This problem is often more acute in arid areas because irrigation water evaporates more quickly and there is less natural leaching and drainage. Salinization generally leads to decreased production levels, although in some cases the problem may be severe enough to obstruct agriculture altogether.

Agriculture can contribute to water quality reduction in several ways, but it can also feel the effects of this pollution as reductions in water quality often lead to decreases in agricultural production. Water-induced soil erosion from cropland can be a major problem for water quality, leading to suspended solids in the water supply and siltation in the channel. Additional ground and surface water pollution from agriculture can be caused by fertilizer, pesticide, and animal manure inputs. Excess nutrients in the water supply can lead to eutrophication, which affects the aquatic ecosystem by depleting oxygen through algae blooms. In addition, excess nitrates contributed by fertilizers and animal manure can have human health effects (Wood, Sebastian, and Scherr 2000). These water quality problems can be intensified by increased water scarcity because there is less water to dilute the pollutants.

GROUNDWATER OVERDRAFT REDUCTION

Groundwater pumping in excess of recharge has caused significant groundwater depletion in many regions including northern China, northern India, the western United States, and some countries in WANA. As discussed, groundwater overdraft can lead to significant problems in both water quality and water availability; thus, excessive groundwater use is a critical policy issue in balancing water uses for food production and the environment. The low groundwater pumping scenario (LGW) discussed in this section examines the effects of the global elimination of groundwater overdraft.[1]

Scenario Specification for Sustainable Groundwater Use

In any given aquifer, groundwater overdraft occurs when the ratio of pumping to recharge is greater than 1.0. However, given the large macrobasins used in the IMPACT-WATER model and the unequal distribution of groundwater resources in them, areas exist within these basins where available groundwater resources are subject to overdraft even if the whole-basin ratio shows pumping to be less than recharge. Postel (1999) draws on several sources to estimate total annual global groundwater overdraft at 163 cubic kilometers; using this estimate we set the threshold at which localized groundwater overdraft occurs at the whole-basin level at 0.55. Using this benchmark, groundwater overdraft occurs in a number of basins and countries in 1995 including the Rio Grande and Colorado River basins in the western United States, where the ratio of annual groundwater pumping to recharge is greater than 0.6; the Haihe in northern China, where the ratio is 0.85, and the middle and downstream areas of the Yellow River basin, where the ratio is greater than 0.6; several river basins in northern and western India with ratios in excess of 0.8; Egypt, with a ratio of 2.5; and WANA, with a ratio of 0.8.

It is possible for regions and countries that are unsustainably pumping their groundwater to return to sustainable use in the future. LGW assumes that groundwater overdraft in all countries and regions using water unsustainably is phased out over 25 years beginning in 2000 by reducing annual groundwater pumping to recharge ratios to below 0.55 at the basin or country level.

Compared with 1995 levels, under LGW, groundwater pumping in the overdrafting countries and regions declines by 163 cubic kilometers including reductions of 30 cubic kilometers in China, 69 cubic kilometers in India, 11 cubic kilometers in the United States, 29 cubic kilometers in WANA, and 24 cubic kilometers in other countries. The projected increase in pumping for areas with more plentiful groundwater resources remains about the same as under BAU. Total global groundwater pumping falls to 753 cubic kilometers in 2021–25, a decline from the 1995 value of 817 cubic kilometers and from the 2021–25 BAU value of 922 cubic kilometers.

Scenario Results for Sustainable Groundwater Use

In this section we analyze projections for water and food under LGW compared with BAU.

Total water withdrawals are projected to increase by 846 cubic kilometers between 1995 and 2021–25 under BAU (Table 7.1). Such increases are smaller under LGW because groundwater overdraft, as discussed, is assumed to fall. The global elimination of groundwater overdraft results in a 161.8 cubic kilometer decrease in water withdrawals in 2021–25 compared with BAU. The decrease is only 5.3 cubic kilometers in developed countries compared with 156.5 cubic kilometers in developing countries. The largest regional impacts are felt in India and China, where water withdrawals under LGW decrease by approximately 10 and 4 percent, respectively, compared with BAU. In most other regions under LGW, water withdrawals decrease by smaller amounts.

Table 7.1—Total water withdrawal under business-as-usual and low groundwater pumping scenarios, 1995 and 2021–25

Region/Country	Total water withdrawal (km³)		
	1995 baseline estimates	2021–2025 projections	
		BAU	LGW
Asia	1,952.7	2,419.8	2,286.1
China	678.8	843.6	812.8
India	674.4	822.0	742.9
Southeast Asia	203.1	278.3	278.3
South Asia excluding India	353.0	416.0	392.2
Latin America (LA)	297.8	402.3	402.3
Sub-Saharan Africa (SSA)	128.4	206.9	208.2
West Asia/North Africa (WANA)	236.1	294.0	269.8
Developed countries	1,144.2	1,271.6	1,266.3
Developing countries	2,761.9	3,480.6	3,324.1
World	**3,906.1**	**4,752.1**	**4,590.3**

Source: IMPACT-WATER assessments and projections, 2002.
Notes: 2021–25 data are annual averages. BAU indicates the business-as-usual scenario and LGW, the low groundwater pumping scenario; and km³, cubic kilometers.

Table 7.2—Consumptive water use by sector under business-as-usual and low groundwater pumping scenarios, 2021–25

Region/Country	Consumptive water use (km³)							
	Irrigation		Domestic		Industrial		Livestock	
	BAU	LGW	BAU	LGW	BAU	LGW	BAU	LGW
Asia	842.2	774.9	146.3	145.9	78.8	78.5	22.9	22.8
China	232.7	220.2	57.7	57.3	31.6	31.4	7.1	7.1
India	338.1	295.0	39.8	39.7	16.2	16.1	7.6	7.5
Southeast Asia	89.8	89.8	29.3	29.3	20.5	20.5	3.9	3.9
South Asia excluding India	168.1	156.5	15.8	15.9	4.5	4.5	3.7	3.8
Latin America (LA)	94.7	94.7	30.0	30.0	29.7	29.7	12.1	12.1
Sub-Saharan Africa (SSA)	61.6	62.3	22.8	22.8	2.3	2.3	3.9	3.9
West Asia/North Africa (WANA)	136.5	121.7	12.8	12.7	8.6	8.5	3.1	3.2
Developed countries	277.7	275.2	68.3	68.2	115.4	115.3	18.0	18.0
Developing countries	1215.7	1134.3	214.6	214.3	121.9	121.6	43.3	43.1
World	**1493.4**	**1409.6**	**282.9**	**282.5**	**237.2**	**236.9**	**61.4**	**61.1**

Source: IMPACT-WATER projections, 2002.
Notes: Data are annual averages. BAU indicates the business-as-usual scenario and LGW, the low groundwater pumping scenario; and km³, cubic kilometers.

The consumptive use of water—water withdrawn from the source that cannot be reused in the same basin—is also projected for each sector under BAU and LGW (Table 7.2). Globally, irrigation is by far the greatest user of water in the four sectors reported in Table 7.2. It also undergoes the greatest overall decrease in water use under LGW. The global elimination of groundwater overdraft leads to a worldwide reduction of consumptive water use in 2021–25 of 5.6 percent in the irrigation sector, 0.5 percent in the livestock sector, 0.1 percent in the domestic sector, and 0.1 percent in the industrial sector compared with BAU. Most of this change occurs in developing countries, where consumptive water use in the irrigation sector under LGW declines by 6.7 percent. Changes in developed country water use are much smaller.

Total cereal area is estimated to be 730 thousand hectares lower in 2021–25 under LGW than projected under BAU (Table 7.3). This is because of the significant difference in irrigated area between the two scenarios (3.3 million hectares less under LGW). Rainfed area is greater under LGW because of the increase in cereal prices induced by the cutback in groundwater pumping, but is not large enough to completely offset the reduction in irrigated area. Most of the difference in irrigated area occurs in developing countries—most significantly in China. Declines in cultivated area also occur for soybeans and roots and tubers under LGW. Absolute

Table 7.3—Cereal area harvested under business-as-usual and low groundwater pumping scenarios, 1995 and 2021–25

Region/Country	Rainfed harvested area (million ha)			Irrigated harvested area (million ha)		
	1995 baseline estimates	2021–25 projections BAU	LGW	1995 baseline estimates	2021–25 projections BAU	LGW
Asia	136.9	130.2	130.5	152.9	167.7	164.8
China	26.2	29.6	29.6	62.4	66.6	64.0
India	62.3	49.8	49.9	37.8	46.7	46.8
Southeast Asia	29.8	31.5	31.6	19.2	20.3	20.4
South Asia excluding India	5.6	5.6	5.6	19.9	21.0	20.3
Latin America (LA)	41.8	55.0	55.3	7.5	9.8	9.8
Sub-Saharan Africa (SSA)	69.8	95.5	95.8	3.3	4.8	4.8
West Asia/North Africa (WANA)	34.0	35.6	35.9	9.8	10.9	10.4
Developed countries	192.1	196.0	197.4	41.8	45.1	45.3
Developing countries	282.2	316.1	317.2	171.3	191.9	188.5
World	**474.3**	**512.1**	**514.7**	**213.1**	**237.0**	**233.7**

Source: IMPACT-WATER assessments and projections, 2002.
Notes: 2021–25 data are annual averages. BAU indicates the business-as-usual scenario; LGW, the low groundwater pumping scenario; and million ha, million hectares.

decreases in irrigated area for these commodities are not as large as those for cereals although the percentage difference for soybeans—at 3 percent—is larger than that for the other commodities (the irrigated area decline for cereals is only 1.4 percent). Reductions in harvested area for soybeans and roots and tubers are also concentrated in China.

In most regions, irrigated cereal yields in 2021–25 are lower under LGW than under BAU (Table 7.4). Globally yields decline by 1.7 percent, in developing countries they decline by 2.5 percent, and in developed countries they increase slightly (by 0.2 percent). In contrast, rainfed yields increase slightly under LGW. World and developing country rainfed yields increase by 0.7 percent while developed country yields increase by 0.6 percent over BAU levels.

Total cereal production under LGW decreases by 18 million metric tons compared with equivalent BAU levels in 2021–25 (Table 7.5). This overall decrease is made up of 35 million metric tons in irrigated cereal production, counteracted by a rainfed production increase of 17 million metric tons. Price increases spurred by lower irrigated production stimulate rainfed production. World wheat prices under LGW reflect a 10 percent increase over BAU equivalents in 2021–25, with rice prices increasing by 6 percent and maize prices by 5 percent (Figure 7.1).

Table 7.4—Cereal yield under business-as-usual and low groundwater pumping scenarios, 1995 and 2021–25

| Region/Country | Rainfed yield (kg/ha) | | | Irrigated yield (kg/ha) | | |
| | 1995 baseline estimates | 2021–25 projections | | 1995 baseline estimates | 2021–25 projections | |
		BAU	LGW		BAU	LGW
Asia	1,699	2,459	2,474	3,227	4,503	4,374
China	3,585	4,647	4,685	4,225	5,881	5,871
India	1,197	1,632	1,643	2,653	3,821	3,449
Southeast Asia	1,609	2,466	2,477	3,054	4,269	4,297
South Asia excluding India	1,239	1,916	1,928	2,187	3,282	3,227
Latin America (LA)	2,067	2,917	2,937	4,066	5,457	5,492
Sub-Saharan Africa (SSA)	848	1,194	1,202	2,157	3,083	3,128
West Asia/North Africa (WANA)	1,397	1,753	1,767	3,578	4,858	4,851
Developed countries	3,167	3,886	3,910	4,439	5,972	5,983
Developing countries	1,506	2,076	2,090	3,249	4,529	4,417
World	2,179	2,769	2,788	3,483	4,803	4,720

Source: IMPACT-WATER assessments and projections, 2002.
Notes: 2021–25 data are annual averages. BAU indicates the business-as-usual scenario; LGW, the low groundwater pumping scenario; and kg/ha, kilograms per hectare.

Table 7.5—Cereal production under business-as-usual and low groundwater pumping scenarios, 1995 and 2021–25

Region/Country	Rainfed production (million mt)			Irrigated production (million mt)		
	1995 baseline estimates	2021–25 projections BAU	LGW	1995 baseline estimates	2021–25 projections BAU	LGW
Asia	232.6	320.2	322.8	493.3	755.3	720.9
China	94.0	137.4	138.6	263.6	391.6	375.9
India	74.6	81.4	82.0	100.3	178.3	161.5
Southeast Asia	47.9	77.8	78.3	58.5	86.6	87.6
South Asia excluding India	6.9	10.6	10.7	43.6	68.9	65.4
Latin America (LA)	86.4	160.6	162.4	30.6	53.4	54.0
Sub-Saharan Africa (SSA)	59.2	114.1	115.2	7.0	14.7	15.0
West Asia/North Africa (WANA)	47.5	62.3	63.4	34.9	53.0	50.3
Developed countries	608.3	761.6	771.9	185.6	269.1	270.7
Developing countries	425.0	656.3	663.0	556.7	869.1	832.4
World	1,033.3	1,418.0	1,434.9	742.3	1,138.2	1,103.2

Source: IMPACT-WATER assessments and projections, 2002.
Notes: 2021–25 data are annual averages. BAU indicates the business-as-usual scenario; LGW, the low groundwater pumping scenario; and million mt, million metric tons.

Figure 7.1—World food prices under business-as-usual and low groundwater pumping scenarios, 2021–25

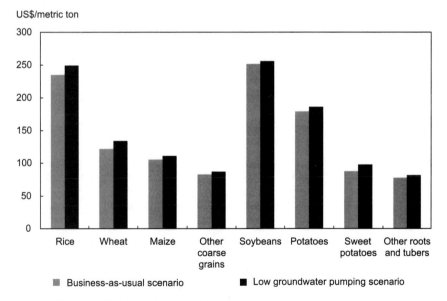

US$/metric ton

Business-as-usual scenario   Low groundwater pumping scenario

Source: IMPACT-WATER projections, 2002.
Note: Data are annual averages; US$/mt indicates U.S. dollars per metric ton.

Total developing country cereal production declines by 30 million metric tons under LGW in 2021–25 compared with BAU; irrigated production declines by 37 million metric tons, and rainfed production increases by 7 million metric tons. Cereal production actually increases in developed countries by 12 million metric tons in response to world price increases, and more than compensates reductions from decreased groundwater pumping.

Under LGW global soybean production falls by 1.9 million metric tons (0.8 percent), potato production decreases by 4.3 million metric tons (1.1 percent), and sweet potato production decreases by 1.5 million metric tons (0.7 percent) compared with BAU. Production of cassava and other roots and tubers—virtually all rainfed—actually increases by 1.8 million metric tons (0.7 percent) because price increases for other staples shift demand toward cassava, boosting prices and inducing slightly higher production.

Although substantial, the estimated decline in global food production from the elimination of groundwater overdraft is not devastatingly high because of the induced increases in food prices that stimulate increases in rainfed production and offset the fall in irrigated production. But, as would be expected, much more serious impacts are felt in countries and basins that currently have large overdrafts. Cereal production falls by 16.2 million metric tons in India, with a few basins particularly hard hit including the Ganges basin—where cereal production declines 8.8 million metric tons—and the Indus basin—where cereal production falls by 4.6 million metric tons. In China, cereal production falls by 14.5 million metric tons including 11 million metric tons in the Haihe River basin and 5.7 million metric tons in the Yellow River basin. The production impacts felt in these and other water-scarce basins are discussed in greater detail in Box 7.1.

Cereal demand also falls in these countries under LGW, with decreases of 3.8 and 4 million metric tons in India and China, respectively (Table 7.6). Globally, demand declines by 23.5 million metric tons. These declines occur in developing countries predominantly, particularly in Asia. Although demand decreases across the board, the declines are not great enough to counteract the predicted decreases in production.

The shortfall in production compared with demand is offset with higher net imports, which increase in the developing world as a whole but are concentrated in particular areas. Compared with BAU, in 2021–25 LGW results in an increase in net cereal imports of 13 million metric tons in India and 14 million metric tons in China (Figure 7.2). Unsurprisingly, net cereal exports in developed countries increase to supply the additional demand in the developing world.

Improved efficiency in overdrafting basins to offset the lost production and consumption from reduced groundwater pumping would require reform beyond the basins most affected. Although improvements directed at the specific overdrafting basins could, in theory, compensate these declines, they would be unlikely in

Box 7.1—Elimination of groundwater overdraft in water scarce basins

Groundwater overdraft is a problem in many of the major water scarce basins around the world. To phase out overdraft by 2025, groundwater pumping in water-scarce basins and countries is significantly reduced under LGW compared with BAU levels, including a reduction of 10.5 cubic kilometers in the Haihe, 15.3 cubic kilometers in the Yellow, 24.5 cubic kilometers in the Indus, and 32.9 cubic kilometers in the Ganges river basins, and 2.7 cubic kilometers in Egypt. The ratio of water withdrawal to renewable water declines across all of the selected water scarce regions, with particularly large declines in the Yellow and Haihe river basins in China (19 and 16 percent respectively). IWSR and relative irrigated yields under LGW are also significantly lower. Although impacts on global food production and demand under LGW are not particularly significant, the effect in these selected water scarce basins and countries is considerable. For example, compared with BAU, total cereal production under LGW drops by 15 percent in the Haihe, 9 percent in the Yellow, 10 percent in the Indus, and 9 percent in the Ganges river basins, and 6 percent in Egypt. These results indicate it will be infeasible to maintain cereal production at BAU levels in water scarce basins through improvement in basin efficiency alone; increases in broader agricultural investments and agricultural policy reform will be necessary.

Table 7.6—Cereal demand under business-as-usual and low groundwater pumping scenarios, 1995 and 2021–25

	Cereal demand (million mt)		
	1995 baseline estimates	2021–25 projections	
Region/Country		BAU	LGW
Asia	794.3	1,205.3	1193.2
China	375.0	571.9	568.1
India	171.3	268.5	264.5
Southeast Asia	113.5	172.9	171.4
South Asia excluding India	54.9	98.6	96.5
Latin America (LA)	137.4	231.0	228.5
Sub-Saharan Africa (SSA)	78.4	158.8	156.9
West Asia/North Africa (WANA)	120.2	196.6	194.5
Developed countries	686.4	794.2	788.9
Developing countries	1,092.2	1,754.4	1,736.1
World	**1,778.6**	**2,548.5**	**2,525.0**

Source: IMPACT-WATER assessments and projections, 2002.
Notes: 2021–25 data are annual averages. BAU indicates the business-as-usual scenario; LGW, the low groundwater pumping scenario; and million mt, million metric tons.

Figure 7.2—Net cereal trade under business-as-usual and low groundwater pumping scenarios, 2021–25

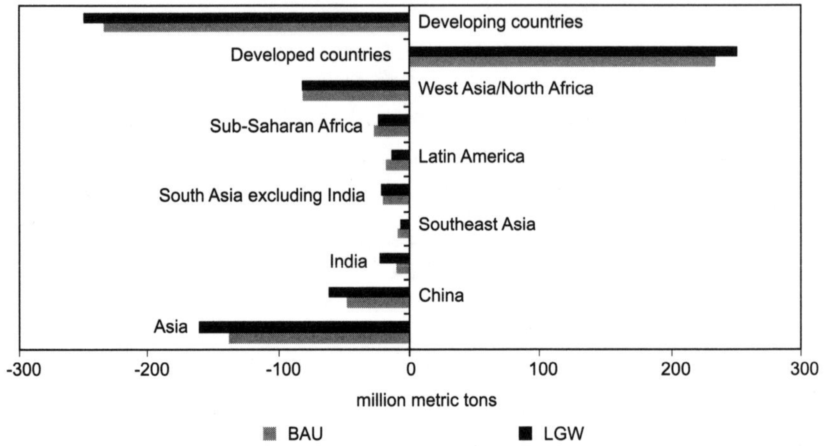

Source: IMPACT-WATER projections, 2002.
Note: Data are annual averages; negative values indicate net imports; positive values, net exports.

reality. For example, in the Indus basin, 2025 basin efficiency (*BE*) values would need to rise from 0.59 to 0.76 to generate enough cereal production to compensate for the reduced groundwater overdraft, and in China's Yellow River, 2021–25 BE values would have to increase from 0.62 to 0.82.

ENVIRONMENTAL DEMANDS FOR WATER

Environmental demands for water have attracted increasing attention in recent years. Smakhtin (2002) defines environmental water requirements as the amount and quality of water required to protect an ecosystem to enable ecologically sustainable development and water resource utilization. Extreme changes in ecosystems may occur if water available for environmental uses falls below a certain threshold.[2] Many countries are beginning to incorporate these concepts into their water resources management strategies to reserve a certain quantity of water for environmental or ecosystem uses.

Water reserved for the environment can help regulate pollution and sustain the riparian ecosystem. Sufficient in-stream water availability can help to temper water pollution through the dilution of contaminants in the watercourse. Water availability is critical to the maintenance of local flora and fauna in a watershed (particularly fish and other aquatic species). Water is also needed to maintain existing wetlands, which can have additional positive impacts on the watershed because they can recharge aquifers, digest organic wastes, and store runoff (Johnson, Revenga, and Echeverría 2001).

INCREASE IN ENVIRONMENTAL WATER FLOWS

The possible tradeoffs between water for food production and water for nature became one of the most contentious issues in discussions of the *Second World Water Forum* in The Hague in 2000. Participants in the "Water for Food" theme stressed the need for slow growth in water consumption in agriculture, while the "Water for Nature" theme called for significant reallocation of water from agriculture to environmental uses. As Rijsberman and Molden (2001) note, the Global Water Partnership's Framework for Action to Achieve the Water Vision in the 21st Century captures the central paradox as follows:

> On the one hand, the fundamental fear of food shortages encourages ever greater use of water resources for agriculture. On the other, there is a need to divert water from irrigated food production to other users and to protect the resource and the ecosystem. Many believe this conflict is one of the most critical problems to be tackled in the early 21st century.
>
> (GWP 2001 cited in Rijsberman and Molden 2001)

But does the solution to this paradox require a zero-sum trade-off between food production and water for environmental purposes? The scenarios that follow address this issue by examining the impact of a mandated increase in environmental flows on total water use and food production. In the first scenario (HENV), a global increase in water reserved as committed flows for the environment is simulated *without* improved river basin efficiency; in the second (HENV-HE), a global increase in water reserved as committed flows for the environment is simulated *with* improved river basin efficiency.

Global Increase in Environmental Water Flows

To model higher environmental water flows, HENV assumes that additional water is freed for the environment by maintaining total water consumption at 1995 levels. To explore the trade-offs between irrigation and environmental flows, the 2021–25 domestic and industrial water demand projections are maintained at BAU levels to ensure that the irrigation sector is the only variable creating water consumption savings under HENV. Hence HENV depicts a trade-off between environmental and irrigation uses worldwide. The reduction in global total water withdrawals in 2021–25 under HENV compared with BAU is 678 cubic kilometers, or 14 percent, and in total consumption the reduction is 340 cubic kilometers, or 16 percent.

HENV-HE adds the dimension of whether the impacts of these water savings on the irrigation sector can be minimized through water use efficiency. Under this second environmental flow scenario, *BE* increases from BAU levels to produce beneficial crop water consumption roughly equivalent to BAU levels during 2021–25 (Table 7.7). *BE* levels under HENV-HE, therefore, are much higher than under BAU, but they are not unreasonable given the advanced irrigation systems available today and potential reforms in water policy and management.

Results for High Environmental Flow Scenarios
A global increase in water committed to environmental uses decreases total water withdrawal in 2021–25 by 14 percent compared with BAU. The 4,074 cubic kilometer total withdrawn under HENV in 2021–25 is still higher than the 1995 level, but only by 4 percent compared with a projected 22 percent increase under BAU (Table 7.8). Total water withdrawal under HENV decreases for both developing and developed countries compared with BAU (slightly more in developing countries).

Table 7.7—Basin efficiency and beneficial irrigation water consumption under business-as-usual, high environmental flows, and high environmental flows and high irrigation efficiency scenarios, 1995 and 2021–25

Region/Country	Basin efficiency				Beneficial Irrigation water consumption (km³)			
	1995 baseline estimates	2021–25 projections			1995 baseline estimates	2021–25 projections		
		BAU	HENV	HENV-HE		BAU	HENV	HENV-HE
Asia	0.53	0.58	0.58	0.77	439.6	486.5	378.0	485.0
China	0.54	0.60	0.60	0.82	130.8	138.5	105.2	136.8
India	0.57	0.63	0.63	0.82	183.4	212.3	165.8	210.6
Southeast Asia	0.47	0.49	0.49	0.65	40.5	44.4	33.2	41.6
South Asia excluding India	0.48	0.50	0.50	0.66	79.0	84.1	68.5	89.0
Latin America (LA)	0.45	0.47	0.47	0.61	39.5	44.4	33.4	41.9
Sub-Saharan Africa (SSA)	0.44	0.46	0.46	0.66	22.2	28.4	17.9	25.2
West Asia/North Africa (WANA)	0.68	0.73	0.73	0.88	82.5	99.6	77.0	88.9
Developed countries	0.65	0.69	0.69	0.79	175.5	190.6	158.1	177.2
Developing countries	0.54	0.58	0.58	0.76	626.6	708.2	553.6	693.7
World	0.56	0.60	0.60	0.76	802.1	898.7	711.7	870.8

Source: IMPACT-WATER assessments and projections, 2002.
Notes: 2021–25 data are annual averages. BAU indicates the business-as-usual scenario; HENV, higher environmental flow; HENV-HE, higher environmental flow and higher irrigation efficiency; and km³, cubic kilometers.

Table 7.8—Total water withdrawal under business-as-usual, high environmental flows, and high environmental flows and high irrigation efficiency scenarios, 1995 and 2021–25

Region/Country	Total water withdrawal (km³)			
	1995 baseline estimates	2021–25 projections		
		BAU	HENV	HENV-HE
Asia	1,952.7	2,419.8	2,026.3	1,996.9
China	678.8	843.6	707.8	695.7
India	674.4	822.0	679.1	664.1
Southeast Asia	203.1	278.3	234.6	232.6
South Asia excluding India	353.0	416.0	352.8	352.5
Latin America (LA)	297.8	402.3	344.4	346.5
Sub-Saharan Africa (SSA)	128.4	206.9	154.9	155.9
West Asia/North Africa (WANA)	236.1	294.0	242.2	236.2
Developed countries	1,144.2	1,271.6	1,154.5	1,155.2
Developing countries	2,761.9	3,480.6	2,919.7	2,887.4
World	**3,906.1**	**4,752.1**	**4,074.2**	**4,042.6**

Source: IMPACT-WATER assessments and projections, 2002.
Notes: 2021–25 data are annual averages. BAU indicates the business-as-usual scenario; HENV, higher environmental flow; and HENV-HE, higher environmental flow and higher irrigation efficiency; and km³, cubic kilometers.

Developing country withdrawals are 16 percent lower under HENV than under BAU in 2021–25, and developed country withdrawals are 9 percent lower; regionally, the impact in India is particularly significant, with a decline of 17 percent.

Understandably, total global water withdrawals also decrease under HENV-HE compared with BAU, and at approximately the same rates as HENV. The global decrease under HENV-HE is 15 percent compared with BAU; developing and developed country decreases are similar, at 17 and 9 percent, respectively, compared with BAU.

Increasing global environmental water flows predominantly affects consumptive use in the irrigation sector. Under HENV, global consumptive use of water for irrigation declines in 2021–25 by 21 percent compared with BAU (Table 7.9). As a result, the irrigation water supply reliability index (IWSR) declines significantly under HENV compared with BAU (Table 7.10). From 0.81 in 1995, IWSR in developing countries declines to 0.58 by 2021–25 under HENV compared with 0.75 under BAU. Sub-Saharan Africa (SSA) and Latin America (LA) show the largest declines in IWSR, with a drop of 0.28 between 1995 and 2021–25.

The reduction in water use for irrigation under HENV-HE is slightly larger, at 24 percent globally compared with BAU. For developing countries, the effects of HENV and HENV-HE are similar—22 and 24 percent declines over BAU levels respectively. Decreases in developed countries are smaller, at 18 and 19 percent

Table 7.9—Consumptive water use by sector under business-as-usual, high environmental flows, and high environmental flows and high irrigation efficiency scenarios, 2021–25

Region/Country	Irrigation			Domestic			Industrial			Livestock		
	BAU	HENV	HENV-HE	BAU	HENV	HENV-HE	BAU	HENV	HENV-HE	BAU	HENV	HENV-HE
Asia	842.2	656.4	633.1	146.3	140.3	143.8	78.8	75.2	77.2	22.9	21.5	22.1
China	232.7	178.2	167.8	57.7	55.3	57.2	31.6	30.1	31.2	7.1	6.8	7.0
India	338.1	264.2	255.8	39.8	38.4	38.4	16.2	15.3	15.4	7.6	6.9	6.9
Southeast Asia	89.8	66.9	63.9	29.3	27.7	28.8	20.5	19.5	20.1	3.9	3.8	3.8
South Asia excluding India	168.1	136.8	135.8	15.8	15.4	15.8	4.5	4.5	4.5	3.7	3.6	3.7
Latin America (LA)	94.7	70.2	68.2	30.0	28.7	29.5	29.7	28.5	29.3	12.1	11.4	11.8
Sub-Saharan Africa (SSA)	61.6	39.3	37.9	22.8	19.8	20.9	2.3	2.0	2.1	3.9	3.5	3.7
West Asia/North Africa (WANA)	136.5	105.3	101.3	12.8	12.6	12.7	8.6	8.4	8.5	3.1	3.1	3.2
Developed countries	277.7	229.0	224.1	68.3	66.1	67.2	115.4	111.9	113.7	18.0	17.5	17.8
Developing countries	1,215.7	948.7	918.0	214.6	204.1	209.6	121.9	116.6	119.6	43.3	40.7	41.9
World	1,493.4	1,177.7	1,142.1	282.9	270.2	276.8	237.2	228.6	233.3	61.4	58.1	59.7

Source: IMPACT-WATER projections, 2002.
Notes: Data are annual averages. BAU indicates the business-as-usual scenario; HENV, higher environmental flow; HENV-HE, higher environmental flow and higher irrigation efficiency; and km³, cubic kilometers.

Table 7.10—Irrigation water supply reliability under business-as-usual, high environmental flows, and high environmental flows and high irrigation efficiency scenarios, 1995 and 2021–25

| Region/Country | Irrigation water supply reliability index (IWSR) | | | |
| | 1995 baseline estimates | 2021–25 projections | | |
		BAU	HENV	HENV-HE
Asia	0.83	0.76	0.59	0.73
China	0.87	0.77	0.59	0.73
India	0.80	0.73	0.57	0.71
Southeast Asia	0.87	0.84	0.63	0.77
South Asia excluding India	0.79	0.75	0.61	0.77
Latin America (LA)	0.83	0.74	0.55	0.68
Sub-Saharan Africa (SSA)	0.73	0.71	0.45	0.62
West Asia/North Africa (WANA)	0.78	0.73	0.57	0.65
Developed countries	0.87	0.90	0.74	0.82
Developing countries	0.81	0.75	0.58	0.72
World	**0.82**	**0.77**	**0.61**	**0.74**

Source: IMPACT-WATER assessments and projections, 2002.
Notes: 2021–25 data are annual averages. BAU indicates the business-as-usual scenario; HENV, higher environmental flow; and HENV-HE, higher environmental flow and higher irrigation efficiency.

for HENV and HENV-HE, respectively, compared with BAU. As assumed, however, beneficial crop water consumption under HENV-HE is close to BAU levels (Table 7.7); hence IWSR values under HENV-HE are also close to, although actually lower than, BAU levels (Table 7.10).

Impacts in non-irrigation sectors under HENV compared with BAU are not nearly as noticable; global consumptive use declines by 4 percent in the domestic sector, 4 percent in the industrial sector, and 5 percent for livestock water uses. These impacts are somewhat smaller under HENV-HE; global consumptive use compared with BAU declines by 2 percent in the domestic sector, 2 percent in the industrial sector, and 3 percent in the livestock sector.

Worldwide, HENV provides a dramatic increase in water for the environment; in 2021–25 compared to the BAU, 680 cubic kilometers of water is transferred from withdrawals for irrigation, livestock, domestic, and industrial uses to environmental flows. This additional environmental water is 14 percent of the global withdrawal in 2021–25 under BAU. In developing countries, the increase in environmental flows is 561 cubic kilometers, 16 percent of the developing country withdrawal in 2021–25 under BAU.

In terms of food outputs overall, compared with BAU, production, demand, and prices are greatly affected under HENV; however, the impacts are not significant under HENV-HE because IWSR levels are close to BAU levels. Specifically, total harvested area for cereals in 2021–25 decreases by 15.2 million hectares under

HENV but only 0.3 million hectares under HENV-HE compared with BAU (Table 7.11). Rainfed area increases slightly under HENV but not sufficiently to compensate declines in irrigated area compared with BAU. Globally, the increase in rainfed area almost compensates the decline in irrigated area under HENV-HE.

Developed country harvested area for cereals decreases only slightly under HENV compared with BAU. Rainfed area in developed countries under HENV increases by 0.4 million hectares, while irrigated area decreases by 2 million hectares compared with BAU, causing a slight decrease in overall cereal area. Developing countries fare far worse, with an overall decrease in cultivated area for cereals of 13.6 million hectares under HENV compared with BAU.

Increased global reservation of water for environmental uses affects cereal yields for both irrigated and rainfed areas. Rainfed yields increase slightly under HENV in 2021–25 (1.1 percent) compared with BAU (Table 7.12). Irrigated yields decline by 8.5 percent under HENV, however, compared with BAU. Under HENV-HE, both rainfed and irrigated yields are minimally affected; irrigated yield decreases 2 percent globally, and rainfed yield increases only slightly over BAU levels.

The differences in cereal yield and cultivated area lead to changes in total cereal production under HENV (Table 7.13). Global irrigated production declines significantly (15 percent) while global rainfed production increases only slightly

Table 7.11—Cereal area harvested under business-as-usual, high environmental flows, and high environmental flows and high irrigation efficiency scenarios, 1995 and 2021–25

Region/Country	Rainfed harvested area (million ha)				Irrigated harvested area (million ha)			
	1995 baseline estimates	2021–25 projections			1995 baseline estimates	2021–25 projections		
		BAU	HENV	HENV-HE		BAU	HENV	HENV-HE
Asia	136.9	130.2	130.2	130.7	152.9	167.7	156.2	165.4
China	26.2	29.6	29.5	29.7	62.4	66.6	59.3	63.8
India	62.3	49.8	49.9	50.0	37.8	46.7	45.6	46.7
Southeast Asia	29.8	31.5	31.6	31.6	19.2	20.3	19.6	20.3
South Asia excluding India	5.6	5.6	5.6	5.6	19.9	21.0	19.0	21.1
Latin America (LA)	41.8	55.0	55.4	55.4	7.5	9.8	8.9	9.8
Sub-Saharan Africa (SSA)	69.8	95.5	96.2	96.1	3.3	4.8	4.1	4.5
West Asia/North Africa (WANA)	34.0	35.6	35.4	35.9	9.8	10.9	9.6	10.4
Developed countries	192.1	196.0	196.4	197.3	41.8	45.1	43.1	45.0
Developing countries	282.2	316.1	317.0	317.8	171.3	191.9	177.4	188.7
World	**474.3**	**512.1**	**513.4**	**515.2**	**213.1**	**237.0**	**220.5**	**233.6**

Source: IMPACT-WATER assessments and projections, 2002.
Notes: 2021-25 data are annual averages. BAU indicates the business-as-usual scenario; HENV, higher environmental flow; HENV-HE, higher environmental flow and higher irrigation efficiency; and million ha, million hectares.

Table 7.12—Cereal yield under business-as-usual, high environmental flows, and high environmental flows and high irrigation efficiency scenarios, 1995 and 2021–25

Region/Country	Rainfed yield (mt/ha)				Irrigated yield (mt/ha)			
	1995 baseline estimates	2021–25 projections			1995 baseline estimates	2021–25 projections		
		BAU	HENV	HENV-HE		BAU	HENV	HENV-HE
Asia	1.70	2.46	2.51	2.49	3.23	4.50	4.06	4.43
China	3.59	4.65	4.75	4.70	4.23	5.88	5.42	5.81
India	1.20	1.63	1.68	1.66	2.65	3.82	3.27	3.77
Southeast Asia	1.61	2.47	2.51	2.48	3.05	4.27	3.96	4.18
South Asia excluding India	1.24	1.92	1.90	1.90	2.19	3.28	3.08	3.32
Latin America (LA)	2.07	2.92	2.99	2.95	4.07	5.46	4.97	5.34
Sub-Saharan Africa (SSA)	0.85	1.19	1.23	1.21	2.16	3.08	2.88	2.99
West Asia/North Africa (WANA)	1.40	1.75	1.80	1.77	3.58	4.86	4.97	4.86
Developed countries	3.17	3.89	3.88	3.89	4.44	5.97	5.51	5.79
Developing countries	1.51	2.08	2.13	2.10	3.25	4.53	4.12	4.46
World	**2.18**	**2.77**	**2.80**	**2.79**	**3.48**	**4.80**	**4.39**	**4.72**

Source: IMPACT-WATER assessments and projections, 2002.
Notes: 2021–25 data are annual averages. BAU indicates the business-as-usual scenario; HENV, higher environmental flow; HENV-HE, higher environmental flow and higher irrigation efficiency; and mt/ha, metric tons per hectare.

Table 7.13—Cereal production under business-as-usual, high environmental flows, and high environmental flows and high irrigation efficiency scenarios, 1995 and 2021–25

Region/Country	Rainfed production (million mt)				Irrigated production (million mt)			
	1995 baseline estimates	2021–25 projections			1995 baseline estimates	2021–25 projections		
		BAU	HENV	HENV-HE		BAU	HENV	HENV-HE
Asia	232.6	320.2	326.9	325	493.3	755.3	633.7	733
China	94.0	137.4	139.8	140	263.6	391.6	321.2	371
India	74.6	81.4	83.9	83	100.3	178.3	149.0	176
Southeast Asia	47.9	77.8	79.3	79	58.5	86.6	77.5	85
South Asia excluding India	6.9	10.6	10.5	11	43.6	68.9	58.4	70
Latin America (LA)	86.4	160.6	165.6	163	30.6	53.4	44.4	52
Sub-Saharan Africa (SSA)	59.2	114.1	118.2	116	7.0	14.7	11.7	13
West Asia/North Africa (WANA)	47.5	62.3	63.8	63	34.9	53.0	47.8	51
Developed Countries	608.3	761.6	762.8	768	185.6	269.1	237.3	260
Developing Countries	425.0	656.3	673.6	667	556.7	869.1	730.2	841
World	**1,033.3**	**1,418.0**	**1,436.4**	**1,435**	**742.3**	**1,138.2**	**967.5**	**1,102**

Source: IMPACT-WATER assessments and projections, 2002.
Notes: 2021–25 data are annual averages. BAU indicates the business-as-usual scenario; HENV, higher environmental flow; HENV-HE, higher environmental flow and higher irrigation efficiency; and million mt, million metric tons.

(1 percent) compared with BAU. This increase is insufficient to offset the decline in irrigated production. Again, rainfed and irrigated cereal production under HENV-HE changes only slightly compared with BAU, with global rainfed production increasing by 17 million metric tons (1 percent), irrigated production decreasing by 36.2 million metric tons (3 percent), and total cereal production decreasing by 19.2 million metric tons (less than 1 percent) (see also Box 7.2).

The high environmental water flow scenarios also result in decreases in total cereal demand compared with BAU levels. The decrease is 6 percent under HENV and only 1 percent under HENV-HE (Table 7.14). The developing world experiences the bulk of this decrease—7 percent under HENV and about 1 percent under HENV-HE. Declines are small for developed countries, at 4 percent under HENV

Box 7.2—Irrigation and environmental uses in water scarce basins

The high environmental flow scenario (HENV) has large effects on irrigation water supply and irrigation production in water scarce basins and countries. Compared with BAU, water withdrawals under HENV decline 22 percent in the Haihe, 25 percent in the Yellow, 23 percent in the Indus, and 17 percent in the Ganges river basins, and 14 percent in Egypt. Irrigated production is significantly reduced in these basins, which leads to a decrease in total cereal production, as it proves virtually impossible to make up the difference with rainfed production. Compared with BAU, total cereal production under HENV is reduced by 15 percent in the Haihe, 18 percent in the Yellow, 21 percent in the Indus, and 15 percent in the Ganges river basins, and 14 percent in Egypt.

Combining high environmental flows and high water use efficiency (HENV-HE) leads to considerable improvement in cereal production in the water scarce basins compared with HENV. In the Indus and Ganges, which have relatively more potential for efficiency improvement, higher BE provides enough additional beneficial water use to almost fully compensate for the water diverted to higher environmental flows. But the potential for boosting efficiency is limited for the other water scarce basins because basin efficiencies are already high, and the IWSR and relative irrigated yields remain lower under HENV-HE than BAU. Compared with BAU, the total cereal production under HENV-HE is 12 percent lower in the Haihe, 8 percent in the Yellow, 2 percent in the Indus, and 1 percent in the Ganges river basins, and 5 percent in Egypt.

Table 7.14—Cereal demand under business-as-usual, high environmental flows, and high environmental flows and high irrigation efficiency scenarios, 1995 and 2021–25

Region/Country	1995 baseline estimates	Cereal demand (million mt) 2021–25 projection		
		BAU	HENV	HENV-HE
Asia	794.3	1,205.0	1,125.4	1,192
China	375.0	572.0	540.7	567
India	171.3	268.0	246.0	265
Southeast Asia	113.5	173.0	161.4	171
South Asia excluding India	54.9	99.0	87.6	97
Latin America (LA)	137.4	231.0	212.2	228
Sub-Saharan Africa (SSA)	78.4	159.0	142.4	155
West Asia/North Africa (WANA)	120.2	197.0	186.0	195
Developed countries	686.4	794.0	765.0	792
Developing countries	1,092.2	1,754.0	1,631.6	1,733
World	**1,778.6**	**2,549.0**	**2,396.6**	**2,525**

Source: IMPACT-WATER assessments and projections, 2002.
Notes: 2021–25 data are annual averages. BAU indicates the business-as-usual scenario; HENV, higher environmental flow; HENV-HE, higher environmental flow and higher irrigation efficiency; and million mt, million metric tons.

and only a slight decline under HENV-HE. Prices further affect these demand levels as shown in Figure 7.3. World food prices are significantly larger under HENV but only slightly larger under HENV-HE than under the BAU. HENV prices are significantly higher than for either BAU or HENV-HE, but especially so for rice, where prices increase 73 percent over BAU and HENV levels. Other cereal prices under HENV increase at slightly lower levels, ranging from 49–54 percent.

Net cereal trade in 2021–25 changes only slightly in most regions under HENV and HENV-HE compared with BAU (Figure 7.4). Net imports decrease slightly in developing countries while, correspondingly, net exports decrease slightly in developed countries under both scenarios. The largest impact occurs in China and the Asian region as a whole under HENV, where net imports increase significantly over BAU levels to compensate for declines in food production.

SUMMARY

Irrigation deficits in many basins and countries increase in severity even under BAU, and further decreases in water available for agriculture—be they from increased environmental reservation or reduced groundwater pumping—further reduce agricultural production growth, increase food prices, and reduce food demand.

Figure 7.3—World food prices under business-as-usual, high environmental flows, and high environmental flows and high irrigation efficiency scenarios, 2021–25

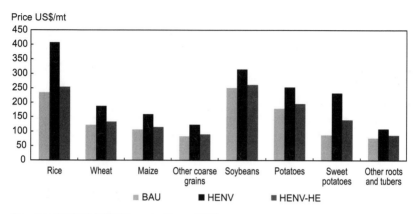

Source: IMPACT-WATER projections, 2002.
Notes: Data are annual averages. BAU indicates the business-as-usual scenario; HENV, higher environmental flow; HENV-HE, higher environmental flow and higher irrigation efficiency; and US$/mt, U.S. dollars per metric ton.

Figure 7.4—Net cereal trade under business-as-usual, high environmental flows, and high environmental flows and high irrigation efficiency scenarios, 2021–25

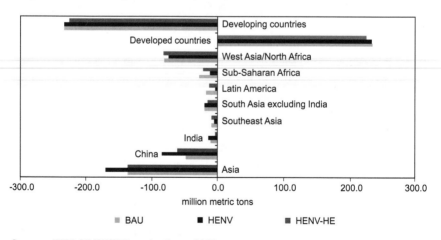

Source: IMPACT-WATER projections, 2002.
Notes: BAU indicates the business-as-usual scenario; HENV, higher environmental flow; HENV-HE, higher environmental flow and higher irrigation efficiency; negative values indicate net imports; positive values, net exports.

The global impact on food production from eliminating groundwater overdraft is relatively small, but the impacts for specific countries and river basins are quite large (see Box 7.1). In China and India, significant reductions in cereal production and consumption are accompanied by increased cereal imports. While the seriousness of these country-level shortfalls in demand and increases in imports should not be minimized, they could very well be a worthwhile tradeoff in restoring sustainability of groundwater supplies. To compensate for reduction in groundwater pumping, agricultural research investments should be increased to boost crop yields, and investment and policy reform—including the elimination of power subsidies for pumping—should be implemented to increase basin efficiency and encourage diversification out of irrigated cereals into crops that give more value per unit of water. This is particularly necessary in the hardest hit river basins such as the Ganges and Yellow River basins.

Irrigation and environmental flow requirements conflict in many regions of the world, and this will only intensify in the future in the absence of more effective policies and investments. HENV shows that reserving an additional 680 cubic kilometers in environmental flow, globally, leads to large reductions in food production and tremendous food price increases. Concerted technological improvements, infrastructure investments, and policy efforts, however, especially directed toward improving basin efficiency, could significantly mitigate these negative effects at a global level as depicted under HENV-HE. Relatively little room exists to improve water use efficiency in the most severely water-scarce basins, however, and food production and farm incomes could fall significantly if water allocated for irrigation is transferred to other uses (see Box 7.2). In these basins, alternative interventions may be required, to compensate farmers for the negative effects of the environmental water diversions including more rapid crop yield growth from agricultural investments, diversification into less water-intensive crops, or broader economic diversification to reduce the relative role of agriculture over time. As shown in Chapter 6, policy reform such as raising water prices in the domestic and industrial sectors to slow the growth in water use would be another option to help balance environmental and irrigation water needs.

NOTES

1. As in previous chapters, BAU and LGW use the climate regime of 1961–90.

2. This lowest threshold is referred to as the resource base by Smakhtin (2002).

Chapter 8

Irrigated and Rainfed Agriculture: Options for Food Production Growth

As already mentioned, world population is expected to reach 7.9 billion by the year 2025. To support this growing population, food production will need to respond to the growing demand. Increases in production could potentially come from increases in irrigated agriculture, which currently produces approximately 40 percent of total cereals, or from increases in rainfed agriculture, which continues to play an important role in total worldwide agricultural production. This chapter presents scenarios dealing with future changes in the growth and levels of investment in both irrigated and rainfed agriculture, along with the impacts these scenarios may have on production, harvested area, demand, prices, water withdrawals, and water use.

INVESTING IN WATER SUPPLY EXPANSION AND EFFICIENCY ENHANCEMENT

As earlier chapters have established, irrigation is the dominant user of water accounting for 72 percent of global water withdrawals, of which 90 percent is used in developing countries. Water availability for irrigation competes in many regions, however, with rapidly increasing nonagricultural water uses in industry, households, and the environment. A portion of the growing demand for water will be met through new investments in irrigation and water supply systems and through improved water management, and some potential exists for the expansion of nontraditional sources of water supply. However, in many arid or semiarid areas—and seasonally in wetter areas—water is no longer abundant, and the high economic and environmental costs of developing new water resources impose limits on supply expansion. Therefore, new supplies may not be sufficient to meet growing demands. As a result, the role of water withdrawals in irrigated agriculture and food security has received substantial attention in recent years. Whether water availability for irrigation—together with feasible production growth in rainfed areas—will provide the food needed to meet the growing demand and improve national and global food security remains a crucial and urgent question for the world.

Low Infrastructure Investment

The low investment in infrastructure scenario (LINV) explores the impact of reduced water supply investments on food production. Comparisons between BAU and LINV in terms of basin efficiency (*BE*), potential irrigated area, increased reservoir storage, and increased maximum allowable surface and groundwater water withdrawal (SMAWW and GMAWW) are presented in Table 8.1. *BE* is lower under LINV than under BAU for all regions, which reduces beneficial crop water consumption by 32 cubic kilometers in the developed world, 147 cubic kilometers in the developing world, and 179 cubic kilometers worldwide. During 1995–2025 under LINV, reservoir storage increases by 40 percent, SMAWW by 35 percent, and GMAWW by 41 percent of the comparable BAU increases.

Global water withdrawals in 2021–25 under LINV increase marginally over the 1995 levels (8 percent), but are 11 percent lower than BAU levels (Table 8.2). The increase is larger in developing countries (10 percent) than in developed countries (3 percent). In contrast, increases over 1995 levels under BAU are 26 percent in developing countries and 11 percent in developed countries.

Table 8.1—Basin efficiency, reservoir storage, and water withdrawal capacity under business-as-usual and low investment in infrastructure scenarios, 1995–2025

Region/Country	Basin efficiency		Storage increase (km³)		SMAWW increase (km³)		GMAWW increase (km³)	
	BAU	LINV	BAU	LINV	BAU	LINV	BAU	LINV
Asia	0.58	0.55	352	156	545	194	64	24
China	0.60	0.55	157	88	180	52	34	11
India	0.63	0.58	135	48	162	54	18	8
Southeast Asia	0.49	0.48	37	12	93	40	10	4
South Asia	0.50	0.49	12	4	72	31	1	0
Latin America (LA)	0.47	0.45	62	21	107	47	14	8
Sub-Saharan Africa (SSA)	0.46	0.44	74	25	68	18	24	10
West Asia/North Africa (WANA)	0.73	0.71	81	27	57	24	3	1
Developed countries	0.69	0.66	44	18	155	47	23	9
Developing countries	0.58	0.55	577	231	772	279	104	43
World	0.60	0.57	621	249	926	326	126	52

Source: IMPACT-WATER projections and assessments, 2002.
Notes: BAU indicates the business-as-usual scenario; LINV, the low investment in infrastructure scenario; and km³, cubic kilometers.

Table 8.2—Total water withdrawal under business-as-usual and low investment in infrastructure scenarios, 1995 and 2021–25

	Total water withdrawal (km³)		
	1995 baseline estimates	2021–25 projections	
Region/Country		BAU	LINV
Asia	1,952.7	2,419.8	2,138.9
China	678.8	843.6	729.2
India	674.4	822.0	742.4
Southeast Asia	203.1	278.3	234.8
South Asia excluding India	353.0	416.0	381.3
Latin America (LA)	297.8	402.3	342.4
Sub-Saharan Africa (SSA)	128.4	206.9	150.3
West Asia/North Africa (WANA)	236.1	294.0	260.1
Developed countries	1,144.2	1,271.6	1,182.0
Developing countries	2,761.9	3,480.6	3,043.8
World	**3,906.1**	**4,752.1**	**4,225.8**

Source: IMPACT-WATER assessments and projections, 2002.
Notes: 2021–25 data are annual averages. BAU indicates the business-as-usual scenario; LINV, the low investment in infrastructure scenario; and km³, cubic kilometers.

LINV has significant negative impacts on irrigation water consumption. Globally it falls by 240 cubic kilometers (16 percent) compared with BAU (Table 8.3). Global consumptive use in all other sectors is also lower under LINV with decreases of 4 percent for the domestic sector, 3 percent for the industrial sector, and 5 percent for livestock compared with BAU. The difference between BAU and LINV once again is greater in developing countries, where irrigation water consumption is 17 percent lower, while developed country consumption is 13 percent lower than under BAU. Consumption in the other three sectors in Table 8.3 ranges from 4 to 6 percent lower than BAU in developing countries and from 2 to 3 percent lower in developed countries.

Worldwide irrigated harvested cereal area in 2021–25 falls by 18.8 million hectares under LINV compared with BAU (Table 8.4), while rainfed harvested cereal area under LINV is 8.4 million hectares larger than under BAU. This results in a global decrease in harvested cereal area of 10.4 million hectares. Irrigated harvested cereal area under LINV increases only slightly over the 1995 levels, at 5.1 million hectares over the period. The impact on irrigated area is felt much more in developing than in developed countries; by 2021–25 LINV results in 9 percent less irrigated area in developing countries and 2 percent less in developed countries compared with BAU.

Irrigated cereal yields under LINV decline slightly compared with BAU. Globally, irrigated yield declines by 0.2 metric tons per hectare by 2021–25 and by

Table 8.3—Consumptive water use by sector under business-as-usual and low investment in infrastructure scenarios, 2021–25

| Region/Country | Consumptive water use (km³) | | | | | | | |
| | Irrigation | | Domestic | | Industrial | | Livestock | |
	BAU	LINV	BAU	LINV	BAU	LINV	BAU	LINV
Asia	842.2	712.0	146.3	141.0	78.8	75.5	22.9	21.5
China	232.7	186.1	57.7	55.8	31.6	30.4	7.1	6.9
India	338.1	298.9	39.8	38.2	16.2	15.3	7.6	6.9
Southeast Asia	89.8	66.9	29.3	27.8	20.5	19.5	3.9	3.7
South Asia excluding India	168.1	150.0	15.8	15.6	4.5	4.5	3.7	3.7
Latin America (LA)	94.7	68.9	30.0	28.8	29.7	28.5	12.1	11.4
Sub-Saharan Africa (SSA)	61.6	37.3	22.8	19.6	2.3	2.0	3.9	3.4
West Asia/North Africa (WANA)	136.5	115.8	12.8	12.7	8.6	8.5	3.1	3.1
Developed countries	277.7	241.8	68.3	66.5	115.4	112.4	18.0	17.6
Developing countries	1,215.7	1,011.7	214.6	204.7	121.9	117.0	43.3	40.9
World	1,493.4	1,253.4	282.9	271.3	237.2	229.4	61.4	58.4

Source: IMPACT-WATER projections, 2002.
Notes: Data are annual averages. BAU indicates the business-as-usual scenario; LINV, the low investment in infrastructure scenario; and km³, cubic kilometers.

Table 8.4—Cereal area harvested under business-as-usual and low investment in infrastructure scenarios, 1995 and 2021–25

| Region/Country | Rainfed harvested area (million ha) | | | Irrigated harvested area (million ha) | | |
| | 1995 baseline estimates | 2021–25 projections | | 1995 baseline estimates | 2021–25 projections | |
		BAU	LINV		BAU	LINV
Asia	136.9	130.2	131.5	152.9	167.7	154.2
China	26.2	29.6	29.8	62.4	66.6	58.7
India	62.3	49.8	50.2	37.8	46.7	42.2
Southeast Asia	29.8	31.5	31.9	19.2	20.3	19.8
South Asia excluding India	5.6	5.6	5.6	19.9	21.0	20.5
Latin America (LA)	41.8	55.0	56.2	7.5	9.8	8.2
Sub-Saharan Africa (SSA)	69.8	95.5	96.9	3.3	4.8	3.4
West Asia/North Africa (WANA)	34.0	35.6	36.4	9.8	10.9	9.8
Developed countries	192.1	196.0	199.7	41.8	45.1	44.0
Developing countries	282.2	316.1	320.8	171.3	191.9	174.2
World	474.3	512.1	520.5	213.1	237.0	218.2

Source: IMPACT-WATER assessments and projections, 2002.
Notes: 2021–25 data are annual averages. BAU indicates the business-as-usual scenario; LINV, the low investment in infrastructure scenario; and million ha, million hectares.

Table 8.5—Cereal yield under business-as-usual and low investment in infrastructure scenarios, 1995 and 2021ñ25

Region/Country	Rainfed yield (mt/ha)			Irrigated yield (mt/ha)		
	1995 baseline estimates	2021ñ25 projections		1995 baseline estimates	2021ñ25 projections	
		BAU	LINV		BAU	LINV
Asia	1.7	2.5	2.5	3.2	4.5	4.3
China	3.6	4.6	4.8	4.2	5.9	5.6
India	1.2	1.6	1.7	2.7	3.8	3.8
Southeast Asia	1.6	2.5	2.5	3.1	4.3	4.1
South Asia excluding India	1.2	1.9	1.9	2.2	3.3	3.3
Latin America (LA)	2.1	2.9	3.0	4.1	5.5	5.2
Sub-Saharan Africa (SSA)	0.8	1.2	1.2	2.2	3.1	3.1
West Asia/North Africa (WANA)	1.4	1.8	1.8	3.6	4.9	4.9
Developed countries	3.2	3.9	3.9	4.4	6.0	5.7
Developing countries	1.5	2.1	2.1	3.2	4.5	4.4
World	**2.2**	**2.8**	**2.8**	**3.5**	**4.8**	**4.6**

Source: IMPACT-WATER assessments and projections, 2002.
Notes: 2021ñ25 data are annual averages. BAU indicates the business-as-usual scenario; LINV, the low investment in infrastructure scenario; and mt/ha, metric tons per hectare.

0.3 and 0.1 metric tons per hectare in developed and developing countries, respectively (Table 8.5). Rainfed yield remains the same as under BAU for virtually all regions. With a decline in irrigated yield and area from lower water use per hectare, global irrigated cereal production drops by 124.2 million metric tons under LINV compared with BAU (Table 8.6); irrigated production in developing countries decreases 12 percent, and in developed countries it decreases 6 percent.

The fall in production results in dramatic price increases for cereals by 2021–25 compared with BAU. Rice prices are the most sensitive to changes in water availability among the cereals, and increase by 35 percent under LINV (Figure 8.1). Maize prices are 28 percent higher and wheat prices 25 percent higher under LINV. The increase in cereal prices raises incentives for expanded rainfed crop area. Rainfed cereal area increases by 8.4 million metric tons under LINV and production increases by 49.1 million metric tons, partially offsetting the drop in irrigated production (Tables 8.4 and 8.6).

The rising food prices projected in these scenarios depress food demand and worsen food security by widening the food supply and demand gaps for developing countries. Across the globe, cereal demand is 79.1 million metric tons lower in 2021–25 under the LINV scenario compared with BAU (Table 8.7). The

Table 8.6—Cereal production under business-as-usual and low investment in infrastructure scenarios, 1995 and 2021–25

Region/Country	Rainfed production (million mt)			Irrigated production (million mt)		
	1995 baseline estimates	2021–25 projections		1995 baseline estimates	2021–25 projections	
		BAU	LINV		BAU	LINV
Asia	232.6	320.2	331.1	493.3	755.3	668.4
China	94.0	137.4	141.7	263.6	391.6	331.6
India	74.6	81.4	84.7	100.3	178.3	160.1
Southeast Asia	47.9	77.8	80.3	58.5	86.6	80.4
South Asia excluding India	6.9	10.6	10.8	43.6	68.9	66.8
Latin America (LA)	86.4	160.6	168.7	30.6	53.4	43.0
Sub-Saharan Africa (SSA)	59.2	114.1	119.5	7.0	14.7	10.6
West Asia/North Africa (WANA)	47.5	62.3	65.4	34.9	53.0	47.7
Developed countries	608.3	761.6	783.2	185.6	269.1	252.7
Developing countries	425.0	656.3	683.9	556.7	869.1	761.3
World	**1,033.3**	**1,418.0**	**1,467.1**	**742.3**	**1,138.2**	**1,014.0**

Source: IMPACT-WATER assessments and projections, 2002.
Notes: 2021–25 data are annual averages. BAU indicates the business-as-usual scenario; LINV, the low investment in infrastructure scenario; and million mt, million metric tons.

Figure 8.1—World food prices under business-as-usual and low investment in infrastructure scenarios, 1995 and 2021–25

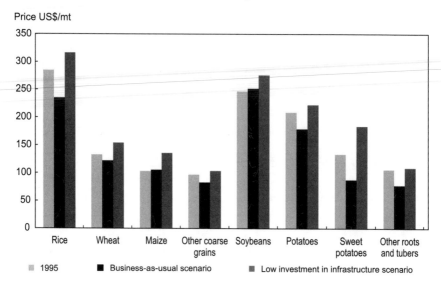

Source: IMPACT-WATER projections, 2002.
Notes: Data are annual averages. US$/mt indicates U.S. dollars per metric ton.

Table 8.7—Cereal demand under business-as-usual and low investment in infrastructure scenarios, 1995 and 2021–25

Region/Country	Cereal demand (million mt)		
	1995 baseline estimates	2021–25 projections	
		BAU	LINV
Asia	794.3	1,205.3	1,161.1
China	375.0	571.9	553.9
India	171.3	268.5	256.3
Southeast Asia	113.5	172.9	166.4
South Asia excluding India	54.9	98.6	92.5
Latin America (LA)	137.4	231.0	220.4
Sub-Saharan Africa (SSA)	78.4	158.8	149.4
West Asia/North Africa (WANA)	120.2	196.6	191.3
Developed countries	686.4	794.2	783.1
Developing countries	1,092.2	1,754.4	1,686.3
World	1,778.6	2,548.5	2,469.4

Source: IMPACT-WATER assessments and projections, 2002.
Notes: 2021–25 data are annual averages. BAU indicates the business-as-usual scenario; LINV, the low investment in infrastructure scenario; and million mt, million metric tons.

majority of this decrease is in developing countries—68.1 million metric tons compared with 11.1 million metric tons in developed countries. Net cereal imports into developing countries increase by an average of 16 million metric tons per year under LINV during 2021–25 (Figure 8.2). At local and regional levels, these price increases could significantly affect poor consumers in developing countries by reducing their incomes and increasing malnutrition given many poor consumers spend a large part of their income on food. Higher international prices also have national level effects because poor countries allocate increasing resources to import large portions of their food.

GETTING MORE FROM RAINFED AGRICULTURE

While irrigation is important in many parts of the world, further expansion of rainfed agriculture will also be crucial to future agricultural growth. Emphasizing increased yields rather than expanding harvested area in rainfed agriculture is essential in most of the world because many environmental problems can develop from further expansion of rainfed production into marginal areas. Biodiversity losses can develop from the clearing of areas for agriculture as many native plants may be lost, and disease and pest problems may also develop through ecosystem alterations. Soil erosion is a particular concern in marginal areas such as hillsides and arid areas where agricultural expansion often occurs in the developing world. Three primary ways to enhance rainfed cereal yields without expanding harvested area are examined in

Figure 8.2—Net cereal trade under business-as-usual and low investment in infrastructure scenarios, 1995 and 2021–25

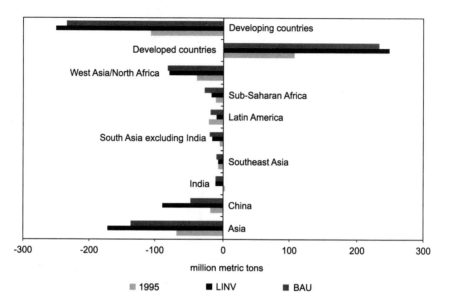

Source: IMPACT-WATER assessments and projections, 2002.
Notes: 2021–25 data are annual averages. Negative net trade indicates imports.

this section including increasing effective rainfall use through improved water management, particularly water harvesting; increasing crop yields in rainfed areas through agricultural research; and reforming policies and increasing investments in rainfed areas.

These methods are represented by the following scenarios, developed to determine the contribution of rainfed agriculture to total food production under low levels of irrigation development and water supply investment.

1) The no improvement in effective rainfall use scenario (NIER), which assumes no improvement in effective rainfall use, compared with the 3–5 percent increase in effective rainfall use assumed under BAU.

2) The low investment in infrastructure but higher increase of rainfed area and yield scenario (LINV-HRF), which adds the dimension of high increases in rainfed area and yield to the LINV scenario discussed above. To examine the potential for rainfed production growth to compensate the effect of reductions in irrigated area and irrigation water supply, we assume that rainfed area and

yield increase to levels that can almost offset the reduction of irrigated production and maintain essentially the same international trade prices. A larger increase is assigned to rainfed yield than area (because of limited potential for area expansion), and a larger increase is assigned to those basins, countries, or regions where irrigation effects are greater.

3)   The low investment in infrastructure but high increase of effective rainfall use scenario (LINV-HIER) looks at the possibility of increasing effective rainfall use to counteract the reduction of irrigated production resulting from low investment in irrigation development and water supply. Effective rainfall use gradually increases by 10–15 percent above 1995 levels from 1995 to 2025 in those basins/countries with rainwater shortages for crop production, including river basins in the western United States, northern and western China, northern and western India, and West Asia and North Africa (WANA). An increase of 5–10 percent is projected for other regions.

Water Harvesting

Water harvesting can increase effective rainfall use by concentrating and collecting rainwater from a larger catchment area onto a smaller cultivated area. The runoff can either be diverted directly and spread on the fields or collected in some way to be used at a later time. Water harvesting techniques include external catchment systems, microcatchments, and rooftop runoff collection, the latter of which is used almost exclusively for nonagricultural purposes. External catchment water harvesting involves the collection of water from a large area a substantial distance from where crops are being grown. Types of external catchment systems include runoff farming, which involves collecting runoff from the hillsides onto flat areas, and floodwater harvesting within a streambed using barriers to divert stream flow onto an adjacent area, thus increasing infiltration of water into the soil. Microcatchment water harvesting methods are those in which the catchment area and cropped area are distinct but adjacent to each other. Some specific microcatchment techniques include contour or semicircular bunds, and meskat-type systems in which the cropped area is immediately below the catchment area that has been stripped of vegetation to increase runoff. (See Rosegrant et al. 2002 for a more extensive discussion of these methods).

While many water harvesting case studies and experiments have shown increases in yield and water use efficiency on experimental plots and some individual farms, it is not clear whether the widespread use of these technologies is feasible. Construction and maintenance costs of water harvesting systems, particularly the labor costs, are very important in determining whether a technique will be widely adopted at the individual farm level. The initial high labor costs of building the water harvesting structure often provide disincentives for adoption (Tabor 1995). The initial labor costs for construction generally occur in the dry season when labor is cheaper but also scarce given worker migration; maintenance costs, on the other hand often occur in the rainy season when labor costs are higher because of competition with conventional agriculture. Thus, while many case studies of water harvesting methods show positive results, these methods have yet to be widely adopted by farmers. Some projects may require inputs that are too expensive for some farmers to supply. In addition, many farmers in arid or semi-arid areas do not have the manpower available to move the large amounts of earth necessary in some of the larger water harvesting systems.

In addition to water harvesting, the use of improved farming techniques has been suggested to help conserve soil and make more effective use of rainfall. Conservation tillage measures such as minimum till and no till have been tested in some developing countries. Precision agriculture, which has been used in the United States, has also been suggested for use in developing countries. Along with research on integrated nutrient management, applied research to adapt conservation tillage technologies for use in unfavorable rainfed systems in developing countries could have a large positive impact on local food security and increased standards of living.

Agricultural Research to Improve Rainfed Cereal Yields

A common perception is that rainfed areas did not benefit much from the Green Revolution, but breeding improvements have enabled modern varieties to spread to many rainfed areas. Over the past 10–15 years most of the area expansion through use of modern varieties has occurred in rainfed areas, beginning first with wetter areas and proceeding gradually to more marginal ones (Byerlee 1996). In the 1980s, modern varieties of the major cereals spread to an additional 20 million hectares in India, a figure comparable to adoption rates at the height of the Green Revolution (1966–75). Three quarters of the more recent adoption took place on rainfed land, and adoption rates for improved varieties of maize and wheat in rainfed environments are approaching those in irrigated areas (Byerlee 1996).

Although adoption rates of modern varieties in rainfed areas are catching up with irrigated areas, the yield gains in rainfed areas remain lower. The high heterogeneity and erratic rainfall of rainfed environments make plant breeding a difficult task. Until recently, potential cereal yield increases appeared limited in the less favorable rainfed areas with poor soils and harsh environmental conditions. However, recent evidence shows dramatic increases in yield potential in even drought-prone and high temperature rainfed environments. For example, the yield potential for wheat in less favorable environments increased by more than 2.5 percent per year between 1979 and 1995, far higher than the rates of increase for irrigated areas (Lantican and Pingali 2002). A change in breeding strategy to directly target rainfed areas, rather than relying on "spill-in" from breeding for irrigated areas was a key to this faster growth.

Both conventional and nonconventional breeding techniques are used to increase rainfed cereal yields. Three major breeding strategies include research to increase harvest index, plant biomass, and stress tolerance (particularly drought resistance). The first two methods increase yields by altering the plant architecture, while the third focuses on increasing the ability of plants to survive stressful environments. The first of these may have only limited potential for generating further yield growth because of physical limitations, but considerable potential exists in the latter two. For example the "New Rice for Africa," a hybrid between Asian and African species, was bred to fit the rainfed upland rice environment in West Africa. It produces over 50 percent more grain than current varieties when cultivated in traditional rainfed systems without fertilizer. In addition to higher yields, these varieties mature 30–50 days earlier than current varieties and are far more disease and drought tolerant than previous varieties (WARDA 2000).

If agricultural research investments can be sustained, the continued application of conventional breeding and the recent developments in nonconventional breeding offer considerable potential for improving cereal yield growth in rainfed environments. Cereal yield growth in farmers' fields will come both from incremental increases in the yield potential in rainfed and irrigated areas and from improved stress resistance in diverse environments, including improved drought tolerance (together with policy reform and investments to remove constraints to attaining higher yield potential, as discussed in the next section). The rate of growth in yields will be enhanced by extending research both downstream to farmers and upstream to the use of tools derived from biotechnology to assist conventional breeding, and, if concerns over risks can be solved, to the use of transgenic breeding.

Participatory plant breeding plays a key role for successful yield increases through genetic improvement in rainfed environments (particularly in dry and remote areas). Farmer participation in the very early stages of selection helps to fit the crop to a multitude of target environments and user preferences (Ceccarelli, Grando, and Booth 1996; Kornegay, Beltran, and Ashby 1996). Participatory plant breeding may be the only possible type of breeding for crops grown in remote regions, where a high level of diversity is required within the same farm, or for minor crops that are often neglected by formal breeding (Ceccarelli, Grando, and Booth 1996).

To assure effective breeding for high stress environments, the availability of diverse genes is essential. It is therefore important that the tools of biotechnology, such as marker-assisted selection and cell and tissue culture techniques, be employed for crops in developing countries, even if these countries stop short of true transgenic breeding. To date, however, application of molecular biotechnology has been limited to a small number of traits of interest to commercial farmers, mainly developed by a few life science companies operating at a global level. Very few applications with direct benefits to poor consumers or to resource-poor farmers in developing countries have been introduced—although the New Rice for Africa described above may pave the way for future use of biotechnology tools to aid breeding for breakthroughs beneficial to production in developing countries. Much of the science and many tools and intermediate products of biotechnology are transferable to solve high priority problems in the tropics and subtropics, but it is generally agreed that the private sector will not invest sufficiently to make the needed adaptations in these regions. Consequently, national and international public sectors will have to play a key role in the developing world, mainly by accessing proprietary tools and products from the private sector. However, there has been little detailed analysis of the incentives and mechanisms by which such public-private partnerships can be realized (Byerlee and Fischer 2000).

Policy Reform and Infrastructure Investment in Rainfed Areas

Cereal yields can also be increased through improved policies and increased investment in areas with exploitable yield gaps (the difference between the genetic yield potential and actual farm yields). Such exploitable gaps may be relatively small in high intensity production areas such as most irrigated areas, where production equal to 70 percent or more of the yield gap is achieved (Cassman 1999). However, with yield potential growing significantly in rainfed environments exploitable yield gaps are considerably higher in rainfed areas, because remoteness, poor policies, and a lack of investments have often isolated these regions from access to output and input markets, so farmers face depressed prices for their crops and high prices or lack of availability of inputs. Riskier soil and water conditions in less favorable areas also depress yields compared with their potential.

Emerging evidence shows that the right kinds of investments can boost agricultural productivity far more effectively than previously thought in many less-favored lands. Increased public investment in many less-favored areas may have the potential to generate competitive, if not greater, agricultural growth on the margin than comparable investments in many high-potential areas, and could have a greater impact on the poverty and environmental problems of the less-favored areas in which they are targeted (Hazell, Jagger, and Knox 2000). Although rainfed areas differ greatly from region to region based on the physical and climatic characteristics of the area, certain development strategies may commonly work in many rainfed areas. Key strategies include the improvement of technology and farming systems, ensuring equitable and secure access to natural resources, ensuring effective risk management, investment in rural infrastructure, providing a policy environment that doesn't discriminate against rainfed areas, and improving the coordination among farmers, NGOs, and public institutions (Rosegrant and Hazell 2000).

Improvements in Rainfed Agriculture

Changes in rainfed yields through improved water management, advancements in agricultural research, and policy reform affect water use and crop production as well as overall contributions of irrigated and rainfed agriculture to total food production. The future outlook for water and food is dependent on policy and investment decisions on agricultural research, irrigation, water supply infrastructure, and other water resource investments, as well as the pace of water demand management improvement and farmers' decisions regarding onfarm management and adoption of new technologies. But what would happen if improvements in effective rainfall use lagged, or there were significant cutbacks in irrigation development and water supply investments? Could more rapid growth in rainfed crop production compensate for reductions in irrigation and water supply investment compared with BAU? Through alternative scenarios, we explore the impacts of these changes and other modifications in policy, technology, and investment.

Rainfed Agriculture Scenario Results

The three scenarios discussed here illustrate the impacts of low irrigation investments and different levels of effective rainfall use and rainfed area and yield on water use and crop production. The amount of irrigation water used under NIER is the same as that used under BAU (Table 8.3). Irrigation water consumption under the two scenarios with improved rainfed agriculture (LINV-HRF and LINV-HIER) declines by 16 percent (240 cubic kilometers) compared with BAU.

The cultivated area using irrigated and rainfed harvesting techniques differs among the three scenarios as well. The amount of rainfed harvested area under NIER is 17.2 million hectares less than under BAU, which has a greater increase in effective rainfall use (Table 8.8). The majority of this decline occurs in developed countries. However, in the low investment in irrigation development and water supply scenarios (again, LINV-HRF and LINV-HIER), an increase in rainfed harvested area occurs. Compared with BAU, this increase is 10.1 million hectares under LINV-HRF, and 27.2 million hectares under LINV-HIER. A slight majority of this area increase occurs in developing countries for both LINV-HRF and LINV-HIER.

Rainfed yields increase under both LINV-HRF and LINV-HIER compared with BAU (Table 8.9). The largest increase in global rainfed yield occurs under

Table 8.8—Rainfed and irrigated cereal area harvested under various scenarios, 2021–25

Region/Country	Rainfed area (million ha)				Irrigated area (million ha)			
	BAU	NIER	LINV-HRF	LINV-HIER	BAU	NIER	LINV-HRF	LINV-HIER
Asia	130.2	126.0	137.1	138.2	167.7	168.2	160.2	161.5
China	29.6	28.4	31.8	31.2	66.6	66.8	60.1	60.4
India	49.8	48.8	51.7	51.9	46.7	46.8	46.4	46.8
Southeast Asia	31.5	30.2	32.8	33.5	20.3	20.3	20.1	20.4
South Asia excluding India	5.6	5.6	6.1	5.6	21.0	21.1	20.7	20.9
Latin America (LA)	55.0	53.4	55.5	59.8	9.8	9.8	8.9	9.0
Sub-Saharan Africa (SSA)	95.5	95.4	94.9	96.7	4.8	4.8	3.7	3.7
West Asia/North Africa (WANA)	35.6	34.1	36.0	36.6	10.9	10.8	10.1	10.3
Developed countries	196.0	186.1	198.7	208.2	45.1	45.6	43.8	44.0
Developing countries	316.1	308.8	323.4	331.1	191.9	192.3	181.6	183.0
World	**512.1**	**494.9**	**522.2**	**539.3**	**237.0**	**237.9**	**225.4**	**227.0**

Source: IMPACT-WATER projections, 2002.
Notes: Data are annual averages. BAU indicates the business-as-usual scenario; NIER, the no improvement in effective rainfall use scenario; LINV-HRF, the low investment in irrigation development and water supply but high increases in rainfed area and yield scenario; LINV-HIER, the low investment in irrigation development and water supply but high increase of effective rainfall use scenario; and million ha, million hectares.

LINV-HRF (11 percent). LINV-HIER produces a somewhat smaller increase (3 percent). With no improvement in effective rainfall use (NIER) rainfed yields decline by 1 percent compared with BAU, while irrigated yields increase slightly.

Total cereal production decreases under NIER by 41 million metric tons compared with BAU (rainfed production reduces by 59 million metric tons, partially offset by an increase of 18 million metric tons in irrigated areas through higher cereal prices). The reduction of rainfed cereal production is most significant in China, Latin America (LA), Sub-Saharan Africa (SSA), and WANA, where decreases are in the 3–5 percent range (Table 8.10). All these regions have large areas of low rainfall rainfed cereal production. The worldwide share of rainfed cereal production declines slightly from 56 percent under BAU to 54 percent under NIER.

Under LINV-HRF, increasing rainfed area and yield can offset low irrigation and water supply investment globally, although some specific regions may not be able to increase production enough to compensate the loss in irrigated area (see Box 8.1). Worldwide, this scenario estimates a net increase of 34 million metric tons of cereal production compared with BAU. China, however, is unable to increase rainfed production enough to offset the irrigated production decline because the

Table 8.9—Rainfed and irrigated cereal yield under various scenarios, 2021–25

Region/Country	Rainfed yield (mt/ha)				Irrigated yield (mt/ha)			
	BAU	NIER	LINV-HRF	LINV-HIER	BAU	NIER	LINV-HRF	LINV-HIER
Asia	2.46	2.47	2.96	2.49	4.50	4.56	4.05	4.13
China	4.65	4.63	5.36	4.67	5.88	5.97	5.33	5.43
India	1.63	1.65	1.99	1.68	3.82	3.86	3.43	3.49
Southeast Asia	2.47	2.50	2.98	2.54	4.27	4.30	3.88	3.95
South Asia excluding India	1.92	1.83	2.51	1.99	3.28	3.32	3.09	3.15
Latin America (LA)	2.92	2.92	3.13	3.08	5.46	5.53	4.85	4.92
Sub-Saharan Africa (SSA)	1.19	1.16	1.22	1.30	3.08	3.14	2.95	2.99
West Asia/North Africa (WANA)	1.75	1.73	1.93	1.89	4.86	4.85	4.55	4.61
Developed countries	3.89	3.88	4.24	3.95	5.97	6.04	5.54	5.59
Developing countries	2.08	2.06	2.36	2.18	4.53	4.58	4.09	4.16
World	**2.77**	**2.75**	**3.07**	**2.86**	**4.80**	**4.86**	**4.37**	**4.43**

Source: IMPACT-WATER projections, 2002.
Notes: Data are annual averages. BAU indicates the business-as-usual scenario; NIER, the no improvement in effective rainfall use scenario; LINV-HRF, the low investment in irrigation development and water supply but high increases in rainfed area and yield scenario; LINV-HIER, the low investment in irrigation but high increase of effective rainfall use scenario; and mt/ha, metric tons per hectare.

dominant share of total cereal harvested area is irrigated. In developed countries, irrigated production is less affected by low irrigation investment, so those countries can make up for the developing country decrease through increased rainfed production. Under LINV-HRF, developed country irrigated production declines by 27 million metric tons, while rainfed production increases by 80 million metric tons. The share of rainfed production increases significantly to 62 percent globally, 51 percent in developing countries, and 78 percent in developed countries, compared with 56, 43, and 74 percent respectively under BAU (Table 8.11).

While increases in rainfed area and yield may be able to offset reductions in irrigation investments, results under LINV-HIER show that the projected increase in effective rainfall water use cannot fully compensate the irrigation decline because of the low investment in irrigation development and water supply. Although global rainfed cereal production under LINV-HIER is 126 million metric tons more than that under BAU, total net cereal production is 5 million metric tons lower. In developing countries, the net decrease in overall production is 42 million metric tons. Although there is no reliable data to justify the potential increase of effective rainfall use in various regions of the world, we think the very large projected increase under LINV-HIER would be difficult, if not impossible, to achieve. As under LINV-HRF, the share of rainfed production also increases under LINV-HIER,

Table 8.10—Rainfed and irrigated cereal production under various scenarios, 2021–25

Region/Country	Rainfed production (million mt)				Irrigated production (million mt)			
	BAU	NIER	LINV-HRF	LINV-HIER	BAU	NIER	LINV-HRF	LINV-HIER
Asia	320	311	405	344	755	767	649	666
China	137	132	170	146	392	398	320	328
India	81	81	103	87	178	181	159	164
Southeast Asia	78	76	98	85	87	87	78	81
South Asia excluding India	11	10	15	11	69	70	64	66
Latin America (LA)	161	156	174	184	53	54	43	44
Sub-Saharan Africa (SSA)	114	111	115	126	15	15	11	11
West Asia/North Africa (WANA)	62	59	70	69	53	53	46	47
Developed countries	762	723	842	822	269	275	242	246
Developing countries	656	636	763	722	869	881	742	761
World	**1,418**	**1,359**	**1,605**	**1,544**	**1,138**	**1,156**	**985**	**1,007**

Source: IMPACT-WATER projections, 2002.
Notes: Data are annual averages. BAU indicates the business-as-usual scenario; NIER, the no improvement in effective rainfall use scenario; LINV-HRF, the low investment in irrigation development and water supply but high increases in rainfed area and yield scenario; LINV-HIER, the low investment in irrigation development and water supply but high increase of effective rainfall use scenario; and million mt, million metric tons.

Table 8.11—Proportion of rainfed cereal production under various scenarios, 2021–25

Region/Country	Proportion of rainfed production (%)			
	BAU	NIER	LINV-HRF	LINV-HIER
Asia	29.8	28.8	38.4	34.1
China	25.9	24.9	34.7	30.8
India	31.3	30.9	39.3	34.7
Southeast Asia	47.3	46.6	55.7	51.2
South Asia excluding India	13.8	12.5	19.0	14.3
Latin America (LA)	75.2	74.3	80.2	80.7
Sub-Saharan Africa (SSA)	88.4	88.1	91.3	92.0
West Asia/North Africa (WANA)	53.9	52.7	60.3	59.5
Developed countries	73.9	72.4	77.7	77.0
Developing countries	43.0	41.9	50.7	48.7
World	**55.5**	**54.0**	**62.0**	**60.5**

Source: IMPACT-WATER projections, 2002.
Notes: Data are annual averages. BAU indicates the business-as-usual scenario; NIER, the no improvement in effective rainfall use scenario; LINV-HRF, the low investment in irrigation development and water supply but high increases in rainfed area and yield scenario; and LINV-HIER, the low investment in irrigation development and water supply but high increase of effective rainfall use scenario.

Box 8.1—Irrigated and rainfed production in selected water scarce basins

Low investment in irrigation leads to declining water withdrawals, irrigation water supply reliability (IWSR), and relative irrigated yields in water scarce areas. Compared with BAU, water withdrawals decline by 5 percent in the Haihe, 15 percent in the Yellow, 13 percent in the Indus, and 7 percent in the Ganges river basins under LINV, and 9 percent in Egypt. IWSR also declines somewhat in all of the water scarce areas under LINV, ranging from 18 percent in the Yellow River basin to 6 percent in the Ganges River basin compared with BAU. Relative irrigated cereal yields also decline under each of the low investment in irrigation scenarios, with the greatest drops occurring under LINV-HRF and LINV-HIER. These reductions in irrigated cereal yields lead to decreased irrigated cereal production across the low investment scenarios.

The LINV-HRF and LINV-HIER scenarios attempt to compensate for the loss in irrigated production by increasing rainfed production through higher rainfed yield and area growth and greater improvements in rainfall harvesting. Under these scenarios, relative rainfed yields and the contribution of rainfed crops to total production increase compared with BAU. However, because of low rainfall, it is impossible to compensate for the irrigated production loss in Egypt under LINV-HRF and LINV-HIER because most of its cropland is irrigated. In the Haihe basin, cereal production is higher under LINV-HRF than under BAU, while production declines in the remaining water-scarce basins. Production is projected to decrease 5 percent in the Yellow, 10 percent in the Indus, and 3 percent in the Ganges River basins, and 10 percent in Egypt. Under LINV-HIER, none of the basins or countries is able to produce enough additional food from rainfed agriculture to compensate for the irrigated production loss from low irrigation and water supply investment. Compared with BAU, cereal production declines by 3 percent in the Haihe, 7 percent in the Yellow, 12 percent in the Indus, and 7 percent in the Ganges River basins, and 7 percent in Egypt. It is clear from these results that irrigation is critical in these basins and countries, and additional contributions from rainfed agriculture may be effective but the impacts will not be enough to offset the loss in irrigated cereal production. Production shifts toward higher-valued, less water intensive crops could help to reduce the negative impacts on farmers in these water scarce basins.

Table 8.12—World food prices under various scenarios, 2021–25

Region/Country	World food prices (US$/mt)			
	BAU	NIER	LINV-HRF	LINV-HIER
Rice	235	247	232	276
Wheat	122	140	113	126
Maize	106	120	100	108
Other coarse grains	83	100	74	79

Source: IMPACT-WATER projections, 2002.
Notes: Data are annual averages. BAU indicates the business-as-usual scenario; NIER, the no improvement in effective rainfall use scenario; LINV-HRF, the low investment in irrigation development and water supply but high increases in rainfed area and yield scenario; LINV-HIER, the low investment in irrigation development and water supply but high increase of effective rainfall use scenario; and (US$/mt), U.S. dollars per metric ton.

although to a lesser degree. Globally, the percentage of rainfed production increases by 5 percent, with increases of 6 and 3 percent in the developing and developed world, respectively (Table 8.11).

Both NIER and LINV-HIER show significant increases in world cereal prices compared with BAU (Table 8.12). Under NIER, in which the small increase in effective rainfall use under BAU is eliminated, world prices increase by 5 percent for rice, 15 percent for wheat, 13 for maize, and 20 percent for other grains compared with their BAU equivalents. Under LINV-HRF—with a strategy of offsetting the reduction in irrigation investment by investing in rainfed area development and increased yield—world prices are lower than under BAU for all cereal crops, with a small decline for rice (1 percent) and a larger decline for other cereals (6–11 percent). World prices for rice, wheat and maize under LINV-HIER are higher than those under BAU, with an especially large 17 percent increase for rice.

SUMMARY

As shown in the scenarios presented in this Chapter, a decline in investment in irrigation and water supply infrastructure reduces production growth and sharply increases world cereal prices, causing negative impacts in low-income developing countries. An important question facing the world is can we compensate the loss of crop production from falling investment with increased rainfed crop production if—as is expected—irrigation input is lower? Analysis in this chapter indicates great potential for increasing rainfed production.

Drops in irrigated area and yield under LINV resulted in decreased production, which would lead to sharply increasing food prices, negatively impacting the poor in developing countries. The LINV-HIER and LINV-HRF scenarios show the importance of rainfed agriculture in attempting to offset irrigated production losses by increasing rainfed production. While rainfed production did increase under LINV-HIER, the level was not sufficient to fully counter the decline in irrigated production. Rainfed production under LINV-HRF was able to offset irrigated production declines globally, but in certain regions where a large percentage of cereal area is irrigated, once again the rainfed production increase could not make up the deficit.

These scenarios show that rainfed agriculture will continue to be important in ensuring food production growth in the future. Combined with emerging insights from the literature on rainfed agriculture, the results here point to a strategy for investments and policy reform to enhance the contribution of rainfed agriculture. Water harvesting has the potential to improve rainfed crop yields in some regions, and could provide farmers with improved water availability (Bruins, Evenari, and Nessler 1986) and increased soil fertility in some local and regional ecosystems, as well as environmental benefits through reduced soil erosion. Nevertheless, despite localized successes, broader farmer acceptance of water harvesting techniques has been limited because of high implementation costs and greater short-term risk from additional inputs and cash and labor requirements (Rosegrant et al. 2002; Tabor 1995). Water harvesting initiatives frequently suffer from lack of hydrological data, insufficient planning regarding important social and economic considerations, and the absence of a long-term government strategy to ensure the sustainability of interventions. Greater farmer involvement at the planning stages for maintenance and data collection, and provision of appropriate educational and extension support could help expand the contribution of water harvesting (Oweis, Hachum and Kijne 1999).

The rate of investment in crop breeding targeted to rainfed environments is crucial to future cereal yield growth. Strong progress has been made in breeding for enhanced crop yields in rainfed areas, even in the more marginal rainfed environments (Byerlee, Heisey and Pingali 1999; Lantican and Pingali 2002). The continued application of conventional breeding and the recent developments in nonconventional breeding offer considerable potential for improving cereal yield growth in rainfed environments. Cereal yield growth in rainfed areas could be further improved by extending research both downstream to farmers (Ceccarelli, Grando, and Booth 1996) and upstream to the use of tools derived from biotechnology to assist conventional breeding, and, if concerns over risks can be solved, from the use of transgenic breeding.

Crop research targeted to rainfed areas should be accompanied by increased investment in rural infrastructure and policies to close the gap between potential yields in rainfed areas and the actual yields achieved by farmers. Important policies include higher priority for rainfed areas in agricultural extension services and access to markets, credit, and input supplies (Rosegrant and Hazell 2000). Successful development of rainfed areas is likely to be more complex than in high-potential irrigated areas because of their relative lack of access to infrastructure and markets, and their more difficult and variable agroclimatic environments. Investment, policy reform, and transfer of technology to rainfed areas, such as water harvesting, will therefore require stronger partnerships between agricultural researchers, local organizations, farmers, community leaders, NGOs, national policymakers, and donors (Rosegrant and Hazell 2000). Progress in rainfed agriculture may also be slower than in the early Green Revolution because new approaches will need to be developed for specific environments and tested on a small scale before wide dissemination, but as shown here, enhanced rainfed crop production growth would be an important source of water savings.

Chapter 9

Implications for the Future: Meeting the Challenge of Water Scarcity

Irrigation is, and will remain, the largest single user of water, but its share of world water consumption is projected to decline from 80 percent in 1995 to 72 percent in 2025 under the business-as-usual scenario (BAU). Economic expansion, population growth, and urbanization will drive demand in the non-irrigation sectors including domestic, industrial, and livestock water demand, which will increase by 62 percent over 1995 levels. In developing countries, non-irrigation water demand will grow even faster, increasing 100 percent between 1995 and 2025. Irrigation water consumption will grow by only 9 percent globally and 12 percent in developing countries because of limited growth in water supply and priority allocation for drinking water and industrial water uses. For the first time in world history, water demand for nonagricultural uses is growing more rapidly in absolute terms than water demand for agriculture. Compared with 1995, global water withdrawal in 2025 declines by 3 percent under the sustainable water use scenario (SUS) and by 36 percent under the water crisis scenario (CRI), according to our projections.

Growing water scarcity in response to rapid domestic and industrial water demand growth, particularly in the developing countries, is worsened by often severe constraints on the water supply. These constraints can be caused, first, by source limits—meaning absolute constraints on water supply—in some dry and highly developed regions including areas of northern China, northwestern India, the western United States, and much of West Asia and North Africa (WANA),[1] and, second, by economic constraints that slow the growth of new water supply infrastructure including dams and water distribution systems. These economic constraints are the result of the high financial, social, and environmental costs of dams, irrigation infrastructure, and domestic and industrial water supply.

Given water supply growth is limited but domestic and industrial water demand is growing rapidly, a significant share of the additional water for domestic and industrial uses will come from the irrigation sector. This transfer will lead to a substantial increase in water scarcity for irrigation, shown by the irrigation water supply reliability index (IWSR), which measures the availability of water relative to full water demand for irrigation. In developing countries, IWSR values decline from 0.81 in 1995 to 0.75 in 2025 under BAU, and in water-scarce basins the decline will be steeper. Increasing water scarcity for agriculture not only limits crop area expansion but also slows irrigated cereal yield growth in developing countries. This fall in the relative crop yield represents an annual yield loss through increased water stress of 0.68 metric tons per hectare in 2025, or an annual cereal production loss of 130 million metric tons. The increasing water scarcity—especially for irrigation— occurs virtually worldwide, but hotspots of extreme water scarcity increases exist including the Indus river basin in India, the Haihe and Yellow river basins in northern China, basins in northwestern China, Egypt, and WANA, and important U.S. food producing basins including the Colorado, Rio Grande, and Texas Gulf basins. Nationally and locally, the decline in irrigated production growth is projected to create food deficits and income losses in regions that depend heavily on irrigation. Globally, the decline reduces the contribution of irrigated production to future food production growth. Under BAU, irrigated production contributes 50 percent of the additional food produced between 1995 and 2025.

Water scarcity could severely—and easily—worsen if policy and investment commitments from national governments and international donors and development banks weaken further. The low investment scenario (LINV) leads to significant declines in irrigation water supply reliability and rising food prices; the water crisis scenario (CRI), under which current trends in water policy and investment deteriorate more broadly, results in the breakdown of domestic water service for hundreds of millions of people, devastating losses of wetlands, dramatic reductions in food production, and skyrocketing food prices that force declining per capita food consumption in much of the world. Uncertainty about increases in industrial and domestic demand, in terms of water-saving technology improvements, policy reform, and political will, could induce non-irrigation water demand to grow even faster than projected, further compounding water scarcity.

Water scarcity can induce increases in food prices and, hence, decreases in food demand. As shown under CRI, major cereal crop prices could more than double BAU projections, significantly reducing food demand especially in developing countries; per capita cereal demand in developing countries could actually drop below 1995 levels. Moreover, price increases have an even larger impact on low-income consumers because food represents such a large proportion of their real incomes and therefore can lead to increased malnutrition as well. Developing countries may experience additional impacts from food price increases through pressure on foreign exchange reserves, inflation, and impacts on macroeconomic stability and investment. Policy reform including agricultural research and management in rainfed areas and changes in the management of irrigation and water supplies would help to circumvent these price effects.

Excessive flow diversion and groundwater overdrafting have already caused environmental problems in many regions of the world. Our analysis shows that problems—locally and globally—will likely worsen in the future. Under current investment plans and with the continuation of recent trends in the water and food sectors, further expansion of environmental uses of water would require reductions in consumption of irrigation water and/or domestic and industrial water. Thus, in the absence of policy and investment reform, water for the environment and for food production will increasingly conflict in many parts of the world. The global decrease in environmental flows under CRI is about 1,490 cubic kilometers compared with SUS—equivalent to five times the annual flow of the Mississippi River and 20 times the annual flow of the Yellow River.

The criticality ratio—the ratio of water withdrawal to total renewable water— is a broad indicator of environmental water stress. High criticality ratios (values above 0.40) signify more intensive use of river basin water, a high probability of lower water availability and quality, and absolute water shortages during low flow periods. This ratio is globally low—only 0.08 in 1995 and 0.10 in 2025—because the global value includes water abundant countries such as Brazil and Canada that together account for 25 percent of the world's renewable freshwater. But environmental water stress is much higher, and is increasing rapidly, in critical areas in China, India, the United States, WANA, and elsewhere at local levels. In the U.S. Rio Grande and Colorado basins, the 1995 criticality ratio is close to 1.5 and remains constant at that high level until 2025 under BAU projections. In China, between 1995 and 2025, the Yellow River basin ratio increases from 0.9 to 1.2, the Haihe basin increases from 1.4 to 1.6, the Indus basin in India increases from 0.7 to 0.9, and in WANA the ratio increases from 0.7 to 0.9.

Even small increases in the criticality ratio may have large impacts on the environment given that usable water for both environmental purposes and offstream consumption is only a small fraction of the total renewable water in some regions because most natural runoff is inaccessible even with large water storage. In addition, the real conflict between water uses and committed environmental flows often occurs in dry periods or periods with large water requirements when the criticality ratio is higher than the annual average.

Nevertheless, the analysis here also points to cause for hope. The various scenarios explored in this book point to three broad strategies that could address the challenge posed by the increasing water scarcity for food production:

1) Increasing the supply of water for irrigation, domestic, and industrial purposes through investment in infrastructure;

2) Conserving water and improving the efficiency of water use in existing systems through water management and policy reform; and

3) Improving crop productivity per unit of water and land through integrated water management and agricultural research and policy efforts, including crop breeding and water management for rainfed agriculture.

INVESTMENT IN INFRASTRUCTURE AND WATER SUPPLY

Although the financial, environmental, and social costs are high for new water supply projects, the selective expansion of water supply capacities, including storage and withdrawal capacities, is still necessary in some regions, especially in developing countries. Storage and water distribution systems such as water lift projects and canals are particularly needed for Sub-Saharan Africa (SSA), some countries in South and Southeast Asia (such as India, Bangladesh, and Viet Nam), and some countries in Latin America. In Bangladesh, storage is needed to reduce the high variance in water supply reliability. Infrastructure constraints will cause water shortages of as much as 60–70 percent in some basins in western and northwestern India after 2015, especially because of insufficient reservoir storage, and the same problem may occur in some basins in south and east India where internal rainfall distribution is uneven. Latin American countries such as Mexico and Argentina will require more storage for intra and interyear regulation after 2010. Thus, hard infrastructure investment has a role to play in the future in some regions but a reduced one compared with past trends, when dam-building and expansion of irrigated area drove rapid increases in irrigated area and crop yields particularly in developing countries.

New investments are increasingly expensive and politically sensitive, however, and appear to have relatively low payoffs. Still, some of the increasing demand for water must be met from carefully selected, economically efficient development of new water, both through impoundment of surface water and sustainable exploitation of groundwater resources, and through expansion in the development of non-traditional water sources.[2] Future construction of irrigation and water supply projects will require balanced development approaches that are acceptable to diverse constituencies. The full social, economic, and environmental costs of development must be considered, but so must the costs of failure to develop new water sources. Project design must ensure comprehensive accounting of full costs and benefits, including not only irrigation benefits but also health, household water use, and catchment improvement benefits. Of utmost importance is improved design and implementation of compensation programs for those who are displaced or negatively affected by water projects.

Sustainable development of groundwater resources also offers significant opportunities for many countries and regions where groundwater extraction remains below natural recharge, including southern China; central, western, and eastern SSA; much of Southeast Asia; and localized regions elsewhere. Groundwater irrigation is more flexible than surface water irrigation and can be used in conjunction with surface water to improve water use efficiency. Conjunctive use of surface and groundwater could be expanded significantly by (1) using wells for supplemental irrigation when canal water is inadequate or unreliable to reduce moisture stress and maximize irrigated crop yields; (2) pumping groundwater into canals to augment the canal water resources, lower the water table, and reduce salinity; and (3) viewing a canal command and its imbedded tubewells as an integrated system thereby optimizing joint use of canal and groundwater resources (Oweis and Hachum 2001; Frederiksen, Berkoff, and Barber 1993). But care must be taken in any expansion of groundwater because the actual extent of groundwater storage and recharge is poorly understood in most developing countries. In many regions, increased investment in exploration and evaluation of aquifer properties such as geometry, boundary and hydraulic characteristics, and recharge rates (including spatial and temporal variability) would have high payoffs.

WATER MANAGEMENT AND POLICY REFORM

Our results show that the most promising avenue for addressing water shortfalls into the future is water management and incentive policy reform to enhance the efficiency of existing water use, supported by infrastructure investment to modernize and upgrade existing irrigation and water delivery systems. As is shown in this book, feasible improvements in basin-scale irrigation water use efficiency can compensate—on a global scale—for reduced irrigation resulting from (1) phasing out groundwater overdraft worldwide; (2) increasing committed environmental flows; (3) raising water prices for agricultural use; and (4) reducing irrigated area development. Further, improving irrigation water use efficiency is shown to be an effective measure for increasing water productivity. In severely water-scarce basins, however, relatively little room exists for improving water use efficiency, and food production and farm incomes could fall significantly if water for irrigation is transferred to other uses. In these basins, governments will need to compensate for the negative impact of growing water scarcity on agriculture by alternative means, such as investing in agriculture to obtain more rapid growth in crop yields, promoting the diversification of farming into less water-intensive crops, and diversifying the economy to reduce the economic role of agriculture over time.

The institutional, technical, and financial feasibility of significant improvements in river basin efficiency in specific river basins requires site-specific research and analysis. Basin efficiency depends on improvements in water-saving technologies and infrastructure and in the institutions governing water allocation, water rights, and water quality. In the industrial sector in developing countries, the amount of water used to produce a given amount of output is far higher than in developed countries. Industrial water recycling could be a major source of water savings in many countries, however. Many industrial water users may be able to decrease their water use by at least 50 percent through water recycling methods (Beekman 1998). Cooling water accounts for more than half the industrial water used and has been one of the major sources for water recycling. Greater adoption of technology for re-circulation of cooling water in developing country factories would reduce the amount of water needed in many industrial processes. In many cases, the cooling water can then be decontaminated and used again for other purposes such as cleaning or landscape irrigation (Beekman 1998). Progress has been made in the urban areas of some water-scarce developing countries. In Beijing, for example, the rate of water recycling increased from 61 percent in 1980 to 72 percent in 1985; and between 1977 and 1991, total industrial water use declined steadily while output increased by 44 percent in real terms (Nickum 1994). Aggressive adoption of such recycling technology could be encouraged by regulations on allowable industrial water discharge and increased prices for water.

In the domestic water sector as well, considerable potential exists for improving water use efficiency. This may include anything from leak detection and repair in municipal systems to installation of low flow showerheads and low water or waterless toilets. It is sometimes argued that water savings from domestic water consumption are not possible because the fraction of water withdrawn actually consumed is small, and most of the water "lost" from systems is reused elsewhere. But a reduction in withdrawals directly saves consumptive use of water in coastal cities—which account for a significant share of the developing (and developed) world's population—where water withdrawn is lost to the oceans. Reduced water withdrawals, which reduce water reuse, also improve water quality, which effectively increases water supply by preventing a proportion of water from reaching such poor quality that it cannot be reused. Reducing withdrawals also generates economic benefits from reduced water treatment and recycling costs as it flows through the river basin (Gleick et al. 2002; Rosegrant 1997).

Reuse of domestic wastewater also has the potential to save freshwater and improve basin efficiency. Treated wastewater can be used for a variety of nonpotable purposes including landscape and recreational irrigation, maintaining urban stream flows and wetlands, and toilet flushing. Other important uses can include wastewater-fed aquaculture and the irrigation of agricultural and forest crops, which can be beneficial in fertilizing crops with wastewater nutrients, reducing overall amounts of chemical fertilizer used and reduce the need for additional pollution control.

Shuval (1990) points to the possible positive economic effects of wastewater reuse for agricultural irrigation by assisting in (water and nutrient) resource conservation, and helping to reduce environmental pollution. Although the reuse of reclaimed wastewater for irrigation has potential benefits, great caution is needed to ensure that water quality is acceptable and that poor quality water is not used to irrigate food for human consumption (particularly those foods that are eaten raw). The rate of expansion of treated wastewater reuse will depend on the quality of the wastewater, public acceptance, and cost-effectiveness. Given the relatively high cost of wastewater treatment, it is likely that treated wastewater could contribute an important share of agricultural water supply only in arid regions where the cost of new water supplies has become very high; nonagricultural uses of treated wastewater are likely to grow faster for the foreseeable future.

Improvements in the irrigation sector to increase water use efficiency must be made at the technical, managerial, and institutional levels. Technical improvements include advanced irrigation systems such as drip irrigation, sprinklers, conjunctive use of surface and groundwater, and precision agriculture, such as computer monitoring of crop water demand. Managerial improvements can include the adoption of demand-based irrigation scheduling systems and improved equipment maintenance. Institutional improvements may involve establishing effective water user associations and water rights, the introduction of water pricing, and improvements in the legal environment for water allocation.

Key to inducing higher water efficiency gains in all sectors is introducing market (or market-style) incentives into water use decisionmaking. Incentive prices for water could have a major impact on water withdrawals and consumptive use in irrigation and urban water uses, thus freeing water for environmental use. As the high price scenario (HP) shows in Chapter 6, even though the water price elasticity of demand is quite low for irrigation, increasing water prices from the low levels prevailing in most countries generates substantial water savings because the total amount of water used in irrigation is so high. The results show that significant water savings are also possible from domestic and industrial uses. A large backlog of water-saving technology for industry in developing countries could come into play with the right incentives. Water savings through incentive policies could provide a significant increase in water for environmental uses. In most regions, the reduction of irrigation water supply through high prices could be balanced with increased irrigation water use efficiency at the basin scale, eliminating the negative impact of high prices on food security.

Nevertheless, implementing policies to increase water prices is politically difficult and could have negative impacts on poor consumers and farmers if badly designed or implemented. But in the domestic and industrial sectors, improving both efficiency and equity through increased water prices is feasible and would provide incentives for conservation, cover the costs of delivery, and generate adequate revenues to finance the needed growth in supplies and expanded coverage of clean piped water. Generalized subsidies should be replaced with subsidies targeted to the poor; other policies, such as increasing block tariffs, could help to ensure water availability to low-income users without direct subsidies. This type of tariff structure has a very low per unit price for water up to a specified volume, after which users pay a higher price for volumetric blocks up to the highest level of consumption. In this way, high-income households that use more water cross subsidize low-income users.

The design of effective and equitable water pricing for agriculture is more difficult. Imposing large increases in administered water prices does not work. High water prices are likely to reduce farm incomes severely (Rosegrant et al. 2000; Perry 2001; Löfgren 1996). Moreover, in existing irrigation systems, the prevailing (formal or informal) water rights significantly increase the value of irrigated land. Water rights holders correctly perceive the imposition of water prices, or an increase in existing prices, as expropriation of those rights, reducing the value of land in established irrigation farms. Attempts to establish or increase water prices are thus met with strong opposition from irrigators (Rosegrant and Binswanger 1994). Finally, implementation of water prices at the farm level is difficult because, with irrigation in much of the developing world consisting of large systems that serve many small farmers, measuring and monitoring deliveries to large numbers of end users—as would be required to charge by volume of water use—is too costly.

Despite these difficulties, it is feasible to design and implement water pricing systems based on water rights that would introduce incentives for efficient water use, recover at least O&M costs, and at the same time protect and even increase farm incomes. For example, a "charge-subsidy" scheme (Pezzey 1992) would establish incentives to use water efficiently without reducing farm incomes and appears to be politically and administratively feasible. A base water right would be established at major turnouts to water user groups or privately run irrigation sub-units (rights could be assigned directly to individual irrigators where administratively feasible). The user group would be responsible for internal water allocation. Subsequently, the base water right would be set based on historical allocation—but likely somewhat lower than the historical allocation in water-scarce basins. A fixed base charge would be applied to this quantity, sufficient to cover O&M and longer term asset replacement (depreciation) costs. For demand greater than the base water right, users would be charged an efficiency price equal to the value of water in alternative uses; for demand below the base right, the same price would be paid to the water user.

The establishment of base water rights would increase the political feasibility of water pricing by formalizing existing water rights rather than being seen as an expropriation of these rights. With efficiency prices paid only on marginal demand above or below the base right, nonpunitive incentives are introduced. Reliance on water user associations to manage water "below the turnout" improves local account-ability, transparency, and the flexibility of water allocation. Information costs would be reduced because local irrigators with expert knowledge of the value of water would bear the costs and generate the necessary information on the value and opportunity costs of water below major turnouts. Reform of water pricing policy in developing countries faces many technical, administrative, and political con-straints, but with increasing water scarcity and declining financial resources avail-able for irrigation and water resource development, reform of water pricing is essential. For both urban and agricultural water, innovative and pragmatic water pricing reform that introduces incentives for efficient use and enhances cost recov-ery while improving equity in water allocation is feasible. Agricultural water pric-ing reform that establishes water rights for users, such as suggested above, would be particularly beneficial, protecting farmers against capricious changes in water allo-cation, ensuring that they benefit from more efficient water use, and in the longer term providing a basis for water trading among farmers and across sectors, further enhancing water use efficiency.

CROP PRODUCTIVITY AND RAINFED AGRICULTURE

Rainfed agriculture emerges from the analysis as a potential key to sustainable development of water and food. Rainfed agriculture still produces about 60 percent of total cereals. Results under BAU show that rainfed agriculture will continue to play an important role in cereal production, contributing half the total increase of cereal production between 1995 and 2025. SUS shows an even higher contribu-tion to the total increase of cereal production by rainfed agriculture. Improved water management and crop productivity in rainfed areas would relieve considerable pressure on irrigated agriculture and on water resources; however, this would be con-tingent on increased investment in research and technology transfer for rainfed areas.

Water harvesting has the potential in some regions to improve rainfed crop yields, and could provide farmers with improved water availability and increased soil fertility in some local and regional ecosystems, as well as environmental benefits through reduced soil erosion. However, greater involvement of farmers from the planning stages and the use of farmers for maintenance and data collection and pro-vision of appropriate educational and extension support are still needed to expand the contribution of water harvesting.

The rate of investment in crop breeding targeted to rainfed environments is cru-cial to future crop yield growth. Strong progress has been made in breeding for enhanced crop yields in rainfed areas, even in more marginal rainfed environments. Continued application of conventional breeding and recent developments in non-conventional breeding offer considerable potential for improving cereal yield growth in rainfed environments. Cereal yield growth in rainfed areas could be further improved by extending research both downstream to farmers and upstream to the use of tools derived from biotechnology to assist conventional breeding, and, if concerns over risks can be solved, to the use of transgenic breeding.

Higher priority for agricultural extension services and access to markets, credit, and input supplies should be given in rainfed areas because successful development of rainfed areas is likely to be more complex than in high-potential irrigated areas given their relative lack of access to infrastructure and markets, and their more difficult and variable agroclimatic environments. Progress may also be slower than in the early Green Revolution because new approaches will need to be developed for specific environments and tested on a small scale prior to broad dissemination. Investment in rainfed areas, policy reform, and transfer of technology, such as water harvesting, will therefore require stronger partnerships between agricultural researchers and other agents of change, including local organizations, farmers, community leaders, NGOs, national policymakers, and donors.

SUMMARY

A large part of the world is facing severe water scarcity. With a continued worsening of water supply and demand trends and water policy and investment performance, water scarcity could become a fully fledged crisis with severe impacts on food production, health, nutrition, and the environment. But solutions to potential water crisis are available, including increasing the supply of water for irrigation, domestic, and industrial purposes through highly selective investments in infrastructure. Even more important, however, are water conservation and water use efficiency improvements in existing irrigation and water supply systems through water management reform, policy reform, and investment in advanced technology and infrastrucure; and improving crop productivity per unit of water and land through integrated efforts in water management and agricultural research and policy, emphasizing crop breeding and water management in rainfed agriculture. The appropriate mix of water policy and management reform and investments, and the feasible institutional arrangements and policy instruments to be used must be tailored to specific countries and basins and will vary across underlying conditions and regions including levels of development, agroclimatic conditions, relative water scarcity, level of agricultural intensification, and degree of competition for water. These solutions are not easy, and will take time, political commitment, and money. One thing is certain; the time to act on fundamental reform of the water sector is now.

NOTES

1. In low rainfall years, for example, water withdrawal in WANA will be significantly higher than the total renewable water in the region, including inflows from other regions.

2. As noted in the opening chapter, nontraditional water sources such as desalination of salt water and brackish water are highly unlikely to make a large contribution to the global water supply over the next several decades. Even an extremely high 20 percent growth in production of desalinated water per year would only account for 1.5 percent of water withdrawal by 2025. Desalination will play an important role in alleviating local water shortages, but even with declining production costs, desalination growth will primarily provide drinking water in coastal regions of countries that are both highly water scarce and relatively wealthy.

References

Alcamo, J. P. 2000. Personal communications on global change and global scenarios of water use and availability: An application of water GAP. Kassel, Germany: Center for Environmental System Research (CESR), University of Kassel.

Alcamo, J., P. Döll, F. Kaspar, and S. Siebert. 1998. *Global change and global scenarios of water use and availability: An application of water GAP 1.0.* Kassel, Germany: Center for Environmental System Research (CESR), University of Kassel.

Alcamo, J., T. Henrichs, and T. Rösch. 2000. World water in 2025: Global modeling and scenario analysis for the world commission on water for the 21st century. Kassel World Water Series Report No. 2. Kassel, Germany: Center for Environmental Systems Research, University of Kassel.

Allan, J. A. 1996. Water security policies and global systems for water scarce regions. In *Sustainability of irrigated agriculture—Transactions, Vol. 1E. Special session: The future of irrigation under increased demand from competitive uses of water and greater needs for food supply—R.7; Symposium: Management information systems in irrigation and drainage.* International Commission on Irrigation and Drainage (ICID) Sixteenth Congress on Irrigation and Drainage, held in Cairo, Egypt, 1996. New Delhi, India: ICID.

Allen, R. G., L. S. Pereira, D. Raes, and M. Smith. 1998. *Crop evapotranspiration, guidelines for computing crop water requirements.* FAO Irrigation and Drainage Paper No. 56. Rome: Food and Agriculture Organization of the United Nations.

Asante, K. 2000. Approaches to continental scale river flow routing. Ph.D. thesis, University of Texas, Austin, U.S.A.

Barker, R., and J. W. Kijne. 2001. Improving water productivity in agriculture: A review of literature. Background paper prepared for SWIM Water Productivity Workshop, November 2001, International Water Management Institute (IWMI), Colombo, Sri Lanka.

Batchelor, C. 1999. Improving water use efficiency as part of integrated catchment management. *Agricultural Water Management* 40 (2): 249–263.

Beckett, J. L., and J. W. Oltjen. 1993. Estimation of the water requirement for beef production in the United States. *Journal of Animal Science* 71 (4) (April): 818–826.

Beekman, G. B. 1998. Water conservation, recycling and reuse. *Water Resources Development* 14 (3): 353–364.

Berbel, J., and J. A. Gomez-Limon. 2000. The impact of water-pricing policy in Spain: An analysis of three irrigated areas. *Agricultural Water Management*. 43: 219–238.

Berger, T. 1994. The independent review of the Sardar Sarovar projects 1991–1992. *Water Resources Development* 10 (1): 55–66.

Bhatia, R., and M. Falkenmark. 1993. Water resource policies and the urban poor: Innovative approaches and policy imperatives. *Water and Sanitation Currents*. United Nations Development Programme and World Bank Water and Sanitation Program. Washington, D.C.: World Bank.

Bird, J., and P. Wallace. 2001. Dams and water storage. Brief No. 7 in *2020 Focus 9: Overcoming water scarcity and quality constraints*. R. S. Meinzen-Dick and M. W. Rosegrant, eds. Washington, D.C.: International Food Policy Research Institute.

Biswas, A. K., J. I. Uitto, and M. Nakayama. 1998. *Sustainable development of the Ganges-Brahmaputra basins*. International Water Resources Association. <Http://www.iwra.siu.edu/committee/ganges-forum.html> accessed June 2002.

Bos, E., and G. Bergkamp. 2001. Water and the environment. In *2020 Focus 9: Overcoming water scarcity and quality constraints*. R. S. Meinzen-Dick and M. W. Rosegrant, eds. Washington, D.C.: International Food Policy Research Institute.

Brown, L. 2000. Falling water tables in China may soon raise food prices everywhere. World Watch Institute. Earth Policy Alerts. <Http://www.earth-policy.org/Alerts/Alert1.htm>. Accessed March 2002.

Bruins, H. J., M. Evenari, and U. Nessler. 1986. Rainwater-harvesting agriculture for food production in arid zones: The challenge of the African famine. *Applied Geography* 6 (1): 13–32.

Byerlee, D. 1996. Modern varieties, productivity and sustainability. *World Development* 24 (4): 697–718.

Byerlee, D., and K. Fischer. 2000. *Accessing modern science: Policy and institutional options for agricultural biotechnology in developing countries.* Agricultural Knowledge and Information Systems (AKIS) Discussion Paper. Washington, D.C.: World Bank.

Byerlee, D., P. Heisey, and P. Pingali. 1999. Realizing yield gains for food staples in developing countries in the early 21st century: Prospects and challenges. Paper presented to the study week on "Food Needs of the Developing World in the Early 21st Century," The Vatican, January 27–30.

Cai, X. 1999. Irrigated and rainfed crop area and yield. International Food Policy Research Institute, Washington, D.C. Mimeo.

Cai, X., and M. W. Rosegrant. 2002. Global water demand and supply projections. Part 1: A modeling approach. *Water International* 27 (3): 159–169.

Cai, X., and M. W. Rosegrant. 1999. Irrigated and rainfed crop area and yield in China, India, and the U.S. International Food Policy Research Institute, Washington D.C. Mimeo.

Carpenter, S., P. Pingali, E. Bennett, and M. Zurek. 2002. Background document for the scenarios working group meeting "Millenium Ecosystem Assessment," held in Tlaxcala, Mexico, February.

Carter, T. R., M. L. Parry, H. Harasawa, and S. Nishioka. 1994. *Intergovernmental Panel on Climate Change (IPCC): Technical guidelines for assessing climate change impacts and adaptations with a summary for policy makers and a technical summary.* London and Japan: Department of Geography, University College London, and Center for Global Environmental Research, National Institute for Environmental Studies.

Cassman, K. G. 1999. Ecological intensification of cereal production systems: Yield potential, soil quality, and precision agriculture. *Proceedings of the National Academy of Sciences of the United States of America* 96 (11): 5952–5959.

Caswell, M., and D. Zilberman. 1986. The effects of well depth and land quality on the choice of irrigation technology. *American Journal of Agricultural Economics* 68: 798–811.

Caswell, M., and D. Zilberman. 1985. The choices of irrigation technologies in California. *American Journal of Agricultural Economics* 67: 224–234.

Ceccarelli, S., S. Grando, and R. H. Booth. 1996. International breeding programmes and resource-poor farmers: Crop improvement in difficult environments. In *Participatory plant breeding.* P. Eyzaguire and M. Iwanaga, eds. Proceedings of a work shop on participatory plant breeding, held in

Wageningen, The Netherlands, July 26–29, 1995. Rome: International Plant Genetics Research Institute.

CMWR (Chinese Ministry of Water Resources). 2002. *Annual reports from major river basins in 2001.* Beijing: CMWR. <Http://www.mwr.gov.cn/english/index.htm> accessed January 2002.

CMWR (Chinese Ministry of Water Resources). 1990 to 1998. *China's water resources annual book.* Beijing: China Water Resources and Hydropower Press.

Cosgrove, W. J., and F. Rijsberman. 2000. *World Water Vision: Making water everybody's business.* London: World Water Council, World Water Vision, and Earthscan.

CRU (Climate Research Unit). 1998. Global Climate Data. CD Rom. East Anglia, U.K.: The University of East Anglia.

Curtin, F. 2000. Transboundary impacts of dams: Conflict prevention strategies. Discussion note prepared for the world commission on dams. Green Cross International, Geneva.

Dalhuisen, J. M., R. J. G. M. Florax, H. L. F. de Groot, and P. Nijkamp. 2002. *Price and income elasticities of water demand: Why empirical estimates differ.* Tinbergen Institute Discussion Paper TI 2001–057/3. Amsterdam: Tinbergen Institute.

de Fraiture, C., and C. Perry. 2002. Why is irrigation water demand inelastic at low price ranges? Paper presented at the workshop, "Irrigation Water Policies: Micro and Macro Considerations" held in Agadir, Morocco, June 15–17, 2002.

de Haen, H. 1997. Environmental consequences of agricultural growth in developing countries. In *Sustainability, growth, and poverty alleviation.* S. A. Vosti and T. Reardon, eds. Baltimore, Md., U.S.A.: Johns Hopkins University Press.

de Moor, A., and P. Calamai. 1997. *Subsidizing unsustainable development: Undermining the earth with public funds.* San Jose, Costa Rica: Earth Council. <Http://www.ecouncil.ac.cr/econ/sud/> accessed July 2002.

Dialogue on Water and Climate. 2002. *Dialogue on water and climate in the Yellow River Basin (China).* Wageningen, the Netherlands: International Secretariat of the Dialogue on Water and Climate Science Support Office.

Dinar, A., and A. Subramanian. 1997. *Water pricing experiences: An international perspective.* World Bank Technical Paper No. 386. Washington, D.C.

Dinar, A., T. K. Balakrishnan, and J. Wambia. 1998. *Political economy and political risks of institutional reform in the water sector.* World Bank Working Paper No. 1987. Washington, D.C.

Doorenbos, J., and A. H. Kassam. 1979. *Crop yield vs. water.* FAO Irrigation and Drainage Paper No. 33. Rome: Food and Agriculture Organization of the United Nations.

Doorenbos, J., and W. O. Pruitt. 1977. *Crop water requirement.* FAO Irrigation and Drainage Paper No. 24. Rome: Food and Agriculture Organization of the United Nations.

Easter, K. W., M. W. Rosegrant, and A. Dinar (eds.). 1998. *Markets for water: Potential and performance.* Boston: Kluwer Academic Publishers.

ECOSOC (United Nations Economic and Social Council). 1997. *Comprehensive assessment of the freshwater resources of the world.* Report No. E/CN17/1997/9. Geneva: Commission on Sustainable Development.

ESCAP (United Nations Economic and Social Commisssion for Asia and the Pacific). 1995. *Guidebook to water resources, use and management in Asia and the Pacific.* Water Resources Series No. 74. New York: United Nations.

Espey, M., J. Espey, and W. D. Shaw. 1997. Price elasticity of residential demand for water: A meta-analysis. *Water Resources Research* 33 (6): 1369–1374.

FAO (Food and Agriculture Organization of the United Nations). 2002. The salt of the earth: Hazardous for food production. World Food Summit Five Years Later. <Http://www.fao.org/worldfoodsummit/english/newsroom/focus/focus1.htm> accessed July 2002.

——. 2000. FAOSTAT database. <Http://apps.fao.org/>.

——. 1999. *Irrigated harvested cereal area for developing countries.* Preliminary data based on work in progress for Agriculture: Towards 2015/30. Technical Interim Report. Global Perspective Studies Unit, Rome.

——. 1998a. *Crop evapotranspiration guidelines for computing crop water requirements.* FAO Irrigation and Drainage Paper No. 56. Rome.

——. 1998b. *FAOSTAT database.* <Http://faostat.fao.org> updated June, accessed September.

——. 1998c. Food outlook: Global information and early warning system on food and agriculture. Various issues. Rome: FAO Commodities and Trade Division.

——. 1996. *Food production: The critical role of water.* World Food Summit, Rome.

——. 1995. *Irrigation in Africa in figures.* Rome.

——. 1992. *Water for sustainable food production and rural development.* UNCED agenda: Targets and cost estimates. Rome.

——. 1986. *Water for animals.* Land and Water Development Division. Rome.

————. 1979. *Crop yield vs. water.* FAO Irrigation and Drainage Paper No. 33. Rome.

Frederiksen, H., J. Berkoff, and W. Barber. 1993. *Water resources management in Asia. Volume I Main Report.* World Bank Technical Paper Number 21. Washington, D. C.: World Bank.

Gallopin, G., and F. R. Rijsberman. 2001. Scenarios and modeling for the World Water Vision, UNESCO, Paris. Mimeo.

Gleick, P. H. 2000. The changing water paradigm: A look at twenty-first century water resources development. *Water International* 25 (1): 127–138.

————. 1999. Water futures: *A review of global water resources projections.* Oakland, Calif., U.S.A.: Pacific Institute for Studies in Development, Environment, and Security.

————. 1998. *The world's water 1998–1999.* The biennial report on freshwater resources. Washington D.C.: Island Press.

Gleick, P. H. (ed.). 1993. *Water in crisis: A guide to the world's water resources.* New York: Oxford University Press.

Gleick, P. H., with W. C. G. Burns, E. L. Chalecki, M. Cohen, K. K. Cushing, A. Mann, R. Reyes, G. H. Wolff, and A. K. Wong. 2002. *The world's water 2002–2003.* The biennial report on freshwater resources. Washington, D.C.: Island Press.

Gracia, F. A., M. A. Garcia Valinas, and R. Martinez-Espineira. 2001. *The literature on the estimation of residential water demand.* St. Francis University, Department of Economics Working Paper Series. <Http://www.stfx.ca/people/rmespi/department/-RoberMarian21NOV.pdf> accessed April 2002.

Gunatilake, H. M., C. Gopalakrishnan, and I. Chandrasena. 2001. The economics of household demand for water: The case of Kandy Municipality, Sri Lanka. *Water Resources Development* 17 (3): 277–288.

GWP (Global Water Partnership). 2001. *Framework for action.* Stockholm: Global Water Partnership.

Hazell, P. B. R., P. Jagger, and A. Knox. 2000. *Technology, natural resource management and the rural poor.* International Fund for Agricultural Development Working Paper. Rome: IFAD.

Hinrichsen, D., B. Robey, and U. D. Upadhyay. 1998. Solutions for a water-short world. *Population Reports,* Series M, No. 14. Baltimore, Md., U.S.A.: Johns Hopkins University School of Public Health, Population Information Program. <Http://www.jhuccp.org/pr/m14edsum.stm>.

HPDGJ (Hydropower Planning and Design General Institute). 1989. *China's water resources and uses.* Beijing: China Water Resources and Hydropower Press.

ICOLD (International Commission on Large Dams). 1998. *World register of dams.* Paris: ICOLD.

IMF (International Monetary Fund). 1997. *International financial statistics (IFS).* Statistics Department. Washington, D.C.: IMF.

IMWR (Indian Ministry of Water Resources). 2002. *Major river basins in India,* New Delhi, India. <Http://www.wrmin.nic.in> accessed in July 2001.

———. 1998 to 2000. Annual Report. New Delhi, India: IMWR.

IWMI (International Water Management Institute). 2000. *Water supply and demand in 2025.* Colombo, Sri Lanka: IWMI.

Johansson, R. B. 2000. *Pricing irrigation water.* A literature survey. Policy Research Working Paper 2449. Washington, D.C: World Bank.

Johnson, N., C. Revenga, and J. Echeverria. 2001. Managing water for people and nature. *Science.* 292 (5519): 1071–1072.

Jones, W. I. 1995. *The World Bank and irrigation.* Washington, D. C.: World Bank.

Keller, J. 1992. Implications of improving agricultural water use efficiency on Egypt's water and salinity balances. In *Roundtable on Egyptian water policy.* M. Abu-Zeid and D. Seckler (eds). Proceedings of a seminar on Egyptian water policy sponsored by the Water Research Center, the Ford Foundation, and Winrock International in Alexandria, Egypt, April 11–13.

Keller, A. A., J. Keller, and D. Seckler. 1996. *Integrated water resources systems: Theory and policy implication.* Research Report No. 3. Colombo, Sri Lanka: International Water Management Institute.

Kite, G., and P. Droogers. 2001. *Integrated basin modeling.* Research Report No. 43. Colombo, Sri Lanka: International Water Management Institute.

Kornegay, J., J. A. Beltran, and J. Ashby. 1996. Farmer selections within segregating populations of common bean in Colombia: Crop improvement in difficult environments. In *Participatory plant breeding.* P. Eyzaguire and M. Iwanaga, eds. Proceedings of a workshop on participatory plant breeding held in Wageningen, the Netherlands, 26–29 July, 1995. Rome: International Plant Genetics Research Institute.

Lantican, M. A., and P. L. Pingali. 2002. Wheat yield potential in marginal environments: Is it improving? *Crop Science,* forthcoming.

Löfgren, H., 1996. The cost of managing with less: Cutting water subsidies and supplies in Egypt's agriculture. TMD Discussion Paper 7. International Food Policy Research Institute, Washington, D.C.

Lohmann, D., E. Raschke, B. Nijssen, D. P. Lettenmaier. 1998. Regional scale hydrology: 1. Formulation of VIC-2L Model coupled to a routing model. *Hydrological Sciences Journal* 43 (1):131–141.

Loucks, D. P., J. R. Stedinger, and H. Douglas. 1981. *Water resource systems planning and analysis.* Englewood Cliffs, NJ, U.S.A: Prentice-Hall.

Maidment, D. 1999. GIS hydro' 99. <Http://www.ce.utexas.edu/prof/maidment/new.html> accessed May 1999.

Mancl, K. 1994. *Water use planning guide.* Report No. AEX-420–94, Columbus, Ohio, U.S.A.: Ohio State University. <Http://ohioline.ag.ohio-state.edu/aexfact/0420.html> accessed March 2001.

Margat, J. 1995. *Water use in the world: Present and future.* Contribution to the IHP Project M-1-3, International Hydrologic Programme, UNESCO.

Martindale, D., and P. Gleick. 2001. Safeguarding our water: How we can do it. *Scientific American.* February: 52–55.

McKinney, D. C., X. Cai , M. W. Rosegrant, C. Ringler, C. A. Scott. 1999. *Modeling water resources management at the basin level: Review and future directions.* System-Wide Initiative on Water Management (SWIM) Paper No. 6. Colombo, Sri Lanka: International Water Management Institute.

McNeeley J. A. 1999. *Freshwater management: From conflict to cooperation.* World Conservation IUCN Bulletin, Issue 2. International Union for Conservation of Nature and Natural Resources. Gland, Switzerland: World Conservation Unit. <Http://www.iucn.org/bookstore/bulletin/1999/wc2/content/conflict.pdf>.

Miller, J. R., G. L. Russell, and G. Caliri. 1994. Continental-scale river flow in climate models. *Journal of Climate* 7: 914–928.

Molden, D. J. 1997. *Accounting for water use and productivity.* System-Wide Initiative on Water Management (SWIM) Paper No. 1. Colombo, Sri Lanka: International Water Management Institute.

Molden, D. J., U. Amarasinjhe, and I. Hussain. 2001. *Water for rural development.* Working paper 32. Colombo, Sri Lanka: International Water Management Institute.

Molden, D., R. Sakthivadivel, and Z. Habib. 2001. *Basin-level use and productivity of water: Examples from South Asia.* Research Report 49. Colombo, Sri Lanka: International Water Management Institute.

Molle, F. 2002. To price or not to price? Thailand and the stigma of "free water." Paper presented at the workshop Irrigation water policies: Macro and micro considerations, Agadir, Morocco, June 15–17.

——. 2001. *Water pricing in Thailand: Theory and practice.* Research Report No. 7, DORAS Project. Bangkok: Kasetsart University. <Http://std.cpc.ku.ac.th/delta/conf/Acrobat/Papers_Eng/pricing.pdf.> accessed March 2002.

Moormann, F. R., and N. van Breemen. 1978. *Rice: Soil, water, land.* Los Baños, the Philippines: International Rice Research Institute.

Moscosco, J. 1996. Aquaculture using treated effluents from the San Juan stabilization ponds, Lima, Peru. In *Abstracts of recycling waste for agriculture: the rural-urban connection.* Washington, D.C.: World Bank.

Nickum, J. E. 1994. Beijing's maturing socialist water economy. In *Metropolitan water use conflicts in Asia and the Pacific.* J. E. Nickum and K. W. Easter, eds. East-West Center and United Nations Centre for Regional Development. Oxford: Westview Press.

NIHWR (Nanjing Institute of Hydrology and Water Resources). 1998. *Water demand and supply in China in the 21ˢᵗ Century.* Beijing: China Water Resources and Hydropower Press.

Nile Basin Initiative. 2002. *Introduction to the Nile River Basin.* Entebbe, Uganda: The Nile Basin Initiative Secretariat. <Http://www.nilebasin.org/IntroNR.htm>.

OECD (Organisation for Economic Co-operation and Development). 1998. *The Athens workshop: Sustainable management of water in agriculture—Issues and policies.* Paris: OECD.

——. 1996. *Guidelines for aid agencies for improved conservation and sustainable use of tropical and sub-tropical wetlands.* Paris: OECD.

Oweis, T. and A. Hachum. 2001. *Coping with increased water scarcity in dry areas: ICARDA's research to increase water productivity.* Aleppo, Syria: International Center for Agricultural Research in the Dry Areas.

Oweis, T., A. Hachum, and J. Kijne. 1999. *Water harvesting and supplementary irrigation for improved water use efficiency in dry areas.* SWIM Paper 7. Colombo, Sri Lanka: International Water Management Institute.

Perry, C. J. 2001. *Charging for irrigation water: The issues and options. (With a case study from Iran).* Research Report 52. Colombo, Sri Lanka: International Water Management Institute.

——. 1996. *Alternative to cost sharing for water service to agriculture in Egypt.* IIMI Research Report No. 2. Colombo: International Water Management Institute.

Perry, C. J., and S. G. Narayanamurthy. 1998. *Farmer response to rationed and uncertain irrigation supplies.* Research Report No. 24. Colombo, Sri Lanka: International Water Management Institute.

Pezzey, J. 1992. The symmetry between controlling pollution by price and controlling it by quantity. *Canadian Journal of Economics* 25 (4): 983–991.

Pingali, P. L., and M. W. Rosegrant. 2000. Intensive food systems in Asia: Can the degradation problems be reversed? In *Tradeoffs or synergies? Agricultural intensification, economic development and the environment,* D. R. Lee and C. B. Barrett, eds. New York: CABI Publishing.

Postel, S. L. 2002. *From Rio to Johannesburg: Securing water for people, crops, and ecosystems.* World Summit Policy Brief No. 8. World Watch Institute. <Http://www.worldwatch.org/worldsummit/briefs/20020716.html>.

———. 1999. *Pillar of sand—Can the irrigation miracle last?* New York: W. W. Norton.

Postel, S. L., and A. T. Wolf. 2001. Dehydrating conflict. *Foreign Policy.* September: 2–9.

Qian Z. (ed.) 1991. *China's water resources.* Beijing: China Water Resources and Hydropower Press.

Raskin, P. D. 2002. Global scenarios and the millenium ecosystem assessment. Discussion paper for the Millenium Ecosystem Assessment First Global Scenarios Workshop held in Trinidad, April 14–17. Boston, Mass., U.S.A.: Stockholm Environment Institute-Boston Center Tellus Institute.

Raskin, P. (ed.) 1997. *Comprehensive assessment of the freshwater resources of the world.* Stockholm: Stockholm Environment Institute.

Raskin, P., E. Hansen, and R. Margolis. 1995. *Water and sustainability.* Polestar Series Report No. 4. Boston: Stockholm Environment Institute.

Repetto, R. 1986. *Skimming the water: Rent-seeking and the performance of public irrigation systems.* Research Report No. 4. Washington, D.C.: World Resources Institute.

Revenga, C., J. Brunner, N. Henninger, K. Kassem, R. Payne. 2000. *Pilot analysis of global ecosystems: Freshwater systems.* Washington, D.C.: World Resources Institute.

Revenga, C., S. Murray, J.Abramovitz, and A. Hammond. 1998. *Watershed of the world: Ecological value and vulnerability.* Washington, D.C.: World Resources Institute.

Rijsberman, F. R., and D. Molden. 2001. Balancing water uses: Water for food and water for nature. Thematic background paper. International Conference on Freshwater. Bonn, Germany.

Rogers, P., R. de Silva, and R. Bhatia. 2002. Water is an economic good: How to use prices to promote equity, efficiency, and sustainability. *Water Policy* 4 (1): 1–17.

Rosegrant, M. W. 1997. *Water resources in the twenty-first century: Challenges and implications for action.* 2020 Discussion Paper No. 20. International Food Policy Research Institute, Washington, D.C.

Rosegrant, M. W., M. Agcaoili-Sombilla, and N. D. Perez. 1995. *Global food projections to 2020: Implications for investment.* 2020 Vision for Food, Agriculture, and the Environment Discussion Paper No. 5. International Food Policy Research Institute, Washington, D.C.

Rosegrant, M., and H. P. Binswanger. 1994. Markets in tradable water rights: potential for efficiency gains in developing country water resource allocation. *World Development* 22 (11): 1613–1625.

Rosegrant, M. W., and X. Cai. 2000. Modeling water availability and food security: A global perspective. The IMPACT-WATER Model. Working paper. International Food Policy Research Institute, Washington, D.C.

Rosegrant, M. W., X. Cai, S. Cline, and N. Nakagawa. 2002. *The role of rainfed agriculture in the future of global food production.* Environment and Production Technology Division Discussion Paper No. 90. International Food Policy Research Institute, Washington, D.C.

Rosegrant, M. W., and S. Cline. 2002. The politics and economics of water pricing in developing countries. *Water Resources IMPACT* 4 (1): 6–8.

Rosegrant, M. W., and P. Hazell. 2000. *Transforming the rural Asian economy: The unfinished revolution.* Hong Kong: Oxford University Press.

Rosegrant, M. W., S. Meijer, and S. A. Cline. 2002. International model for policy analysis of agricultural commodities and trade (IMPACT): Model description. Washington, D.C.: International Food Policy Research Institute. <Http://www.ifpri.org/themes/impact/impactmodel.pdf>.

Rosegrant, M. W., M. S. Paisner, S. Meijer, and J. Witcover. 2001. *Global food projections to 2020: Emerging trends and alternative futures.* Washington, D.C.: International Food Policy Research Institute.

Rosegrant, M. W., C. Ringler, D. C. McKinney, X. Cai, A. Keller, and G. Donoso, 2000. Integrated economic-hydrologic water modeling at the basin scale: The Maipo river basin. *Agricultural Economics* 24 (1): 33–46.

Rosegrant, M. W., R. G. Schleyer, and S. Yadav. 1995. Water policy for efficient agricultural diversification: Market-based approaches. *Food Policy* 20 (3): 203–233.

Rosegrant, M. W., and S. Shetty. 1994. Production and income benefits from improved irrigation efficiency: What is the potential? *Irrigation and Drainage Systems* 8: 251–270.

Rosegrant, M. W., and M. Svendsen. 1993. Asian food production in the 1990s: Irrigation investment and management policy. *Food Policy* 18 (February): 13–32.

Saghir, J., M. Schiffler, and M. Woldu. 1999. *World Bank urban water and sanitation in the Middle East and North Africa region: The way forward.* Washington, D.C.: The World Bank, Middle East and North Africa Region Infrastructure Development Group. December. <Http://www.worldbank.org/wbi/mdf/mdf3/papers/finance/Saghir.pdf> accessed April 2002.

Saleth, R. M. 2001. Water pricing: Potential and problems. *In 2020 Focus 9: Overcoming water scarcity and quality constraints.* R. S. Meinzen-Dick and M. W. Rosegrant, eds. Washington, D.C.: International Food Policy Research Institute.

Saleth, R. M., and A. Dinar. 1997. *Satisfying urban thirst: Water supply augmentation and pricing policy in Hyderabad City, India.* World Bank Technical Paper. Washington, D.C.: World Bank.

Scott, C. A., J. A. Zarazúa, and G. Levine. 2000. *Urban-wastewater reuse for crop production in the water-short Guanajuato River Basin, Mexico.* IWMI Research Report No. 41. Colombo, Sri Lanka: International Water Management Institute.

SCOWR (Scientific Committee on Water Research). 1997. Water resources research: Trends and needs in 1997. *Hydrologic Sciences-Journal* 43 (1): 19–46.

Seckler, D. 1996. *The new era of water resources management.* Research Report No. 1. Colombo, Sri Lanka: International Irrigation Management Institute.

———. 1992. *The Sardar Sarovar project in India: A commentary on the report of the independent review.* Center for Economic Policy Studies Discussion Paper No. 8. Winrock International Institute for Agricultural Development, Morrilton, Ark., U.S.A.

Seckler, D., U. Amarasinghe, D. Molden, de S. Rhadika, and R. Barker. 1998. *World water demand and supply, 1990 to 2025: Scenarios and issues.* Research Report No. 19. Colombo, Sri Lanka: International Water Management Institute.

Shah, F., D. Zilberman, and U. Chakravorty. 1995. Technology Adoption in the presence of an exhaustible resource: The case of groundwater extraction. *American Journal of Agricultural Economics* 77: 291–299.

Shiklomanov, I. A. 1999. Electronic data. Provided to the Scenario Development Panel, World Commission on Water for the 21st Century. Mimeo.

———. 1998. World water resources: A new appraisal and assessment for the 21st Century. International Hydrological Programme (IHP) report. Paris: UNESCO.

Shuval, H. I. 1990. *Wastewater irrigation in developing countries: Health effects and technical solutions.* Summary of World Bank Technical Paper Number 51. Water and Sanitation Discussion Paper Series Report Number 11433. Washington, D.C.: World Bank.

Smakhtin, V. U. 2002. *Environmental water needs and impacts of irrigated agriculture in river basins: A framework for a new research program.* Working Paper 42. Colombo, Sri Lanka: International Water Management Institute.

Smith, A. H., E. O. Lingas, and M. Rahman. 2000. Contamination of drinking-water by arsenic in Bangladesh: A public health emergency. *Bulletin of the World Health Organization* 78 (9): 1093–1103.

Solley, W. B., R. R. Pierce, and H. A. Perlman. 1998. *Estimated water use in the United States in 1995.* U.S. Department of the Interior, U.S. Geological Survey. Denver, Colo., U.S.A.: United States Government Printing Office. <Http://water.usgs.gov/watuse/pdf1995/html/> accessed March 2001.

Tabor, J. A. 1995. Improving crop yields in the Sahel by means of water-harvesting. *Journal of Arid Environments* 30: 83–106.

UN (United Nations). 1998. *World population prospects: The 1998 revision.* New York: United Nations.

———. 1997. *Comprehensive assessment of water resources and water availability in the world.* I. A. Shiklomanov, ed. Geneva: World Meterological Organization (WMO). <Http://www.un.org/esa/sustdev/freshwat.htm> accessed March 2000.

USDA-NASS (United States Department of Agriculture, National Agricultural Statistics Service). 1998. *Commodity reports.* Various issues. Washington, D.C.: USDA, NASS.

USDA-SCS (United States Department of Agriculture, Soil Conservation Service). 1967. Irrigation water requirement. Technical Release No. 21. Washington, D.C.: USDA.

USDA-WAOB (United States Department of Agriculture, World Agricultural Outlook Board). 1998. *Major world crop areas and climatic profiles,* Agricultural Handbook No. 664. Washington, D.C.: USDA.

USGS (United States Geological Survey). 1998. *U.S. water use in 1995.* Washington, D.C.: USGS.

van Hofwegen, P., and M. Svendsen. 2000. *A vision of water for food and rural development,* World Water Vision Sector Report. <Http://www.worldwatercouncil.org/Vision/Documents/WaterforFoodVisionDraft2.PDF> accessed June 2001.

Varela-Ortega, C., J. M. Sumpsi, A. Garrido, M. Blanco, and E. Iglesias. 1998. Water pricing, public decision making and farmers' response: implications for water policy. *Agricultural Economics* 19: 193–202.

Vorosmarty, C. J., B. Fekete, and B. A. Tucker. 1996. River discharge database, version 1.0 (RivDIS v1.0) Volumes 0–6. A contribution to IHP-V Theme 1, Technical Documents in Hydrology Series, UNESCO, Paris. <Http://www.rivdis.sr.unh.edu>.

Wallingford, H. R. 2000. Guidelines of the flushing of sediment from reservoirs. Report of H. R. Wallingford, SR 563, Wallingford, U.K.

WARDA (West Africa Rice Development Association). 2000. Consortium formed to rapidly disseminate New Rice for Africa. <Http://www.warda.cgiar.org/News/NERICAConsortium.htm> updated April 2001, accessed August 2001.

Wetlands International. 1996. A global overview of wetland loss and degradation. Preliminary paper presented at "technical session B" of the Sixth Meeting of the Contracting Parties held in Brisbane, Australia, March 1996. Published in Vol. 10 of the conference proceedings. <Http://www.ramsar.org/about_wetland_loss.htm>.

WHO (World Health Organization). 2000. *WHO guidelines for drinking water quality training pack.* Rome: WHO.

WHO (World Health Organization) and UNICEF (United Nations Children's Fund). 2000. *Global Water supply and sanitation assessment 2000 Report.* Geneva: UN.

Wood, S., K. Sebastian, and S. J. Scherr. 2000. *Pilot analysis of global ecosystems: Agroecosystems.* Washington D.C.: International Food Policy Research Institute and World Resources Institute. <Http://www.ifpri.org> and <Http://www.wri.org/wr2000>.

Working Group on Environment in U.S.-China Relations. 1998. *Water and agriculture in China/Chinese watershed management practices.* China Environment Series. <Http://ecsp.si.edu/pdf/China2c.pdf> accessed June 2002.

World Bank. 2000. *World development indicators 2000* (CD-ROM). Washington, D.C.

———. 1998. *World development indicators 1998.* Washington, D.C.

———. 1997. Commodity price data (pinksheets). Economic Policy and Prospects Group, Development Economics Vice Presidency. Washington, D.C.

———. 1995. *Learning from Narmada.* Washington D.C.: Operations Evaluation Department, World Bank.

———. 1993. *Water resources management.* A World Bank policy paper. Washington, D. C.

WRI (World Resources Institute). 2000. People and ecosystems: The fraying web of life. In *World Resources 2000–2001.* New York: Elsevier Science.

———. 1998. *World resources 1998–99.* New York: Oxford University Press. <Http://www.wri.org> accessed March 2000.

Yepes, G. 1995. *Reduction of unaccounted for water: The job can be done!* Water and Sanitation Division Working Paper. Washington, D.C.: World Bank.

Yevjevich, V. 1991. Tendencies in hydrology research and its applications for 21st century. *Water Resources Management* 5: 1–23.

Zilberman, D., U. Chakravorty, and F. Shah. 1997. Efficient management of water in agriculture. In *Decentralization and coordination of water resources.* D. Parker and Y. Tsur eds. Boston: Kluwer Academic Publishers.

Model Formulation and Implementation: The Business-as-Usual Scenario

This appendix is based on three methodology papers and describes the equations used in the IMPACT model and the Water Simulation Model (WSM)—in particular, the connection between the water demand and supply components and the food production, demand, and trade components is highlighted. The data requirements are also described. For IMPACT, see Rosegrant, Meijer, and Cline (2002); for WSM, see Cai and Rosegrant (2002); and for the combined IMPACT and WSM model, see Rosegrant and Cai (2000).

INTERNATIONAL MODEL FOR POLICY ANALYSIS OF AGRICULTURAL COMMODITIES AND TRADE (IMPACT)

Basic IMPACT Methodology

IFPRI's IMPACT model offers a methodology for analyzing baseline and alternative scenarios for global food demand, supply, trade, income and population. IMPACT covers 36 countries and regions (which account for virtually all the world's food production and consumption, see Boxes A.1 and A.2), and 16 commodities including all cereals, soybeans, roots and tubers, meats, milk, eggs, oils, oilcakes and meals (Box A.1). IMPACT is a representation of a competitive world agricultural market for crops and livestock. It is specified as a set of country or regional submodels, within each of which supply, demand, and prices for agricultural commodities are determined. The country and regional agricultural submodels are linked through trade, a specification that highlights the interdependence of countries and commodities in the global agricultural markets.

The model uses a system of supply and demand elasticities incorporated into a series of linear and nonlinear equations to approximate the underlying production and demand functions. World agricultural commodity prices are determined

Box A.1—IMPACT countries, regions, and commodities

1. United States of America
2. European Union (EU15)
3. Japan
4. Australia
5. Other developed countries
6. Eastern Europe
7. Central Asia
8. Other former Soviet Union (other FSU)
9. Mexico
10. Brazil
11. Argentina
12. Colombia
13. Other Latin America (other LA)

14. Nigeria
15. Northern Sub-Saharan Africa
16. Central and western Sub-Saharan Africa
17. Southern Sub-Saharan Africa
18. Eastern Sub-Saharan Africa
19. Egypt
20. Turkey
21. Other West Asia and North Africa (WANA)
22. India
23. Pakistan
24. Bangladesh
25. Other South Asia
26. Indonesia
27. Thailand
28. Malaysia
29. Philippines
30. Viet Nam
31. Myanmar
32. Other South East Asia
33. China
34. South Korea
35. Other East Asia

1. Beef
2. Pork
3. Sheep and goats
4. Poultry
5. Eggs
6. Milk
7. Wheat
8. Rice
9. Maize
10. Other coarse grains
11. Potatoes
12. Sweet potato and yams
13. Cassava and other roots and tubers
14. Soybeans
15. Meals
16 Oils

Box A.2—Definitions of IMPACT countries and regions

WESTERN WORLD
1. Australia
2. European Union (EU 15): Austria, Belgium, Denmark, Finland, France, Germany, Greece, Ireland, Italy, Luxembourg, the Netherlands, Portugal, Spain, Sweden, and the United Kingdom
3. Japan
4. United States
5. Other developed countries:
   Canada, Iceland, Israel, Malta, New Zealand, Norway, South Africa, and Switzerland
6. Eastern Europe:
   Albania, Bosnia-Herzegovina, Bulgaria, Croatia, Czech Republic, Hungary, Macedonia, Poland, Romania, Slovakia, Slovenia, and Yugoslavia

FORMER SOVIET UNION (FSU)
7. Central Asia:
   Kazakhstan, Kyrgyzstan, Tajikistan, Turkmenistan, Uzbekistan
8. Other Former Soviet Union:
   Armenia, Azerbaijan, Belarus, Estonia, Georgia,
   Latvia, Lithuania, Moldova, Russian Federation, and Ukraine

DEVELOPING COUNTRIES AND REGIONS
Central and Latin America
9. Argentina
10. Brazil
11. Colombia
12. Mexico
13. Other Latin America:
    Antigua and Barbuda, Bahamas, Barbados, Belize, Bolivia, Chile, Costa Rica, Cuba, Dominica, Dominican Republic, Ecuador, El Salvador, French Guiana, Grenada, Guadeloupe, Guatemala, Guyana, Haiti, Honduras, Jamaica, Martinique, Netherlands Antilles, Nicaragua, Panama, Paraguay, Peru, Saint Kitts and Nevis, Saint Lucia, Saint Vincent, Suriname, Trinidad and Tobago, Uruguay and Venezuela
Sub-Saharan Africa
14. Central and western Sub-Saharan Africa:
    Benin, Cameroon, Central African Republic, Comoros Island, Congo Republic, Democratic Republic of Congo, Gabon, Gambia, Ghana, Guinea, Guinea-Bissau, Ivory Coast, Liberia, Sao Tome and Principe, Senegal, Sierra Leone, and Togo

(continued)

Box A.2—Continued

15. Eastern Sub-Saharan Africa: Burundi, Kenya, Rwanda, Tanzania, and Uganda
16. Nigeria
17. Northern Sub-Saharan Africa:
    Burkina Faso, Chad, Djibouti, Eritrea, Ethiopia, Mali, Mauritania, Niger, Somalia, and Sudan
18. Southern Sub-Saharan Africa: Angola, Botswana, Lesotho, Madagascar, Malawi, Mauritius, Mozambique, Namibia, Reunion, Swaziland, Zambia, and Zimbabwe

West Asia and North Africa (WANA)

19. Egypt
20. Turkey
21. Other West Asia and North Africa:
    Algeria, Cyprus, Iran, Iraq, Jordan, Kuwait, Lebanon, Libya, Morocco, Saudi Arabia, Syria, Tunisia, United Arab Emirates, and Yemen

South Asia

22. Bangladesh
23. India
24. Pakistan
25. Other South Asia:
    Afghanistan, Maldives, Nepal, and Sri Lanka

Southeast Asia

26. Indonesia
27. Malaysia
28. Myanmar
29. Philippines
30. Thailand
31. Viet Nam
32. Other Southeast Asian countries:
    Brunei, Cambodia, and Laos

East Asia

33. China (including Taiwan and Hong Kong)
34. Republic of Korea
35. Other East Asia:
    Democratic People's Republic of Korea, Macao, and Mongolia

Rest of the world (ROW)

36. Cape Verde, Fiji, French Polynesia, Kiribati, New Guinea, Papua New Guinea, Seychelles, and Vanuatu

annually at levels that clear international markets. Demand is a function of prices, income, and population growth. Growth in crop production in each country is determined by crop prices and the rate of productivity growth. Future productivity growth is estimated by its component sources, including crop management research, conventional plant breeding, wide-crossing and hybridization breeding, and biotechnology and transgenic breeding. Other sources of growth considered include private sector agricultural research and development, agricultural extension and education, markets, infrastructure, and irrigation.

IMPACT TECHNICAL METHODOLOGY

Crop Production

Domestic crop production is determined by the area and yield response functions. Harvested area is specified as a response to the crop's own price, the prices of other competing crops, the projected rate of exogenous (nonprice) growth trend in harvested area, and water (Equation 1). The projected exogenous trend in harvested area captures changes in area resulting from factors other than direct crop price effects, such as expansion through population pressure and contraction from soil degradation or conversion of land to nonagricultural uses. Yield is a function of the commodity price, the prices of labor and capital, a projected nonprice exogenous trend factor reflecting technology improvements, and water (Equation 2). Annual production of commodity i in country n is then estimated as the product of its area and yield (Equation 3).

Area response:

$$AC_{tni} = \alpha_{tni} \times (PS_{tni})^{\varepsilon_{iin}} \times \prod_{j \neq i}(PS_{tnj})^{\varepsilon_{ijn}} \times (1 + gA_{tni}) - \Delta AC_{tni}(WAT_{tni}); \quad (1)$$

Yield response:

$$YC_{tni} = \beta_{tni} \times (PS_{tni})^{\gamma_{iin}} \times \prod_{k}(PF_{tnk})^{\gamma_{ikn}} \times (1 + gCY_{tni}) - \Delta YC_{tni}(WAT_{tni}); \quad (2)$$

Production:

$$QS_{tni} = AC_{tni} \times YC_{tni}; \quad (3)$$

where AC = crop area
             YC = crop yield
             QS = quantity produced
             PS = effective producer price

PF = price of factor or input k (for example labor and capital)

Π = product operator

i, j = commodity indices specific for crops

k = inputs such as labor and capital

n = country index

t = time index

gA = growth rate of crop area

gCY = growth rate of crop yield

ε = area price elasticity

γ = yield price elasticity

α = crop area intercept

β = crop yield intercept

ΔAC = crop area reduction due to water stress

ΔYC = crop yield reduction due to water stress

WAT = water variable

Incorporation of Water in Crop Area Functions

Reduction of crop harvested area ΔAC is calculated as:

$$\Delta AC_i = 0, \ \ if \ \ \frac{ETA}{ETM} > E^*, \ otherwise \tag{4}$$

$$\Delta AC_i = AC_i \cdot \left[1 - \left(\frac{ETA^i}{ETM^i} / E^{*i}\right) \right] \ \ for \ irrigated \ areas \tag{5}$$

$$\Delta AC_i = AC_i \cdot \left[1 - \left(ky^i \cdot (1 - \frac{ETA^i}{ETM^i} / E^{*i}) \right)^{\gamma} \right] \ \ for \ rainfed \ areas \tag{6}$$

where ETA = actual crop evapotranspiration in the crop growth season

ETM = potential crop evapotranspiration in the crop growth season (see description later in Equation 24)

E^* = threshold of relative evapotranspiration, below which farmers reduce crop area

ky = crop response coefficient to water stress.

Actual crop evapotranspiration includes irrigation water which can be used for crop evapotranspiration (NIW) and effective rainfall (PE),

$$ETA^i = NIW^i + PE^i$$

where for rainfed crops, NIW = 0. The determination of NIW for irrigated crops and PE for both rainfed and irrigated crops will be described later. The determination of E* is empirical. For irrigated area, farmers can reduce area and increase water application per unit of the remaining area. Assuming E* = ky - 0.25, Figure A.1 shows relative irrigated yield, area and production versus relative ET. As can be seen, for irrigated area, when ETA/ETM > E*, farmers will maintain the entire crop area, and yield is reduced linearly with ETA/ETM; and when ETA/ETM < E*, farmers will reduce the crop area linearly with ETA/ETM, and maintain constant crop yield corresponding to E*. Equation 5 is derived based on the assumption that the total available water can be totally applied in the remained irrigated area.

For the same crop, the value of E* is generally much lower for rainfed areas than for irrigated areas. For rainfed area, theoretically, when ETA/ETM < E*, farmers will give up all the area. However, in the real world this may not true. Historic records show that in a region with arid or semi-arid climate, even in a very dry region, the harvested rainfed area did not reduce to zero. However, a general empirical relationship between rainfed harvested area and ETA/ETM is not available from the existing studies. We assume the FAO yield-water relationship can be applied to harvested area and water, which is shown in Equation 6, but with a calibration coefficient (g). This coefficient for a crop is estimated based on evaluation of rainfed harvested area and effective rainfall in recent years.

Figure A.1—Relative irrigated yield, area, and production versus relative crop evapotranspiration

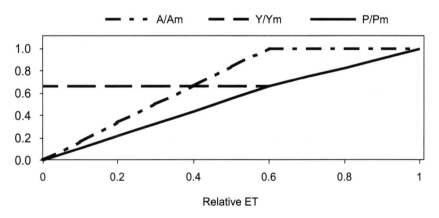

Source: Authors' assessments.
Notes: E* = 0.6; A indicates area; Am, maximum area; Y, yield; Ym, maximum yield; P, production; and Pm, maximum production.

Equations 5 and 6 capture the effect of extreme water shortages on the crop area decision. The parameter E* will vary with respect to the sensitivity of crops to water stress. When E* equals 1 all adjustments to water shortages are realized through area reduction while crop yield is maintained. For crops that are highly sensitive to water stress, (that is, ky > 1.0), E* in fact approaches a value of 1.0 (for example, 0.9 or more). For these crops, water shortages are handled by leaving a portion of the land fallow while maintaining yields on the remaining area, a strategy that maximizes crop production and returns given the constrained water availability. For relatively drought-tolerant crops, E* has a lower value. For these crops, maximization of production and returns requires spreading the water over as broad an area as possible to maintain production while reducing crop yields. E* can be estimated based on a yearly series of historical data including crop area and yield in different basins/countries, or can be estimated through a field survey. The modeling framework currently only incorporates a relationship between E* and the crop response to water stress (ky). The assumed relationship is E* = ky - 0.25 for irrigated crops and approximately E* = ky*0.6 for rainfed crops.

Incorporation of Water in Crop Yield Function

Reduction of crop yield is calculated as:

$$\Delta YC = YC^i \cdot ky^i \cdot (1 - ETA^i / ETM^i) \cdot \left[\frac{\min\limits_{t \subset growthstages} \left((1 - ETA_m^i / ETM_m^{it}) \right)}{(1 - ETA^i / ETM^i)} \right]^{\beta} \quad (7)$$

in which b is the coefficient to characterize the penalty item, which should be estimated based on local water application in crop growth stages and crop yield. Here crop yield reduction is calculated based on seasonal water availability (that is, seasonal ETA), but they are "penalized" if water availability in some crop growth stages (month) is particularly lower than the seasonal level. All other items have been previously defined.

Livestock Production

Livestock production is modeled similarly to crop production except that livestock yield reflects only the effects of expected developments in technology (Equation 9). Total livestock slaughter is a function of the livestock's own price and the price of competing commodities, the prices of intermediate (feed) inputs, and a trend variable reflecting growth in the livestock slaughtered (Equation 8). Total production is calculated by multiplying the slaughtered number of animals by the yield per head (Equation 10).

Number slaughtered:

$$AL_{tni} = \alpha_{tni} \times (PS_{tni})^{\varepsilon_{iin}} \times \prod_{j \neq i}(PS_{tnj})^{\varepsilon_{ijn}}$$
$$\times \prod_{b \neq i}(PI_{tnb})^{\gamma_{ibn}} \times (1 + gSL_{tni}); \tag{8}$$

Yield:

$$YL_{tni} = (1 + gLY_{tni}) \times YL_{t-1,ni}; \tag{9}$$

Production:

$$QS_{tni} = AL_{tni} \times YL_{tni}; \tag{10}$$

where	AL	=	number of slaughtered livestock
	YL	=	livestock product yield per head
	PI	=	price of intermediate (feed) inputs
	i, j	=	commodity indices specific for livestock
	b	=	commodity index specific for feed crops
	gSL	=	growth rate of number of slaughtered livestock
	gYL	=	growth rate of livestock yield
	α	=	intercept of number of slaughtered livestock
	ε	=	price elasticity of number of slaughtered livestock
	γ	=	feed price elasticity

The remaining variables are defined as for crop production.

Demand Functions

Domestic demand for a commodity is the sum of its demand for food, feed, and other uses (Equation 16). Food demand is a function of the price of the commodity and the prices of other competing commodities, per capita income, and total population (Equation 11). Per capita income and population increase annually according to country-specific population and income growth rates as shown in Equations 12 and 13. Feed demand is a derived demand determined by the changes in livestock production, feed ratios, and own- and cross-price effects of feed crops (Equation 14). The equation also incorporates a technology parameter that indicates improvements in feeding efficiencies. The demand for other uses is estimated as a proportion of food and feed demand (Equation 15). Note that total demand for livestock consists only of food demand.

Demand for food:

$$QF_{tni} = \alpha_{tni} \times (PD_{tni})^{\varepsilon_{iin}} \times \prod_{j \neq i}(PD_{tnj})^{\varepsilon_{ijn}} \times (INC_{tn})^{\eta_{in}} \times POP_{tn}; \qquad (11)$$

where

$$INC_{tn} = INC_{t-1,ni} \times (1 + gI_{tn}); \text{ and} \qquad (12)$$

$$POP_{tn} = POP_{t-1,ni} \times (1 + gP_{tn}); \qquad (13)$$

Demand for feed:

$$QL_{tnb} = \beta_{tnb} \times \sum_{l}(QS_{tnl} \times FR_{tnbl}) \times (PI_{tnb})^{\gamma_{bn}}$$

$$\times \prod_{o \neq b}(PI_{tnb})^{\gamma_{bon}} \times (1 + FE_{tnb}); \qquad (14)$$

Demand for other uses:

$$QE_{tni} = QE_{t-1,ni} \times \frac{(QF_{tni} + QL_{tni})}{(QF_{t-1,ni} + QL_{t-1,ni})}; \qquad (15)$$

Total demand:

$$QD_{tni} = QF_{tni} + QL_{tni} + QE_{tni}; \qquad (16)$$

where

QD	=	total demand
QF	=	demand for food
QL	=	derived demand for feed
QE	=	demand for other uses
PD	=	the effective consumer price
INC	=	per capita income
POP	=	total population
FR	=	feed ratio
FE	=	feed efficiency improvement
PI	=	the effective intermediate (feed) price
i,j	=	commodity indices specific for all commodities
l	=	commodity index specific for livestock
b,o	=	commodity indices specific for feed crops

gI = income growth rate
gP = population growth rate
ε = price elasticity of food demand
γ = price elasticity of feed demand
η = income elasticity of food demand
α = food demand intercept
β = feed demand intercept

The rest of the variables are as defined earlier.

Prices

Prices are endogenous in the model. Domestic prices are a function of world prices, adjusted by the effect of price policies and expressed in terms of the producer subsidy equivalent (PSE), the consumer subsidy equivalent (CSE), and the marketing margin (MI). PSEs and CSEs measure the implicit level of taxation or subsidy borne by producers or consumers relative to world prices and account for the wedge between domestic and world prices. MI reflects other factors such as transport and marketing costs. In the model, PSEs, CSEs, and MIs are expressed as percentages of the world price. To calculate producer prices, the world price is reduced by the MI value and increased by the PSE value (Equation 17). Consumer prices are obtained by adding the MI value to the world price and reducing it by the CSE value (Equation 18). The MI of the intermediate prices is smaller because wholesale instead of retail prices are used, but intermediate prices (reflecting feed prices) are otherwise calculated the same as consumer prices (Equation 19).

Producer prices:

$$PS_{tni} = [PW_i \ (1 - MI_{tni})](1 + PSE_{tni}); \tag{17}$$

Consumer prices:

$$PD_{tni} = [PW_i \ (1 + MI_{tni})](1 - CSE_{tni}); \tag{18}$$

Intermediate (feed) prices:

$$PI_{tni} = [PW_i \ (1 + 0.5 \ MI_{tni})](1 - CSE_{tni}); \tag{19}$$

where PW =   the world price of the commodity
         MI =   the marketing margin

PSE =   the producer subsidy equivalent
CSE =   the consumer subsidy equivalent

The rest of the variables are as defined earlier.

International Linkage—Trade

The country and regional submodels are linked through trade. Commodity trade by country is the difference between domestic production and demand (Equation 20). Countries with positive trade are net exporters, while those with negative values are net importers. This specification does not permit a separate identification of both importing and exporting countries of a particular commodity. In the 1995 base year, changes in stocks are computed at the 1994-96 average levels. Therefore, production and demand values are not equal in the base year. Stock changes in the base year are phased out during the first three years of the projection period to achieve long-run equilibrium—that is, a supply-demand balance is achieved with no annual changes in stocks.

Net trade:

$$QT_{tni} = QS_{tni} - QD_{tni};$$

(20)

where QT =   volume of trade
        QS =   domestic supply of the commodity
        QD =   domestic demand of the commodity
        i =   commodity index specific for all commodities

The rest of the variables are as defined earlier.

ALGORITHM FOR SOLVING THE EQUILIBRIUM CONDITION

The model is written in the General Algebraic Modeling System (GAMS) programming language. The solution of the system of equations is achieved by using the Gauss-Seidel method algorithm. This procedure minimizes the sum of net trade at the international level and seeks a world market price for a commodity that satisfies Equation 17, the market-clearing condition.

$$\sum_{n} QT_{tni} = 0;$$

(21)

The world price (PW) of a commodity is the equilibrating mechanism such that when an exogenous shock is introduced in the model, PW will adjust and each adjustment is passed back to the effective producer (PS) and consumer (PD) prices via the price transmission equations (Equations 17–19). Changes in domestic prices subsequently affect commodity supply and demand, necessitating their iterative readjustments until world supply and demand balance, and world net trade again equals zero.

Determination of Malnutrition

To explore food security effects, IMPACT projects the percentage and number of malnourished preschool children (0–5 years old) in developing countries. A malnourished child is a child whose weight-for-age is more than two standard deviations below the weight-for-age standard set by the U.S. National Center for Health Statistics/World Health Organization. The estimated functional relationship used to project the percentage of malnourished children in the model is as follows:

$$MAL = -25.24 * ln(KCAL_t) - 71.76 \, LFEXPRAT_t - 0.22 \, SCH_t - 0.08 \, WATER_t \tag{22}$$

where MAL = percentage of malnourished children
  $KCAL$ = per capita kilocalorie availability
  $LFEXPRAT$ = ratio of female to male life expectancy at birth
  SCH = total female enrollment in secondary education (any age group) as a percentage of the female age-group corresponding to national regulations for secondary education, and
  $WATER$ = percentage of population with access to safe water.

The percentage of malnourished children derived is then applied to the projected population of children 0-5 years of age to compute the number of malnourished children:

$$NMAL_t = MAL_t \times POP5_t, \tag{23}$$

where $NMAL$ = number of malnourished children, and
  $POP5$ = number of children 0-5 years old in the population.

WATER SIMULATION MODEL

The model is based on a river basin approach. Figure A.2 presents maps of the spatial units used in the modeling exercise, including 9 basins in China, 13 basins in

Figure A.2—IMPACT-WATER spatial elements

(a) Combined basins

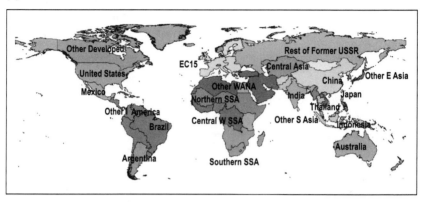

Source : Authors' assessments.

(b) Major basins in China

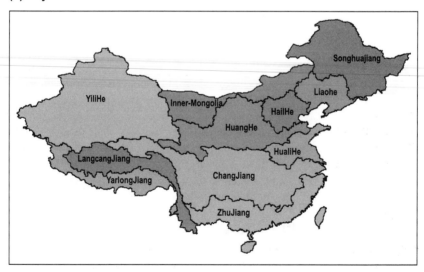

Source : Authors' assessments based on HPDGJ (1989) and Qian (1991).

Figure A.2—Continued

(c) Major basins in India

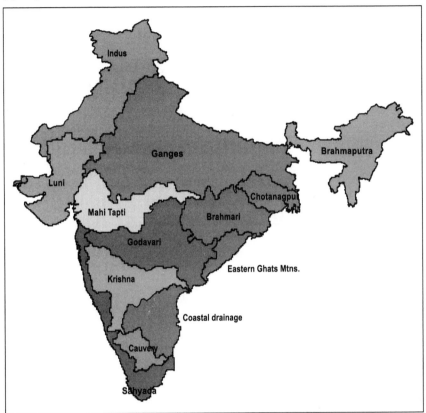

Source : Authors' assessments based on Revenga et al. (1998).

India, 14 basins in the United States (not pictured), and 33 "aggregated basins" in other countries or regions (See Box A.1). 1995 is treated as the base year, in which all demand and supply items are assessed and calibrated. Projections of water demand and supply are made for the 30 years from 1995 to 2025.

WATER DEMAND

Irrigation Water Demand

Irrigation water demand is assessed as crop water requirement based on hydrologic and agronomic characteristics. Net crop water demand (NCWD) in a basin in a year is calculated based on an empirical crop water requirement function (Doorenbos and Pruitt 1979):

$$NCWD = \sum_{cp} \sum_{ct} kc^{cp,ct} \cdot ET_0^{ct} \cdot A^{cp} = \sum_{cp} \sum_{ct} ETM^{ct,cp} \cdot A^{cp} \quad (24)$$

in which cp is the index of crops, ct is the index of crop growth stages, ET_0 is the reference evapotranspiration [L], kc is the crop coefficient, and A is the crop area.

Part or all of crop water demand can be satisfied by effective rainfall (PE), which is the rainfall infiltrated into the root zone and available for crop use. Effective rainfall for crop growth can be increased through rainfall harvesting technology. Then net irrigation water demand (NIRWD), with consideration of effective rainfall use and salt leaching requirement, is:

$$NIRWD = \sum_{cp} \sum_{st} \left(kc^{cp,st} \cdot ET_0^{st} - PE^{cp,st}\right) \cdot AI^{cp} \cdot (1 + LR) \quad (25)$$

in which AI is the irrigated area., LR is the salt leaching factor, which is characterized by soil salinity and irrigation water salinity.

Total irrigation water demand represented in water depletion (IRWD) is calculated as:

$$IRWD = NIRWD / BE \quad (26)$$

in which *BE* is defined as basin efficiency. The concept of basin efficiency was discussed, and various definitions were provided by Molden, Sakthivadivel, and Habib (2001). The basin efficiency used in this study measures the ratio of beneficial water depletion (crop evapotranspiration and salt leaching) to the total irrigation water depletion at the river basin scale. Basin efficiency in the base year (1995) is calculated as the ratio of the net irrigation water demand (NIRWD, Equation 25) to the total irrigation water depletion estimated from records. Basin efficiency in future years is assumed to increase at a prescribed rate in a basin, depending on water infrastructure investment and water management improvement in the basin.

The projection of irrigation water demand depends on the changes of irrigated area and cropping patterns, water use efficiency, and rainfall harvest technology. Global climate change can also affect future irrigation water demand through temperature and precipitation change, but is not considered in the current modeling framework.

Livestock Water Demand

Livestock water demand (LVWD) in the base year is estimated based on livestock production (QS_{lv}) and water consumptive use per unit of livestock production (w_{lv}), including beef, milk, pork, poultry, eggs, sheep and goats, and aquaculture fish production. For all of the livestock products except fish, it is assumed that the projection of livestock water demand in each basin, country, or region follows the same growth rate of livestock production. Then livestock water demand is determined as a linear function of livestock production, assuming no change in consumptive water use per unit of livestock production

$$LVWD = QS_{lv} \cdot w_{lv} \tag{27}$$

The water demand for fish production is assumed to grow at the weighted average of livestock water demand growth.

Industrial Water Demand

Projection of industrial water demand depends on income (gross domestic production per capita (GDPC) and water use technology improvement. A linear relationship between industrial water demand intensity (IWDI per cubic meter of water per $1,000 GDP) and GDP per capita and a time variable (T) is estimated by regression based on historical records (Shiklomanov 1999 for industrial water consumption; World Bank 1998) and adjusted according to our perspectives on future industrial water demand in different regions and countries.

$$IWDI = \alpha + \beta \cdot GDPC + \gamma \cdot T \tag{28}$$

in which α is the intercept; β is the income coefficient, reflecting how industrial water use intensity changes with GDPC; and g is the time coefficient, mainly reflecting the change of water use technology with technology change. It is found that $\alpha > 0$, $\dfrac{\partial IWDI}{\partial GDPC} = \beta < 0$, and $\dfrac{\partial IWDI}{\partial T} =$ for all basins and countries, which shows that in future years, the industrial water use intensity will reduce with the $GDPC$ and T (T = 95 for 1995; 100 for 2000; and so on).

Domestic Water Demand

Domestic water demand (DOWD) includes municipal water demand and rural domestic water demand. Domestic water demand in the base year is estimated based on the same sources and method as those used for industrial water demand assessment. Domestic water demands in future years are projected based on projections of population and income growth. In each country or basin, income elasticities (η) of demand for domestic use are synthesized based on the literature and available estimates. These elasticities of demand measure the propensity to consume water with respect to increases in per capita income. The elasticities utilized are defined to capture both direct income effects and conservation of domestic water use through technological and management change. The annual growth rate of domestic water demand (ϕ_{dwd}) is a function of the growth rate of population (ϕ_{pop}) and that of income (GDPC, ϕ_{gdpc}), as

$$\phi_{dwd} = \phi_{pop} + \eta \cdot \phi_{gdpc} \tag{29}$$

where $\partial \phi_{dwd} / \partial \phi_{gdpc} = \eta < 0$ implies that per capita domestic water demand will actually decline with income growth, which happens with some developed countries where current per capita domestic water consumption is high; and $\partial \phi_{dwd} / \partial \phi_{gdpc} = \eta > 0$ implies that per capita domestic water demand will increase with income growth, which happens in all developing countries.

Committed Flow for Environmental, Ecological, and Navigational Uses

In the modeling framework here, committed flow is specified as a percentage of average annual runoff. Data is lacking on this variable for most basins and countries, so an iterative procedure is used to specify this variable where data is lacking. The base value for committed flows is assumed to be 10 percent, with additional increments of 20–30 percent if navigation requirements are significant (for example, Yangtze River basin); 10–15 percent if environmental reservation is significant, as in most developed countries; and 5–10 percent for arid and semi-arid regions where ecological requirements, such as salt leaching, are high (for example, Central Asia). The estimated values for committed flows are then calibrated for the base year relative to basin inflow, outflow, and consumptive use.

Demand for Water Withdrawals

Offstream water demand items described above are all expressed in water depletion/consumption. The demand for water withdrawal is calculated as total water depletion demand (DWP) divided by the water depletion coefficient:

$$DWW = DWP / DC = (IRWD + INWD + DOWD + LVWD) / DC \tag{30}$$

The value of the water depletion coefficient in the context of the river basin mainly depends on the relative fraction of agricultural and nonagricultural water use (that is, larger agricultural water use corresponds to a higher value of water depletion coefficient), as well as water conveyance/distribution/recycling systems and pollution discharge and treatment facilities. In the base year, DC is calculated by given water depletion (WDP) and water withdrawal (WITHD), and DC in the future is projected as a function of the fraction of non-irrigation water use:

$$DC = \rho \cdot \left(\frac{WDPDO + WDPIN + WDPLV}{WDPT} \right)^{\psi} \qquad (31)$$

This regression function is made based on historical non-irrigation water depletion and total water depletion in different basins or countries, resulting in regression coefficients $\rho > 0$, and $\psi < 0$ for all basins and countries.

Price Impact on Water Demand

A classic Cobb-Douglas function is used to specify the relationship between water demand (W) and water price (P), based on price elasticity (ξ):

$$W = W_0 \cdot (\frac{P}{P_0})^{\xi} \qquad (32)$$

where W_0 and P_0 represent a baseline water demand and water price, respectively. This relationship is applied to agricultural, industrial, and domestic sectors, with price elasticity (ξ) estimated for each of the sectors.

Committed Flow for Environmental, Ecological, and Navigational Uses

In the modeling framework here, committed flow is specified as a percentage of average annual runoff. Data is lacking on this variable for most basins and countries, so an iterative procedure is used to specify this variable. The base value for committed flows is assumed to be 10 percent, with additional increments of 20–30 percent if navigation requirements are significant (for example, the Yangtze River Basin); 10–15 percent if environmental reservation is significant, as in most developed countries; and 5–10 percent for arid and semi-arid regions where ecological requirements, such as salt leaching, are high (for example, Central Asia). The estimated values for committed flows are then calibrated for the base year relative to basin inflow, outflow, and consumptive use.

WATER SUPPLY

Assuming minimum environmental and ecological flow requirements as a prede-termined hard constraint in water supply, we focus on the determination of off-stream water supply for domestic, industrial, livestock, and irrigation sectors. Two steps are undertaken to determine offstream water supply by sectors. The first is to determine the total water supply represented as depletion/consumption (WDP) in each month of a year; and the second is to allocate the total to different sectors. Particularly, irrigation water supply is further allocated to different crops in the basin.

To determine the total amount of water available for various offstream uses in a basin, hydrologic processes, such as precipitation, evapotranspiration, and runoff are taken into account to assess total renewable water (TRW). Moreover, anthro-pogenic impacts are combined to define the fraction of the total renewable water that can be used. These impacts can be classified into (1) water demands; (2) flow regulation through storage, flow diversion, and groundwater pumping; (3) water pollution and other water losses (sinks); and (4) water allocation policies, such as committed flows for environmental purposes, or water transfers from agricultural to municipal and industrial uses. Therefore, water supply is calculated based on both hydrologic processes and anthropogenic impacts through the model, including the relationships listed above.

A simple network with a two-basin framework can be used as an example (Figure A.3). Water availability in the downstream basin depends on the rainfall drainage in the basin and the inflow from the upstream basin(s). Then surface water balance at the basin scale can be represented as:

$$ST^t - ST^{t-1} = ROFF^t + INF^t + OS^t - SWDP^t - RL^t - EL^t \qquad (33)$$

in which t is the modeling time interval; ST is the change of basin reservoir stor-age; INF is the inflow from other basin(s); OS represents other sources entering water supply system, such as desalinized water; RL is the total release, including the committed instream flow and spill in flooding periods; EL is the evaporation loss (mainly from surface reservoir surface); and $SWDP$ is the total water depletion from surface water sources which is equal to water withdrawal minus return flow. $SWDP$ is determined from this water balance equation, with an upper bound constrained by surface maximum allowed water withdrawal ($SMAWW$) as:

$$\sum_t SWDP^t / DC \le SMAWW \qquad (34)$$

Other constraints related to the items in Equation 8 include that flow release (RL) must be equal or greater than the committed instream flow; monthly reservoir evap-oration is calculated based on reservoir surface area, and climate characteristics.

Figure A.3—Connected flow among river basins, countries, regions

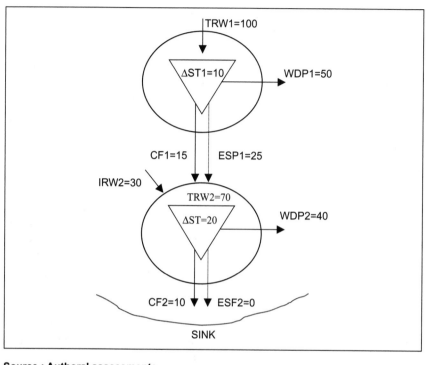

Source : Authors' assessments.
Notes : TRW indicates total renewable water; IRW, internal renewable water; WDP;
water consumption; CF, committed flow; ESP, excess spill; and ∆ST, storage change.

Depletion from the groundwater source (*GWDP*) is constrained by maximum allowed water withdrawal from groundwater (*GMAWW*):

$$\sum_t GWDP^t / DC \leq GMAWW \qquad (35)$$

The estimation of the *SMAWW* and *GMAWW* in the base year (1995) is based on the actual annual water withdrawal and annual groundwater pumping in 1995 (WRI 2000). Projections of *SMAWW* and *GMAWW* are based on assumptions on future surface and ground water development in different countries and regions. In particular, the projection of *GMAWW* is based on historic pumping and potential groundwater source (measured by groundwater recharge).

A traditional reservoir operation model is developed, including all of the above relationships of natural water availability, storage regulation, withdrawal capacity, and committed flow requirements. The model is formulated as an optimization model. The model is run for individual years with month as the time period. The objective is to maximize the reliability of water supply (that is, ratio of water supply over demand, less or equal to 1.0), as

$$
\max \left[\frac{\sum_t (SWDP^t + GWDP^t)}{\sum_t \left(DOWD^t + INWD^t + LVWD^t + IRWD^t\right)^+} + \omega \cdot \min_t \left(\frac{SWDP^t + GWDP^t}{DOWD^t + INWD^t + LVWD^t + IRWD^t}\right) \right] \tag{36}
$$

and as can be seen, the objective function also drives the water application according to the water demand in crop growth stages (months) by maximizing the minimum ratio among time periods (12 months). The weight item w is determined by trial-and-error until water supply is distributed to months approximately proportional to monthly water demand.

Once the model solves for total water that could be depleted in each month ($SWDP$ and $GWDP$) for various off-stream uses under constraints described above, the next step is to determine water supply for different sectors. Assuming domestic water demand is satisfied first, followed in priority by industrial and livestock water demand, irrigation water supply is the residual claimant. Monthly non-irrigation water demands are calculated based on their annual value multiplied by monthly distribution coefficients. Water supply represented in depletion for different sectors is calculated as:

$$
\begin{aligned}
EFPFO^t &= min\ (DOWD^t, SWDP^t + GWDP^t) \\
WDPIN^t &= min\ (INWD^t, SWDP^t + GWDP^t - WDPDO^t) \\
WDPLV^t &= min\ (LVWD^t, SWDP^t + GWDP^t - WDPDO^t - WDPIN^t)\ and \\
WDIR^t &= min\ (IRWD^t, SWDP^t + GWDP^t - WDPDO^t - WDPLV^t)
\end{aligned} \tag{37}
$$

Finally, total water available for crop evapotranspiration (NIW) is calculated by introducing the basin efficiency (BE) for irrigation systems and discount of salinity leaching requirement, that is,

$$
TNIW^t = BE \cdot WDIR^t / (1 + LR) \tag{38}
$$

TET can be further allocated to crops according to crop irrigation water demand, yield response to water stress (ky), and average crop price (P_c) for each of the major crops considered in a basin, including rice, wheat, maize, other coarse grains, soybeans, potatoes, sweet potatoes, and roots and tubers.

The allocation fraction is defined as:

$$\pi^{i,t} = \frac{ALLO^{i,t}}{\sum\limits_{cp} ALLO^{i,t}} \quad \text{and,} \tag{39}$$

$$ALLO^i = AI^i \cdot ky^i \cdot \left[1 - PE^{i,t} / ETM^{i,t}\right] PC^i \tag{40}$$

in which $ETM^{cp,t} = ET_o^{cp,t} \cdot kc^{cp,t}$ is the maximum crop evapotranspiration; π is a scaled number in the range of $(0,1)$ and the sum of over all crops is set to equal 1. The effective water supply allocated to each crop is then calculated by

$$NIW^{i,t} = TNIWt \cdot \pi^{i,t} \tag{41}$$

Thus, irrigation water is allocated based on profitability of the crop, sensitivity to water stress, and irrigation water demand (total demand minus effective rainfall) of the crop. Higher priority is given to the crops with higher profitability, which are more drought sensitive, and/or that require more irrigation water.

Effective Rainfall
Effective rainfall (PE) depends on total rainfall (PT), previous soil moisture content (SMo), maximum crop evapotranspiration (ETM), and soil characteristics (hydraulic conductivity K, moisture content at field capacity Z_s, and others). PE is calculated by an SCS method (USDA, SCS 1967), given PT, ETM, and effective soil water storage:

$$PE^{cp,st} = f \cdot \left(1.253 PT^{st \, 0.824} - 2.935\right) \cdot 10^{(0.001 ETM^{cp,st})} \tag{42}$$

in which f is the correction factor that depends on the depth of irrigation, that is,

$f = 1.0$ if depth of irrigation per application, DI, is 75mm, $\tag{43}$

$f = 0.133 + 0.201*ln(Da)$ if $DI<75$mm per application, and $\tag{44}$

$f = 0.946 + 0.00073*Da$ if $DI>75$mm per application. $\tag{45}$

Depth of irrigation application is 75mm to 100mm for irrigated land, and 150mm to 200mm for rainfed land.

If the above results in PE greater than ET_m or PT, PE equals the minimum of ET_m or PT. When $PT<12.5$mm, $PE=PT$.

Global precipitation grids (half degree) (1961–90, monthly data) from the University of East Anglia are used to extract the total rainfall on the crop land in IMPACT regions/countries/basins. With crop-wise ETM and total rainfall, crop-wise monthly effective rainfall (time series over 30 years) is calculated by the SCS method described above.

Moreover, the effective rainfall for crop growth can be increased through rainfall harvesting technology. Rainfall harvesting is the capture, diversion, and storage of rainwater for plant irrigation and other uses, and can be an effective water conservation tool, especially in arid and semi-arid regions. Water harvesting can provide farmers with improved water availability, increased soil fertility, and higher crop production in some local and regional ecosystems, and can also provide broader environmental benefits through reduced soil erosion. Although improved water harvesting is often considered in connection with traditional agriculture, it also has potential in highly developed agriculture. Advanced tillage practices can also increase the share of rainfall that goes to infiltration and evapotranspiration. Contour plowing, which is typically a soil-preserving technique, should also act to detain and infiltrate a higher share of the precipitation. Precision leveling can also lead to greater relative infiltration, and therefore a higher percentage of effective rainfall. A coefficient (l, $\lambda > 1$) is used to reflect the addition of effective rainfall from rainfall harvesting at various levels,

$$PE *^{cp,st} = \lambda \cdot PE^{cp,st} \tag{46}$$

MODEL IMPLEMENTATION

The model implementation procedure is shown in Box A.3. The model is applied for a monthly water balance within one year. It is run through a series of years by solving individual years in sequence and connecting the outputs from year to year. The time series of climate parameters are derived based on past 30-year historical records, 1961–90. In addition to a basic scenario that overlays the single historic time series over the 1995–2025 projection period, a number of scenarios of hydrologic time series can be generated by changing the sequence of the yearly records. Water supply uncertainty from various hydrologic levels can then be identified from the statistics of multiple hydrologic scenarios.

The ending storage of one year is taken as the initial storage of the next year, with assumed initial water storage for the base year. For those basins that have large storage, interyear flow regulation is active in this modeling framework.

Water demand for non-irrigation sectors ($DOWD$, $INWD$, and $LVWD$) is updated year by year (see Equations 27, 28, and 29) Infrastructure is updated by

---

Box A.3—Model implementation procedure

Base Year (such as 1995)

For each group i of (group1 .. group5)

For each individual/aggregated basin j in group i

Given water demand and supply parameters in the base year

(including estimated initial reservoir storage and external inflow)

Solve WSM for water supply

Calculate outflow from basin j

End of group i

End of all groups

Projected years (such as 1996-2025)

For each year k of (1996 -2025)

For each group i of (group1 .. group5)

For each individual/aggregated basin j in group i

Update water demand and supply parameters, including initial reservoir storage from the end of year k-1, and inflow from other units in the groups previously solved (for group 1, inflow is equal to 0)

Solve WSM for water supply

Calculate outflow basin j

End of group i

End of all groups in year k

End of all years

---

projections of reservoir storage, water use efficiency, and maximum allowed water withdrawal (*MAWW*).

The model is run for individual basins, but with interbasin/international flow simulated. The outflow (*RL*) from one basin becomes a source to downstream basins, which is important to many international river basins such as the Nile (Sudan, Ethiopia, Egypt, Uganda, Burundi, Tanzania, Kenya, Zaire, and Rwanda); Mekong (China, Laos, Burma, Thailand, Cambodia, and Viet Nam); Indus (Pakistan, India, Afghanistan, and China); Ganges-Brahmaputra (China, India, Bangladesh, Bhutan, and Nepal); Amazon (Brazil, Peru, Bolivia, Colombia, Ecuador, Venezuela, and Guyana); Danube (Romania, Yugoslavia, Hungry, Albania,

Italy, Austria, Czechoslovakia, Germany, Russia, Poland, Bulgaria, and Switzerland); Niger (Mali, Nigeria, Niger, Algeria, Guinea, Chad, Cameroon, Burkina Faso, Benin, Côte D'Ivoire); Tigris-Euphrates (Iraq, Iran, Turkey, and Syria); and Rio Grande (United States and Mexico).

To trace the flow connection between major international river basins, we classify the 69 basins or aggregated basins (see Figure A.2) into five groups according to the flow direction between those basins:

Group 1 : without upstream inflow,

Group 2 : with upstream inflow only from group 1,

Group 3 : with upstream inflow from group 2, and with/inflow from group 1,

Group 4 : with upstream inflow from group 3 and with/ inflow from group 1 and 2, and

Group 5 : with upstream inflow from group 4 and with/ inflow from group 1, 2, and 3.

Group 1, without any inflow, is first solved; and then group 2, with inflow from one or more basins of group 1, and so on. One group is ready to be solved with inflows from all the groups that have flow release to basins in the current group. The implementation of this spatial connection allows the model to deal with water transfer between basins and water sharing in international river basins.

CONNECTING IMPACT AND WSM

The WSM calculates effective irrigation water supply in each basin by crop and by period ($NIW_{i,t}$), over a 30-year time horizon. The results from the WSM are then incorporated into IMPACT for simulating food production, demand, and trade.

Figure A.4 shows the flow chart of the IMPACT-WATER program. For each year, initially, it is assumed that there is no water shortage, $\Delta AC(W)$ and $\Delta YC(W)$ are zero, and crop area harvested and crop yields are determined based on price, labor, fertilizer, and other inputs, and technological change. Then water availability for crops is computed, $\Delta AC(W)$ and $\Delta YC(W)$ are calculated, and crop area (A) and yield (Y) are updated, based on equations 39–40. Next, crop production and stock are updated, and net food trade and the global trade balance calculated (global net trade should equal zero). If the trade balance is violated, then crop prices are adjusted, and the model undertakes a new iteration. The loop stops when net trade equals zero. Thus, crop area and yield are determined endogenously based on water availability, price, and other agricultural inputs.

Figure A.4—Flow chart of the IMPACT-WATER program

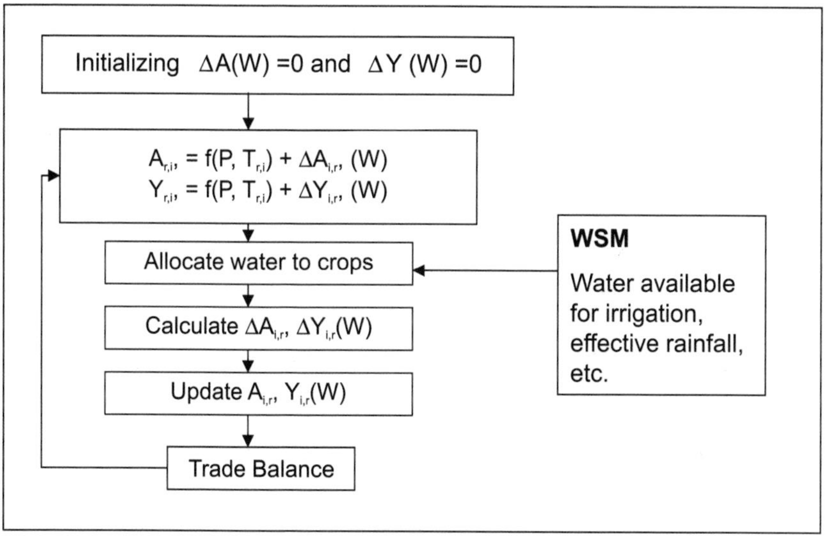

Source : Compiled by authors.

INPUT DATA

Extensive data are required for the IMPACT-WATER modeling framework. The information is drawn from highly disparate databases and requires an interdisciplinary and international collaboration of professionals in agronomy, economics, engineering, and public policy. Table A.1 describes the major data and their sources, which are classified into six classes: water supply infrastructure, hydrology, agronomy, crop production and non-irrigation water demand, and water policies. The data have been prepared for river basins (in China, India and the United States) and countries and regions. Some data have been estimated for a 30-year time horizon including precipitation, runoff, and evapotranspiration; other data are calibrated for the base year and are then determined by the model for future years (including irrigated and rainfed crop area and yield, and crop area and yield reduction from to water shortages). As indicated above and in Table A.1, some data came directly from other sources, some are treated based on other sources, and some are estimated according to related literature.

Table A.1—Input Data

Category	Details	Sources
Infrastructure	Reservoir storage	ICOLD (1998)
	Withdrawal capacity	WRI (2000); Gleick (1993)
	Groundwater pumping capacity	WRI (2000)
	Water distribution, use and recycling situation	Scenario Development Panel, World Water Vision
Hydrology	Watershed delineation	WRI
	Precipitation	CRU (1998)
	Potential evapotranspiration	Alcamo et al. (2000)
	Runoff	Alcamo et al. (2000)
	Groundwater recharge	WRI (2000); Gleick (1999)
	Committed flow	Authors' assessments
	Water pollution (salinity)	Authors' assessments
Agronomy	Crop growth stages	Rice provided by FAO; wheat and maize by CIMMYT; and other crops by USDA
	Crop evapotranspiration coefficients (kc)	FAO (1998); Doorenbos and Kassam (1977)
	Yield-water response coefficient (ky)	FAO (1998); Doorenbos and Pruitt (1979)
Crop production	Irrigated and rainfed area (baseline): actual harvested and potential	FAO (1999); Cai (1999)
	Irrigated and rainfed yield (baseline): actual and potential	FAO (1999); Cai (1999)
Non-irrigation water demand	Industry	Shiklomanov (1999) for the Scenario Development Panel, World Water Vision
	Domestic	Shiklomanov (1999) for the Scenario Development Panel, World Water Vision
	Livestock	Mancl (1994); Beckett and Oltjen (1993); FAO (1986)
Water policies	Committed flows	Authors' assessments
	Water demand growth	Authors' assessments
	International water sharing agreements	Authors' assessments based on WRI (2000)
	Investment	Authors' assessments

Source: Compiled by authors.
Notes: CIMMYT indicates the International Wheat and Maize Improvement Center; FAO, the Food and Agriculture Organization of the United Nations; ICOLD, International Commission on Large Dams; WRI, World Resources Institute; and USDA, the United States Department of Agriculture.

GIS and other methods are used to treat these parameters. For example, original hydrologic data are represented in a grid, and a GIS program is used to extract the value and aggregate grids into IMPACT spatial units. Other data are given in smaller spatial units (such as for China, the United States, and districts in India), and the GIS program is applied to overlay the data at the smaller scales. Many other intermediate programs were developed to estimate the required data or transfer the original data to the format required by the models. Data required for agricultural modeling by IMPACT are described in Rosegrant et al. (2001).

Table A.2—Water demand and supply data

Region/ Country	Average annual precipitation (mm)	Average annual ET_0 (mm)	Internal water (km³)		Inflow (km³)		
			average	variance	average	maximum	minimum
United States							
Ohio and							
Tennessee	1,160	970	235.3	48.2	148.0	178.0	107.0
Rio Grande	405	1,795	9.7	4.0	0.0	0.0	0.0
Columbia	596	1,005	270.8	34.0	0.0	0.0	0.0
Colorado	268	1,452	32.1	8.4	0.0	0.0	0.0
Great Basin	549	947	44.0	10.9	0.0	0.0	0.0
California	558	1,685	101.3	38.2	0.0	0.0	0.0
White-Red	827	1,360	127.9	46.7	0.0	0.0	0.0
Mid Atlantic	1,072	871	252	38.3	0.0	0.0	0.0
Mississippi							
Downstream	1,278	1,216	116.5	31.6	95.0	105.0	50.0
Upstream	826	848	191.2	40.1	0.0	0.0	0.0
Great Lakes-Red	760	768	202.8	18.6	0.0	0.0	0.0
South Atlantic-Gulf	1323	1365	285.4	58.4	0.0	0.0	0.0
Texas-Gulf	824	1512	78.1	25.3	0.0	0.0	0.0
Missouri	592	996	150.6	41.7	0.0	0.0	0.0
U.S. average/total	n.a.	n.a.	**2,098**	**444**	**243**	**283**	**157**
China							
Huaihe	880	957	93.8	7.8	0.0	0.0	0.0
Haihe	503	1,196	42.3	9.1	0.0	0.0	0.0
Huanghe	529	1,099	71.6	16.0	0.0	0.0	0.0
Changjian	1,236	945	908.1	79.9	0.0	0.0	0.0
Songliao	530	877	198.9	24.4	0.0	0.0	0.0
Inland	235	1,035	59.9	8.7	0.0	0.0	0.0
Southwest	1,707	1,074	702.8	53.7	0.0	0.0	0.0
ZhuJiang	1,513	1,118	407.6	54.3	0.0	0.0	0.0
Southeast	1,611	1,075	145.2	34.2	0.0	0.0	0.0
China average/total	n.a.	n.a.	**2,630**	**288**	**0**	**0**	**0**
India							
Sahyadri Ghats	1,095	2,311	109.7	16.9	0.0	0.0	0.0
Eastern Ghats	1,133	2,259	15.7	3.8	0.0	0.0	0.0
Cauvery	964	2,291	14.4	4.0	0.0	0.0	0.0
Godavari	1,030	2,242	111.4	26.3	0.0	0.0	0.0
Krishna	847	2,322	90.6	15.5	0.0	0.0	0.0
Indian-Coastal-							
Drain	905	2,328	28.6	7.9	0.0	0.0	0.0
Chotanagpur	1,449	2,065	42.6	10.0	0.0	0.0	0.0
Brahmari	1,322	2,133	105.3	17.3	0.0	0.0	0.0
Luni River Basin	641	2,290	24.5	11.2	0.0	0.0	0.0
Mahi-Tapti-							
Narmada	1,007	2,205	87.1	19.4	0.0	0.0	0.0
Brahmaputra	2,453	1,320	624.4	62.9	290.5	348.5	254.0
Indus	737	1,799	75.6	9.7	174.3	209.1	152.4
Ganges	1036	2,035	391.3	57.7	116.2	139.4	101.6
India average/total	n.a.	n.a.	**1,721**	**263**	**581**	**697**	**508**

(continued)

Table A.2—Continued

Region/ Country	Average annual precipitation (mm)	Average annual ET_0 (mm)	Internal water (km³)		Inflow (km³)		
			average	variance	average	maximum	minimum
European Union 15	1,013	783	1,124.6	128.9	0.0	0.0	0.0
Japan	1,512	798	274.3	56.8	0.0	0.0	0.0
Australia	512	1,580	548.1	282.9	0.0	0.0	0.0
Other developed countries	1,138	1,128	4,395.9	132.1	0.0	0.0	0.0
Eastern Europe	697	705	264.7	66	112.0	0.0	0.0
Central Asia	288	1080	204	45.6	20.0	0.0	0.0
Rest of former Soviet Union	512	661	4,005.9	241	222.0	330.0	144.0
Mexico	1,306	1,781	325.8	49.8	2.5	5.0	0.3
Brazil	1,740	1,873	6,454.9	441.3	1,900	2,350	1,600
Argentina	875	1,407	389.6	112.4	623.0	1,410.0	343.0
Colombia	2,233	1,517	1,627.8	105.6	0.0	0.0	0.0
Other Latin America	1,592	1,708	4,371.9	200	0.0	0.0	0.0
Nigeria	1,077	2,280	260.3	32.9	43.7	69.0	23.4
Northern Sub-Saharan Africa	832	2,399	610.2	114.5	224.8	352.0	70.0
Central and western Sub-Saharan Africa	1,552	1,982	2,479.1	179.7	313.5	420.0	248.3
Southern Sub-Saharan Africa	960	2,104	1,125.9	125.1	0.0	0.0	0.0
Eastern Sub-Saharan Africa	1,114	2,093	327.6	66.1	24.5	80.0	10.0
Egypt	57	1,621	2.3	0.7	58.8	184.0	27.5
Turkey	586	1,304	114.9	31.9	0.0	0.0	0.0
Other WANA	417	1,605	77.4	16.9	50.5	143.0	21.5
Pakistan	424	1,952	110.5	26.3	186.0	372.0	55.8
Bangladesh	2,222	1,787	166.5	22	1,167	2,334	350.1
Other South Asia	1,257	1,467	279.1	15.7	31.2	62.0	6.2
Indonesia	2,643	1,819	2,005.3	236	0.0	0.0	0.0
Thailand	1,506	2,323	229.1	25.9	120.0	240.0	36.0
Malaysia	2,792	1,790	399.3	47.6	0.0	0.0	0.0
Philippines	2,342	1,756	199.6	29.1	0.0	0.0	0.0
Viet Nam	1,913	1,517	219.6	24.2	546.0	1092.	163.8
Myanmar	2,105	1,976	942.1	107	110.0	220.0	33.0
Other Southeast Asia	1,995	2,150	345.7	24.3	420.0	840.0	126.0
South Korea	1,358	952	43.8	12	2.5	5.0	0.5
Other East Asia	891	824	136	15	7.7	14.0	2.0
Rest of the world	1,622	1,504	685.3	72.4	0.0	0.0	0.0

Sources: Compiled by authors based on WRI (1998), Shiklomanov (1999), HPDGJ (1989), Qian (1991), NIHWR (1998), and CMWR (1990-98) for river basins in China; USGS (1998) for river basins in the united States; and ESCAP (1995) and IMWR (1998-2000) for river basins in India.

Notes: AGR indicates the fraction of agricultural water consumption; DC, the consumption coefficient (th ratio of consumption over withdrawal); and BE, basin efficiency.

Aside from some parameters already presented above, Table A.2 summarizes the water demand and supply parameters. (These items have all been previously described.

NOTES
1. For i belonging to livestock, QL and QE are equal to zero.

Formulation and Business-as-Usual Scenario Projections for 1995, 2010, and 2025

Following are business-as-usual scenario (BAU) projections for water and food for 1995, 2010, and 2025 for 69 spatial units, by crop, as average results from 30 hydrologic climate scenarios (Tables B.1-28)

Table B.1—Water consumption, total and irrigation

Region/Country	Total water consumption (km³)			Irrigation water consumption (km³)		
	1995	2010	2025	1995	2010	2025
Ohio and Tennessee	9.3	10	10	1.1	1	1.3
Rio Grande	4.8	4.8	4.8	3.2	2.9	2.9
Columbia	16.9	16.9	17.1	15.2	14.8	15
Colorado	16.8	15.9	16	13.5	11.9	11.9
Great Basin	7.2	7.7	7.8	5.8	6	6.1
California	29.7	30.4	31	25.1	25.2	25.4
White-Red	16.5	16	17.1	12.5	10.4	10.5
Mid Atlantic	9.3	10.2	9.9	1.1	1.1	1.3
Mississippi						
Downstream	8.2	8.7	9.1	5.8	5.9	6.2
Upstream	5.3	5.6	5.5	1.4	1.4	1.4
Great Lakes-Red	6.6	7.1	6.9	0.9	1	1
South Atlantic-Gulf	14.7	16	16.8	6.4	6.5	6.9
Texas-Gulf	14.1	14.4	14.9	9.3	8.9	9
Missouri	25.7	24.6	24.3	22.6	21.2	20.8
U.S. total	**185.1**	**188.3**	**191.2**	**123.8**	**118.3**	**119.8**
Huaihe	30.2	32.9	36.6	24.4	22.3	22.4
Haihe	25.4	24.4	23.9	22.1	19.3	17.9
Huanghe	25	26.1	28.7	21.3	20.7	22.3
Changjian	101.7	107.9	115.8	82.5	75.7	77.4
Songliao	23.4	25.5	28.6	18.9	18.7	20.2
Inland	32.7	32.7	34.9	31.8	31.2	32.7
Southwest	2.8	3.1	3.8	2.3	2	2.2
ZhuJiang	32.9	34.1	38.1	26.6	23.1	23.3
Southeast	16.6	16.5	18.4	14.4	12.4	12.4
China total	**290.7**	**303.2**	**328.8**	**244.2**	**225.5**	**230.9**
Sahyadri Ghats	7.6	9.3	10.1	5	5.3	5.3
Eastern Ghats	5.4	7	5.7	5	6.4	5
Cauvery	6.3	6.5	6.5	5.7	5.5	5.2
Godavari	15.8	16.5	18.8	13.9	13.2	14.3
Krishna	24.3	25.7	28.3	22.6	22.7	24.5
Indian-Coastal-Drain	17.9	23.9	21.6	15.8	20.8	18
Chotanagpur	3.2	4.8	6.2	0.7	0.7	0.8
Brahmari	13	13.3	15.1	12	11.6	13.3
Luni River Basin	19.9	20.1	23.6	19.2	19.1	22.4
Mahi-Tapti-Narmada	17	17.8	18.5	15.9	16	16.4
Brahmaputra	2.5	3.2	4	0.6	0.5	0.4
Indus	79.2	84.1	90.9	77.3	81.1	86.8
Ganges	140.5	140.9	147	127.5	118.7	119.5
India total	**352.8**	**372.9**	**396.3**	**321.3**	**321.6**	**331.7**

(continued)

Table B.1—Continued

Region/Country	Total water consumption (km³)			Irrigation water consumption (km³)		
	1995	2010	2025	1995	2010	2025
European Union 15	86.4	93.4	96.8	48.4	50.2	51.7
Japan	29.9	29.9	29	16.7	15	14.8
Australia	12.8	13.5	14.6	10.2	10.4	11
Other developed countries	28.4	29.8	31.6	13.7	13	14
Eastern Europe	33.9	39.2	41.9	20.6	21.7	24.8
Central Asia	82.1	84.6	87.3	77.9	79.2	80.9
Rest of former Soviet Union	63.8	67.3	72.5	38.2	38.4	40.8
Mexico	38.9	40.2	43.1	31.3	29.9	31.1
Brazil	27.8	34.5	39	13.6	14.9	15.3
Argentina	19.8	22.1	24.2	15.2	15.7	16.9
Colombia	3.6	4.7	5.8	0.7	0.8	0.9
Other Latin America	41.3	47.9	57.7	27.5	28.3	32.8
Nigeria	5.6	8.6	11.8	3.5	5	6.7
Northern Sub-Saharan Africa	30.8	33.7	37.5	27.7	28.6	29.7
Central and western Sub-Saharan Africa	5.4	8.1	11.3	2.6	3.1	3.6
Southern Sub-Saharan Africa	16	18.8	24.2	14	15.7	19.6
Eastern Sub-Saharan Africa	4.6	6.4	8.5	2.6	2.9	3.2
Egypt	27.9	30	31.9	25.4	26.4	27.2
Turkey	22.8	28.6	34.4	18.1	21.7	25.8
Other West Asia/North Africa (WANA)	84.4	88.9	95.9	78.1	79.9	84.2
Pakistan	123.7	129.2	133.1	118	119.9	120.1
Bangladesh	20.8	23.5	25.1	18	19.1	19.2
Other South Asia	29.3	32.8	35.8	27.2	29.1	30
Indonesia	40.5	46.4	52.2	29.5	30.3	30.3
Thailand	27.4	28.4	32	24.1	22.9	24.7
Malaysia	4.8	6.4	7.2	2.8	3.2	3.3
Philippines	20.1	23.7	27.7	15.9	16.4	17.1
Viet Nam	14.7	16.2	19.7	10.2	11.9	13.1
Myanmar	3.3	4.3	5.6	2.2	2.3	2.6
Other Southeast Asia	1.5	2	2.8	0.9	0.9	1
South Korea	9.4	12.5	12.9	4.9	5.7	6.2
Other East Asia	8.5	9.6	10.6	6.7	7.4	7.5
Rest of the world	0.2	0.2	0.3	0.1	0	0
Developed countries	440.3	461.3	477.5	271.7	267.1	276.9
Developing countries	1,358.3	1,468.2	1,603.0	1,163.8	1,168.3	1,215.5
World	**1,798.6**	**1,929.5**	**2,080.5**	**1,435.5**	**1,435.5**	**1,492.3**

Source: 1995 baseline data for water consumption by sector are author estimates based on Shiklomanov (1999) and Gleick (1993) for individual countries and regions; HPDGJ (1989), Qian (1991), NIHWR (1998), and CMWR (1990-98) for river basins in China; USGS (1998) for river basins in the United States; and ESCAP (1995) and IMWR (1998-2000) for river basins in India. Livestock data are from FAO (1986), Mancl (1994), and Beckett and Oltjen (1993). 2010 and 2025 data are IMPACT-WATER projections, 2002.

Notes: Km³ indicates cubic kilometers.

Table B.2—Water consumption, non-irrigation

Region/Country	Domestic (km³)			Industry (km³)			Livestock (km³)			Total Non-Irrigation (km³)		
	1995	2010	2025	1995	2010	2025	1995	2010	2025	1995	2010	2025
Ohio and Tennessee	1.3	1.3	1.3	6.7	7.4	7	0.3	0.3	0.4	8.2	9	8.7
Rio Grande	0.7	0.8	0.8	0.8	0.9	0.9	0.1	0.1	0.1	1.6	1.8	1.9
Columbia	1	1.2	1.3	0.7	0.9	0.7	0.1	0.1	0.1	1.8	2.1	2.1
Colorado	1.7	1.9	2.1	1.4	1.8	1.7	0.2	0.2	0.2	3.3	3.9	4.1
Great Basin	0.7	0.8	0.9	0.6	0.8	0.8	0.1	0.1	0.1	1.3	1.6	1.7
California	3	3.3	3.6	1.2	1.4	1.5	0.4	0.4	0.5	4.5	5.2	5.6
White-Red	1.8	2.9	3.5	1.5	1.9	2.2	0.7	0.8	0.9	4.1	5.6	6.6
Mid Atlantic	2.6	2.6	2.7	5.4	6.3	5.7	0.2	0.2	0.2	8.1	9.1	8.6
Mississippi												
Downstream	1.1	1.1	1.2	0.9	1	1	0.5	0.6	0.7	2.5	2.8	2.9
Upstream	1.1	1.2	1.2	2.5	2.7	2.5	0.3	0.4	0.4	3.9	4.3	4.1
Great Lakes-												
Red	1.4	1.4	1.4	4.1	4.6	4.2	0.1	0.2	0.2	5.7	6.2	5.9
South Atlantic-												
Gulf	3.9	4.3	4.8	3.6	4.2	4.1	0.8	0.9	1	8.3	9.5	10
Texas-Gulf	2.4	2.6	2.7	2.3	2.8	3	0.1	0.1	0.1	4.8	5.5	5.9
Missouri	1.5	1.6	1.7	1.1	1.2	1.1	0.5	0.6	0.7	3.1	3.4	3.5
U.S. total	**24.2**	**27**	**29.4**	**32.6**	**37.9**	**36.4**	**4.4**	**5.1**	**5.7**	**61.3**	**69.9**	**71.5**
Huaihe	4	6.9	7.9	1.2	2.9	5.2	0.5	0.8	1	5.7	10.5	14.2
Haihe	1.9	2.8	3.6	1.1	2	1.8	0.3	0.4	0.6	3.3	5.1	6
Huanghe	2.4	3.4	4	1	1.5	1.8	0.3	0.5	0.7	3.7	5.4	6.5
Changjian	12.3	20.3	24.3	5.7	10	11.3	1.2	2	2.8	19.2	32.2	38.4
Songliao	2.2	3.2	3.5	2	2.9	4.1	0.4	0.6	0.8	4.5	6.7	8.4
Inland	0.7	1.2	1.5	0.1	0.2	0.4	0.1	0.2	0.2	0.9	1.5	2.2
Southwest	0.4	0.6	0.8	0.1	0.3	0.7	0	0.1	0.1	0.5	1	1.6
ZhuJiang	4.3	6.9	10.3	1.6	3.4	3.5	0.4	0.7	1	6.4	11	14.7
Southeast	1.9	2.8	3.5	0.3	1.1	2.2	0.1	0.2	0.3	2.3	4.1	6
China total	**30**	**48**	**59.4**	**13.1**	**24.4**	**31.1**	**3.4**	**5.3**	**7.4**	**46.5**	**77.7**	**97.9**
Sahyadri Ghats	1.3	1.8	2.3	0.8	1.5	1.6	0.4	0.6	0.9	2.5	3.9	4.8
Eastern Ghats	0.3	0.4	0.5	0.1	0.1	0.1	0.1	0.1	0.2	0.4	0.6	0.7
Cauvery	0.4	0.6	0.9	0.1	0.2	0.3	0.1	0.1	0.1	0.6	1	1.3
Godavari	1.4	2.2	3	0.2	0.6	0.9	0.3	0.4	0.7	1.9	3.3	4.5
Krishna	1.2	1.9	2.5	0.3	0.7	0.6	0.3	0.5	0.7	1.8	3	3.8
Indian-Coastal-												
Drain	1.1	1.3	1.5	0.8	1.4	1.5	0.3	0.4	0.6	2.1	3.2	3.7
Chotanagpur	1.9	2.8	3.4	0.6	1.3	2	0	0	0	2.5	4	5.4
Brahmari	0.9	1.2	1.5	0.2	0.3	0.3	0.1	0.1	0.1	1.1	1.6	1.9
Luni River Basin	0.7	0.8	1	0.1	0.1	0.1	0	0	0	0.8	1	1.1
Mahi-Tapti-Narmada	0.9	1.3	1.5	0.2	0.4	0.5	0.1	0.1	0.1	1.1	1.8	2.1
Brahmaputra	0.6	0.8	1	0.4	0.5	0.6	0.8	1.3	2.1	1.9	2.7	3.6
Indus	0.9	1.4	1.8	0.4	0.6	0.7	0.6	1	1.6	1.9	3	4.1
Ganges	9.6	15.6	20.1	3	6	6.5	0.4	0.6	1	13	22.2	27.6
India total	**21**	**32.1**	**40.9**	**7.2**	**13.8**	**15.7**	**3.3**	**5.3**	**8.1**	**31.5**	**51.3**	**64.7**

(continued)

Table B.2—Continued

Region/Country	Domestic (km³) 1995	2010	2025	Industry (km³) 1995	2010	2025	Livestock (km³) 1995	2010	2025	Total Non-Irrigation (km³) 1995	2010	2025
European Union 15	12.5	13.1	13.3	21	25.2	26.8	4.6	4.9	5	38	43.2	45.1
Japan	3.4	3.6	3.6	9.5	10.9	10.3	0.3	0.3	0.3	13.2	14.8	14.2
Australia	0.5	0.6	0.7	1.2	1.4	1.5	0.9	1.1	1.3	2.6	3.1	3.6
Other developed countries	6	6.8	7.2	7	8.1	8.4	1.7	1.9	2	14.7	16.7	17.6
Eastern Europe	2.9	3.3	3.6	9	12.7	11.9	1.4	1.5	1.6	13.3	17.5	17
Central Asia	1.6	2.1	2.6	1.7	2.2	2.5	0.9	1.1	1.3	4.2	5.4	6.4
Rest of former Soviet Union	9.1	10.1	10.9	14.4	16.7	18.6	2.1	2.1	2.2	25.6	28.9	31.6
Mexico	3.1	4.2	4.9	3.5	4.8	5.4	0.9	1.3	1.8	7.5	10.3	12.1
Brazil	5.7	7.8	9.6	6.1	8.5	9.7	2.5	3.4	4.4	14.2	19.6	23.7
Argentina	1.1	1.5	1.7	2	3.1	3.3	1.4	1.8	2.2	4.6	6.4	7.3
Colombia	1.5	2.1	2.6	0.5	0.7	0.9	0.8	1.1	1.4	2.9	3.9	4.9
Other Latin America	6.7	9.5	11.8	5.7	8.2	10.5	1.3	1.9	2.6	13.7	19.5	25
Nigeria	1.7	2.8	3.8	0.2	0.4	0.7	0.2	0.4	0.6	2.1	3.6	5.1
Northern Sub-Saharan Africa	2.4	3.9	5.9	0.2	0.3	0.5	0.5	0.9	1.3	3.1	5.1	7.8
Central and western Sub-Saharan Africa	2.4	4.2	6.4	0.2	0.4	0.6	0.2	0.4	0.6	2.8	5	7.7
Southern Sub-Saharan Africa	1.5	2.3	3.4	0.2	0.3	0.5	0.3	0.5	0.7	2	3.1	4.6
Eastern Sub-Saharan Africa	1.6	2.8	4.3	0.1	0.1	0.2	0.3	0.5	0.8	2	3.5	5.3
Egypt	1.6	2.3	2.9	0.7	1.1	1.5	0.2	0.2	0.3	2.5	3.6	4.7
Turkey	2.1	3.1	4	1.9	2.9	3.6	0.7	0.9	1.1	4.7	6.9	8.7
Other West Asia/North Africa (WANA)	3.4	4.8	6.3	2	2.9	3.5	0.9	1.3	1.9	6.2	9	11.7
Pakistan	3.1	5.1	7	1.6	2.7	3.9	0.9	1.4	2.1	5.7	9.2	13
Bangladesh	2.3	3.6	4.7	0.2	0.3	0.5	0.3	0.5	0.8	2.8	4.4	5.9
Other South Asia	1.6	2.8	4.6	0.1	0.2	0.3	0.5	0.7	1	2.2	3.7	5.8
Indonesia	6.9	9.5	13.5	3.6	5.7	7.1	0.6	0.9	1.3	11	16.1	22
Thailand	1.9	3.1	4.3	1.1	1.9	2.5	0.2	0.4	0.6	3.3	5.4	7.3
Malaysia	1	1.5	2	0.9	1.6	1.9	0.1	0.1	0.1	1.9	3.2	4
Philippines	1.3	2.1	3	2.8	4.9	7.3	0.2	0.3	0.4	4.2	7.3	10.7
Viet Nam	1.8	3.2	4.5	2.5	0.7	1.4	0.3	0.4	0.6	4.6	4.3	6.6
Myanmar	0.7	1.4	2.1	0.1	0.1	0.2	0.3	0.5	0.7	1.1	2	3
Other Southeast Asia	0.4	0.6	1	0.2	0.3	0.5	0.1	0.2	0.3	0.7	1.1	1.8
South Korea	1.6	2	2.3	2.7	4.5	4.2	0.2	0.2	0.3	4.5	6.8	6.8
Other East Asia	0.7	1.1	1.4	0.9	0.9	1.4	0.2	0.2	0.3	1.8	2.2	3
Rest of the world	0.1	0.1	0.2	0	0	0	0	0.1	0.1	0.1	0.2	0.3
Developed countries	58.7	64.5	68.6	94.7	112.8	113.8	15.3	16.9	18.2	168.6	194.2	200.6
Developing countries	110.6	169.5	221	62.2	98.3	121.4	21.8	32.1	45.2	194.5	299.9	387.6
World	169.2	234	289.6	156.9	211	235.2	37	49	63.4	363.1	494.1	588.2

Source: 1995 baseline data for water consumption by sector are author estimates based on Shiklomanov (1999) and Gleick (1993) for individual countries and regions; HPDGJ (1989), Qian (1991), NIHWR (1998), and CMWR (1990-98) for river basins in China; USGS (1998) for river basins in the United States; and ESCAP (1995) and IMWR (1998-2000) for river basins in India. Livestock data are from FAO (1986), Mancl (1994), and Beckett and Oltjen (1993). 2010 and 2025 data are IMPACT-WATER projections, 2002.
Notes: Km³ indicates cubic kilometers.

Table B.3—Water withdrawal and the share of total renewable water

Region/Country	Total water withdrawal (km³)			Ratio of withdrawal to TRW		
	1995	2010	2025	1995	2010	2025
Ohio and Tennessee	36.6	39.7	39.2	0.16	0.17	0.17
Rio Grande	11.6	11.8	11.9	1.39	1.42	1.43
Columbia	52	53.7	54.3	0.19	0.2	0.2
Colorado	37.5	36.2	36.6	1.63	1.58	1.59
Great Basin	14.3	15.7	16.2	0.46	0.51	0.52
California	57.3	60.1	62	0.56	0.59	0.61
White-Red	39.9	42.1	46.1	0.37	0.39	0.43
Mid Atlantic	39.6	43.6	42.3	0.16	0.17	0.17
Mississippi						
Downstream	20.3	21.4	22.6	0.1	0.1	0.11
Upstream	22.4	24.1	23.3	0.14	0.15	0.15
Great Lakes-Red	22.9	24.7	23.7	0.11	0.12	0.12
South Atlantic-Gulf	48.9	53.8	56.6	0.17	0.19	0.2
Texas-Gulf	32.7	34	35.5	0.51	0.53	0.56
Missouri	60.8	59.8	59.5	0.44	0.46	0.45
U.S. total	**496.6**	**520.8**	**529.7**	**0.24**	**0.25**	**0.26**
Huaihe	77.9	93.7	108.3	0.83	1	1.15
Haihe	59.2	62.1	62.9	1.4	1.47	1.49
Huanghe	64	71.1	79.5	0.89	0.99	1.11
Changjian	212.6	238.5	259.1	0.23	0.26	0.29
Songliao	51.5	59.2	67.6	0.26	0.3	0.34
Inland	89.5	98.9	111.2	2.99	3.3	3.71
Southwest	8.3	9.7	12.3	0.01	0.01	0.02
ZhuJiang	77.1	84.9	96.9	0.19	0.21	0.24
Southeast	38.8	41.4	47.7	0.27	0.29	0.33
China total	**678.8**	**759.4**	**845.5**	**0.26**	**0.29**	**0.33**
Sahyadri Ghats	14.9	18.7	20.8	0.14	0.17	0.19
Eastern Ghats	10.5	13.7	11.6	0.67	0.87	0.74
Cauvery	11.8	12.8	13.1	0.82	0.89	0.91
Godavari	30.2	33.3	38.8	0.27	0.3	0.35
Krishna	46.2	51.4	57.5	0.51	0.57	0.63
Indian-Coastal-Drain	34.8	46.9	43.6	1.08	1.45	1.35
Chotanagpur	7.2	10.9	14.3	0.17	0.26	0.34
Brahmari	25.5	27.2	31	0.24	0.22	0.26
Luni River Basin	41.9	43.1	50.8	1.48	1.4	1.66
Mahi-Tapti-Narmada	31.4	34.3	36.3	0.36	0.39	0.42
Brahmaputra	5.5	7.2	9.2	0.01	0.01	0.01
Indus	159.1	178.7	198.6	0.72	0.81	0.9
Ganges	255.3	271.9	289.3	0.5	0.54	0.57
India total	**674.4**	**750**	**814.8**	**0.3**	**0.33**	**0.35**

(continued)

Table B.3—Continued

Region/Country	Total water withdrawal (km³)			Ratio of withdrawal to TRW		
	1995	2010	2025	1995	2010	2025
European Union 15	231.4	253.6	263.4	0.21	0.23	0.23
Japan	65.3	66.3	64.2	0.24	0.24	0.23
Australia	26	28.1	30.5	0.05	0.05	0.06
Other developed countries	78.5	84.4	89.5	0.02	0.02	0.02
Eastern Europe	85.6	101.1	105.5	0.23	0.27	0.28
Central Asia	146.6	152.2	157.8	0.67	0.69	0.72
Rest of former Soviet Union	160.7	168.3	182.1	0.04	0.04	0.04
Mexico	78.6	86.2	94.2	0.24	0.26	0.29
Brazil	69.5	88.2	101.4	0.01	0.01	0.01
Argentina	37.7	43.8	48.4	0.04	0.04	0.05
Colombia	9.9	13	16	0.01	0.01	0.01
Other Latin America	102	123.2	150.3	0.02	0.03	0.03
Nigeria	10.9	16.9	23.2	0.04	0.06	0.08
Northern Sub-Saharan Africa	52.2	59.4	68.3	0.06	0.07	0.08
Central and western Sub-Saharan Africa	11	17.2	24.7	0	0.01	0.01
Southern Sub-Saharan Africa	44.4	57.9	78.3	0.04	0.05	0.07
Eastern Sub-Saharan Africa	9.9	14.3	19.6	0.03	0.04	0.06
Egypt	54.3	60.4	65.6	0.89	0.99	1.08
Turkey	38.6	49.3	59.6	0.25	0.32	0.38
Other West Asia/North Africa (WANA)	143.2	156	171.5	1.16	1.25	1.39
Pakistan	267.3	291.2	309.3	0.9	0.98	1.05
Bangladesh	32.6	37.8	41.4	0.02	0.03	0.03
Other South Asia	53.2	62	70.3	0.17	0.2	0.23
Indonesia	53	62.9	73.1	0.03	0.03	0.04
Thailand	40.2	44.1	51	0.12	0.13	0.15
Malaysia	13.3	18.3	20.9	0.03	0.05	0.05
Philippines	47	58.2	70	0.24	0.29	0.35
Viet Nam	38.6	41.5	52	0.05	0.05	0.07
Myanmar	7.9	10.6	14.1	0.01	0.01	0.01
Other Southeast Asia	3.1	4.1	5.8	0	0.01	0.01
South Korea	25.8	34.9	35.9	0.56	0.75	0.78
Other East Asia	17.6	20.2	23.2	0.12	0.14	0.16
Rest of the world	0.4	0.5	0.7	0	0	0
Developed countries	1,144.2	1,222.6	1,264.9	0.09	0.09	0.1
Developing countries	2,761.9	3,133.6	3,506.8	0.08	0.09	0.1
World	**3,906.1**	**4,356.2**	**4,771.7**	**0.08**	**0.09**	**0.1**

Sources: 1995 baseline data for water consumption by sector are author estimates based on Shiklomanov (1999) and Gleick (1993) for individual countries and regions; HPDGJ (1989), Qian (1991), NIHWR (1998), and CMWR (1990-98) for river basins in China; USGS (1998) for river basins in the United States; and ESCAP (1995) and IMWR (1998-2000) for river basins in India. Livestock data are from FAO (1986), Mancl (1994), and Beckett and Oltjen (1993). 2010 and 2025 data are IMPACT-WATER projections, 2002.
Notes: TRW indicates total renewable water; km³, cubic kilometers.

Table B.4—Water supply reliability, irrigation and non-irrigation

Region/Country	Irrigation water supply reliability			Non-irrigation water supply reliability		
	1995	2010	2025	1995	2010	2025
Ohio and Tennessee	1	0.87	1	1	0.99	1
Rio Grande	0.84	0.8	0.83	0.99	0.98	0.99
Columbia	0.94	0.94	0.99	1	1	1
Colorado	0.91	0.83	0.86	1	0.99	0.99
Great Basin	0.94	0.97	1	0.99	1	1
California	0.93	0.95	1	0.99	0.99	1
White-Red	0.94	0.74	0.75	0.99	0.95	0.95
Mid Atlantic	1	0.92	1	1	0.99	1
Mississippi						
Downstream	0.86	0.87	0.93	0.95	0.96	0.98
Upstream	1	0.94	0.99	1	0.99	1
Great Lakes-Red	1	0.99	1	1	1	1
South Atlantic-Gulf	1	0.96	1	1	0.99	1
Texas-Gulf	0.91	0.84	0.86	0.99	0.97	0.98
Missouri	0.97	0.88	0.88	1	0.99	0.99
U.S. total	0.93	0.89	0.91	0.99	0.99	0.99
Huaihe	0.83	0.71	0.66	0.99	0.95	0.94
Haihe	0.78	0.66	0.62	1	0.97	0.97
Huanghe	0.8	0.74	0.75	0.99	0.95	0.95
Changjian	0.92	0.84	0.9	1	0.99	0.99
Songliao	0.85	0.71	0.71	0.98	0.93	0.93
Inland	0.81	0.77	0.79	1	1	1
Southwest	0.99	0.89	0.96	0.99	0.98	0.99
ZhuJiang	0.98	0.88	0.91	1	0.99	0.99
Southeast	1	0.85	0.84	1	0.98	0.98
China total	0.87	0.78	0.79	0.99	0.97	0.97
Sahyadri Ghats	0.77	0.72	0.66	0.96	0.91	0.88
Eastern Ghats	0.62	0.81	0.67	0.99	0.98	0.98
Cauvery	0.84	0.71	0.59	0.99	1	1
Godavari	0.99	0.81	0.8	1	1	1
Krishna	0.73	0.64	0.62	1	1	1
Indian-Coastal-Drain	0.63	0.75	0.64	1	1	1
Chotanagpur	0.71	0.64	0.64	0.96	0.95	0.97
Brahmari	0.74	0.64	0.68	1	1	1
Luni River Basin	0.73	0.7	0.8	1	0.99	1
Mahi-Tapti-Narmada	0.9	0.83	0.79	1	0.99	1
Brahmaputra	0.88	0.82	0.85	0.98	0.96	0.97
Indus	0.83	0.78	0.79	1	1	1
Ganges	0.83	0.7	0.67	1	0.99	1
India total	0.8	0.73	0.71	0.99	0.98	0.99

(continued)

Table B.4—Continued

Region/Country	Irrigation water supply reliability			Non-irrigation water supply reliability		
	1995	2010	2025	1995	2010	2025
European Union 15	0.9	0.94	0.99	1	1	1
Japan	1	0.95	0.98	1	0.99	1
Australia	0.88	0.88	0.93	0.98	0.98	0.99
Other developed countries	0.92	0.88	0.97	1	1	1
Eastern Europe	0.83	0.84	0.96	0.96	0.96	0.99
Central Asia	0.67	0.69	0.72	1	1	1
Rest of former Soviet Union	0.66	0.65	0.71	0.91	0.91	0.93
Mexico	0.84	0.73	0.75	1	0.99	0.99
Brazil	0.72	0.74	0.73	0.99	0.99	0.99
Argentina	0.75	0.72	0.73	0.98	0.96	0.96
Colombia	0.89	0.76	0.72	0.99	0.96	0.95
Other Latin America	0.93	0.74	0.79	1	1	1
Nigeria	0.59	0.65	0.72	0.94	0.93	0.95
Northern Sub-Saharan Africa	0.74	0.71	0.7	0.97	0.95	0.95
Central and western Sub-Saharan Africa	0.96	0.91	0.88	1	1	1
Southern Sub-Saharan Africa	0.72	0.68	0.72	1	1	1
Eastern Sub-Saharan Africa	0.8	0.78	0.74	0.99	0.99	0.98
Egypt	0.73	0.72	0.71	1	1	1
Turkey	0.8	0.76	0.77	1	0.98	0.97
Other West Asia/North Africa (WANA)	0.79	0.76	0.75	1	1	1
Pakistan	0.78	0.76	0.73	1	1	1
Bangladesh	0.8	0.79	0.76	0.91	0.92	0.91
Other South Asia	0.88	0.88	0.86	1	1	0.99
Indonesia	0.83	0.83	0.81	0.96	0.96	0.95
Thailand	0.94	0.82	0.86	1	0.98	0.98
Malaysia	0.79	0.93	1	0.97	0.99	1
Philippines	0.89	0.9	0.91	0.98	1	1
Viet Nam	0.86	0.94	0.96	0.97	0.99	0.99
Myanmar	0.78	0.74	0.76	0.99	0.98	0.99
Other Southeast Asia	0.89	0.79	0.82	0.98	0.95	0.96
South Korea	0.78	0.87	0.96	0.95	0.97	0.98
Other East Asia	0.79	0.9	0.93	0.99	0.99	0.99
Rest of the world	0.83	0.87	0.93	0.95	0.98	0.98
Developed countries	0.87	0.85	0.9	0.98	0.97	0.98
Developing countries	0.81	0.75	0.75	0.99	0.98	0.98
World	**0.82**	**0.77**	**0.78**	**0.98**	**0.98**	**0.98**

Sources: 1995 baseline data for water consumption by sector are author estimates based on Shiklomanov (1999) and Gleick (1993) for individual countries and regions; HPDGJ (1989), Qian (1991), NIHWR (1998), and CMWR (1990-98) for river basins in China; USGS (1998) for river basins in the United States; and ESCAP (1995) and IMWR (1998-2000) for river basins in India. Livestock data are from FAO (1986), Mancl (1994), and Beckett and Oltjen (1993). 2010 and 2025 data are IMPACT-WATER projections, 2002.

Table B.5—Irrigated and rainfed rice area, yield, and production,1995

Region/Country	AI (000ha)	YI (kg/ha)	PI (10^6-mt)	AR (000ha)	YR (kg/ha)	PR (10^6-mt)
Ohio and Tennessee	1	4,251	0	0	0	0
Rio Grande	21	4,095	0.08	0	0	0
Columbia	0	6,033	0	0	0	0
Colorado	37	6,033	0.23	0	0	0
Great Basin	19	6,033	0.12	0	0	0
California	172	6,033	1.04	0	0	0
White-Red	381	4,059	1.55	0	0	0
Mid Atlantic	0	0	0	0	0	0
Mississippi						
Downstream	383	4,101	1.57	0	0	0
Upstream	6	3,982	0.02	0	0	0
Great Lakes-Red	0	0	0	0	0	0
South Atlantic-Gulf	76	4,019	0.31	0	0	0
Texas-Gulf	121	3,832	0.47	0	0	0
Missouri	26	3,982	0.1	0	0	0
U.S. total	1,242	4,409	5.48	0	0	0
Huaihe	1,869	5,104	9.54	0	0	0
Haihe	252	4,499	1.14	0	0	0
Huanghe	296	3,930	1.16	0	0	0
Changjian	15,941	4,153	66.2	0	0	0
Songliao	1,073	4,816	5.17	625	3,612	2.26
Inland	96	4,097	0.39	0	0	0
Southwest	314	3,609	1.13	0	0	0
ZhuJiang	7,706	3,525	27.16	0	0	0
Southeast	2,960	3,680	10.89	0	0	0
China total	30,508	4,025	122.79	625	3,612	2.26
Sahyadri Ghats	950	3,090	2.93	1,879	1,800	3.38
Eastern Ghats	859	2,670	2.29	675	1,160	0.78
Cauvery	480	3,160	1.52	155	2,470	0.38
Godavari	2,105	2,550	5.37	1,442	990	1.43
Krishna	1,209	2,920	3.53	476	1,600	0.76
Indian-Coastal-Drain	1,591	3,050	4.85	371	2,240	0.83
Chotanagpur	98	1,940	0.19	4,597	1,940	8.92
Brahmari	2,140	1,920	4.11	4,499	1,030	4.63
Luni River Basin	75	1,480	0.11	26	1,530	0.04
Mahi-Tapti-Narmada	115	2,130	0.24	865	960	0.83
Brahmaputra	950	1,800	1.71	808	1,270	1.03
Indus	2,379	3,340	7.95	428	1,420	0.61
Ganges	5,023	2,040	10.25	8,444	1,420	11.99
India total	17,974	2,507	45.06	24,664	1,444	35.61

(continued)

Table B.5—Continued

Region/Country	AI (000ha)	YI (kg/ha)	PI (10^6-mt)	AR (000ha)	YR (kg/ha)	PR (10^6-mt)
European Union 15	391	3,980	1.56	0	0	0
Japan	2,093	4,385	9.18	10	1,485	0.01
Australia	127	5,306	0.67	0	0	0
Other developed countries	1	1,539	0	0	0	0
Eastern Europe	15	2,364	0.03	0	0	0
Central Asia	321	1,603	0.51	0	0	0
Rest of former Soviet Union	203	1,785	0.36	0	0	0
Mexico	35	3,558	0.12	50	2,595	0.13
Brazil	1,192	2,935	3.5	3,044	1,167	3.55
Argentina	173	3,225	0.56	0	0	0
Colombia	280	3,403	0.95	127	1,569	0.2
Other Latin America	1,292	2,908	3.76	526	1,655	0.87
Nigeria	281	1,889	0.53	1,484	764	1.13
Northern Sub-Saharan Africa	251	1,432	0.36	187	737	0.14
Central and western Sub-Saharan Africa	190	1,997	0.38	2,172	778	1.69
Southern Sub-Saharan Africa	449	1,540	0.69	894	1,199	1.07
Eastern Sub-Saharan Africa	82	2,000	0.16	440	945	0.42
Egypt	586	5,412	3.17	0	0	0
Turkey	48	3,120	0.15	0	0	0
Other West Asia/North Africa (WANA)	737	2,519	1.86	0	0	0
Pakistan	2,179	1,793	3.91	0	0	0
Bangladesh	5,504	2,868	15.78	1,460	1,354	1.98
Other South Asia	940	2,221	2.09	1,509	1,379	2.08
Indonesia	8,794	3,378	29.71	2,453	1,258	3.09
Thailand	2,099	2,668	5.6	7,278	1,221	8.89
Malaysia	454	2,362	1.07	231	1,407	0.33
Philippines	2,620	2,175	5.7	1,230	1,368	1.68
Viet Nam	3,682	3,135	11.54	3,113	1,641	5.11
Myanmar	824	2,868	2.36	4,950	1,948	9.64
Other Southeast Asia	170	2,026	0.34	2,165	1,210	2.62
South Korea	986	4,404	4.34	83	2,298	0.19
Other East Asia	390	3,353	1.31	192	1,230	0.24
Rest of the world	8	1,602	0.01	0	0	0
Developed countries	4,072	4,244	17.28	10	1,485	0.01
Developing countries	83,049	3,231	268.33	58,876	1,408	82.91
World	**87,120**	**3,278**	**285.61**	**58,886**	**1,408**	**82.92**

Sources: For cereals in developing countries, FAO (1998b and 1999); for crops in basins in the United States, China, and India, and non-cereal crops in all countries and regions, Cai and Rosegrant (1999).
Notes: AI indicates irrigated area; YI, irrigated yield; PI, irrigated production; AR, rainfed area; YR, rainfed yield; PR, rainfed production; 000ha, thousand hectares; kg/ha, kilograms per hectare; and 10^6-mt, million metric tons.

Table B.6—Irrigated and rainfed wheat area, yield, and production, 1995

Region/Country	AI (000ha)	YI (kg/ha)	PI (10^6-mt)	AR (000ha)	YR (kg/ha)	PR (10^6-mt)
Ohio and Tennessee	2	3,842	0.01	986	3,468	3.42
Rio Grande	73	2,719	0.2	236	1,730	0.41
Columbia	563	6,321	3.56	1,755	3,245	5.69
Colorado	146	5,070	0.74	383	2,150	0.82
Great Basin	58	5,813	0.34	39	2,061	0.08
California	160	5,534	0.89	67	3,213	0.21
White-Red	238	2,790	0.66	4,600	1,858	8.55
Mid Atlantic	4	4,578	0.02	290	3,618	1.05
Mississippi						
Downstream	17	3,530	0.06	425	3,067	1.3
Upstream	4	3,309	0.01	1,134	2,648	3
Great Lakes-Red	10	2,932	0.03	3,138	2,291	7.19
South Atlantic-Gulf	12	3,498	0.04	552	3,035	1.68
Texas-Gulf	205	2,540	0.52	595	1,528	0.91
Missouri	276	3,142	0.87	9,075	2,130	19.33
U.S. total	**1,767**	**4,492**	**7.94**	**23,275**	**2,305**	**53.65**
Huaihe	6,728	4,774	32.12	2,467	3,343	8.25
Haihe	2,842	4,336	12.32	1,027	2,860	2.94
Huanghe	3,070	3,139	9.64	1,809	2,211	4
Changjian	5,655	3,269	18.49	1,404	3,266	4.59
Songliao	379	3,659	1.39	1,002	2,206	2.21
Inland	1,325	3,667	4.86	287	2,075	0.6
Southwest	235	2,739	0.64	33	2,678	0.09
ZhuJiang	455	1,975	0.9	179	1,903	0.34
Southeast	254	2,638	0.67	0	0	0
China total	**20,943**	**3,869**	**81.02**	**8,208**	**2,803**	**23.01**
Sahyadri Ghats	29	1,390	0.04	22	650	0.01
Eastern Ghats	1	1,840	0	0	1,100	0
Cauvery	0	780	0	0	840	0
Godavari	388	1,550	0.6	202	630	0.13
Krishna	194	1,460	0.28	198	560	0.11
Indian-Coastal-Drain	1	1,460	0	1	650	0
Chotanagpur	13	1,850	0.02	53	2,020	0.11
Brahmari	58	1,560	0.09	83	750	0.06
Luni River Basin	659	2,680	1.77	155	820	0.13
Mahi-Tapti-Narmada	929	1,950	1.81	508	1,090	0.55
Brahmaputra	0	0	0	52	1,510	0.08
Indus	3,873	4,090	15.84	1,328	2,570	3.41
Ganges	12,149	2,570	31.22	4,427	1,460	6.46
India total	**18,295**	**2,825**	**51.68**	**7,028**	**1,573**	**11.06**

(continued)

Table B.6—Continued

Region/Country	AI (000ha)	YI (kg/ha)	PI (10^6-mt)	AR (000ha)	YR (kg/ha)	PR (10^6-mt)
European Union 15	3,460	6,726	23.27	13,020	5,203	67.74
Japan	0	0	0	154	3,220	0.5
Australia	1,486	2,090	3.11	7,996	1,661	13.28
Other developed countries	1,334	2,689	3.59	11,596	2,231	25.87
Eastern Europe	1,898	4,237	8.04	7,671	3,066	23.52
Central Asia	6,011	1,109	6.67	8,280	594	4.92
Rest of former Soviet Union	4,173	1,937	8.08	26,643	1,583	42.18
Mexico	765	4,429	3.39	136	2,032	0.28
Brazil	14	3,299	0.05	1,374	1,662	2.28
Argentina	57	3,721	0.21	5,668	2,123	12.03
Colombia	0	0	0	40	2,119	0.08
Other Latin America	164	3,315	0.54	881	2,168	1.91
Nigeria	28	1,426	0.04	0	0	0
Northern Sub-Saharan Africa	319	1,535	0.49	1,159	1,429	1.66
Central and western Sub-Saharan Africa	0	0	0	9	958	0.01
Southern Sub-Saharan Africa	64	4,034	0.26	33	960	0.03
Eastern Sub-Saharan Africa	0	0	0	229	1,785	0.41
Egypt	987	5,371	5.3	0	0	0
Turkey	95	3,295	0.31	9,422	1,879	17.7
Other West Asia/North Africa (WANA)	3,821	3,179	12.15	11,781	1,095	12.9
Pakistan	7,519	2,134	16.05	675	487	0.33
Bangladesh	280	2,527	0.71	372	1,455	0.54
Other South Asia	2,441	1,384	3.38	105	543	0.06
Indonesia	0	0	0	0	0	0
Thailand	0	0	0	1	661	0
Malaysia	0	0	0	0	0	0
Philippines	0	0	0	0	0	0
Viet Nam	0	0	0	0	0	0
Myanmar	80	1,010	0.08	24	457	0.01
Other Southeast Asia	0	0	0	0	0	0
South Korea	0	0	0	2	4,109	0.01
Other East Asia	333	967	0.32	102	577	0.06
Rest of the world	0	0	0	0	1,906	0
Developed countries	14,119	3,827	54.03	90,354	2,509	226.73
Developing countries	62,215	2,936	182.64	55,529	1,608	89.28
World	**76,334**	**3,101**	**236.68**	**145,884**	**2,166**	**316.01**

Sources: For cereals in developing countries, FAO (1998b and 1999); for crops in basins in the United States, China, and India, and noncereal crops in all countries and regions, Cai and Rosegrant (1999).

Notes: AI indicates irrigated area; YI, irrigated yield; PI, irrigated production; AR, rainfed area; YR, rainfed yield; PR, rainfed production; 000ha, thousand hectares; kg/ha, kilograms per hectare; and 10^6-mt, million metric tons.

Table B.7—Irrigated and rainfed maize area, yield and production, 1995

Region/Country	AI (000ha)	YI (kg/ha)	PI (10^6-mt)	AR (000ha)	YR (kg/ha)	PR (10^6-mt)
Ohio and Tennessee	83	8,838	0.73	4,147	7,917	32.83
Rio Grande	100	10,548	1.06	79	4,001	0.32
Columbia	24	12,424	0.3	44	9,424	0.41
Colorado	135	9,610	1.29	30	5,066	0.15
Great Basin	12	9,098	0.1	0	2,749	0
California	57	10,266	0.58	0	2,749	0
White-Red	501	10,228	5.12	309	5,226	1.61
Mid Atlantic	25	8,457	0.22	756	7,070	5.35
Mississippi						
Downstream	88	8,134	0.72	537	7,655	4.11
Upstream	185	8,968	1.66	9,819	8,399	82.47
Great Lakes-Red	135	8,142	1.1	3,327	7,525	25.04
South Atlantic-Gulf	97	7,851	0.76	741	5,681	4.21
Texas-Gulf	254	10,839	2.76	303	4,159	1.26
Missouri	2,578	8,850	22.82	4,093	7,250	29.67
U.S. total	**4,273**	**9,176**	**39.21**	**24,185**	**7,750**	**187.43**
Huaihe	2,492	6,325	15.76	1,989	4,428	8.81
Haihe	1,668	6,310	10.53	1,950	4,417	8.61
Huanghe	883	5,202	4.6	1,377	3,641	5.01
Changjian	1,610	3,917	6.31	2,070	3,917	8.11
Songliao	1,246	8,308	10.35	5,047	4,990	25.19
Inland	575	5,930	3.41	249	3,557	0.89
Southwest	56	3,464	0.19	284	3,463	0.98
ZhuJiang	311	3,304	1.03	1,013	3,301	3.34
Southeast	58	3,231	0.19	0	0	0
China total	**8,899**	**5,883**	**52.36**	**13,981**	**4,359**	**60.95**
Sahyadri Ghats	34	2,800	0.1	46	1,850	0.08
Eastern Ghats	8	1,930	0.01	56	1,110	0.06
Cauvery	14	1,810	0.03	22	2,860	0.06
Godavari	99	3,210	0.32	374	1,750	0.65
Krishna	153	2,930	0.45	87	2,190	0.19
Indian-Coastal-Drain	31	3,100	0.1	67	2,510	0.17
Chotanagpur	1	1,810	0	57	1,170	0.07
Brahmari	11	1,560	0.02	155	1,090	0.17
Luni River Basin	20	1,870	0.04	192	790	0.15
Mahi-Tapti-Narmada	34	3,030	0.1	883	1,190	1.05
Brahmaputra	0	0	0	41	2,340	0.1
Indus	142	3,340	0.48	589	1,430	0.84
Ganges	434	2,610	1.13	2,485	1,180	2.93
India total	**982**	**2,819**	**2.77**	**5,055**	**1,292**	**6.53**

(continued)

Table B.7—Continued

Region/Country	AI (000ha)	YI (kg/ha)	PI (10^6-mt)	AR (000ha)	YR (kg/ha)	PR (10^6-mt)
European Union 15	1,004	8,773	8.81	2,960	7,829	23.18
Japan	0	0	0	0	2,481	0
Australia	50	5,040	0.25	0	0	0
Other developed countries	0	0	0	5,031	3,403	17.12
Eastern Europe	1,967	4,893	9.62	5,043	3,143	15.85
Central Asia	265	2,467	0.65	0	0	0
Rest of former Soviet Union	441	3,143	1.38	1,491	2,272	3.39
Mexico	1,775	4,993	8.86	5,935	1,498	8.89
Brazil	0	0	0	13,704	2,455	33.64
Argentina	756	5,230	3.95	1,767	3,849	6.8
Colombia	21	2,709	0.06	669	1,537	1.03
Other Latin America	304	6,600	2.01	3,751	1,542	5.78
Nigeria	652	3,402	2.22	4,405	887	3.91
Northern Sub-Saharan Africa	45	1,866	0.08	2,420	1,380	3.34
Central and western Sub-Saharan Africa	1	2,003	0	4,225	1,075	4.54
Southern Sub-Saharan Africa	52	2,335	0.12	5,314	1,095	5.82
Eastern Sub-Saharan Africa	41	2,414	0.1	3,717	1,632	6.07
Egypt	781	6,318	4.94	0	0	0
Turkey	108	6,927	0.75	409	2,859	1.17
Other West Asia/North Africa (WANA)	341	3,207	1.09	278	485	0.13
Pakistan	718	1,548	1.11	162	1,080	0.18
Bangladesh	0	0	0	3	906	0
Other South Asia	239	1,628	0.39	809	1,632	1.32
Indonesia	337	4,960	1.67	3,165	2,044	6.47
Thailand	0	0	0	1,334	3,162	4.22
Malaysia	0	0	0	23	1,829	0.04
Philippines	0	0	0	2,719	1,549	4.21
Viet Nam	94	4,054	0.38	475	1,905	0.9
Myanmar	19	4,416	0.08	146	1,430	0.21
Other Southeast Asia	0	0	0	75	1,560	0.12
South Korea	5	5,619	0.03	14	3,584	0.05
Other East Asia	402	3,536	1.42	230	2,453	0.57
Rest of the world	0	0	0	35	397	0.01
Developed countries	7,734	7,664	59.28	38,711	6,380	246.97
Developing countries	16,838	5,051	85.05	74,819	2,231	166.9
World	**24,572**	**5,874**	**144.33**	**113,530**	**3,645**	**413.87**

Sources: For cereals in developing countries, FAO (1998b and 1999); for crops in basins in the United States, China, and India, and noncereal crops in all countries and regions, Cai and Rosegrant (1999).
Notes: AI indicates irrigated area; YI, irrigated yield; PI, irrigated production; AR, rainfed area; YR, rainfed yield; PR, rainfed production; 000ha, thousand hectares; kg/ha, kilograms per hectare; and 10⁶-mt, million metric tons.

Table B.8—Irrigated and rainfed other coarse grain area, yield, and production, 1995

Region/Country	AI (000ha)	YI (kg/ha)	PI (10^6-mt)	AR (000ha)	YR (kg/ha)	PR (10^6-mt)
Ohio and Tennessee	0	4,932	0	117	2,891	0.34
Rio Grande	56	4,908	0.27	234	2,059	0.48
Columbia	252	5,952	1.5	385	3,203	1.23
Colorado	71	5,806	0.41	74	2,093	0.16
Great Basin	37	5,806	0.21	23	2,600	0.06
California	34	5,037	0.17	56	3,278	0.19
White-Red	106	5,732	0.61	1,166	3,294	3.84
Mid Atlantic	2	5,919	0.01	146	2,829	0.41
Mississippi						
Downstream	7	6,316	0.04	155	3,613	0.56
Upstream	2	4,321	0.01	488	3,115	1.52
Great Lakes-Red	3	3,399	0.01	820	3,167	2.6
South Atlantic-Gulf	3	3,936	0.01	122	1,906	0.23
Texas-Gulf	166	5,157	0.86	746	2,249	1.68
Missouri	191	5,423	1.03	2,700	3,344	9.03
U.S total	**929**	**5,548**	**5.16**	**7,232**	**3,086**	**22.32**
Huaihe	451	3,852	1.74	0	0	0
Haihe	402	2,171	0.87	994	1,518	1.51
Huanghe	128	2,893	0.37	1,152	2,021	2.33
Changjian	679	4,552	3.09	67	4,551	0.31
Songliao	0	0	0	767	3,480	2.67
Inland	65	3,075	0.2	311	1,848	0.57
Southwest	83	3,496	0.29	82	3,496	0.29
ZhuJiang	118	3,678	0.43	35	3,677	0.13
Southeast	115	3,883	0.45	0	0	0
China total	**2,041**	**3,646**	**7.44**	**3,407**	**2,289**	**7.8**
Sahyadri Ghats	7	1,760	0.01	665	893	0.59
Eastern Ghats	0	0	0	244	778	0.19
Cauvery	0	3,883	0	964	1,088	1.05
Godavari	1	955	0	4,596	1,053	4.84
Krishna	19	2,158	0.04	5,264	655	3.45
Indian-Coastal-Drain	0	3,193	0	1,220	1,114	1.36
Chotanagpur	0	0	0	32	770	0.02
Brahmari	0	761	0	92	681	0.06
Luni River Basin	63	778	0.05	3,634	513	1.86
Mahi-Tapti-Narmada	15	1,353	0.02	2,156	1,238	2.67
Brahmaputra	0	0	0	11	867	0.01
Indus	76	1,557	0.12	1,907	593	1.13
Ganges	363	1,415	0.51	4,760	867	4.13
India total	**544**	**1,389**	**0.76**	**25,545**	**836**	**21.37**

(continued)

Table B.8—Continued

Region/Country	AI (000ha)	YI (kg/ha)	PI (10^6-mt)	AR (000ha)	YR (kg/ha)	PR (10^6-mt)
Japan	0	0	0	61	3,749	0.23
Australia	943	2,097	1.98	3,814	1,594	6.08
Other developed countries	784	3,095	2.43	6,816	2,567	17.5
Eastern Europe	2,055	3,603	7.41	5,270	2,314	12.19
Central Asia	2,770	1,037	2.87	3,669	525	1.93
Rest of former Soviet Union	6,616	1,848	12.23	29,851	1,435	42.84
Mexico	531	4,416	2.35	1,326	2,319	3.07
Brazil	0	0	0	441	1,509	0.67
Argentina	0	0	0	1,068	2,599	2.78
Colombia	8	4,506	0.04	202	2,925	0.59
Other Latin America	158	1,586	0.25	1,079	1,665	1.8
Nigeria	334	2,668	0.89	10,709	917	9.82
Northern Sub-Saharan Africa	454	1,496	0.68	25,272	539	13.62
Central and western Sub-Saharan Africa	0	0	0	3,174	776	2.46
Southern Sub-Saharan Africa	7	2,119	0.02	1,839	421	0.77
Eastern Sub-Saharan Africa	12	1,254	0.02	2,069	1,098	2.27
Egypt	257	3,472	0.89	0	0	0
Turkey	0	0	0	3,858	2,069	7.98
Other West Asia/North Africa (WANA)	2,000	2,157	4.31	8,232	922	7.59
Pakistan	0	0	0	0	0	0
Bangladesh	10	607	0.01	82	703	0.06
Other South Asia	83	1,604	0.13	429	940	0.4
Indonesia	0	0	0	0	0	0
Thailand	0	0	0	156	1,398	0.22
Malaysia	0	0	0	0	0	0
Philippines	0	0	0	0	206	0
Viet Nam	0	0	0	4	1,312	0.01
Myanmar	0	0	0	218	645	0.14
Other Southeast Asia	0	0	0	0	0	0
South Korea	0	0	0	91	4,144	0.38
Other East Asia	14	2,540	0.04	122	1,278	0.16
Rest of the world	0	0	0	1	1,649	0
Developed countries	15,886	3,462	55	63,020	2,136	134.61
Developing countries	9,222	2,243	20.68	92,992	923	85.88
World	**25,108**	**3,014**	**75.68**	**156,012**	**1,413**	**220.49**

Sources: For cereals in developing countries, FAO (1998b and 1999); for crops in basins in the United States, China, and India, and noncereal crops in all countries and regions, Cai and Rosegrant (1999).
Notes: AI indicates irrigated area; YI, irrigated yield; PI, irrigated production; AR, rainfed area; YR, rainfed yield; PR, rainfed production; 000ha, thousand hectares; kg/ha, kilograms per hectare; and 10^6-mt, million metric tons.

Table B.9—Irrigated and rainfed soybean area, yield, and production, 1995

Region/Country	AI (000ha)	YI (kg/ha)	PI (10^6-mt)	AR (000ha)	YR (kg/ha)	PR (10^6-mt)
Ohio and Tennessee	28	2,806	0.08	4,056	2,621	10.63
Rio Grande	12	2,289	0.03	53	1,432	0.08
Columbia	220	3,336	0.73	339	3,419	1.16
Colorado	48	3,802	0.18	80	2,662	0.21
Great Basin	12	3,815	0.05	40	3,557	0.14
California	21	3,195	0.07	59	3,084	0.18
White-Red	379	2,486	0.94	1,042	1,902	1.98
Mid Atlantic	17	2,377	0.04	564	2,052	1.16
Mississippi						
Downstream	402	2,383	0.96	1,378	2,092	2.88
Upstream	85	2,839	0.24	7,446	2,844	21.18
Great Lakes-Red	51	2,819	0.14	2,590	2,532	6.56
South Atlantic-Gulf	123	2,274	0.28	1,184	1,817	2.15
Texas-Gulf	31	2,204	0.07	123	1,802	0.22
Missouri	628	3,106	1.95	4,067	2,436	9.91
U.S. total	**2,056**	**2,800**	**5.76**	**23,020**	**2,539**	**58.44**
Huaihe	919	2,345	2.15	58	2,094	0.12
Haihe	720	1,468	1.06	355	1,175	0.42
Huanghe	431	916	0.39	493	733	0.36
Changjian	1,360	1,430	1.95	467	1,430	0.67
Songliao	272	3,107	0.85	2,258	2,272	5.13
Inland	1	1,148	0	1	690	0
Southwest	54	349	0.02	89	340	0.03
ZhuJiang	305	1,226	0.37	322	1,226	0.39
Southeast	159	1,879	0.3	13	1,874	0.02
China total	**4,222**	**1,679**	**7.09**	**4,056**	**1,762**	**7.15**
Sahyadri Ghats	0	0	0	11	468	0.01
Eastern Ghats	0	1,142	0	0	1,016	0
Cauvery	0	507	0	0	439	0
Godavari	99	1,186	0.12	711	957	0.68
Krishna	4	672	0	20	513	0.01
Indian-Coastal-Drain	0	1,161	0	0	0	0
Chotanagpur	0	0	0	0	815	0
Brahmari	0	0	0	23	1,222	0.03
Luni River Basin	6	482	0	0	0	0
Mahi-Tapti-Narmada	376	1,295	0.49	1,186	882	1.05
Brahmaputra	0	0	0	0	0	0
Indus	0	466	0	0	0	0
Ganges	0	0	0	2,376	981	2.33
India total	**485**	**1,258**	**0.61**	**4,328**	**948**	**4.1**

(continued)

Table B.9—Continued

Region/Country	AI (000ha)	YI (kg/ha)	PI (10^6-mt)	AR (000ha)	YR (kg/ha)	PR (10^6-mt)
European Union 15	49	3,927	0.19	287	3,059	0.88
Japan	0	0	0	70	1,731	0.12
Australia	12	2,591	0.03	15	1,262	0.02
Other developed countries	93	3,031	0.28	807	2,515	2.03
Eastern Europe	50	2,268	0.11	127	1,456	0.19
Central Asia	5	845	0	0	0	0
Rest of former Soviet Union	131	839	0.11	442	606	0.27
Mexico	9	2,020	0.02	148	1,603	0.24
Brazil	0	0	0	11,303	2,186	24.71
Argentina	1,335	2,980	3.98	4,524	1,794	8.12
Colombia	3	2,561	0.01	40	2,005	0.08
Other Latin America	90	3,130	0.28	1,187	2,434	2.89
Nigeria	572	372	0.21	0	0	0
Northern Sub-Saharan Africa	9	2,614	0.02	0	0	0
Central and western Sub-Saharan Africa	0	0	0	30	853	0.03
Southern Sub-Saharan Africa	0	0	0	83	1,537	0.13
Eastern Sub-Saharan Africa	4	1,286	0.01	80	1,037	0.08
Egypt	22	2,638	0.06	0	0	0
Turkey	27	2,422	0.06	0	0	0
Other West Asia/North Africa (WANA)	94	1,640	0.15	0	0	0
Pakistan	5	1,029	0.01	0	0	0
Bangladesh	0	0	0	0	0	0
Other South Asia	2	864	0	20	633	0.01
Indonesia	0	0	0	1,388	1,144	1.59
Thailand	0	0	0	323	1,315	0.42
Malaysia	0	0	0	0	333	0
Philippines	0	0	0	4	1,357	0.01
Viet Nam	0	0	0	121	1,001	0.12
Myanmar	0	0	0	58	857	0.05
Other Southeast Asia	0	0	0	24	1,171	0.03
South Korea	0	0	0	108	1,459	0.16
Other East Asia	21	1,580	0.03	301	1,242	0.37
Rest of the world	0	0	0	0	0	0
Developed countries	2,390	2,713	6.49	24,769	2,501	61.94
Developing countries	6,905	1,817	12.55	28,125	1,788	50.28
World	**9,296**	**2,048**	**19.04**	**52,894**	**2,122**	**112.22**

Sources: For cereals in developing countries, FAO (1998b and 1999); for crops in basins in the United States, China, and India, and noncereal crops in all countries and regions, Cai and Rosegrant (1999).
Notes: AI indicates irrigated area; YI, irrigated yield; PI, irrigated production; AR, rainfed area; YR, rainfed yield; PR, rainfed production; 000ha, thousand hectares; kg/ha, kilograms per hectare; and 10^6-mt, million metric tons.

Table B.10—Irrigated and rainfed rice area, yield, and production, 2010

Region/Country	AI (000ha)	YI (kg/ha)	PI (10^6-mt)	AR (000ha)	YR (kg/ha)	PR (10^6-mt)
Ohio and Tennessee	1	4,284	0	0	0	0
Rio Grande	19	4,548	0.09	0	0	0
Columbia	0	6,157	0	0	0	0
Colorado	35	6,598	0.23	0	0	0
Great Basin	20	6,883	0.13	0	0	0
California	175	6,919	1.21	0	0	0
White-Red	350	4,530	1.59	0	0	0
Mid Atlantic	0	0	0	0	0	0
Mississippi						
Downstream	391	4,543	1.78	0	0	0
Upstream	7	4,051	0.03	0	0	0
Great Lakes-Red	0	0	0	0	0	0
South Atlantic-Gulf	79	4,477	0.35	0	0	0
Texas-Gulf	119	4,635	0.55	0	0	0
Missouri	29	3,950	0.11	0	0	0
U.S. total	**1,224**	**4,968**	**6.08**	**0**	**0**	**0**
Huaihe	1,771	5,989	10.6	0	0	0
Haihe	233	4,481	1.05	0	0	0
Huanghe	280	4,298	1.2	0	0	0
Changjian	14,978	5,067	75.89	0	0	0
Songliao	1,417	4,487	6.36	706	3,326	2.34
Inland	107	3,907	0.42	0	0	0
Southwest	292	4,478	1.31	0	0	0
ZhuJiang	7,118	4,416	31.43	0	0	0
Southeast	2,724	4,493	12.24	0	0	0
China total	**28,920**	**4,858**	**140.5**	**706**	**3,321**	**2.34**
Sahyadri Ghats	1,171	3,614	4.23	1,559	2,048	3.19
Eastern Ghats	862	3,685	3.18	928	1,467	1.36
Cauvery	597	3,262	1.95	154	2,347	0.36
Godavari	2,512	3,468	8.71	1,223	1,654	2.02
Krishna	1,469	3,296	4.84	492	2,180	1.07
Indian-Coastal-Drain	1,822	3,189	5.81	373	2,282	0.85
Chotanagpur	182	1,979	0.36	3,434	1,589	5.47
Brahmari	2,583	2,743	7.08	3,553	1,677	5.96
Luni River Basin	102	1,764	0.18	21	1,180	0.03
Mahi-Tapti-Narmada	151	3,032	0.46	713	1,703	1.21
Brahmaputra	813	2,556	2.08	1,082	2,124	2.3
Indus	2,897	3,595	10.41	350	1,680	0.59
Ganges	6,137	2,748	16.86	7,018	1,971	13.83
India total	**21,299**	**3,106**	**66.15**	**20,902**	**1,830**	**38.25**

(continued)

Table B.10—Continued

Region/Country	AI (000ha)	YI (kg/ha)	PI (10^6-mt)	AR (000ha)	YR (kg/ha)	PR (10^6-mt)
European Union 15	397	4,675	1.85	0	0	0
Japan	1,474	5,595	8.25	5	3,981	0.02
Australia	122	6,346	0.78	0	0	0
Other developed countries	1	1,990	0	0	0	0
Eastern Europe	15	2,377	0.04	0	0	0
Central Asia	279	1,886	0.53	0	0	0
Rest of former Soviet Union	167	2,083	0.35	0	0	0
Mexico	40	4,288	0.17	45	3,418	0.15
Brazil	1,211	3,245	3.93	2,984	1,617	4.83
Argentina	199	4,447	0.9	0	0	0
Colombia	345	4,336	1.49	141	1,922	0.27
Other Latin America	1,835	3,013	5.53	493	2,292	1.13
Nigeria	412	2,213	0.91	1,711	1,059	1.81
Northern Sub-Saharan Africa	304	1,446	0.44	248	1,047	0.25
Central and western Sub-Saharan Africa	289	2,160	0.62	2,803	1,028	2.85
Southern Sub-Saharan Africa	613	1,728	1.06	1,110	1,331	1.46
Eastern Sub-Saharan Africa	121	2,193	0.26	453	1,105	0.5
Egypt	670	6,347	4.25	0	0	0
Turkey	45	3,817	0.17	0	0	0
Other West Asia/North Africa (WANA)	652	3,394	2.21	0	0	0
Pakistan	2,239	2,213	4.95	0	0	0
Bangladesh	5,984	3,564	21.33	1,295	1,845	2.39
Other South Asia	990	2,710	2.68	1,570	1,847	2.9
Indonesia	8,834	3,982	35.18	2,476	1,781	4.41
Thailand	2,273	2,643	6.01	7,568	1,390	10.35
Malaysia	432	3,085	1.33	243	1,533	0.37
Philippines	2,740	2,538	6.95	1,270	1,887	2.4
Viet Nam	3,919	4,147	16.25	3,073	2,484	7.63
Myanmar	880	3,746	3.3	5,216	2,511	13.1
Other Southeast Asia	228	2,641	0.6	2,271	1,702	3.86
South Korea	949	4,519	4.29	49	1,994	0.1
Other East Asia	389	3,886	1.51	131	1,604	0.21
Rest of the world	8	1,753	0.01	0	0	0
Developed countries	3,400	5,101	17.35	5	3,984	0.02
Developing countries	87,097	3,829	333.54	56,757	1,790	101.58
World	**90,497**	**3,877**	**350.88**	**56,762**	**1,790**	**101.6**

Source: IMPACT-WATER projections, 2002.

Notes: AI indicates irrigated area; YI, irrigated yield; PI, irrigated production; AR, rainfed area; YR, rainfed yield; PR, rainfed production; 000ha, thousand hectares; kg/ha, kilograms per hectare; and 10^6-mt, million metric tons.

Table B.11—Irrigated and rainfed wheat area, yield, and production, 2010

Region/Country	AI (000ha)	YI (kg/ha)	PI (10^6-mt)	AR (000ha)	YR (kg/ha)	PR (10^6-mt)
Ohio and Tennessee	2	4,216	0.01	1,010	3,412	3.45
Rio Grande	56	3,616	0.2	256	2,440	0.62
Columbia	533	6,905	3.68	1,645	4,196	6.92
Colorado	121	6,122	0.75	392	2,792	1.08
Great Basin	60	7,346	0.44	41	2,588	0.11
California	158	6,798	1.08	58	4,328	0.25
White-Red	193	3,350	0.65	4,651	2,252	10.55
Mid Atlantic	5	5,214	0.02	356	4,321	1.54
Mississippi						
Downstream	18	3,927	0.07	500	3,052	1.52
Upstream	4	3,954	0.01	978	2,850	2.81
Great Lakes-Red	10	3,969	0.04	3,408	2,400	8.21
South Atlantic-Gulf	12	4,069	0.05	629	2,943	1.85
Texas-Gulf	174	4,086	0.73	670	1,856	1.25
Missouri	282	3,792	1.07	9,302	2,554	23.75
U.S. total	**1,627**	**5,410**	**8.8**	**23,893**	**2,676**	**63.93**
Huaihe	7,013	5,963	41.93	3,097	4,352	13.6
Haihe	2,622	5,807	15.26	749	3,938	2.94
Huanghe	3,434	3,454	11.87	1,413	2,782	3.93
Changjian	6,505	4,210	27.39	1,400	3,117	4.38
Songliao	379	4,398	1.67	758	2,330	1.75
Inland	1,318	4,493	5.92	246	2,775	0.68
Southwest	260	3,576	0.93	26	2,652	0.07
ZhuJiang	487	2,256	1.11	138	1,503	0.21
Southeast	247	3,088	0.77	0	0	0
China total	**22,264**	**4,799**	**106.86**	**7,826**	**3,521**	**27.56**
Sahyadri Ghats	34	1,691	0.06	18	965	0.02
Eastern Ghats	2	2,000	0	0	1,434	0
Cauvery	0	1,180	0	0	989	0
Godavari	503	1,701	0.86	183	981	0.18
Krishna	165	2,104	0.35	94	843	0.08
Indian-Coastal-Drain	1	1,801	0	1	1,054	0
Chotanagpur	15	1,779	0.03	37	1,383	0.05
Brahmari	74	2,030	0.15	56	1,076	0.06
Luni River Basin	521	3,878	2.14	144	1,187	0.17
Mahi-Tapti-Narmada	1,022	2,185	2.23	515	1,438	0.74
Brahmaputra	0	0	0	54	1,896	0.1
Indus	4,358	4,765	20.77	1,033	3,399	3.49
Ganges	14,099	2,768	39.03	3,244	1,970	6.44
India total	**20,794**	**3,155**	**65.61**	**5,378**	**2,107**	**11.33**

(continued)

Table B.11—Continued

Region/Country	AI (000ha)	YI (kg/ha)	PI (10^6-mt)	AR (000ha)	YR (kg/ha)	PR (10^6-mt)
European Union 15	3,661	7,680	28.12	13,789	4,989	68.86
Japan	0	0	0	147	3,513	0.51
Australia	2,118	2,584	5.48	10,386	2,094	22.11
Other developed countries	1,645	3,706	6.1	11,569	2,498	28.71
Eastern Europe	2,295	4,471	10.26	9,105	2,736	24.99
Central Asia	6,247	1,258	7.86	9,530	717	6.72
Rest of former Soviet Union	4,725	2,346	11.1	23,214	1,809	42.2
Mexico	751	4,661	3.5	140	2,542	0.36
Brazil	6	3,796	0.02	1,633	2,369	3.81
Argentina	98	3,959	0.39	6,729	2,621	17.67
Colombia	0	0	0	48	2,775	0.13
Other Latin America	207	3,230	0.67	1,055	2,723	2.84
Nigeria	25	1,618	0.04	0	0	0
Northern Sub-Saharan Africa	421	1,576	0.66	1,352	1,483	2
Central and western Sub-Saharan Africa	0	0	0	13	1,180	0.02
Southern Sub-Saharan Africa	80	3,646	0.29	41	1,179	0.05
Eastern Sub-Saharan Africa	0	0	0	297	2,422	0.72
Egypt	790	6,514	5.15	0	0	0
Turkey	77	3,892	0.3	9,941	2,213	22.1
Other West Asia/North Africa (WANA)	4,400	3,764	16.56	12,675	1,145	14.61
Pakistan	7,747	2,620	20.31	689	710	0.49
Bangladesh	290	2,709	0.79	326	1,949	0.64
Other South Asia	2,527	1,839	4.65	67	1,247	0.08
Indonesia	0	0	0	0	0	0
Thailand	0	0	0	1	903	0
Malaysia	0	0	0	0	0	0
Philippines	0	0	0	0	0	0
Viet Nam	0	0	0	0	0	0
Myanmar	97	822	0.08	23	544	0.01
Other Southeast Asia	0	0	0	0	0	0
South Korea	0	0	0	2	4,847	0.01
Other East Asia	344	1,012	0.35	113	651	0.07
Rest of the world	0	0	0	0	2,295	0
Developed countries	16,071	4,347	69.86	92,102	2,729	251.32
Developing countries	67,166	3,485	234.09	57,879	1,922	111.23
World	**83,237**	**3,652**	**303.94**	**149,981**	**2,417**	**362.54**

Source: IMPACT-WATER projections, 2002.
Notes: AI indicates irrigated area; YI, irrigated yield; PI, irrigated production; AR, rainfed area; YR, rainfed yield; PR, rainfed production; 000ha, thousand hectares; kg/ha, kilograms per hectare; and 10^6-mt, million metric tons.

Table B.12—Irrigated and rainfed maize area, yield, and production, 2010

Region/Country	AI (000ha)	YI (kg/ha)	PI (10^6-mt)	AR (000ha)	YR (kg/ha)	PR (10^6-mt)
Ohio and Tennessee	90	10,254	0.93	4,316	8,518	36.84
Rio Grande	100	13,131	1.31	96	5,964	0.57
Columbia	27	14,634	0.39	56	12,058	0.67
Colorado	141	12,548	1.78	35	3,695	0.13
Great Basin	12	10,753	0.13	0	3,897	0
California	59	11,925	0.7	0	3,767	0
White-Red	572	9,887	5.66	353	6,614	2.29
Mid Atlantic	26	9,917	0.26	746	8,295	6.22
Mississippi						
Downstream	94	9,803	0.92	528	7,751	4.11
Upstream	207	10,572	2.19	10,213	7,904	80.9
Great Lakes-Red	151	9,902	1.49	3,679	7,797	28.93
South Atlantic-Gulf	100	10,207	1.02	747	8,427	6.32
Texas-Gulf	264	12,114	3.2	381	5,622	2.1
Missouri	2,818	10,541	29.7	4,627	7,797	35.35
U.S. total	**4,660**	**10,661**	**49.68**	**25,776**	**7,931**	**204.44**
Huaihe	3,338	7,968	26.64	2,440	5,376	13.09
Haihe	2,122	7,108	15.12	2,477	5,173	12.68
Huanghe	1,163	5,647	6.57	1,519	4,396	6.57
Changjian	2,248	5,196	11.68	2,829	4,341	12.28
Songliao	1,959	9,268	18.16	6,147	5,651	34.07
Inland	712	5,559	3.96	294	4,809	1.42
Southwest	60	3,758	0.23	311	3,308	1.03
ZhuJiang	367	4,610	1.7	1,129	3,890	4.4
Southeast	70	4,303	0.3	11	1,359	0.01
China total	**12,039**	**7,007**	**84.36**	**17,157**	**4,987**	**85.56**
Sahyadri Ghats	31	3,277	0.1	49	2,192	0.11
Eastern Ghats	12	3,041	0.04	54	1,453	0.08
Cauvery	20	2,908	0.06	23	2,101	0.05
Godavari	92	5,061	0.47	418	2,274	0.95
Krishna	219	4,519	0.99	103	2,106	0.22
Indian-Coastal-Drain	41	4,890	0.2	72	2,003	0.14
Chotanagpur	1	2,980	0	61	1,683	0.1
Brahmari	14	2,632	0.04	169	1,546	0.26
Luni River Basin	26	3,000	0.08	195	821	0.16
Mahi-Tapti-Narmada	45	4,560	0.2	895	1,619	1.45
Brahmaputra	0	0	0	49	3,043	0.15
Indus	180	5,226	0.94	583	1,271	0.74
Ganges	558	4,041	2.25	2,397	1,580	3.79
India total	**1,239**	**4,336**	**5.37**	**5,068**	**1,617**	**8.2**

(continued)

Table B.12—Continued

Region/Country	AI (000ha)	YI (kg/ha)	PI (10^6-mt)	AR (000ha)	YR (kg/ha)	PR (10^6-mt)
European Union 15	1,074	10,598	11.38	2,653	8,642	22.95
Japan	0	0	0	0	3,869	0
Australia	63	5,307	0.34	0	0	0
Other developed countries	0	0	0	5,327	3,883	20.74
Eastern Europe	2,478	6,100	15.12	5,965	3,403	20.43
Central Asia	264	3,119	0.82	0	0	0
Rest of former Soviet Union	542	3,847	2.09	1,525	3,017	4.55
Mexico	2,282	5,138	11.72	6,233	1,919	11.96
Brazil	0	0	0	19,419	2,631	51.02
Argentina	978	6,712	6.57	2,328	4,453	10.27
Colombia	22	2,973	0.07	702	1,906	1.34
Other Latin America	397	6,737	2.67	4,278	2,105	8.96
Nigeria	714	4,529	3.23	5,142	1,194	6.14
Northern Sub-Saharan Africa	65	2,266	0.15	2,926	1,676	4.9
Central and western Sub-Saharan Africa	1	2,023	0	5,385	1,163	6.26
Southern Sub-Saharan Africa	63	2,530	0.16	6,223	1,409	8.77
Eastern Sub-Saharan Africa	31	2,677	0.09	3,948	2,028	7.99
Egypt	763	8,621	6.58	0	0	0
Turkey	136	6,217	0.85	450	3,565	1.6
Other West Asia/North Africa (WANA)	489	3,662	1.79	220	668	0.15
Pakistan	749	2,039	1.53	157	1,523	0.24
Bangladesh	0	0	0	3	1,144	0
Other South Asia	346	2,027	0.7	935	1,845	1.72
Indonesia	472	5,530	2.61	3,340	2,493	8.29
Thailand	0	0	0	1,323	5,066	6.7
Malaysia	0	0	0	24	2,679	0.06
Philippines	0	0	0	3,202	2,079	6.63
Viet Nam	145	4,362	0.63	488	2,006	0.98
Myanmar	33	4,332	0.14	158	1,821	0.29
Other Southeast Asia	0	0	0	82	2,080	0.17
South Korea	6	7,281	0.05	13	5,253	0.07
Other East Asia	407	3,631	1.48	207	2,504	0.51
Rest of the world	0	0	0	35	488	0.02
Developed countries	8,818	8,914	78.6	41,247	6,622	273.12
Developing countries	21,641	6,079	131.57	89,448	2,670	238.81
World	**30,459**	**6,900**	**210.17**	**130,695**	**3,917**	**511.93**

Source: IMPACT-WATER projections, 2002.
Notes: AI indicates irrigated area; YI, irrigated yield; PI, irrigated production; AR, rainfed area; YR, rainfed yield; PR, rainfed production; 000ha, thousand hectares; kg/ha, kilograms per hectare; and 10^6-mt, million metric tons.

Table B.13—Irrigated and rainfed other coarse grain area, yield, and production, 2010

Region/Country	AI (000ha)	YI (kg/ha)	PI (10^6-mt)	AR (000ha)	YR (kg/ha)	PR (10^6-mt)
Ohio and Tennessee	0	5,861	0	80	3,806	0.31
Rio Grande	57	5,086	0.29	269	2,869	0.77
Columbia	274	6,584	1.8	349	4,863	1.7
Colorado	70	7,583	0.54	80	3,348	0.27
Great Basin	42	6,632	0.28	25	3,931	0.1
California	39	5,273	0.21	67	4,560	0.3
White-Red	151	5,748	0.87	1,286	3,914	5.05
Mid Atlantic	2	7,279	0.01	137	4,298	0.6
Mississippi						
Downstream	7	7,210	0.05	158	4,990	0.8
Upstream	3	5,071	0.01	475	3,952	1.9
Great Lakes-Red	3	4,248	0.01	886	3,385	3.03
South Atlantic-Gulf	3	4,868	0.01	93	2,608	0.24
Texas-Gulf	182	6,005	1.09	770	2,763	2.11
Missouri	213	6,303	1.34	2,885	3,557	10.37
U.S. total	**1,045**	**6,240**	**6.52**	**7,560**	**3,644**	**27.55**
Huaihe	528	4,444	2.35	0	0	0
Haihe	377	2,543	0.96	976	2,120	2.07
Huanghe	151	2,883	0.43	1,081	2,042	2.22
Changjian	855	6,188	5.29	104	4,562	0.47
Songliao	0	0	0	905	3,627	3.29
Inland	65	3,719	0.24	351	2,840	1
Southwest	117	3,900	0.46	93	3,507	0.32
ZhuJiang	153	3,934	0.6	40	3,362	0.13
Southeast	147	4,408	0.65	0	0	0
China total	**2,393**	**4,589**	**10.98**	**3,550**	**2,678**	**9.51**
Sahyadri Ghats	9	2,589	0.02	591	940	0.55
Eastern Ghats	0	0	0	272	853	0.23
Cauvery	0	5,088	0	660	1,298	0.85
Godavari	2	1,630	0	4,037	1,167	4.66
Krishna	23	3,399	0.08	3,967	1,020	4.04
Indian-Coastal-Drain	0	3,066	0	1,166	1,181	1.36
Chotanagpur	0	0	0	62	1,139	0.07
Brahmari	0	1,310	0	103	1,010	0.1
Luni River Basin	66	1,417	0.09	3,207	721	2.28
Mahi-Tapti-Narmada	20	1,717	0.03	2,330	1,437	3.35
Brahmaputra	0	0	0	21	1,583	0.03
Indus	77	2,254	0.17	1,793	843	1.5
Ganges	368	2,197	0.81	4,912	1,112	5.46
India total	**565**	**2,151**	**1.21**	**23,121**	**1,060**	**24.51**

(continued)

Table B.13—Continued

Region/Country	AI (000ha)	YI (kg/ha)	PI (10^6-mt)	AR (000ha)	YR (kg/ha)	PR (10^6-mt)
European Union 15	4,723	6,580	31.08	9,694	3,989	38.7
Japan	0	0	0	58	3,896	0.22
Australia	1,117	2,959	3.31	3,994	1,873	7.58
Other developed countries	903	4,855	4.39	6,303	3,013	18.98
Eastern Europe	2,500	3,828	9.57	5,890	2,720	16.13
Central Asia	2,806	1,053	2.96	2,613	991	2.59
Rest of former Soviet Union	6,691	1,970	13.19	25,335	1,492	38.11
Mexico	663	4,614	3.06	1,420	3,295	4.68
Brazil	0	0	0	504	2,149	1.08
Argentina	0	0	0	1,159	4,018	4.66
Colombia	10	4,564	0.05	219	3,643	0.8
Other Latin America	313	2,356	0.74	1,238	1,995	2.44
Nigeria	497	3,234	1.61	13,442	1,121	15.06
Northern Sub-Saharan Africa	463	1,914	0.89	30,607	710	21.74
Central and western Sub-Saharan Africa	0	0	0	4,298	880	3.79
Southern Sub-Saharan Africa	11	2,571	0.03	2,312	568	1.31
Eastern Sub-Saharan Africa	12	1,446	0.02	2,650	1,174	3.11
Egypt	207	3,832	0.79	0	0	0
Turkey	0	0	0	3,012	3,259	9.81
Other West Asia/North Africa (WANA)	2,078	2,367	4.92	8,648	1,139	9.85
Pakistan	0	0	0	147	416	0.06
Bangladesh	14	655	0.01	81	571	0.05
Other South Asia	83	1,827	0.15	454	1,291	0.59
Indonesia	0	0	0	0	0	0
Thailand	0	0	0	155	1,642	0.25
Malaysia	0	0	0	0	0	0
Philippines	0	0	0	0	219	0
Viet Nam	0	0	0	5	1,658	0.01
Myanmar	0	0	0	235	738	0.17
Other Southeast Asia	0	0	0	0	0	0
South Korea	0	0	0	87	5,547	0.48
Other East Asia	14	2,693	0.04	126	1,344	0.17
Rest of the world	0	0	0	1	2,053	0
Developed countries	16,979	4,008	68.05	58,834	2,503	147.26
Developing countries	10,128	2,709	27.44	100,084	1,166	116.7
World	27,107	3,523	95.48	158,918	1,661	263.96

Source: IMPACT-WATER projections, 2002.
Notes: AI indicates irrigated area; YI, irrigated yield; PI, irrigated production; AR, rainfed area; YR, rainfed yield; PR, rainfed production; 000ha, thousand hectares; kg/ha, kilograms per hectare; and 10⁶-mt, million metric tons.

Table B.14—Irrigated and rainfed soybean area, yield, and production, 2010

Region/Country	AI (000ha)	YI (kg/ha)	PI (10^6-mt)	AR (000ha)	YR (kg/ha)	PR (10^6-mt)
Ohio and Tennessee	33	3,106	0.1	4,372	2,493	10.98
Rio Grande	11	2,698	0.03	60	2,045	0.12
Columbia	226	3,787	0.85	452	3,129	1.41
Colorado	48	4,686	0.22	96	3,675	0.35
Great Basin	13	4,472	0.06	52	3,551	0.19
California	23	3,612	0.08	72	3,129	0.22
White-Red	420	2,556	1.07	1,130	1,843	2.07
Mid Atlantic	17	2,745	0.05	551	2,411	1.34
Mississippi						
Downstream	416	3,215	1.34	1,169	2,601	3.1
Upstream	97	3,315	0.32	7,371	2,706	20.21
Great Lakes-Red	54	3,530	0.19	2,820	2,920	8.32
South Atlantic-Gulf	123	2,928	0.36	972	2,442	2.38
Texas-Gulf	31	2,774	0.09	129	1,989	0.25
Missouri	694	3,063	2.13	4,412	2,092	9.15
U.S. total	2,206	3,126	6.9	23,656	2,541	60.1
Huaihe	767	2,875	2.21	62	2,603	0.16
Haihe	844	1,854	1.57	490	1,624	0.8
Huanghe	459	1,240	0.57	541	1,134	0.62
Changjian	1,340	2,148	2.88	494	2,029	1
Songliao	311	3,015	0.94	2,670	2,801	7.53
Inland	2	1,433	0	1	1,377	0
Southwest	64	540	0.03	127	475	0.06
ZhuJiang	333	1,671	0.56	387	1,434	0.56
Southeast	182	2,201	0.4	17	1,865	0.03
China total	4,303	2,128	9.16	4,790	2,246	10.76
Sahyadri Ghats	0	0	0	19	702	0.01
Eastern Ghats	0	1,290	0	0	974	0
Cauvery	0	785	0	0	652	0
Godavari	90	1,687	0.15	1,069	1,336	1.43
Krishna	4	1,049	0	26	782	0.02
Indian-Coastal-Drain	0	1,498	0	0	0	0
Chotanagpur	0	0	0	0	1,170	0
Brahmari	0	0	0	31	1,491	0.05
Luni River Basin	5	682	0	0	0	0
Mahi-Tapti-Narmada	316	1,897	0.6	1,571	1,318	2.07
Brahmaputra	0	0	0	0	0	0
Indus	0	790	0	0	0	0
Ganges	0	0	0	2,584	1,359	3.51
India total	415	1,827	0.76	5,301	1,338	7.09

(continued)

Table B.14—Continued

Region/Country	AI (000ha)	YI (kg/ha)	PI (10^6-mt)	AR (000ha)	YR (kg/ha)	PR (10^6-mt)
European Union 15	51	5,068	0.26	275	3,438	0.94
Japan	0	0	0	67	1,875	0.13
Australia	13	2,929	0.04	16	1,937	0.03
Other developed countries	98	3,477	0.34	936	3,309	3.1
Eastern Europe	55	2,494	0.14	122	1,906	0.23
Central Asia	5	1,232	0.01	0	0	0
Rest of former Soviet Union	139	876	0.12	374	727	0.28
Mexico	12	2,388	0.03	168	2,196	0.37
Brazil	0	0	0	12,563	3,264	41.04
Argentina	1,333	3,711	4.95	5,640	2,577	14.63
Colombia	3	3,127	0.01	46	2,701	0.12
Other Latin America	90	3,354	0.3	1,463	2,296	3.36
Nigeria	633	504	0.32	0	0	0
Northern Sub-Saharan Africa	9	2,613	0.02	0	0	0
Central and western Sub-Saharan Africa	0	0	0	37	1,136	0.04
Southern Sub-Saharan Africa	0	0	0	92	1,908	0.17
Eastern Sub-Saharan Africa	4	1,853	0.01	100	1,527	0.15
Egypt	23	2,968	0.07	0	0	0
Turkey	27	3,315	0.09	0	0	0
Other West Asia/North Africa (WANA)	102	1,910	0.2	0	0	0
Pakistan	6	1,194	0.01	0	0	0
Bangladesh	0	0	0	0	0	0
Other South Asia	2	1,109	0	21	875	0.02
Indonesia	0	0	0	1,537	1,602	2.46
Thailand	0	0	0	340	1,719	0.58
Malaysia	0	0	0	0	464	0
Philippines	0	0	0	4	1,849	0.01
Viet Nam	0	0	0	136	1,293	0.18
Myanmar	0	0	0	65	1,080	0.07
Other Southeast Asia	0	0	0	27	1,439	0.04
South Korea	0	0	0	108	1,914	0.21
Other East Asia	21	1,930	0.04	325	1,777	0.58
Rest of the world	0	0	0	0	0	0
Developed countries	2,562	3,041	7.79	25,447	2,547	64.81
Developing countries	6,987	2,284	15.96	32,760	2,499	81.88
World	**9,549**	**2,487**	**23.75**	**58,206**	**2,520**	**146.69**

Source: IMPACT-WATER projections, 2002.
Notes: AI indicates irrigated area; YI, irrigated yield; PI, irrigated production; AR, rainfed area; YR, rainfed yield; PR, rainfed production; 000ha, thousand hectares; kg/ha, kilograms per hectare; and 10^6-mt, million metric tons.

Table B.15—Irrigated and rainfed rice area, yield, and production, 2025

Region/Country	AI (000ha)	YI (kg/ha)	PI (10^6-mt)	AR (000ha)	YR (kg/ha)	PR (10^6-mt)
Ohio and Tennessee	1	4,842	0	0	0	0
Rio Grande	21	4,946	0.1	0	0	0
Columbia	0	6,986	0	0	0	0
Colorado	36	7,455	0.27	0	0	0
Great Basin	19	7,813	0.15	0	0	0
California	168	8,414	1.41	0	0	0
White-Red	348	5,034	1.76	0	0	0
Mid Atlantic	0	0	0	0	0	0
Mississippi						
Downstream	386	5,273	2.04	0	0	0
Upstream	7	4,583	0.03	0	0	0
Great Lakes-Red	0	0	0	0	0	0
South Atlantic-Gulf	76	4,975	0.38	0	0	0
Texas-Gulf	116	5,198	0.61	0	0	0
Missouri	27	4,430	0.12	0	0	0
U.S. total	**1,205**	**5,697**	**6.86**	**0**	**0**	**0**
Huaihe	1,675	6,309	10.56	0	0	0
Haihe	226	4,694	1.06	0	0	0
Huanghe	263	4,625	1.22	0	0	0
Changjian	13,359	5,536	73.95	0	0	0
Songliao	1,499	4,858	7.28	672	3,442	2.31
Inland	108	4,535	0.49	0	0	0
Southwest	279	5,025	1.4	0	0	0
ZhuJiang	6,732	4,923	33.15	0	0	0
Southeast	2,582	4,960	12.81	0	0	0
China total	**26,723**	**5,311**	**141.92**	**672**	**3,440**	**2.31**
Sahyadri Ghats	1,293	4,226	5.46	1,231	2,102	2.59
Eastern Ghats	818	4,495	3.68	1,012	1,584	1.6
Cauvery	663	3,631	2.41	120	2,434	0.29
Godavari	2,681	4,459	11.96	954	1,916	1.83
Krishna	1,570	3,740	5.87	394	2,400	0.95
Indian-Coastal-Drain	1,825	3,332	6.08	276	2,322	0.64
Chotanagpur	191	2,525	0.48	2,630	1,752	4.62
Brahmari	2,807	3,583	10.06	2,594	1,760	4.57
Luni River Basin	105	2,298	0.24	20	1,300	0.03
Mahi-Tapti-Narmada	163	3,734	0.61	522	1,922	1
Brahmaputra	653	3,349	2.19	1,160	2,367	2.74
Indus	3,104	4,414	13.7	298	1,851	0.55
Ganges	6,603	3,423	22.6	5,396	2,286	12.34
India total	**22,477**	**3,796**	**85.33**	**16,606**	**2,032**	**33.74**

(continued)

Table B.15—Continued

Region/Country	AI (000ha)	YI (kg/ha)	PI (10^6-mt)	AR (000ha)	YR (kg/ha)	PR (10^6-mt)
European Union 15	390	6,302	2.46	0	0	0
Japan	1,327	5,617	7.45	5	4,114	0.02
Australia	136	7,706	1.04	0	0	0
Other developed countries	1	2,552	0	0	0	0
Eastern Europe	15	2,878	0.04	0	0	0
Central Asia	311	2,201	0.68	0	0	0
Rest of former Soviet Union	188	2,275	0.43	0	0	0
Mexico	43	5,718	0.25	45	4,314	0.19
Brazil	1,158	4,131	4.78	3,183	1,806	5.76
Argentina	238	6,142	1.49	0	0	0
Colombia	348	5,135	1.79	146	2,213	0.32
Other Latin America	1,821	3,656	6.66	482	2,875	1.39
Nigeria	549	3,053	1.68	1,828	1,280	2.34
Northern Sub-Saharan Africa	346	1,863	0.65	297	1,362	0.4
Central and western Sub-Saharan Africa	361	2,932	1.06	3,354	1,278	4.29
Southern Sub-Saharan Africa	781	2,193	1.71	1,366	1,598	2.18
Eastern Sub-Saharan Africa	173	2,467	0.43	498	1,299	0.65
Egypt	674	7,731	5.21	0	0	0
Turkey	46	4,853	0.22	0	0	0
Other West Asia/North Africa (WANA)	658	4,015	2.64	0	0	0
Pakistan	2,219	2,912	6.46	0	0	0
Bangladesh	6,116	4,138	25.3	1,180	2,141	2.53
Other South Asia	983	3,227	3.17	1,567	2,314	3.63
Indonesia	8,722	4,581	39.96	2,460	2,083	5.12
Thailand	2,248	3,150	7.08	8,306	1,432	11.72
Malaysia	396	3,533	1.4	258	1,733	0.45
Philippines	2,762	3,146	8.69	1,270	2,123	2.7
Viet Nam	4,060	5,286	21.47	3,012	3,421	10.3
Myanmar	898	4,972	4.46	5,284	3,016	15.93
Other Southeast Asia	275	3,609	0.99	2,324	2,265	5.26
South Korea	858	4,934	4.24	24	2,073	0.05
Other East Asia	383	4,763	1.82	135	1,675	0.23
Rest of the world	7	2,004	0.01	0	0	0
Developed countries	3,261	5,609	18.29	5	4,090	0.02
Developing countries	86,634	4,404	381.55	54,297	2,053	111.48
World	**89,895**	**4,448**	**399.84**	**54,302**	**2,053**	**111.5**

Source: IMPACT-WATER projections, 2002.
Notes: AI indicates irrigated area; YI, irrigated yield; PI, irrigated production; AR, rainfed area; YR, rainfed yield; PR, rainfed production; 000ha, thousand hectares; kg/ha, kilograms per hectare; and 10^6-mt, million metric tons.

Table B.16—Irrigated and rainfed wheat area, yield, and production, 2025

Region/Country	AI (000ha)	YI (kg/ha)	PI (10^6-mt)	AR (000ha)	YR (kg/ha)	PR (10^6-mt)
Ohio and Tennessee	2	4,809	0.01	1,007	3,639	3.67
Rio Grande	55	5,012	0.28	245	2,828	0.69
Columbia	521	7,539	3.93	1,564	5,106	7.99
Colorado	125	7,355	0.93	392	3,088	1.2
Great Basin	59	9,007	0.53	41	3,046	0.12
California	155	8,662	1.34	59	4,868	0.29
White-Red	185	4,590	0.86	4,720	2,540	12.05
Mid Atlantic	4	6,253	0.03	381	5,483	2.09
Mississippi						
Downstream	19	4,770	0.09	509	3,352	1.71
Upstream	3	4,780	0.02	957	3,067	2.94
Great Lakes-Red	10	5,127	0.05	3,727	2,883	10.8
South Atlantic-Gulf	13	4,982	0.06	641	3,325	2.13
Texas-Gulf	172	5,956	1.05	722	2,203	1.61
Missouri	276	4,839	1.34	9,301	2,999	27.89
U.S. total	**1,599**	**6,571**	**10.5**	**24,265**	**3,099**	**75.19**
Huaihe	7,168	6,483	46.68	2,573	4,674	12.12
Haihe	2,211	6,351	14.08	511	4,027	2.05
Huanghe	3,993	3,841	15.34	1,077	2,831	3.05
Changjian	7,478	4,776	35.72	994	3,316	3.3
Songliao	361	4,815	1.74	577	2,314	1.33
Inland	1,302	4,844	6.31	176	2,803	0.49
Southwest	303	4,060	1.23	20	2,653	0.05
ZhuJiang	570	2,436	1.4	101	1,456	0.15
Southeast	246	3,269	0.82	0	0	0
China total	**23,633**	**5,218**	**123.32**	**6,030**	**3,739**	**22.55**
Sahyadri Ghats	38	1,938	0.07	15	994	0.02
Eastern Ghats	2	2,276	0	0	1,437	0
Cauvery	0	1,421	0	0	1,084	0
Godavari	602	2,030	1.22	136	1,053	0.14
Krishna	169	2,662	0.45	70	885	0.06
Indian-Coastal-Drain	2	1,941	0	1	1,109	0
Chotanagpur	13	2,270	0.03	29	1,405	0.04
Brahmari	83	2,131	0.17	41	1,128	0.05
Luni River Basin	643	4,623	3.12	111	1,229	0.14
Mahi-Tapti-Narmada	1,080	2,255	2.44	405	1,482	0.6
Brahmaputra	0	0	0	56	2,041	0.11
Indus	4,621	5,460	25.23	814	3,546	2.88
Ganges	15,256	3,083	47.04	2,425	2,044	5
India total	**22,510**	**3,544**	**79.78**	**4,103**	**2,202**	**9.04**

(continued)

Table B.16—Continued

Region/Country	AI (000ha)	YI (kg/ha)	PI (10^6-mt)	AR (000ha)	YR (kg/ha)	PR (10^6-mt)
European Union 15	3,615	8,173	29.55	13,476	5,191	69.97
Japan	0	0	0	150	3,433	0.51
Australia	2,081	3,410	7.1	10,249	2,644	27.52
Other developed countries	1,599	5,300	8.47	11,883	3,076	36.47
Eastern Europe	2,302	5,516	12.7	9,174	2,928	26.87
Central Asia	6,294	1,527	9.61	10,438	802	8.27
Rest of former Soviet Union	4,841	2,866	13.88	24,847	1,929	48.25
Mexico	748	5,174	3.88	130	2,514	0.33
Brazil	6	4,856	0.03	2,062	2,893	5.9
Argentina	103	5,417	0.56	7,973	3,444	27.66
Colombia	0	0	0	49	3,155	0.16
Other Latin America	228	4,009	0.92	1,337	3,043	4.03
Nigeria	25	2,532	0.06	0	0	0
Northern Sub-Saharan Africa	533	1,845	0.98	1,476	1,729	2.55
Central and western Sub-Saharan Africa	0	0	0	16	1,282	0.02
Southern Sub-Saharan Africa	107	4,063	0.44	47	1,205	0.06
Eastern Sub-Saharan Africa	0	0	0	428	2,511	1.08
Egypt	834	7,893	6.58	0	0	0
Turkey	77	4,309	0.33	10,249	2,290	23.54
Other West Asia/North Africa (WANA)	4,663	4,359	20.33	13,528	1,316	17.9
Pakistan	7,612	3,387	25.81	604	833	0.5
Bangladesh	287	3,167	0.91	333	2,301	0.77
Other South Asia	2,526	2,148	5.43	66	1,465	0.1
Indonesia	0	0	0	0	0	0
Thailand	0	0	0	1	1,014	0
Malaysia	0	0	0	0	0	0
Philippines	0	0	0	0	0	0
Viet Nam	0	0	0	0	0	0
Myanmar	114	961	0.11	17	563	0.01
Other Southeast Asia	0	0	0	0	0	0
South Korea	0	0	0	2	5,175	0.01
Other East Asia	344	1,308	0.45	123	650	0.08
Rest of the world	0	0	0	0	2,562	0
Developed countries	16,036	5,126	82.2	94,043	3,028	284.77
Developing countries	70,641	3,957	279.51	59,014	2,110	124.54
World	**86,677**	**4,173**	**361.71**	**153,057**	**2,674**	**409.31**

Source: IMPACT-WATER projections, 2002.
Notes: AI indicates irrigated area; YI, irrigated yield; PI, irrigated production; AR, rainfed area; YR, rainfed yield; PR, rainfed production; 000ha, thousand hectares; kg/ha, kilograms per hectare; and 10^6-mt, million metric tons.

Table B.17—Irrigated and rainfed maize area, yield, and production, 2025

Region/Country	AI (000ha)	YI (kg/ha)	PI (10^6-mt)	AR (000ha)	YR (kg/ha)	PR (10^6-mt)
Ohio and Tennessee	91	13,418	1.23	4,338	9,886	42.92
Rio Grande	98	15,871	1.56	93	7,277	0.68
Columbia	27	19,403	0.52	55	15,243	0.83
Colorado	144	16,093	2.32	35	4,479	0.16
Great Basin	12	12,900	0.16	0	4,525	0
California	58	14,603	0.85	0	4,261	0
White-Red	578	11,355	6.57	386	7,539	2.87
Mid Atlantic	26	12,357	0.33	753	9,802	7.42
Mississippi						
Downstream	96	12,660	1.21	539	9,535	5.15
Upstream	211	12,923	2.72	10,323	9,432	97.31
Great Lakes-Red	153	12,053	1.85	3,901	9,169	35.76
South Atlantic-Gulf	100	13,454	1.34	748	10,521	7.89
Texas-Gulf	266	14,304	3.8	415	6,593	2.69
Missouri	2,748	13,428	37.07	5,080	9,105	45.6
U.S. total	**4,608**	**13,351**	**61.52**	**26,667**	**9,348**	**249.28**
Huaihe	4,119	9,602	39.63	2,618	5,652	14.83
Haihe	2,225	8,887	19.86	2,762	5,729	15.68
Huanghe	1,331	6,880	9.17	1,663	4,813	7.87
Changjian	2,596	6,981	18.12	2,900	5,162	14.97
Songliao	2,499	12,382	30.95	7,080	5,783	40.28
Inland	848	5,868	4.98	306	5,724	1.75
Southwest	64	3,808	0.24	312	3,227	1.01
ZhuJiang	423	5,537	2.35	1,162	4,555	5.3
Southeast	81	5,441	0.44	11	1,700	0.02
China total	**14,186**	**8,864**	**125.75**	**18,816**	**5,406**	**101.72**
Sahyadri Ghats	28	4,080	0.12	51	2,673	0.14
Eastern Ghats	16	4,348	0.07	53	1,738	0.09
Cauvery	26	4,189	0.11	23	2,595	0.06
Godavari	84	7,331	0.62	433	2,763	1.2
Krishna	302	6,151	1.86	108	2,520	0.27
Indian-Coastal-Drain	50	6,936	0.35	71	2,339	0.16
Chotanagpur	1	4,500	0.01	59	1,955	0.12
Brahmari	17	3,921	0.07	173	1,862	0.32
Luni River Basin	32	4,509	0.15	200	1,000	0.2
Mahi-Tapti-Narmada	54	6,215	0.34	868	1,917	1.66
Brahmaputra	0	0	0	52	3,623	0.19
Indus	218	7,581	1.66	570	1,511	0.86
Ganges	667	5,857	3.9	2,326	1,949	4.53
India total	**1,496**	**6,169**	**9.23**	**4,986**	**1,966**	**9.8**

(continued)

Table B.17—Continued

Region/Country	AI (000ha)	YI (kg/ha)	PI (10^6-mt)	AR (000ha)	YR (kg/ha)	PR (10^6-mt)
European Union 15	1,082	12,073	13.06	2,530	9,042	22.89
Japan	0	0	0	0	4,800	0
Australia	68	5,970	0.4	0	0	0
Other developed countries	0	0	0	5,279	4,212	22.3
Eastern Europe	2,542	7,462	18.97	6,267	3,846	24.14
Central Asia	274	3,831	1.05	0	0	0
Rest of former Soviet Union	592	5,134	3.04	1,678	3,528	5.86
Mexico	2,362	6,001	14.17	6,190	2,196	13.59
Brazil	0	0	0	21,096	3,039	64.11
Argentina	1,127	10,085	11.37	2,638	5,374	14.11
Colombia	22	3,519	0.08	709	2,159	1.53
Other Latin America	438	8,877	3.89	4,766	2,204	10.4
Nigeria	762	6,037	4.6	5,488	1,505	8.26
Northern Sub-Saharan Africa	75	3,011	0.22	3,136	2,114	6.63
Central and western Sub-Saharan Africa	1	2,589	0	6,055	1,528	9.25
Southern Sub-Saharan Africa	71	3,135	0.22	6,596	1,584	10.45
Eastern Sub-Saharan Africa	28	2,906	0.08	4,591	2,212	10.14
Egypt	770	10,539	8.11	0	0	0
Turkey	162	6,903	1.12	397	3,667	1.46
Other West Asia/North Africa (WANA)	655	3,780	2.48	178	720	0.13
Pakistan	756	2,598	1.97	157	1,762	0.28
Bangladesh	0	0	0	3	1,347	0
Other South Asia	387	2,451	0.95	950	2,239	2.13
Indonesia	545	6,509	3.55	3,364	2,865	9.62
Thailand	0	0	0	1,392	6,343	8.79
Malaysia	0	0	0	24	3,415	0.08
Philippines	0	0	0	3,323	2,749	9.14
Viet Nam	193	4,824	0.93	495	2,188	1.08
Myanmar	49	4,658	0.23	165	2,264	0.37
Other Southeast Asia	0	0	0	87	2,627	0.23
South Korea	7	11,254	0.08	13	7,668	0.1
Other East Asia	408	4,040	1.65	185	2,458	0.45
Rest of the world	0	0	0	34	579	0.02
Developed countries	8,892	10,908	96.99	42,420	7,649	324.47
Developing countries	24,776	7,739	191.74	95,833	3,067	293.88
World	**33,668**	**8,576**	**288.73**	**138,253**	**4,473**	**618.35**

Source: IMPACT-WATER projections, 2002.
Notes: AI indicates irrigated area; YI, irrigated yield; PI, irrigated production; AR, rainfed area; YR, rainfed yield; PR, rainfed production; 000ha, thousand hectares; kg/ha, kilograms per hectare; and 10^6-mt, million metric tons.

Table B.18—Irrigated and rainfed other coarse grain area, yield, and production, 2025

Region/Country	AI (000ha)	YI (kg/ha)	PI (10^6-mt)	AR (000ha)	YR (kg/ha)	PR (10^6-mt)
Ohio and Tennessee	0	6,915	0	69	4,570	0.32
Rio Grande	56	6,191	0.34	255	3,310	0.84
Columbia	265	8,157	2.16	308	6,014	1.85
Colorado	66	9,153	0.61	74	4,218	0.31
Great Basin	43	8,078	0.34	26	4,912	0.13
California	40	6,446	0.26	67	5,251	0.35
White-Red	155	6,747	1.04	1,388	4,813	6.72
Mid Atlantic	2	8,677	0.02	140	5,545	0.79
Mississippi						
Downstream	8	8,468	0.06	165	6,149	1.03
Upstream	3	6,195	0.02	489	4,536	2.23
Great Lakes-Red	3	5,094	0.01	946	4,045	3.86
South Atlantic-Gulf	3	5,737	0.02	83	3,227	0.27
Texas-Gulf	176	7,216	1.27	827	3,404	2.8
Missouri	203	7,272	1.48	2,920	4,257	12.62
U.S. total	**1,020**	**7,485**	**7.63**	**7,756**	**4,399**	**34.12**
Huaihe	559	4,970	2.78	0	0	0
Haihe	362	2,962	1.07	966	2,397	2.32
Huanghe	148	3,188	0.47	990	2,305	2.29
Changjian	926	6,912	6.4	108	5,188	0.56
Songliao	0	0	0	966	4,164	4.03
Inland	64	4,385	0.28	327	3,538	1.16
Southwest	132	4,494	0.59	97	3,898	0.38
ZhuJiang	171	4,426	0.76	41	3,580	0.15
Southeast	158	5,293	0.84	0	0	0
China total	**2,521**	**5,235**	**13.2**	**3,496**	**3,111**	**10.88**
Sahyadri Ghats	10	3,202	0.03	524	1,109	0.58
Eastern Ghats	0	0	0	278	1,034	0.29
Cauvery	0	6,276	0	728	1,518	1.1
Godavari	2	2,141	0	4,115	1,297	5.28
Krishna	28	4,467	0.12	3,933	1,207	4.71
Indian-Coastal-Drain	0	3,956	0	1,157	1,286	1.48
Chotanagpur	0	0	0	68	1,343	0.09
Brahmari	0	1,784	0	110	1,283	0.14
Luni River Basin	67	1,938	0.13	3,262	839	2.69
Mahi-Tapti-Narmada	24	1,848	0.04	2,401	1,553	3.73
Brahmaputra	0	0	0	22	1,916	0.04
Indus	77	2,732	0.21	1,825	959	1.73
Ganges	365	2,879	1.05	4,816	1,326	6.39
India total	**573**	**2,788**	**1.6**	**23,239**	**1,216**	**28.25**

(continued)

Table B.18—Continued

Region/Country	AI (000ha)	YI (kg/ha)	PI (10^6-mt)	AR (000ha)	YR (kg/ha)	PR (10^6-mt)
European Union 15	4,594	7,180	32.98	8,613	4,281	36.87
Japan	0	0	0	59	3,843	0.23
Australia	1,149	4,685	5.38	4,373	2,476	10.91
Other developed countries	903	7,293	6.59	6,460	3,801	24.58
Eastern Europe	2,469	4,571	11.29	5,897	3,054	18.09
Central Asia	2,943	1,066	3.14	2,349	976	2.29
Rest of former Soviet Union	6,552	2,098	13.74	26,107	1,551	40.83
Mexico	749	5,643	4.22	1,463	4,073	5.97
Brazil	0	0	0	520	2,658	1.38
Argentina	0	0	0	1,205	5,348	6.47
Colombia	10	5,075	0.05	221	4,231	0.94
Other Latin America	351	3,137	1.1	1,395	2,107	2.9
Nigeria	569	4,053	2.31	14,541	1,244	18.08
Northern Sub-Saharan Africa	455	2,637	1.2	36,686	917	33.63
Central and western Sub-Saharan Africa	0	0	0	5,581	1,035	5.78
Southern Sub-Saharan Africa	14	3,664	0.05	2,669	736	1.96
Eastern Sub-Saharan Africa	12	1,861	0.02	3,046	1,404	4.27
Egypt	204	4,202	0.86	0	0	0
Turkey	0	0	0	3,129	4,099	12.83
Other West Asia/North Africa (WANA)	2,044	2,497	5.1	8,508	1,258	10.7
Pakistan	0	0	0	147	497	0.07
Bangladesh	17	733	0.01	79	633	0.05
Other South Asia	82	2,003	0.16	448	1,516	0.68
Indonesia	0	0	0	0	0	0
Thailand	0	0	0	163	1,863	0.3
Malaysia	0	0	0	0	0	0
Philippines	0	0	0	0	242	0
Viet Nam	0	0	0	5	2,118	0.01
Myanmar	0	0	0	242	902	0.22
Other Southeast Asia	0	0	0	0	0	0
South Korea	0	0	0	86	6,799	0.59
Other East Asia	14	3,240	0.04	131	1,613	0.21
Rest of the world	0	0	0	1	2,451	0
Developed countries	16,686	4,651	77.62	59,265	2,795	165.64
Developing countries	10,557	3,132	33.07	109,352	1,358	148.46
World	27,244	4,063	110.68	168,617	1,863	314.11

Source: IMPACT-WATER projections, 2002.
Notes: AI indicates irrigated area; YI, irrigated yield; PI, irrigated production; AR, rainfed area; YR, rainfed yield; PR, rainfed production; 000ha, thousand hectares; kg/ha, kilograms per hectare; and 10⁶-mt, million metric tons.

Table B.19—Irrigated and rainfed soybean area, yield, and production, 2025

Region/Country	AI (000ha)	YI (kg/ha)	PI (10^6-mt)	AR (000ha)	YR (kg/ha)	PR (10^6-mt)
Ohio and Tennessee	36	4,019	0.14	4,737	2,860	13.62
Rio Grande	10	3,254	0.03	64	2,403	0.15
Columbia	234	4,535	1.06	458	3,572	1.63
Colorado	49	5,539	0.27	99	4,247	0.42
Great Basin	13	5,358	0.07	55	4,070	0.22
California	25	4,366	0.11	77	3,615	0.28
White-Red	452	3,096	1.4	1,287	2,135	2.77
Mid Atlantic	18	3,316	0.06	585	2,719	1.6
Mississippi						
Downstream	433	4,064	1.76	1,022	3,057	3.16
Upstream	105	3,974	0.42	8,132	3,071	25.21
Great Lakes-Red	59	4,354	0.26	3,197	3,587	11.55
South Atlantic-Gulf	127	3,646	0.46	814	3,071	2.5
Texas-Gulf	33	3,443	0.11	146	2,317	0.34
Missouri	734	3,277	2.41	5,017	2,139	10.77
U.S. total	2,329	3,683	8.58	25,691	2,889	74.22
Huaihe	648	3,311	2.15	65	3,021	0.2
Haihe	936	2,456	2.3	604	2,155	1.31
Huanghe	481	1,812	0.87	582	1,693	0.99
Changjian	1,359	3,432	4.66	510	3,130	1.6
Songliao	344	3,320	1.14	3,109	3,019	9.42
Inland	2	2,096	0	2	2,007	0
Southwest	73	891	0.06	151	775	0.12
ZhuJiang	355	2,355	0.84	426	2,019	0.86
Southeast	201	2,626	0.53	20	2,255	0.05
China total	4,397	2,856	12.56	5,468	2,658	14.53
Sahyadri Ghats	0	0	0	25	997	0.03
Eastern Ghats	0	1,647	0	0	1,182	0
Cauvery	0	1,136	0	0	921	0
Godavari	86	2,150	0.18	1,345	1,623	2.18
Krishna	4	1,611	0.01	30	1,131	0.03
Indian-Coastal-Drain	0	1,912	0	0	0	0
Chotanagpur	0	0	0	0	1,609	0
Brahmari	0	0	0	37	1,757	0.07
Luni River Basin	6	1,149	0.01	0	0	0
Mahi-Tapti-Narmada	282	2,402	0.68	1,858	1,839	3.42
Brahmaputra	0	0	0	0	0	0
Indus	0	1,170	0	0	0	0
Ganges	0	0	0	2,787	1,798	5.01
India total	378	2,317	0.88	6,083	1,765	10.74

(continued)

Table B.19—Continued

Region/Country	AI (000ha)	YI (kg/ha)	PI (10^6-mt)	AR (000ha)	YR (kg/ha)	PR (10^6-mt)
European Union 15	52	6,423	0.34	298	4,109	1.22
Japan	0	0	0	69	2,294	0.16
Australia	13	3,987	0.05	15	2,436	0.04
Other developed countries	102	4,493	0.46	1,033	4,131	4.27
Eastern Europe	57	3,335	0.19	126	2,416	0.31
Central Asia	5	1,888	0.01	0	0	0
Rest of former Soviet Union	144	1,095	0.16	407	836	0.34
Mexico	14	3,266	0.05	181	2,959	0.54
Brazil	0	0	0	13,649	4,287	58.53
Argentina	1,366	5,234	7.15	6,673	3,538	23.71
Colombia	3	4,227	0.01	48	3,494	0.17
Other Latin America	92	4,526	0.42	1,773	2,843	5.05
Nigeria	648	657	0.43	0	0	0
Northern Sub-Saharan Africa	9	2,753	0.02	0	0	0
Central and western Sub-Saharan Africa	0	0	0	41	1,418	0.06
Southern Sub-Saharan Africa	0	0	0	95	2,336	0.22
Eastern Sub-Saharan Africa	4	2,381	0.01	110	1,960	0.22
Egypt	23	3,758	0.09	0	0	0
Turkey	27	4,291	0.12	0	0	0
Other West Asia/North Africa (WANA)	107	2,471	0.27	0	0	0
Pakistan	6	1,554	0.01	0	0	0
Bangladesh	0	0	0	0	0	0
Other South Asia	2	1,359	0	21	1,107	0.02
Indonesia	0	0	0	1,634	2,094	3.42
Thailand	0	0	0	351	2,175	0.76
Malaysia	0	0	0	0	597	0
Philippines	0	0	0	4	2,372	0.01
Viet Nam	0	0	0	145	1,674	0.24
Myanmar	0	0	0	70	1,351	0.09
Other Southeast Asia	0	0	0	28	1,781	0.05
South Korea	0	0	0	108	2,448	0.26
Other East Asia	21	2,503	0.05	345	2,300	0.79
Rest of the world	0	0	0	0	0	0
Developed countries	2,697	3,622	9.77	27,637	2,915	80.55
Developing countries	7,102	3,107	22.06	36,828	3,243	119.42
World	**9,799**	**3,249**	**31.83**	**64,466**	**3,102**	**199.97**

Source: IMPACT-WATER projections, 2002.

Notes: AI indicates irrigated area; YI, irrigated yield; PI, irrigated production; AR, rainfed area; YR, rainfed yield; PR, rainfed production; 000ha, thousand hectares; kg/ha, kilograms per hectare; and 10⁶-mt, million metric tons.

Table B.20—Irrigated and rainfed roots and tubers area, yield, and, production, 1995

Region/Country	AI (000ha)	YI (kg/ha)	PI (10^6-mt)	AR (000ha)	YR (kg/ha)	PR (10^6-mt)
Ohio and Tennessee	2	26,432	0.05	7	20,857	0.15
Rio Grande	10	37,431	0.36	2	16,894	0.04
Columbia	109	63,440	6.92	8	36,642	0.28
Colorado	36	34,791	1.27	0	0	0
Great Basin	10	35,562	0.35	0	0	0
California	24	38,811	0.91	1	16,000	0.02
White-Red	18	36,198	0.66	1	14,711	0.02
Mid Atlantic	16	27,977	0.46	65	28,175	1.84
Mississippi						
Downstream	0	10,718	0	2	18,721	0.04
Upstream	55	37,734	2.09	18	23,165	0.41
Great Lakes-Red	62	36,772	2.28	47	20,712	0.97
South Atlantic-Gulf	2	11,277	0.03	12	19,591	0.23
Texas-Gulf	9	27,909	0.25	3	15,179	0.04
Missouri	43	38,508	1.64	33	16,755	0.55
U.S. total	**397**	**43,557**	**17.27**	**199**	**23,084**	**4.58**
Huaihe	497	18,779	9.34	861	12,169	10.48
Haihe	196	19,126	3.75	353	12,563	4.44
Huanghe	1,458	20,085	29.29	2,125	14,547	30.92
Changjian	282	22,711	6.41	451	12,166	5.49
Songliao	769	24,563	18.88	305	20,221	6.16
Inland	238	25,254	6.01	321	21,265	6.83
Southwest	775	17,543	13.59	668	15,030	10.04
ZhuJiang	284	15,069	4.28	153	8,584	1.31
Southeast	42	16,795	0.71	77	12,491	0.97
China total	**4,541**	**20,315**	**92.26**	**5,315**	**14,418**	**76.63**
Sahyadri Ghats	0	0	0	23	14,541	0.33
Eastern Ghats	0	0	0	13	12,885	0.17
Cauvery	0	0	0	17	14,474	0.24
Godavari	1	11,328	0.01	22	16,566	0.36
Krishna	3	10,243	0.03	49	14,918	0.73
Indian-Coastal-Drain	10	11,948	0.12	0	0	0
Chotanagpur	0	0	0	252	22,189	5.59
Brahmari	0	0	0	124	16,597	2.06
Luni River Basin	20	22,813	0.45	20	23,600	0.47
Mahi-Tapti-Narmada	19	14,857	0.28	25	17,900	0.45
Brahmaputra	0	0	0	122	9,602	1.17
Indus	9	18,861	0.16	62	20,815	1.29
Ganges	66	19,130	1.27	615	16,077	9.88
India total	**128**	**18,198**	**2.33**	**1,343**	**16,937**	**22.75**

(continued)

Table B.20—Continued

Region/Country	AI (000ha)	YI (kg/ha)	PI (10^6-mt)	AR (000ha)	YR (kg/ha)	PR (10^6-mt)
European Union 15	275	37,930	10.45	1,340	28,583	38.29
Japan	0	0	0	190	26,047	4.96
Australia	41	29,942	1.21	0	0	0
Other developed countries	50	33,559	1.69	216	24,610	5.33
Eastern Europe	599	20,199	12.1	1,676	13,307	22.3
Central Asia	309	9,358	2.89	0	0	0
Rest of former Soviet Union	1,281	14,231	18.22	4,729	10,499	49.65
Mexico	4	24,911	0.1	63	19,775	1.25
Brazil	0	0	0	2,172	13,031	28.3
Argentina	32	29,336	0.93	104	16,917	1.76
Colombia	18	12,704	0.23	358	12,778	4.57
Other Latin America	80	11,044	0.88	1,375	8,318	11.44
Nigeria	5,276	10,040	52.97	0	0	0
Northern Sub-Saharan Africa	846	3,891	3.29	0	0	0
Central and western Sub-Saharan Africa	136	11,468	1.56	5,713	7,364	42.07
Southern Sub-Saharan Africa	2,075	5,014	10.41	225	6,608	1.49
Eastern Sub-Saharan Africa	167	8,829	1.48	2,257	6,388	14.42
Egypt	116	21,276	2.47	0	0	0
Turkey	200	23,417	4.68	0	9,535	0
Other West Asia/North Africa (WANA)	127	25,676	3.26	303	13,997	4.24
Pakistan	103	14,219	1.46	0	0	0
Bangladesh	0	0	0	177	10,729	1.9
Other South Asia	13	12,526	0.16	179	8,355	1.5
Indonesia	117	14,321	1.68	1,589	11,153	17.73
Thailand	0	0	0	1,323	13,676	18.09
Malaysia	0	0	0	54	9,641	0.52
Philippines	0	0	0	424	6,793	2.88
Viet Nam	0	0	0	627	6,847	4.29
Myanmar	0	0	0	29	9,068	0.26
Other Southeast Asia	0	0	0	47	7,262	0.34
South Korea	0	0	0	41	21,767	0.9
Other East Asia	15	13,559	0.2	180	10,422	1.88
Rest of the world	4	11,877	0.05	192	7,015	1.35
Developed countries	2,643	23,065	60.95	8,350	14,984	125.11
Developing countries	14,307	12,811	183.29	24,091	10,815	260.54
World	16,950	14,410	244.25	32,440	11,888	385.65

Source: IMPACT-WATER projections, 2002.
Notes: AI indicates irrigated area; YI, irrigated yield; PI, irrigated production; AR, rainfed area; YR, rainfed yield; PR, rainfed production; 000ha, thousand hectares; kg/ha, kilograms per hectare; and 106-mt, million metric tons.

Table B.21—Irrigated and rainfed roots and tubers area, yield, and production, 2010

Region/Country	AI (000ha)	YI (kg/ha)	PI (10^6-mt)	AR (000ha)	YR (kg/ha)	PR (10^6-mt)
Ohio and Tennessee	2	28,167	0.06	7	23,538	0.17
Rio Grande	10	45,567	0.44	2	24,558	0.06
Columbia	111	71,966	8.01	10	48,675	0.49
Colorado	37	42,130	1.57	0	0	0
Great Basin	10	41,489	0.42	0	0	0
California	24	45,480	1.08	1	20,742	0.02
White-Red	19	36,645	0.68	1	18,289	0.02
Mid Atlantic	17	31,642	0.53	63	28,023	1.78
Mississippi						
Downstream	0	12,278	0	2	26,542	0.05
Upstream	57	43,138	2.45	17	30,296	0.53
Great Lakes-Red	63	43,076	2.73	49	28,438	1.39
South Atlantic-Gulf	2	11,846	0.03	12	14,944	0.18
Texas-Gulf	9	32,513	0.31	3	16,810	0.05
Missouri	44	43,968	1.92	35	19,400	0.68
U.S. total	405	49,928	20.22	203	26,638	5.41
Huaihe	509	23,534	11.98	812	15,997	12.99
Haihe	201	22,882	4.59	324	14,862	4.81
Huanghe	1,285	26,080	33.5	2,008	16,393	32.91
Changjian	289	28,904	8.35	428	16,436	7.03
Songliao	571	28,694	16.37	297	21,919	6.5
Inland	244	32,082	7.82	301	28,733	8.64
Southwest	793	20,900	16.57	626	18,548	11.6
ZhuJiang	290	19,223	5.58	142	11,353	1.61
Southeast	43	21,266	0.92	74	16,023	1.18
China total	4,224	25,021	105.68	5,010	17,423	87.29
Sahyadri Ghats	0	0	0	24	18,701	0.45
Eastern Ghats	0	0	0	13	16,551	0.21
Cauvery	0	0	0	19	21,374	0.4
Godavari	1	16,505	0.02	22	20,637	0.46
Krishna	4	12,392	0.05	52	17,551	0.92
Indian-Coastal-Drain	15	14,871	0.23	0	0	0
Chotanagpur	0	0	0	283	30,852	8.72
Brahmari	0	0	0	124	20,674	2.57
Luni River Basin	23	30,768	0.69	24	32,110	0.77
Mahi-Tapti-Narmada	29	16,817	0.49	29	24,341	0.72
Brahmaputra	0	0	0	136	12,646	1.72
Indus	14	21,120	0.29	65	23,472	1.53
Ganges	105	22,828	2.39	691	20,402	14.1
India total	192	21,790	4.18	1,483	21,964	32.56

(continued)

Table B.21—Continued

Region/Country	AI (000ha)	YI (kg/ha)	PI (10^6-mt)	AR (000ha)	YR (kg/ha)	PR (10^6-mt)
European Union 15	282	43,669	12.32	1,241	35,433	43.97
Japan	0	0	0	191	31,806	6.06
Australia	42	33,003	1.38	0	0	0
Other developed countries	56	30,808	1.74	215	27,988	6.03
Eastern Europe	631	21,576	13.62	1,570	14,664	23.02
Central Asia	319	10,026	3.2	0	0	0
Rest of former Soviet Union	1,336	14,049	18.77	4,428	11,994	53.11
Mexico	5	26,941	0.13	67	21,037	1.4
Brazil	0	0	0	2,157	17,698	38.18
Argentina	53	30,442	1.61	81	19,551	1.59
Colombia	21	14,168	0.3	368	18,095	6.65
Other Latin America	96	11,803	1.14	1,497	11,040	16.52
Nigeria	6,258	12,522	78.36	0	0	0
Northern Sub-Saharan Africa	846	3,954	3.34	0	0	0
Central and western Sub-Saharan Africa	140	13,346	1.87	7,058	9,779	69.02
Southern Sub-Saharan Africa	2,335	5,871	13.71	265	8,744	2.32
Eastern Sub-Saharan Africa	168	11,171	1.88	2,789	8,570	23.9
Egypt	121	23,137	2.81	0	0	0
Turkey	216	29,217	6.32	0	12,400	0
Other West Asia/North Africa (WANA)	182	35,942	6.55	308	20,782	6.4
Pakistan	125	16,872	2.1	0	0	0
Bangladesh	0	0	0	216	14,331	3.09
Other South Asia	13	18,440	0.24	202	12,555	2.53
Indonesia	117	16,662	1.96	1,531	13,548	20.74
Thailand	0	0	0	1,095	15,784	17.29
Malaysia	0	0	0	54	12,196	0.66
Philippines	0	0	0	430	8,140	3.5
Viet Nam	0	0	0	647	9,124	5.91
Myanmar	0	0	0	31	11,507	0.35
Other Southeast Asia	0	0	0	50	9,144	0.46
South Korea	0	0	0	41	27,945	1.16
Other East Asia	15	16,980	0.25	175	14,056	2.46
Rest of the world	4	14,381	0.06	210	8,532	1.79
Developed countries	2,753	24,722	68.06	7,848	17,534	137.6
Developing countries	15,451	15,254	235.69	25,765	13,421	345.78
World	**18,204**	**16,686**	**303.74**	**33,613**	**14,381**	**483.38**

Source: IMPACT-WATER projections, 2002.
Notes: AI indicates irrigated area; YI, irrigated yield; PI, irrigated production; AR, rainfed area; YR, rainfed yield; PR, rainfed production; 000ha, thousand hectares; kg/ha, kilograms per hectare; and 10⁶-mt, million metric tons.

Table B.22—Irrigated and rainfed roots and tubers area, yield, and production, 2025

Region/Country	AI (000ha)	YI (kg/ha)	PI (10^6-mt)	AR (000ha)	YR (kg/ha)	PR (10^6-mt)
Ohio and Tennessee	2	34,803	0.07	7	26,819	0.19
Rio Grande	10	57,602	0.55	2	28,457	0.06
Columbia	110	90,847	10	10	57,863	0.55
Colorado	37	53,031	1.94	0	0	0
Great Basin	10	51,522	0.51	0	0	0
California	24	59,310	1.4	1	22,930	0.02
White-Red	18	44,544	0.82	1	21,099	0.03
Mid Atlantic	17	38,955	0.65	63	32,827	2.07
Mississippi						
Downstream	0	14,500	0	2	31,693	0.06
Upstream	56	52,442	2.93	17	37,278	0.64
Great Lakes-Red	63	51,411	3.23	50	34,656	1.73
South Atlantic-Gulf	2	14,556	0.03	12	16,669	0.19
Texas-Gulf	9	39,785	0.36	3	18,895	0.05
Missouri	42	53,885	2.28	37	23,334	0.87
U.S. total	**399**	**62,072**	**24.77**	**204**	**31,606**	**6.46**
Huaihe	506	26,238	13.28	775	18,194	14.1
Haihe	200	25,333	5.05	311	16,333	5.08
Huanghe	1,282	29,003	37.17	1,946	18,499	36
Changjian	287	32,469	9.32	409	18,760	7.68
Songliao	568	32,110	18.24	302	23,522	7.11
Inland	242	38,128	9.24	279	31,104	8.69
Southwest	789	23,619	18.63	593	19,507	11.57
ZhuJiang	289	21,638	6.25	133	12,855	1.71
Southeast	43	23,710	1.02	71	18,275	1.29
China total	**4,206**	**28,108**	**118.22**	**4,819**	**19,343**	**93.22**
Sahyadri Ghats	0	0	0	24	21,777	0.52
Eastern Ghats	0	0	0	12	18,655	0.22
Cauvery	0	0	0	20	27,523	0.54
Godavari	2	21,408	0.03	22	23,204	0.52
Krishna	6	16,451	0.09	53	19,001	1.01
Indian-Coastal-Drain	20	17,822	0.35	0	0	0
Chotanagpur	0	0	0	295	38,881	11.49
Brahmari	0	0	0	122	23,076	2.81
Luni River Basin	34	45,398	1.55	24	33,547	0.81
Mahi-Tapti-Narmada	38	20,771	0.79	30	25,449	0.75
Brahmaputra	0	0	0	141	15,284	2.16
Indus	18	28,242	0.51	70	26,315	1.84
Ganges	137	30,058	4.1	722	25,234	18.21
India total	**254**	**29,309**	**7.43**	**1,535**	**26,635**	**40.89**

(continued)

Table B.22—Continued

Region/Country	AI (000ha)	YI (kg/ha)	PI (10^6-mt)	AR (000ha)	YR (kg/ha)	PR (10^6-mt)
European Union 15	279	46,678	13.02	1,182	39,738	46.97
Japan	0	0	0	186	34,474	6.42
Australia	41	44,707	1.85	0	0	0
Other developed countries	53	41,655	2.2	211	33,407	7.05
Eastern Europe	641	24,670	15.81	1,494	16,539	24.71
Central Asia	325	11,860	3.85	0	0	0
Rest of former Soviet Union	1,350	14,936	20.16	4,216	12,734	53.69
Mexico	6	35,798	0.2	67	26,728	1.78
Brazil	0	0	0	2,135	21,567	46.04
Argentina	72	37,281	2.67	71	23,882	1.71
Colombia	18	15,937	0.28	370	22,753	8.41
Other Latin America	102	15,709	1.6	1,559	12,578	19.61
Nigeria	6,644	15,091	100.27	0	0	0
Northern Sub-Saharan Africa	833	5,020	4.18	0	0	0
Central and western Sub-Saharan Africa	129	16,166	2.09	7,596	11,559	87.8
Southern Sub-Saharan Africa	2,578	7,091	18.28	282	10,431	2.94
Eastern Sub-Saharan Africa	163	12,877	2.1	2,971	10,222	30.37
Egypt	128	28,273	3.61	0	0	0
Turkey	228	35,811	8.17	0	17,944	0
Other West Asia/North Africa (WANA)	190	47,278	8.96	309	28,666	8.85
Pakistan	139	21,352	2.97	0	0	0
Bangladesh	0	0	0	236	19,134	4.52
Other South Asia	13	24,932	0.32	213	17,503	3.73
Indonesia	114	18,851	2.14	1,454	15,703	22.83
Thailand	0	0	0	982	16,502	16.2
Malaysia	0	0	0	54	15,366	0.83
Philippines	0	0	0	429	10,248	4.4
Viet Nam	0	0	0	622	11,543	7.18
Myanmar	0	0	0	31	14,111	0.44
Other Southeast Asia	0	0	0	49	10,861	0.54
South Korea	0	0	0	41	34,307	1.4
Other East Asia	15	22,651	0.33	168	17,892	3.01
Rest of the world	4	17,430	0.07	207	9,867	2.04
Developed countries	2,763	28,164	77.82	7,494	19,389	145.29
Developing countries	16,158	17,809	287.75	26,202	15,600	408.76
World	**18,921**	**19,321**	**365.57**	**33,696**	**16,443**	**554.05**

Source: IMPACT-WATER projections, 2002.
Notes: AI indicates irrigated area; YI, irrigated yield; PI, irrigated production; AR, rainfed area; YR, rainfed yield; PR, rainfed production; 000ha, thousand hectares; kg/ha, kilograms per hectare; and 10^6-mt, million metric tons.

Table B.23—Food demand and net trade for wheat, 1995, 2010, and 2025

Region/Country	Demand (million metric tons)			Trade (million metric tons)		
	1995	2010	2025	1995	2010	2025
United States	42.77	36.66	42.77	30.01	35.76	42.7
European Union 15	82.94	81.17	82.94	15.11	15.96	16.58
Japan	7.6	6.69	7.6	-5.87	-6.19	-7.12
Australia	6.58	5.8	6.58	11.68	21.66	27.92
Other developed countries	18.74	16.67	18.74	15.48	17.89	25.91
Eastern Europe	32.28	31.86	32.28	1.43	3.23	7.13
Central Asia	18.09	15.47	18.09	-1.47	-1	-0.3
Rest of former Soviet Union	53.14	54.64	53.14	-4.38	-1.45	9.29
Mexico	7.74	6.31	7.74	-1.34	-2.46	-3.55
Brazil	13.78	11.51	13.78	-6.94	-7.7	-7.88
Argentina	10.21	8.64	10.21	5.49	9.3	18.04
Colombia	1.62	1.33	1.62	-0.96	-1.21	-1.47
Other Latin America	14.54	11.44	14.54	-6.34	-7.96	-9.64
Nigeria	3.13	1.96	3.13	-0.72	-1.92	-3.09
Northern Sub-Saharan Africa	9.41	5.47	9.41	-1.61	-2.82	-5.91
Central and western Sub-Saharan Africa	4.03	2.35	4.03	-1.46	-2.34	-4.02
Southern Sub-Saharan Africa	3.17	1.9	3.17	-1.06	-1.58	-2.72
Eastern Sub-Saharan Africa	1.99	1.23	1.99	-0.45	-0.51	-0.92
Egypt	17.39	14.46	17.39	-5.96	-9.33	-10.82
Turkey	24.47	21.81	24.47	0.12	0.52	-0.61
Other West Asia/North Africa (WANA)	69.91	54.02	69.91	-15.04	-23.1	-31.91
India	103.57	81.85	103.57	0.73	-5.25	-15.25
Pakistan	37.41	26.72	37.41	-2.21	-6.04	-11.23
Bangladesh	5.01	3.4	5.01	-1.21	-2	-3.36
Other South Asia	9.51	6.46	9.51	-1.05	-1.73	-4
Indonesia	6.69	5	6.69	-3.95	-5.03	-6.72
Thailand	1.12	0.84	1.12	-0.66	-0.84	-1.12
Malaysia	1.77	1.27	1.77	-0.88	-1.27	-1.78
Philippines	3.86	2.61	3.86	-1.8	-2.62	-3.88
Viet Nam	0.91	0.57	0.91	-0.4	-0.58	-0.92
Myanmar	0.28	0.19	0.28	-0.06	-0.1	-0.16
Other Southeast Asia	0.07	0.04	0.07	-0.03	-0.04	-0.07
China	146.74	137.46	146.74	-9.95	-3.86	-2.44
South Korea	5.27	4.4	5.27	-3.58	-4.42	-5.28
Other East Asia	1.27	0.93	1.27	-0.36	-0.52	-0.75
Rest of the world	0.67	0.46	0.67	-0.33	-0.46	-0.67
Developed countries	244	233	244	63	87	122
Developing countries	524	430	524	-63	-87	-122
World	**768**	**664**	**768**	**0**	**0**	**0**

Sources : For 1995, FAO (1998b); for 2010 and 2025, IMPACT-WATER projections, 2002.

Table B.24—Food demand and net trade for maize, 1995, 2010, and 2025

Region/Country	Demand (million metric tons)			Trade (million metric tons)		
	1995	2010	2025	1995	2010	2025
United States	229.26	202.43	229.26	48.97	51.16	80.7
European Union 15	35.32	34.99	35.32	-1.62	-0.69	0.64
Japan	15.71	16.12	15.71	-16.4	-16.12	-15.7
Australia	0.32	0.29	0.32	0.01	0.05	0.08
Other developed countries	21.04	19.53	21.04	0.14	1.13	1.25
Eastern Europe	29.33	27.52	29.33	-0.19	7.92	13.75
Central Asia	0.81	0.72	0.81	0	0.1	0.24
Rest of former Soviet Union	5.28	5.24	5.28	-0.58	1.42	3.59
Mexico	33.07	25.86	33.07	-3.73	-2.2	-5.35
Brazil	67.39	50.28	67.39	-0.89	0.65	-3.28
Argentina	9.11	7.1	9.11	5.46	9.66	16.32
Colombia	3.94	3.07	3.94	-1.32	-1.68	-2.33
Other Latin America	22.04	16.47	22.04	-4.35	-5.07	-7.83
Nigeria	13.38	9.17	13.38	0	0.21	-0.47
Northern Sub-Saharan Africa	7.5	4.94	7.5	-0.06	0.1	-0.66
Central and western Sub-Saharan Africa	10.34	6.73	10.34	-0.13	-0.49	-1.1
Southern Sub-Saharan Africa	13.09	8.83	13.09	-0.57	0.1	-2.46
Eastern Sub-Saharan Africa	13.19	9.03	13.19	-0.31	-0.98	-3
Egypt	11.47	9.28	11.47	-2.34	-2.77	-3.42
Turkey	3.3	2.85	3.3	-0.49	-0.4	-0.73
Other West Asia/North Africa (WANA)	11.78	8.58	11.78	-5.09	-6.67	-9.2
India	20.78	13	20.78	0.03	0.48	-1.87
Pakistan	2.45	1.86	2.45	0	-0.09	-0.21
Bangladesh	0.01	0.01	0.01	0	0	0
Other South Asia	3.39	2.5	3.39	-0.07	-0.07	-0.31
Indonesia	14	11.8	14	-0.91	-0.95	-0.88
Thailand	9.51	6.83	9.51	-0.1	-0.14	-0.71
Malaysia	4.35	3.51	4.35	-2.25	-3.45	-4.27
Philippines	11	7.58	11	-0.23	-0.98	-1.86
Viet Nam	2.25	1.75	2.25	0.03	-0.14	-0.24
Myanmar	0.36	0.28	0.36	0.08	0.15	0.25
Other Southeast Asia	0.21	0.16	0.21	-0.01	0.01	0.02
China	264.33	187.35	264.33	-5.04	-18.66	-37.55
South Korea	12.95	11.09	12.95	-7.89	-11	-12.76
Other East Asia	2.65	2.5	2.65	-0.12	-0.51	-0.55
Rest of the world	0.11	0.09	0.11	-0.06	-0.07	-0.09
Developed countries	336	306	336	30	45	84
Developing countries	569	413	569	-30	-45	-84
World	**905**	**719**	**905**	**0**	**0**	**0**

Sources : For 1995, FAO (1998b); for 2010 and 2025, IMPACT-WATER projections, 2002.

Table B.25—Food demand and net trade for other coarse grains, 1995, 2010, and 2025

Region/Country	Demand (million metric tons)			Trade (million metric tons)		
	1995	2010	2025	1995	2010	2025
United States	33.13	30.17	33.13	3.92	3.76	8.52
European Union 15	55.08	55.88	55.08	8.71	13.85	14.78
Japan	6.44	5.95	6.44	-5.68	-5.73	-6.21
Australia	5.9	5.14	5.9	3.94	5.74	10.37
Other developed countries	21.81	19.65	21.81	3.27	3.43	9.2
Eastern Europe	23.17	21.9	23.17	-0.61	3.65	5.75
Central Asia	5.46	4.6	5.46	0.94	0.94	-0.04
Rest of former Soviet Union	58.32	56.8	58.32	-0.08	-5.51	-3.76
Mexico	16.24	12.05	16.24	-2.88	-4.34	-6.08
Brazil	2.96	2.32	2.96	-1.03	-1.24	-1.58
Argentina	3.98	3.04	3.98	0.61	1.61	2.48
Colombia	1.66	1.27	1.66	-0.29	-0.44	-0.68
Other Latin America	5.11	3.77	5.11	-0.55	-0.63	-1.14
Nigeria	24.55	16.32	24.55	0.02	0.21	-4.12
Northern Sub-Saharan Africa	33.06	20.61	33.06	0.08	1.96	1.71
Central and western Sub-Saharan Africa	6.43	3.92	6.43	-0.21	-0.15	-0.65
Southern Sub-Saharan Africa	1.9	1.24	1.9	-0.1	0.09	0.11
Eastern Sub-Saharan Africa	4.97	3.36	4.97	-0.04	-0.26	-0.68
Egypt	1.79	1.32	1.79	-0.05	-0.54	-0.94
Turkey	12.44	9.78	12.44	0.44	-0.02	0.28
Other West Asia/North Africa (WANA)	34.92	26.29	34.92	-7.08	-11.6	-19.18
India	29.73	25.78	29.73	0.11	-0.07	0.05
Pakistan	1.22	0.89	1.22	0	-0.83	-1.15
Bangladesh	0.11	0.09	0.11	0	-0.03	-0.05
Other South Asia	1	0.77	1	-0.01	-0.03	-0.16
Indonesia	0.15	0.1	0.15	-0.06	-0.1	-0.15
Thailand	0.78	0.59	0.78	-0.17	-0.34	-0.48
Malaysia	0.1	0.1	0.1	-0.08	-0.1	-0.1
Philippines	0.3	0.27	0.3	-0.22	-0.27	-0.3
Viet Nam	0.02	0.02	0.02	-0.08	-0.02	-0.01
Myanmar	0.21	0.17	0.21	0	0.01	0.01
Other Southeast Asia	0.01	0.01	0.01	-0.01	-0.01	-0.01
China	27.93	22.1	27.93	-1.83	-1.61	-3.9
South Korea	2.4	1.75	2.4	-0.91	-1.29	-1.82
Other East Asia	0.27	0.24	0.27	-0.01	-0.04	-0.02
Rest of the world	0.06	0.05	0.06	-0.04	-0.05	-0.06
Developed countries	204	195	204	13	19	39
Developing countries	220	163	220	-13	-19	-39
World	424	358	424	0	0	0

Sources : For 1995, FAO (1998b); for 2010 and 2025, IMPACT-WATER projections, 2002.

Table B.26—Food demand and net trade for soybeans, 1995, 2010, and 2025

Region/Country	Demand (million metric tons)			Trade (million metric tons)		
	1995	2010	2025	1995	2010	2025
United States	63.7	50.75	63.7	21.92	15.97	18.84
European Union 15	21.09	17.54	21.09	-14.19	-16.36	-19.56
Japan	7.3	5.8	7.3	-4.86	-5.68	-7.15
Australia	0.23	0.2	0.23	-0.12	-0.13	-0.14
Other developed countries	4.05	3.31	4.05	-0.47	0.08	0.65
Eastern Europe	0.73	0.59	0.73	-0.2	-0.22	-0.24
Central Asia	0.04	0.03	0.04	-0.02	-0.03	-0.03
Rest of former Soviet Union	0.46	0.44	0.46	-0.05	-0.04	0.03
Mexico	5.08	3.85	5.08	-2.62	-3.46	-4.5
Brazil	40.23	28.56	40.23	3.22	12.42	18.24
Argentina	19.17	13.28	19.17	2.48	6.24	11.62
Colombia	0.59	0.39	0.59	-0.18	-0.26	-0.41
Other Latin America	4.62	3.07	4.62	1.02	0.51	0.64
Nigeria	0.49	0.33	0.49	0	-0.01	-0.07
Northern Sub-Saharan Africa	0.05	0.03	0.05	0	-0.01	-0.03
Central and western Sub-Saharan Africa	0.06	0.04	0.06	0	0	0
Southern Sub-Saharan Africa	0.31	0.2	0.31	-0.01	-0.03	-0.09
Eastern Sub-Saharan Africa	0.19	0.12	0.19	0	0.04	0.04
Egypt	0.31	0.21	0.31	-0.09	-0.14	-0.23
Turkey	0.45	0.29	0.45	-0.13	-0.2	-0.33
Other West Asia/North Africa (WANA)	0.61	0.4	0.61	-0.12	-0.2	-0.35
India	11.5	7.39	11.5	-0.01	0.47	0.07
Pakistan	0.09	0.05	0.09	-0.03	-0.04	-0.08
Bangladesh	0	0	0	0	0	0
Other South Asia	0.06	0.03	0.06	0	-0.01	-0.03
Indonesia	4.03	3.06	4.03	-0.73	-0.6	-0.61
Thailand	1.41	0.95	1.41	-0.24	-0.37	-0.65
Malaysia	1.23	0.72	1.23	-0.45	-0.73	-1.23
Philippines	0.35	0.21	0.35	-0.12	-0.2	-0.34
Viet Nam	0.28	0.15	0.28	0.03	0.02	-0.04
Myanmar	0.1	0.07	0.1	0	0	-0.01
Other Southeast Asia	0.06	0.04	0.06	0	0	-0.01
China	38.76	25.08	38.76	-2.61	-5.28	-11.77
South Korea	2.41	1.95	2.41	-1.4	-1.75	-2.15
Other East Asia	0.94	0.63	0.94	-0.04	-0.01	-0.09
Rest of the world	0	0	0	0	0	0
Developed countries	98	79	98	2	-6	-8
Developing countries	133	91	133	-2	6	8
World	231	170	231	0	0	0

Sources : For 1995, FAO (1998b); for 2010 and 2025, IMPACT-WATER projections, 2002.

Table B.27—Food demand and net trade for rice, 1995, 2010, and 2025

Region/Country	Demand (million metric tons)			Trade (million metric tons)		
	1995	2010	2025	1995	2010	2025
United States	4.21	3.45	4.21	2.54	2.62	2.64
European Union 15	2.76	2.36	2.76	-0.6	-0.51	-0.32
Japan	8.98	9.68	8.98	-0.87	-1.42	-1.51
Australia	0.17	0.14	0.17	0.56	0.63	0.85
Other developed countries	1.2	0.99	1.2	-0.82	-0.99	-1.2
Eastern Europe	0.38	0.35	0.38	-0.29	-0.31	-0.33
Central Asia	0.81	0.62	0.81	0.02	-0.09	-0.13
Rest of former Soviet Union	0.68	0.62	0.68	-0.23	-0.27	-0.26
Mexico	1.08	0.73	1.08	-0.29	-0.41	-0.64
Brazil	11.66	9.32	11.66	-0.85	-0.56	-1.14
Argentina	0.55	0.38	0.55	0.28	0.52	0.93
Colombia	2.52	1.74	2.52	-0.17	0.02	-0.43
Other Latin America	9.53	6.58	9.53	-0.3	0.04	-1.57
Nigeria	4.65	3.29	4.65	-0.32	-0.57	-0.64
Northern Sub-Saharan Africa	2.08	1.38	2.08	-0.41	-0.69	-1.04
Central and western Sub-Saharan Africa	9.72	6.38	9.72	-2.06	-2.91	-4.39
Southern Sub-Saharan Africa	4.3	2.98	4.3	-0.3	-0.47	-0.41
Eastern Sub-Saharan Africa	1.53	1.06	1.53	-0.12	-0.3	-0.46
Egypt	5.58	4.01	5.58	0.24	0.23	-0.39
Turkey	0.65	0.52	0.65	-0.26	-0.35	-0.43
Other West Asia/North Africa (WANA)	8.26	5.76	8.26	-2.3	-3.57	-5.66
India	120.61	102.44	120.61	2.7	1.64	-1.99
Pakistan	5.03	3.66	5.03	1.46	1.27	1.4
Bangladesh	27.87	24.37	27.87	-0.5	-0.7	-0.2
Other South Asia	8.55	6.27	8.55	-0.22	-0.7	-1.77
Indonesia	48.88	43.01	48.88	-1.99	-3.5	-3.83
Thailand	9.51	9.47	9.51	5.64	6.86	9.25
Malaysia	2.79	2.36	2.79	-0.47	-0.66	-0.94
Philippines	11.55	10.03	11.55	-0.39	-0.71	-0.2
Viet Nam	22.57	19.64	22.57	1.62	4.21	9.14
Myanmar	17.15	14.61	17.15	0.46	1.77	3.21
Other Southeast Asia	5.66	4.22	5.66	-0.13	0.24	0.58
China	142.38	141.76	142.38	-0.61	0.98	1.85
South Korea	3.81	4.5	3.81	-0.03	-0.11	0.48
Other East Asia	2	2.6	2	-0.76	-0.88	0.05
Rest of the world	0.47	0.34	0.47	-0.23	-0.33	-0.46
Developed countries	18	18	18	0	0	0
Developing countries	492	434	492	0	0	0
World	**510**	**452**	**510**	**0**	**0**	**0**

Sources : For 1995, FAO (1998b); for 2010 and 2025, IMPACT-WATER projections, 2002.

Table B.28—Food demand and net trade for roots and tubers, 1995, 2010, and 2025

Region/Country	Demand (million metric tons)			Trade (million metric tons)		
	1995	2010	2025	1995	2010	2025
United States	29.42	24.52	29.42	0.14	0.93	1.46
European Union 15	51.98	53.61	51.98	-11	2.79	7.82
Japan	5.95	5.92	5.95	-1.08	0.3	0.47
Australia	1.9	1.59	1.9	-0.07	-0.21	-0.05
Other developed countries	8.94	7.84	8.94	0.28	-0.08	0.41
Eastern Europe	38.69	37.66	38.69	-0.17	-1.02	1.47
Central Asia	4.51	3.66	4.51	-0.13	-0.46	-0.65
Rest of former Soviet Union	66.94	68.04	66.94	-0.02	2.2	6.7
Mexico	2.5	1.95	2.5	-0.1	-0.43	-0.52
Brazil	41.6	35.96	41.6	-0.09	3.09	4.67
Argentina	3.9	3.21	3.9	0.06	-0.03	0.41
Colombia	7.67	6.22	7.67	0	1.24	1
Other Latin America	20.64	16.46	20.64	-0.05	1.22	0.61
Nigeria	106.61	78.85	106.61	0	-3.92	-3.36
Northern Sub-Saharan Africa	7.11	4.9	7.11	-0.01	-1.56	-2.93
Central and western Sub-Saharan Africa	93.19	64.74	93.19	0.02	1.91	-2.89
Southern Sub-Saharan Africa	22.93	17.29	22.93	-0.04	-1.54	-1.69
Eastern Sub-Saharan Africa	32.52	22.6	32.52	0.09	1.19	-0.66
Egypt	4.28	3.05	4.28	0.33	-0.24	-0.67
Turkey	7.38	6.26	7.38	0.21	0.05	0.79
Other West Asia/North Africa (WANA)	15.69	11.4	15.69	-0.18	1.44	2.16
India	60.01	38.81	60.01	0.16	-1.92	-11.77
Pakistan	3.55	2.38	3.55	-0.01	-0.27	-0.58
Bangladesh	4.83	2.69	4.83	-0.02	0.03	-0.36
Other South Asia	3.59	2.47	3.59	-0.04	0.28	0.46
Indonesia	23.5	22.18	23.5	1.85	0.35	1.41
Thailand	11.84	8.19	11.84	13.23	9.1	4.36
Malaysia	1.36	1.28	1.36	-0.49	-0.62	-0.53
Philippines	3.65	3.57	3.65	0.08	-0.07	0.75
Viet Nam	6.67	5.33	6.67	0.09	0.08	0.08
Myanmar	0.43	0.34	0.43	0	0	0
Other Southeast Asia	0.59	0.45	0.59	0	-0.03	-0.07
China	218.95	205.57	218.95	-1.86	-12.6	-7.52
South Korea	2.23	2.25	2.23	-1.14	-1.1	-0.83
Other East Asia	3.24	2.67	3.24	-0.01	-0.06	0.07
Rest of the world	2.16	1.92	2.16	-0.02	-0.06	-0.08
Developed countries	204	199	204	-12	5	18
Developing countries	717	577	717	12	-5	-18
World	921	776	921	0	0	0

Sources : For 1995, FAO (1998b); for 2010 and 2025, IMPACT-WATER projections, 2002.

Contributors

Mark W. Rosegrant is a senior research fellow in the Environment and Production Technology Division of IFPRI. He also holds a joint appointment as a principal researcher with the International Water Management Institute (IWMI). Mark received his Ph.D. in public policy from the University of Michigan and has 24 years of experience in research and policy analysis in agriculture and economic development, emphasizing critical water issues as they impact world food security, rural livelihoods, and environmental sustainability. He also developed IFPRI's International Model for Policy Analysis of Agricultural Commodities and Trade (IMPACT) and the IMPACT-WATER model, which are world-recognized models for projecting global and regional food demand, supply, trade, and prices, and water supply and demand to 2020 and 2025. Mark continues to lead the team that maintains the models, which have been used to examine key policy options concerning food prices, food security, livestock and fisheries demand, agricultural research allocation, water resources, environment, and trade. He currently coordinates a joint modeling team between IFPRI and IWMI, developing state-of-the-art integrated global water and food models, and is the author or editor of five books and over 100 professional papers in agricultural economics, water resources, and food policy analysis.

Ximing Cai is a research fellow in the Environment and Production Technology Division of IFPRI. He also holds a joint research position with the International Water Management Institute. He received B.S. and M.S. degrees in water resources engineering from Tsinghua University, Beijing, China, and a Ph.D. degree in environmental and water resources engineering from the University of Texas at Austin. Ximing's current research interests include water resource planning and management, operations research and their application to integrated water resources, and agricultural and economic systems.

Sarah Cline is a research analyst in the Environment and Production Technology Division of IFPRI. She received an M.S. degree in agricultural and resource economics from West Virginia University, and prior to joining IFPRI was a research assistant at Resources for the Future. Sarah's work at IFPRI focuses primarily on water resources policy and management.

Index